The Art of *La Celestina*

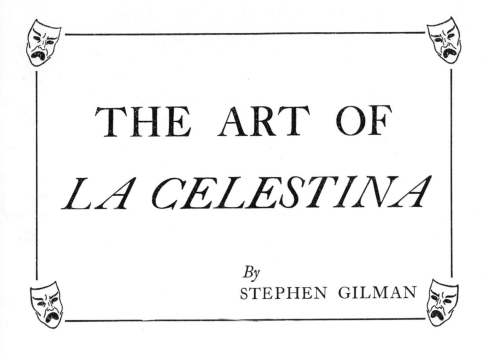

THE ART OF
LA CELESTINA

By
STEPHEN GILMAN

MADISON, 1956
THE UNIVERSITY OF WISCONSIN PRESS

Published by

THE UNIVERSITY OF WISCONSIN PRESS

811 State Street, Madison 5

Copyright © 1956 by the Regents of the University of Wisconsin. Copyright, Canada, 1956. Distributed in Canada by Burns and MacEachern, Toronto

Library of Congress Catalog Card Number 55-9089

MANUFACTURED IN THE UNITED STATES OF AMERICA BY
THE WILLIAM BYRD PRESS, INC., RICHMOND, VIRGINIA

PREFACE

THE LEAST common denominator of prefaces is a cry of warning—warning to the reader to beware of the pitfalls, the peculiarities, the apparent errors, and erring appearances which the author knows to be lying in wait in the text to follow. This preface is no exception. And since cries of warning, unlike either criticism or creation, must be both brief and few to be effective, I shall limit myself to two, each of a single paragraph.

The first is that this book is not about *La Celestina*. It may have things in it which would be interesting or suitable in such a book, but it is not one. Instead it was conceived and completed as a discussion of the art of Fernando de Rojas as I perceive it in the words he wrote. This shift of emphasis—as María Rosa Lida de Malkiel testifies—has been overdue for a long time. The never ending debate about the authorship as well as Rojas' own enigmatic modesty have shadowed the greatness of the creator of *La Celestina*. Although "semi-anonymous"—the word is Menéndez Pidal's—Fernando de Rojas is hardly a nonentity; instead he is a major Spanish writer and a major world writer. He is a writer worthy to be ranked with the best that have written. And it is my purpose to show how and why. I assume that my reader already knows and loves *La Celestina;* I assume that he needs no preliminary explanations, reminders, summaries, or explanations; and having assumed so much I shall now try to discuss the art of the artist who made such an extraordinary, such a profound, such an ironic, and such a beautiful work.

My second warning emerges from the first. The order of what is to follow —the structure of this criticism—is based on the several aspects or planes of Rojas' art: style, characterization, structure, theme, and genre. It would have been possible to proceed in another fashion, to study the composition of *La Celestina* by external comparison or contrast with the notions of literary art prevalent at the time, particularly those emerging from commentaries on Terence. This possibility is an attractive one and would underline significantly the originality of Rojas. Nevertheless, I have rejected it in favor of an

v

internal approach. I have traced from within the contours of Rojas' unique art and have relinquished that striking silhouette of creative behavior which might have resulted from the contrast between what Rojas actually did and what he was told to do by the theorists. As a result, the reader will find that I start with a discussion of minimal traits of style and only arrive at a general assessment in the last chapters. He must resign himself to what I intend as a gradual accretion of insight and information and must forbear to look for sudden illumination. The initial discussion, in effect, has to do with such an ostensibly limited problem as Rojas' peculiar use of the pronoun *tú,* and only much later on is there a consideration of problems of meaning, vision, and historical form.

These warnings having been made, let me now acknowledge the contributions for which I am indebted. One name must lead the rest: that of Américo Castro who introduced me to literary studies—indeed to the very nature of literature—in his first Princeton seminar. This was, as a matter of fact, a seminar on *La Celestina,* and those of us who participated in it remember it as a decisive experience. In my own case, I must confess that that semester became such a part of my life that the originality of these essays (originality in the sense of ultimate responsibility) is impossible for me to determine. My reading of *La Celestina* began by being the reading of Don Américo.

If spiritually the major debt is to Américo Castro, materially this book exists because its author was granted a Guggenheim fellowship. I am exceedingly grateful to the Guggenheim Foundation and to those who recommended me to it. At this point, too, I ought to thank my departmental chairman, Robert E. Rockwood, who solved without complaint all the problems which arose from my leaves, voyagings, and unreasonable requests. His friendship and help have been essential.

Specific contributions to these pages were made by one of my students, Mrs. Jane Johnson Chandler, and my brother-in-law, Claudio Guillén. The first presented me with an excellent thesis which was invaluable for its interpretation of some of Rojas' self-corrections, and the second suggested the rapprochement of Rojas to Marlowe—a suggestion which clarified much of my thinking. I also want to thank María Rosa Lida de Malkiel and Juan David García Bacca who made available the articles cited in the text. I hope they will not disapprove of the use I make of their words.

In relation to the pruning and presentation of the text let me name my friend Roy Harvey Pearce, my father-in-law, Jorge Guillén, and my wife, Teresa. Each in his own way has done his best to make me readable. For this they deserve all my gratitude. Finally may I mention Dean J. Homer Herriott, of the University of Wisconsin, whose interest and help were responsible for the appearance of this book in English.

Zürich, Switzerland
June 8, 1954   S. G.

CONTENTS

	Preface	v
I	In Search of an Artist	3
II	The Art of Style	17
III	The Art of Character	56
IV	The Art of Structure	88
V	The Art of Theme - Creation	119
VI	The Art of Theme - Tradition	154
VII	The Art of Genre	194
	Appendix	
	A. The Authorship Problem: Final Considerations	209
	B. The *Argumentos*	212
	Notes	217
	Index	258

The Art of *La Celestina*

CHAPTER ONE

IN SEARCH OF AN ARTIST

THE FUTURE of *La Celestina* as a major classic of European literature was jeopardized by none other than Fernando de Rojas. His account of its birth had such an atmosphere of mystery that successive generations of readers have doubted not only his identity but also (and this is a doubt which is far more corrosive) that of the work itself. In the *Carta* and verses preceding the text, both the unity of the whole and the very act of creation are thrown open to question. As a result the corpus of critical estimation and discussion—which accompanies a masterpiece as pilot fish accompany a shark—has been hindered and at odds with itself in the centuries following the first edition. Attention has consistently been turned away from literary values and problems and towards suppositions of creative responsibility for this or that segment of the whole. It is both sad and safe to say that if the original anonymity had been maintained or if Rojas had defined conclusively his role as author many more people would read *La Celestina* today.

It will be unnecessary here to retell in detail the involved and somewhat distasteful critical history of the work. Whatever parts of it may be unfamiliar to the reader can easily be found elsewhere. Nevertheless, since the circumstances of the early editions and the several interpretations of these circumstances necessarily shape any attempt to think about *La Celestina,* we cannot avoid them completely. The critic, in other words, must not only have, but also be ready to defend, an opinion as to the number (if not the identities) of the authors. This in turn makes him responsible for the varieties of available opinion as well as the facts which lie behind their divergence. It is the misfortune of *La Celestina* that before evaluating it or even discussing it, it is necessary to define it.

Let us begin with those classroom facts which may be recited briefly and without offense. The first known edition of the work was printed anonymously at Burgos in 1499. Although the first folio of the only existent copy (known to scholars at the turn of the century as the Heber copy) is missing,

3

it apparently had no extensive prefatory or prologue material—aside from the *argumentos* or summaries which introduce each of the sixteen acts. The presence of these *argumentos* leads us to suppose that the missing folio contained on one side the title as it appeared in the Seville, 1501, edition:

> Comedia de Calisto e Melibea con sus argumentos *nuevamente añadidos* la qual contiene, demás de su agradable y dulce estilo, muchas sentencias filosofales y avisos muy necessarios para mancebos, mostrándoles los engaños que están encerrados en siruientes y alcahuetas.[1]

The other side probably contained the "Argumento de toda la obra" and possibly the second title or *incipit* appearing in later editions:

SÍGUESE

> La Comedia de Calisto y Melibea, compuesta en reprehensión de los locos enamorados, que, vencidos en su desordenado apetito, a sus amigas llaman e dizen ser su dios. Assí mesmo fecha en auiso de los engaños de las alcahuetas e malos e lisonjeros siruientes.[2]

Thus, the first appearance of *La Celestina* was as an anonymous *comedia* in sixteen acts with an irreproachably moral purpose.

In the second known edition, Seville, 1501 (referred to above), the author of the sixteen-act *Comedia* reveals his identity in a tentative and hesitant manner. In a prefatory letter, "El auctor a vn su amigo," he begins by explaining that he had found a fragment of an earlier *comedia* by an author unknown to him, a fragment which impressed him with its manifold excellencies:

> E como mirasse su primor, sotil artificio, su fuerte e claro metal, su modo e manera de lauor, su estilo elegante, jamás en nuestra castellana lengua visto ni oydo, leylo tres o quatro vezes. E tantas quantas mas lo leya, tanta más necessidad me ponía de releerlo e tanto más me agradaua y en su processo nueuas sentencias sentía. Vi no sólo ser dulce en su principal hystoria o ficíón toda junta pero avn de algunas sus particularidades salían deleytables fontezicas de filosofía, de otros agradables donayres, de otros auisos e consejos contra lisonjeros e malos siruientes e falsas mugeres hechizeras. (5)

Qualities of style, composition, structure, thematic intention, and even of significance in depth (the progressive revelation of repeated readings) are all praised in the highest possible terms. The writer of the letter goes on to explain that because of these qualities he completed the *Comedia* during a vacation of two weeks. It was merely a "recreación de mi principal estudio," the law. The long first act is identified as the original fragment, while the added fifteen contain his own "maldoladas razones," so carelessly composed. In accordance with this modesty, he continues the camouflage of his identity: "E pues él con temor de detractores e nocibles lenguas, mas aparejadas a reprehender que a saber inuentar, quiso celar e encubrir su nombre, no me culpeys, si en el fin baxo que lo pongo, no espressare el mío." (6)

However the letter is not the only prefatory innovation to be found in the 1501 edition of the *Comedia*. There are also verses in *arte mayor* at the beginning and end of the text, verses less important for what they say (for the most part they stress again the writer's modesty and his fear of adverse "murmuros") than for the fact that they contain an acrostic revealing the identity of the continuing author. The key is given in one of the closing stanzas attributed to Alonso de Proaza (a Valencian humanist fairly well known at the time) and in a manner quite opposed to Rojas' own modesty:

> No quiere mi pluma ni manda razón
> Que quede la fama de aqueste gran hombre
> Ni su digna fama ni su claro nombre
> Cubierto de oluido por nuestra ocasión.
> Por ende juntemos de cada renglón
> De sus onze coplas la letra primera,
> Las quales descubren por sabia manera
> Su nombre, su tierra, su clara nación.
>   (217)

By following these simple directions, we receive the following information: "El Bachiller Fernando de Rojas acabó la Comedia de Calisto y Melibea y fué nascido en la puebla de Montalván."

Thus, in the second known presentation of *La Celestina,* literary and aesthetic considerations have been added to the previous didactic justification. Not only is the moral intention of the work underlined but also the artistry whereby that purpose is achieved. It almost seems as if the change in century resulted in a Renaissance letter being added to a previously mediaeval title. In any case, Rojas is revealed as an artist aware of art and fame in the approved fashion of the new times. This widening of the critical focus, however, is applied to only the first of the sixteen acts of the *Comedia,* a first act separate in authorship, still anonymous, and supposedly of much greater value than the rest. And when in spite of this, Rojas allows his own identity as author of the "inferior" fifteen-act continuation to be revealed, his very excess of modesty seems dubious and rather assertive. The emphasis on mystery, the discovery of a fragmentary masterpiece written by an unknown hand, the impossible "quinze dias de unas vacaciones," the alternate concealment and display of self, all permit and even provoke a certain amount of disbelief. Whether or not one is inclined to accept these statements as true, it is, as we said, undeniable that Rojas himself has contributed to that lack of definition as a single work of art, which has so long plagued *La Celestina*. Unlike attempts to subdivide the *Poema del Cid,* this is one sin which can hardly be charged to scholarship.

In his third and final presentation of *La Celestina* (Salamanca, Sevilla, Toledo, 1502), Rojas not only modifies the prefatory material and the title, but also—and very seriously—the text itself. In the first place, he inserts in the *Carta,* the suggestion that the first act may have been written by either Juan de Mena or Rodrigo de Cota. It is a suggestion which has resulted in much earnest debate and which, rather than clarifying, seems to have added to the previous mystification.[3] In the second place, an entirely new *Prólogo* (copied in large part from Petrarch's *De remediis utriusque fortunae*) comments on a number of new things about the work, including the titular change from *Comedia* to *Tragicomedia*. Not only is the author uncertain of the value of his work and of the authorship, but also now of its very genre: "El primer auctor quiso darle denominación del principio, que fué plazer, e llamóla comedia. Yo viendo estas discordias, entre estos extremos partí agora por medio la porfía, e llaméla tragicomedia." (25) Related to this proposition of the *tragicomedia* as a new sort of generic hybrid, the prologue suggests that Rojas was not now so sure of the moral purpose implied in other parts of the prefatory material. He, following Petrarch, remarks on the inconstancy of nature, on the uninterrupted warring of species and elements that is reflected and amplified in the world of man: "¿Pués qué diremos entre los hombres a quién todo lo sobredicho es subjeto? ¿Quién explanará sus guerras, sus enemistades, sus embidias, sus aceleramientos e mouimientos e descontentamientos? ¿Aquel mudar de trajes, aquel derribar e renouar edificios e otros muchos affectos diuersos e variedades que desta nuestra flaca humanidad nos prouienen?" (22) Is the theme, then, to be exemplary punishment, a castigation of the foolish and the evil and a reassurance of the wise and the good, or is it to be, rather, a desperate exposition of those hazards of existence which correspond to a no longer exemplary fortune? Is *La Celestina* a comedy of vice and folly justly exposed and punished, or does it present in its own way the external and always original theme of tragedy: the human condition in and of itself? Again Rojas' prefatory remarks seem to obscure, to render doubtful, his relationship to his work.

If the inevitable effect on the reader of all these prefatory remarks is one of doubt, of invitation to uncertainty, perhaps the dominant note running through them is that of fear. In the *Carta,* Rojas dwells on "detractores e nocibles lenguas" and he devotes half his space to excusing himself for having written at all. The acrostic verses are given the following title: "El autor escusándose de su yerro en esta obra que escrivió, contra si arguye e compara." As for the *Prólogo,* it closes with a rather frightening picture of the opposing reactions awakened by the *Comedia.* The final sentence is typical:

Assí que viendo estas contiendas, estos díssonos e varios juyzios, miré adonde la mayor parte acostaua, e hallé que querían que se alargasse en el processo de su deleyte destos amantes, sobre lo qual fuy muy importunado; de manera que acordé, aunque contra mi voluntad, meter segunda vez la pluma en tan estraña lauor e tan agena de mi facultad, hurtando algunos ratos a mi principal estudio, con otras horas destinadas para recreación, puesto que no han de faltar nueuos detractores a la nueua adición. (25-26)

Since only Alonso de Proaza's verses show any degree of confidence and valor, we are tempted to conclude that the mystery of the genesis of *La Celestina* is orbitally bound to the note of caution and precaution which is ever present in these prefatory statements and devices.

Only one thing appears to be clear and beyond dispute: Rojas, in order to lengthen "en el processo de su deleyte destos amantes," added five new acts to the sixteen of the *Comedia.* Furthermore, although he does not mention it in the prologue, he deleted some thirty-five lines from his previous text (according to Foulché Delbosc's calculation) and interpolated numerous passages ranging in size from single words to lengthy paragraphs. The entire text was gone over, corrected, and amplified to such an extent that the *Tragicomedia* may be considered to be a new version of *La Celestina.* Yet in spite of the fact that Rojas fairly and openly accepts responsibility for the added acts, this too has been denied him by certain critics. The pervading atmosphere of doubt has not failed to affect the one plain statement of the *Prólogo.*

These then are the facts of the matter, facts susceptible of many interpretations. Mine, I freely admit, is prejudiced—prejudiced by a desire to understand the artistry of Fernando de Rojas. My search for what might have been called several generations ago Rojas' peculiar "genius" must necessarily condition my conclusions. Yet at the same time it would be wrong to dispense arbitrarily with recognized traditions of thought on the matter, traditions which have grown up in the centuries of *La Celestina*'s life as a masterpiece of Spanish literature. They furnish the only guide possible to the labyrinth of facts just outlined. In other words, my approach to the question of authorship must be both privately serviceable and not less publicly reasonable and convincing; past and present opinion must be integrated to my own critical needs. To accomplish this it will be helpful to remember that each traditional point of view as to the authorship involves an implicit attitude towards the work, an attitude which may be measured against my own, and so used or discarded. Thus, I shall select six critics, Juan de Valdés, Blanco White, Foulché Delbosc, Menéndez Pelayo, R. E. House, and lastly Menéndez Pidal, each of whom represents a distinct point of view or variety of opinion, and then try to determine the suppositions and results of what they have to say. While an exhaustive study of the authorship problem would involve many more names and details than are necessary here, these six have expressed themselves decisively and with full responsibility. They should be sufficient for present purposes.

Juan de Valdés in the *Diálogo de la lengua* (although critical of the somewhat adolescent pedantry of the humanism of Rojas' time) is in general pleased with *La Celestina*: "ningún libro ay escrito en castellano donde la lengua sté más natural, más propia ni más elegante."[4] He goes on to accept the statements of the *Carta* at their face value and, as a result, is forced into an oversubtle distinction between the merits of the first act and those of the rest of the work: "*Celestina,* me contenta el ingenio del autor que la començó, y no tanto él del que la acabó; el juicio de todos dos me satisfaze mucho, porque sprimieron a mi ver muy bien y con mucha destreza las naturales condiciones de las personas que introduxeron en su tragicomedia, guardando el decoro dellas desde el principio hasta el fin."[5] Thus, Juan de Valdés admits literary unity and, at the same time, for reasons he finds difficult to explain, denies it. Those who, following his lead, believe in Rojas' discovery of an anonymous fragment tend towards the same hesitant dismembering of the text in their estimations of its value. They are forced to contradict their own realization that (unlike the two parts of the *Roman de la Rose*) the two *Celestinas* are joined in structure, uncontradictory in characterization, and unique in style. Hence, such judgments as that of Juan de Valdés involve a kind of aesthetic comparison which is not only weak but also odious to the reputation of the work as a whole. If we admit without reservations the existence of two authors, it is natural to find the "razones" of one more "maldoladas" than those of the other; it is an adjectival rather than an enlightening literary distinction.

To Blanco White writing from London three centuries later at the height of English Romanticism, the coexistence of two such texts seemed incredible. So instead of inventing a preference for one part or the other, he chose to deny the *Carta,* to imagine a unity of inspiration more suitable to his apparent conception of the artist: "Lo que me parece a mí más cierto es, que los que hablan de la *Celestina* pocos la han leido con atención; pues a haberlo hecho, bien pronto se persuadirían que la invención y estilo nacen de una misma fuente, desde el principio hasta el fin."[6] Although Blanco White's specific arguments may seem naive, his article in the *Mensajero de Londres* stimulated the renewed interest of the nineteenth century in *La Celestina*. By defending the artistic integrity of the work, he once more launched it as a masterpiece among his contemporaries. Thus, Blanco White and Juan de Valdés represent two opposing varieties of a somewhat *a priori* criticism. Without examining either the text or the prefatory material adequately (in spite of Blanco White's assertion to the contrary) each denies one or the other. The intelligent and rather skeptical humanist pretends to choose between the "ingenio," (or inventiveness,) of the author of the first act and that of the author of the rest (while equating them in "juicio" or creative discretion), and the Romantic convert proposes a literary fraud to support that unity of inspiration which seemed indispensable to literary greatness.

Curiously enough, one of the first detailed examinations of the text from the point of view of the authorship question was made not in connection with the first act but with the additions and interpolations of 1502. Foulché Delbosc, after having taken the trouble to edit the 1501 text of the *Comedia,* compared it carefully to the amplified *Tragicomedia,* and, in spite of the unequivocal responsibility assumed by Rojas for his revision, he found much of the added material "unworthy of the original author." The interpolated proverbs, the repetitions and erudite references, as well as certain changes in the characters as they appear in the new acts all seemed to indicate that *La Celestina* was in 1502 padded unmercifully by a second and far inferior author. Foulché Delbosc, accordingly, conceives of the sixteen-act *Comedia* as a single and perfect artistic unit and the statements of the *Carta* as completely false and misleading. Until the publication of the Serrano y Sanz documents establishing the identity of Rojas as a *converso,* a lawyer, for a time the mayor of Talavera, and relating him to *La Celestina,* Foulché Delbosc even went so far as to consider the acrostic a fabrication.[7]

Behind the opinions of Foulché Delbosc (opinions shared by Cejador, House, Azorín, and Delpy) [8] one may detect the presence of at least two unexpressed critical suppositions. On the one hand, there is the ingrained tradition of Malherbe and Boileau, the belief that good taste, pruning, and rigid control of language are indispensable to the making of literature. The *mauvais gout* of the interpolated proverbs and *redites,* the *invraisemblance* of the added erudition in terms of the characters, the lack of *bienséance* displayed by Melibea in the second garden scene, all play their part in the making up of

Foulché Delbosc's mind. They determine what he calls the "côté éstetique de la question." Along with these implicit national criteria, there is the slightly superstitious belief of many positivistic scholars—a belief going back to the beginnings of Romanticism—that the oldest and the most primitive is necessarily the best version of any text. The task of the scholar, therefore, is to reestablish the form of the original inspiration and to cut away the misinterpretations, the faulty readings, the false corrections, imposed on the text by those who copied it or rewrote it in later centuries. The *Comedia* has the virtue of being the primitive pure form of *La Celestina,* while the *Tragicomedia* represents its later corruption and distortion. Thus, Foulché Delbosc seems to combine the faith in inspiration of a Blanco White with notions of Neoclassic good taste remotely related to those of Juan de Valdés—adding for good measure a laudable quantity of philological investigation. The result is the willing attribution to Rojas (or to someone resembling him) of the first act and the denial to him of the additions of 1502. The evidence of both the *Carta and* the *Prólogo* is rejected!

Menéndez Pelayo, in his splendid study of *La Celestina,* undoubtedly had his share of unexpressed criteria for literary judgment, but he is much less rash in applying them to the authorship problem. He realizes the twin dangers of arguing a matter of fact aesthetically and of allowing factual statements to affect reading appreciation. Thus, while agreeing with many of Foulché Delbosc's objections to the additions of 1502, he refuses to admit the conclusion that they are the product of a second author. Not all the added material is necessarily bad, and much that is regrettable finds its parallel in the *Comedia.* One may wish that Rojas had decided to let well enough alone, but the text of the *Tragicomedia* hardly justifies disbelief in the plain statements of the *Prólogo.* As for the authorship of the first act, Menéndez Pelayo defends the unity of the whole basing himself on the doubtful caution of the *Carta* (among other things, the claim to have finished the work in fifteen days) as well as the identity of characters from one act to another. Although he admits, "En absoluto rigor crítico la cuestión del primer acto es insoluble, y a quién se atenga estrictamente a las palabras del bachiller ha de ser muy difícil refutarle,"[9] he, himself, believes that

El bachiller Rojas se mueve dentro de la fábula de la Celestina, no como quién continua obra ajena, sino como quién dispone libremente de su labor propia. Sería el más extraordinario de los prodigios literarios el que un continuador llegase a penetrar de tal modo en la concepción ajena y a identificarse de tal suerte con el espíritu del primitivo autor y con los tipos primarios que el había creado. No conocemos composición alguna donde tal prodigio se verifique; cualquiera que sea el ingenio del que intenta soldar su invención con la ajena, siempre queda visible el punto de la soldadura; siempre en manos del continuador pierden los tipos algo de su valor y pureza primitivos, y resultan o lánguidos y descoloridos, o recargados y caricaturescos. Tal acontece con el falso *Quijote,* de Avellaneda; tal con el segundo *Guzmán de Alfarache* de Mateo Luján de Sayavedra; tal con las dos continuaciones del *Lazarillo de Tormes.* ¿Pero quién sería capaz de notar diferencia alguna entre el Calisto, la Celestina, el Sempronio o el Pármeno del primer acto y los personajes que con iguales nombres figuran en los actos siguientes? ¿Dónde se ve la menor huella de afectación o de esfuerzo para sostenerlos ni para recargarlos? En el primer acto está en germen toda le tragicomedia, y los siguientes son el unico desarrollo natural y legítimo de las premisas sentadas en el primero.[10]

It is important to note that the reasoning of Menéndez Pelayo on this point is of a comparative nature. He does not assert a likeness or a quality and from that deduce a necessary unity of inspiration; rather, in view of a particular continuity, that of character, he compares *La Celestina* with other known sequels. The result is not theoretical impossibility but practical incredibility. If the first act is not by Rojas, given the failure of similar attempts at continuation, it is a unique and highly extraordinary case of literary grafting. The conclusion becomes a question: in view of this, is it not more reasonable to assume that Rojas was the author of the first act?

To Menéndez Pelayo and those who preceded him the problem of authorship, although historical and factual on its own terms, was literary in its importance, a problem of poetic creation and aesthetic value. And, lacking positive historical data, literary considerations were appealed to for its solution. We have just witnessed the great care used by Menéndez Pelayo in approximating these two points of view. R. E. House on the other hand, after placing himself among the followers of the literary doctrines of Foulché Delbosc, proposed to prove his beliefs with linguistic evidence. He would provide himself with facts for the solution of a factual problem, and the results were at once more and less startling than he might have wished. House began by dividing the *Tragicomedia* into five approximately equal parts, the first act, the added acts of 1502, and three from the remaining fifteen acts of the *Comedia.* Then, using a number of linguistic checks (word order, length of speeches, alteration of *le* and *lo* as a direct object referring to things), he totaled their percentages in each of the five parts. In almost every case his results showed approximately equal proportions for the three parts taken from the *Comedia,* but the first act and the additions of 1502 varied appreciably. Furthermore for most of the factors tabulated, House found a statistical progression of regular increase or decrease in the three major divisions of the work. The conclusions of *le* and *lo* are typical in this respect: " 'Lo' appears as against 'le' referring to things in proportion of one to six in the first act, at the ratio of two to three in acts II–XVI, and of more than two to one in the additions."[11]

It is not surprising that, on the basis of these "facts," House's conclusions are hesitant; linguistic evidence has led him into literary absurdity:

It is far from the intention of the writer of these observations to render a final decison on a question which has been so ably discussed by others. The facts presented tell their own story more clearly than he can tell it. However, until something more convincing is offered on the other side of the question, he takes side with those who believe that Alonso de Proaza was the author of the additions of 1502.

The differences between the first act and the remainder of the 1499 version that have come to light unexpectedly offer a new field for study. How does it happen that act I stands apart from acts II–XVI in the eight types of word order studied? . . . It does not seem likely that Rojas found the first act, as is testified, in the form in which he has passed it on to us, but the prefatory letter "el auctor a vn su amigo" may have more truth in it than has commonly been supposed.[12]

"Unexpectedly" and with apparent reluctance, House finds himself faced with three authors for *La Celestina*. In judging his conclusions we must remember that he does not take into account the possibility that the uncertain length of time (the date of writing of the *Comedia* is unknown) between the completion of the first sixteen acts and that of the final version may have changed certain of Rojas' linguistic habits. This would even seem to be likely in a period of linguistic uncertainty, and a similar investigation of the language of such a work as the *Tractado de amores* and that of the *Carcel de amor* (probably composed at different times in spite of their respective dates of publication—1491 and 1492)[13] might well bring out comparable changes. In any case rather than admit three authors, it would seem reasonable to believe the direct evidence of the *Prólogo*. In all factual good faith, House seems to have weakened the literary deductions of Foulché Delbosc.

Lastly, Menéndez Pidal in a recent article on the transformation of style during the reign of Ferdinand and Isabella gives a résumé of his thought on the authorship problem. He returns, curiously enough, to the opinion of Juan de Valdés but sustains it in a very different manner. After surveying linguistic archaisms in the first act, he continues:

Así esta comedia genial, que en el siglo XVI formó escuela, y en su turbia profundidad fué admirada universalmente, se publica como obra anónima y escrita en colaboración, al igual de otras producciones españolas que, a pesar de una poderosa fuerza creadora, aparecen ligadas a la estilística colectiva. En lo que toca a la *Celestina,* se fuerte unidad de concepción artística (argumento único de los que impugnan la multiplicidad de autores) se explica bién porque en el auto primero está, como en semilla, la obra entera, siendo probable además que ese auto fuera acompañado del argumento de la comedia...

De igual modo que la idea directriz, el autor anónimo del primer auto impone un estilo al autor medio anónimo de los autos restantes...[14]

It is worth noting in the first place that this explanation of *La Celestina*'s unity of conception, style, and character (that is to say, of the lack of perceptible literary frontiers between the first act and those which follow it) reflects Menéndez Pidal's long and intense experience of traditional poetry. There, literary unity (as he himself has shown with both erudition and persuasive eloquence) is often the result of the collaboration of many creative minds within a single structure and style. A sacred or unique inspiration is not indispensable. And, as the history of the seventeenth century *comedia* demonstrates, this so-called popular characteristic appears in other sectors of literature in Spanish, becoming in fact an item on Menéndez Pidal's well-known list of "características generales." Secondly we may notice that he accords the added acts to Rojas almost as a matter of course, as a matter hardly worth discussing seriously in spite of Foulché Delbosc and of House.[15]

In evaluating the reasoning of Menéndez Pidal, we may notice his avoidance of many of the pitfalls of his predecessors. He neither denies the unity of *La Celestina* nor does he make a liar of Rojas because of his private intuitions of literary unity. We may doubt the responsibility, for such a personal work as *La Celestina,* of a variety of creation usually assumed in the epic, ballad, or *comedia,* but the reminder that such creative collaboration has existed makes the possibility of continuation by Rojas seem a little less incredible than it did to Menéndez Pelayo. Then too, the several examples of failure mentioned by the latter (the *Quijote apócrifo,* the *Guzmán de Alfarache* of Juan Martí, etc.) were invariable sequels, imitations from without, and not second growths from an original creative germ. In the case of the *Quijote apócrifo,* at any rate, the stated intention was not to write another *Quijote* but to improve upon it, and it is likely that for several of the others no strenuous effort was made to reproduce the original. *La Celestina,* on the other hand, if we are to believe Rojas, did not involve imitation but completion, completion from within an identical literary structure. In this sense, Menéndez Pidal can with greater justification point to certain resemblances to the techniques of traditional creation.

After having glanced at the description of the genesis of *La Celestina* in the *Carta,* in the *Prólogo,* and in the acrostic verses, and after having passed hasty review of the opinions thereby stimulated, some sort of conclusion would seem necessary. It is this: *that the authorship problem, as such a problem, must be by-passed if we hope to discover the way of Rojas' creation, his particular and personal art.* Two things support this conclusion: first, the problem is unsolvable as far as any positive proof is concerned; and, second, any hypothesis which may be proposed must satisfy not only the historical and linguistic facts but also the demands of literary appreciation. As we have seen, for *La Celestina* these two paths to the truth are antagonistic, and their rapprochement brings peril of distortion to either or both. Juan de Valdés, trusting in the *Carta,* draws artificial frontiers across the text, while Blanco White disbelieves Rojas himself for the sake of Romantic literary theory. Foulché Delbosc denies the least doubtful statement of the *Prólogo* and, for the sake of literary criteria apparently alien to *La Celestina,* rejects Rojas' lengthening and improvement of his text. Menéndez Pelayo corrects these errors but cannot conceive of a previous fragment as anything but incredible. House attempts to solve the problem apart from literature and ends with literary absurdity. Only Menéndez Pidal proposes a solution which offers the comprehension of the facts on literary terms. But even so, he implies a variety of poetic creation apparently quite different from that of *La Celestina.* Hence, the belief that the authorship problem renders impossible the evaluation of the text and the conclusion that for the present we must leave it, suitably bracketed, behind us.

To act upon such a conclusion requires the collaboration of the reader. He must be willing to assume (here the opinions of Menéndez Pidal may ease his conscience) that Rojas was telling the truth in the *Carta* and the *Prólogo.* It is not necessary, of course, to accept Rojas' low estimate of his own contribution or to believe that the *Comedia* was finished in fifteen days. As Rojas, himself, says, "aún mas tiempo y menos acepto." But the major assertions, unknown authorship for the first act and complete responsibility for the additions of 1502, must be taken at their face value. If this assumption is made, we shall perhaps for the first time be free to work with all of *La Celestina* confidently and according to our pleasure.

Such an assumption as the above gives new importance to the additions of 1502. If Rojas be admitted as their author without hesitation or questioning,[16] they may be seen as constituting an invaluable key both to his conception of *La Celestina* as a whole and to individual phases of his artistry. We may begin by imagining Rojas sitting down to read, revise, and amplify a text which he had completed some four or five years previously (1498 would perhaps be the latest possible date for termination of the *Comedia*). We may imagine him not now immersed intuitively in his own creation but rather as having gained with time a new critical perspective into his previous accomplishment. Like the Cervantes of the second part of the *Quixote,* the years between first completion and later continuation allowed Rojas to overtake himself intellectually and then to chart new profundities of creative inspiration. It does not matter that this awareness may not correspond entirely to later interpretations of *La Celestina* or that Rojas in 1502 often seems to have had less insight into his own creation than had Cervantes in 1615. What matters is that we understand the shift in the relationship between artist and work of art, a shift which was, we may assume, responsible for the changes and variations of emphasis that are so evident in the additions and interpolations of 1502.

Looked at from this point of view, the changes in the *Tragicomedia* provoke a number of significant questions, questions which will implicitly or explicitly guide us in our reconstruction of Rojas' art. What errors and obscure passages did Rojas find to correct? What themes did he desire to strengthen in view of his new realization of the nature of his masterpiece? What features of his style does he choose to repeat or to underline? What new aspects does he bring out in his portrayal of characters on the basis of his long acquaintance with them? How does he strengthen individual acts and scenes, and to what extent does this strengthening reveal the inner structure of his work? In addition to these limited queries, Calisto's second monologue, Areusa's new capacity for intrigue, and the final rendezvous in the garden, in their turn, invite comparison with their previous incarnations in the *Comedia.* The interpolations and the added acts, in other words, may or may not improve *La Celestina,* but, once Rojas is accepted as their author, they are invaluable to an understanding of his artistry. We may imagine how the discovery of a revised edition of *Hamlet* would affect Shakespearian scholarship; and it is precisely such an opportunity that students of literature in Spanish have disregarded for so long.

It has unfortunately been impossible to carry out the original intention: to organize these essays only on the basis of the added material. In the first place, such an ordering tends to produce an undesirable polemic with those who have denied its major premise, the authenticity of the revision. Each change, treated separately, inevitably suggests separate evaluation as well as the problem of its consistency with other parts of the *Comedia.* But even more important than this is the fact that such aspects of artistry as structure, characterization, or theme are integrated to the whole of the work and so can not be fully developed from the disperse evidence of interpolation or deletion. As for the added acts, the absence of three of the five major characters results naturally in an entirely new approach to structure as well as in modification of the theme. On these levels, neither acts nor interpolations can do more than suggest the nature of Rojas' artistry, and, while such suggestions may be interesting, they are also a limited and inconvenient basis for presentation of the art of the whole. Yet in spite of this change of plan, some sections of the essays on structure, style, and theme will reveal clearly their genesis in meditation on the added material. It was precisely in the course of such meditation that this book was conceived.

Only on the level of style can the interpolations and deletions be used as a basis for discussion. So many of these lesser changes (often no more than a word or two) betray such an evidently stylistic preoccupation—so many are related significantly to their stylistic context—that their study traces without hesitation the contours of *La Celestina*'s art of composition. Many of these minimal self-corrections have the further advantage of reassuring us that Rojas was, in fact, their author. Only a person creatively aware of each line could have made them or would have thought it worth while to do so. And while it is not my purpose to argue with Foulché Delbosc, Delpy, or anyone else, both motivation and manner of revision correspond to a writer preoccupied with his own style. On this level the interpolations are visibly not the scribbling of a literary hack, but rather the result of hours of thought about language by one of the most conscientious of great authors in Spanish. Support for our authorship assumption is, however, a mere by-product of the first essay; in turning to the interpolations and additions in general we may revive these few decisive hours in the history of Spanish literature and, in so doing, may attempt to rediscover the great and unique art of Fernando de Rojas.

CHAPTER TWO

THE ART OF STYLE

─────────

1. Dialogue and Life

THE REDISCOVERY of *La Celestina* in terms of Rojas' art imposes its own definition upon the word "style." For our purposes, style has a sense that is closer to its ancestral "stylus" than those suggested by either Juan de Valdés or Leo Spitzer—to mention two critics concerned with this aspect of the work of art. Style, here, means the written result of those criteria of artistry which control the suggestion, acceptance or erasure of a word in a text. It must have to do with those notions of order, propriety, and pleasing effect which guide the pen of a literary artist. It is the product of his conscious, although not necessarily scholastic, concern with the written word, and while the tacit "manual of style" of an era or of a group plays its part in any such definition, we assume that the individual author's word awareness must surpass recipes. This approach to style as choice of words based on a special consciousness of language falls somewhere in between those of the two critics mentioned above. Juan de Valdés was perhaps less concerned with the writer's artistry than with the effects of the "stilo" on the reader, effects which depended on its adherence to essential and apparently absolute principles of taste. Spitzer (and each of these represents two possible and widely accepted notions of style), on the contrary, relates style so intimately to the creator and his time that he prefers to emphasize its possibilities of unwitting betrayal of them—a betrayal which the critic's intuition can turn to an advantage. But for this essay, neither reader nor writer is in himself adequate. Rojas' artistry of style is based on the individual, and at the same time impersonal, judgment which from sentence to sentence controls the language of *La Celestina.*

The proposition of such an elementary definition of style does not imply the arbitrary rejection of the points of view of either Spitzer or Juan de Valdés. Rather, as we said, it corresponds to our particular approach to *La Celestina,* to the fact that Rojas' art of words is the first and most available level of his artistry. Much of what we shall have to say is derived from contemporary methods of stylistic analysis; at the same time, we must recognize that Rojas' awareness of language was surely governed by general notions of style which in a sense predicted those held fifty years later by a Juan de Valdés. We admit the validity and the need of both points of view but prefer, at least in this case, to forego both aesthetic judgment and elaboration of intuition. Neither will lead us to the reconstruction of Rojas' conscious preoccupation with the words of his text, a preoccupation that is evident in the interpolations and deletions of 1502. Rojas, one of the world's great artists of human awareness, seems himself (at least by the time he corrected the *Comedia* in 1502) to have been very much aware of the nature of his art. And on these terms, the making for him of a personal "manual of style" may also be a worth-while way of studying the words he wrote.

It goes without saying that the interpolations by their very presence in *La Celestina* result from Rojas' belief that a change was advisable in the passages in which they are to be found. In that sense, all the interpolations are potentially indicative of his stylistic art. All not only add but, in adding, correct; and it is interesting to compare the corrected later style with that of the original context. Nevertheless, in considering the interpolations as a group, it results that, from Rojas' standpoint they may be divided into two separate kinds, one of which is more closely related to problems of style than the other. If the rewriting was the outgrowth of years of meditation on what had been created, it follows that certain changes reflect Rojas' new knowledge of the whole, its thematic unity, its structure in acts, the evolution of its personalities, while others correspond to a careful reading of the lesser components: the word, the sentence, the paragraph, or at most the speech. It is these latter which best reveal Rojas' sense of style, which, by the very immediacy of the faults they correct, show off his mind managing his language. One kind of interpolation is related to an awareness of creative patterns above the plane of words; another, to word patterns themselves.[1]

If we set apart all the interpolations of one or two words (interpolations that are almost by definition stylistic) and glance over them, one particular group will assert itself:

CEL.—¿Qué penssavas *Sempronio?* ¿Avíame de mantener el viento? (III, 133)

CEL.—¡Para adalid eres *tú* bueno, cargado de agüeros y recelo! (III, 140)

CEL.—¡Oh *mis enamorados,* mis perlas de oro! ¡Tal me venga el año cual me parece vuestra venida! (IX, 26)

Mel.—Amiga Lucrecia e mi *leal criada* e fiel secretaria, ya has visto como no ha sido más en mi mano. (X, 63)

Cal.—Descuelga *Pármeno* mis coraças *e armaos vosotros e assí yremos a buen recaudo, porque como dizen: el hombre apercibido, medio combatido.* (XII, 77)

Sos.—*Señor,* una mujer que se llamaba Celestina. (XIII, 109)[2]

In these inconspicuous and little noted interpolations, Rojas' awareness of the fundamental stylistic requirement of dialogue is evident. He insists that each speech be adequately directed to the second person, that it exist in function of speaker and listener and not merely for the instruction or entertainment of the reader. These inserted signs of direction, in effect, bring out the inner intentionality of language in *La Celestina*. It is a spoken language (although not always popular) in the sense that it is written as if emerging from one life towards another. Each word, as we shall see, is supported by and gives access to both a *yo* and a *tú*. Dialogue is for Rojas the language which results from the meeting of two lives.

This governing of the style by the requirements of living dialogue is so central to Rojas' art that it must be exemplified with adequate detail. Let us examine two of the above insertions in order to bring out the real need for their presence, the fact they are not just mechanical or surface additions designed to give the appearance of dialogue. The full text of the first is as follows:

Cel.—¿El primero, hijo? Pocas vírgenes, a Diós gracias, has visto tú en esta cibdad, que hayan abierto tienda a vender, de quién yo no aya sido corredora de su primer hilado. En nasciendo la mochacha, la hago escrivir en mi registro, *e esto* para saber quantas se me salen de la red. ¿Qué penssavas, *Sempronio*? ¿Avíame de mantener del viento? ¿Heredé otra herencia? ¿Tengo otra casa o viña? ¿Conócesme otra hazienda más deste oficio? ¿De qué como e beuo? ¿De qué visto y calço? ¿En esta cibdad nascida, en ella criada, manteniendo honrra, como todo el mundo sabe, conoscida, pues, no soy? Quién no supiere mi nombre e mi casa, tenle por extranjero. (III, 133)

This speech consists evidently of two parts: one indicative, a boasting narration, and the other interrogative, a series of more or less rhetorical questions requiring no answers. The first part has its initial note of direction, "¿El primero, hijo?" but this by itself is hardly enough to maintain Sempronio's listening presence (as the person whom these words were designed to impress) all throughout the speech. Hence, the first question of the second part, "¿Qué pensavas?" no matter how rhetorical, is directed point plank at him as the target for the questions to come. But Rojas in 1502 was still unsatisfied and chose to strengthen the note of direction, the authenticity of the speech as dialogue, at this strategic point. "¿Qué pensavas, *Sempronio?*" in effect, is stylistically necessary not only for Rojas but for Celestina, and the absence of the name in the *Comedia* is almost tangible.

Perhaps even more necessary to expression in dialogue is the *tú* of the second example. Sempronio has continued to doubt Celestina's professional capabilities and recalls indirectly the tarring and feathering which resulted from a previous failure. Celestina answers angrily: "¡Alahé, en malora a tí he yo menester para compañero! ¡Aún si quisieses auisar a Celestina en su oficio! Pues quando tú nasciste ya comía yo pan con corteza. ¡Para adalid eres *tú* bueno, cargado de agüeros e recelo!" (III, 140) Little explanation is necessary. The pronouns *yo* and *tú* are central to the expression in dialogue of Celestina's violent reaction, her spontaneous reply not just to Sempronio's doubts but to his implied insult. And Rojas underlines the effective opposition of the first and second persons with an added *tú* in the last sentence; he ends the speech with final stress on the living indignation, the indignation in dialogue, of Celestina. Thus, in both cases, it is apparent that the insertion does not furnish a secondhand veneer of dialogue but rather strengthens a fundamental note of direction that was already present. In both cases, the *yo* of the speaker not only expresses itself but also impresses itself upon the *tú* of the listener, and Rojas, as the corrector of his own text, brings out the extent to which this requirement of dialogue was a part of his artistry of style.

What we have pointed out is, of course, hardly a virtue specific to *La Celestina*. Any good writer of dramatic, epic, or novelistic dialogue knows intuitively such relationships between style and fictional speech. But Rojas is, I think, unique in his conscious and conscientious development of style on this basis; indeed the fine subtleties of his dialogue have not been given the full critical attention they deserve. We may select, more or less at random, any passage from the work (with the exception of Act I and the frequent monologues) and observe immediately the mutual presence of *yo* and *tú* as decisive in word arrangement. The word in *La Celestina* is a bridge between speaker and listener, the meeting place of two lives. The following is typical. Celestina has been talking in a low voice to Lucrecia at the close of her first interview with Melibea:

MELIB.—¿Qué le dizes, madre?
CEL.—Señora, acá nos entendemos.
MELIB.—Dímelo, que me enojo, quando yo presente, se habla cosa de que no aya parte.
CEL.—Señora, que te acuerde la oración, para que la mandes escriuir e que

aprenda de mí a tener mesura en el tiempo de tu yra, en la qual yo vsé lo que se dize: que del ayrado es de apartar por poco tiempo, del enemigo por mucho. Pues tú, señora, tenías yra con lo que sospechaste de mis palabras, no enemistad. Porque, avnque fueran las que tu pensauas, en sí no eran malas: que cada día ay hombres penados por mugeres e mugeres por hombres, e esto obra la natura e la natura ordenóla Diós e Diós no hizo cosa mala. E assí quedaua mi demanda, como quiera que fuesse, en si loable, pues de tal tronco procede, e yo libre de pena. ... (IV, 191–92)

At this point Melibea is no longer able to dominate Celestina, even though she threatens weakly to become angry again. Her feminine querulousness is, in itself, a sign of defeat and permits Celestina's reply. The latter in complete control of the situation, prepares the next step of the coming surrender. First she gives a flimsy explanation of her aside to Lucrecia, ". . . que te acuerde la oración . . . ," and then, without giving Melibea time to think, begins to sum up the interview for her. She does so in the form which she would like to leave impressed on her listener's mind, preparing with her usual canniness the rationalizations to come: "You are not my enemy; you were only temporarily angered." Then more bravely: "Even if what angered you were true, looked at in the proper light, it would not necessarily have been bad." And finally there is the suggestion that Melibea's suspicions may after all have been justified, a suggestion Celestina dares to imply but not yet to confirm: ". . . mi demanda como quiera que fuesse . . ."

But to return to the style, outwardly it is one of rational and objective argument, one of general statement and particular application. From within and upon closer reading, however, we may notice a number of seemingly irrational transitions. The "e que" in Celestina's first sentence with its introduction of "mesura" and the distinction between anger and enmity hardly corresponds to anything Celestina might have been whispering to Lucrecia. The "porque" which introduces the third sentence is equally misleading: there is certainly no causal relationship between Melibea's angry reaction to her suspicions and Celestina's attempt to give them legitimacy even if they were "las que tú pensauas." Argumentative logic is an appearance, a fiction; the actual choice of words depends on the living presence of Melibea as the listener. Each word is, in effect, calculated in terms of the living reaction it is designed to stimulate (although, at the same time, it may betray the sentiments of the speaker), and, as a result, the real structure of the above speech, rather than logical, is based on the vital alternation of the first and second persons. We may notice the following: "*Señora,* que *te* acuerde . . ."; "que aprenda de *mí* a tener mesura en el tiempo de *tu* ira en la qual *yo vsé* . . ." "Pues *tú, señora, tenías* yra . . ."; "avnque fueran las que *tú* pensavas . . ."; *yo* libre de pena". This abundance of first and

second person pronouns indicates the subordination of precedent or generality
("del ayrado es de apartar por poco tiempo," or "Dios no hizo cosa mala")
to the confrontation of two lives. Rojas' artistry of style is primarily an artistry
of living dialogue.

This is true to such an extent that we might apply to the whole of the
style one of the most acute of the interpolated remarks about Celestina: "Lo
que en sus cuentas reza es . . . qué despenseros *le dan ración e qual lo mejor e
cómo les llaman por nombre porque quando los encontrare no hable como
extraña. ...*" (IX, 25) Sempronio then goes on to point out: "Quando
menea los labios es fengir mentiras, ordenar cautelas para hauer dineros: por
aquí le entraré, esto me responderá, estotro replicaré. Assí viue ésta . . ." Celestina's life, like all life in the work, is dedicated to dialogue.

So many other interpolations confirm this as central to Rojas' style that it
is impossible to list them all. But it is hard to resist the temptation to speak of
the first interpolation in Act IV. Alisa has announced that she must leave
Celestina alone with Melibea: "CEL.—(*Aparte*) Por aquí anda el diablo
aparejando oportunidad, arreziando el mal a la otra. *¡Ea! buen amigo, ¡tener
rezio! Agora es mi tiempo o nunca. No la dexes, lléuamela de aquí a quien
digo.*" (IV, 163) In the sixteen-act *Comedia* this aside (and the one preceding
"*Ce, hermano, que se va todo a perder!*" later in the same act) amounted to
little more than a reference to the formal invocation of Satan ending Act III.
But the interpolation with its note of intimate direction imparts Celestina's
actual feeling of an unseen diabolic presence. Her reliance on the supernatural
emerges from the realm of formulas and ritual-conjuring and comes alive in
terms of the hope and despair of these two moments. No longer does Celestina
speak of "Triste Plutón"; she talks instead *to* her "buen amigo" and "hermano"
as her superstition is given circumstantial direction. How much more forceful
is this murmuring than that of the original, and, at the same time, how much
in accord with the most inherent features of Rojas' style!

The presentation of Rojas' stylistic intentions in this way suggests new
significance for a number of other curious features of his language and technique. In the first place, there is the extraordinary abundance of interrogatives. More than half the sentences are surrounded by question marks, and it
may well be that *La Celestina* has for its length more such constructions than
any other work in occidental literature.[3] Of course, these questions are only
infrequently intended to bring forth informative answers from the listener.
But, as we saw in the first interpolation discussed, each of them invokes his
presence. Just as the frequent exclamations express the sentiments of the *yo,*
so these questions enfold the *tú* in what is being said. Language is almost

never allowed an existence on its own terms apart from speech, the speech of two persons facing each other.

This same principle of artistic government necessarily extends beyond the levels of style and language and is betrayed in many other ways. One example is the constant reoccurrence of the topic of cosmetics all through *La Celestina*. Although this topic was frequent in the satire of this and previous periods (e.g., in the *Corbacho* of the Arcipreste de Talavera) and was mentioned briefly by Jorge Manrique to express the evanescence of life, here it seems to answer different necessities. Cosmetics represent a kind of plastic dialogue, a dialogue of vision which accompanies that of hearing. As Areusa says when slandering Melibea, "Por vna vez que aya de salir donde pueda ser vista, enuiste su cara con hiel e miel, con vnas tostadas e higos passados e con otras cosas . . ." (IX, 32) The same function for cosmetics is apparent in Elicia's decision in the added acts to relinquish her mourning for Celestina:

Más para esto es el buen seso, viendo la pérdida al ojo, viendo que los atauíos hazen la muger hermosa, avnque no lo sea, tornan de vieja moça e a la moça más. No es otra cosa la color e aluayalde, sino pegajosa liga en que se trauan los hombres. Ande, pues, mi espejo e alcohol, que tengo dañados estos ojos; anden mis tocas blancas, mis gorgueras labradas, mis ropas de plazer. Quiero adereçar lexía para estos cabellos, que perdían ya la ruuia color y, esto hecho, contaré mis gallinas, haré mi cama, porque la limpieza alegra el coraçón, barreré mi puerta e regaré la calle, porque los que passaren vean que es ya desterrado el dolor. (XVII, 155)

Cosmetics, like clothes, exist here in terms of personal encounter; hence, their constant reoccurrence in all parts of *La Celestina* not as a topic or commonplace but as a vital preoccupation.

Finally, and with all brevity, we may call attention to the running dialogue of attitude and gesture all throughout the work. Each inhabitant of *La Celestina* is constantly alerted to the appearance of the others, not only to that appearance prepared for him artificially by cosmetics, but also to those momentary physical expressions which reveal the other in the intimacy of his life. If cosmetics are directed to the *tú*, gestures emerge, like exclamations, from the *yo*. Although Rojas avoids individual faces and nuances of their expression (a limitation that we cannot begin to explain here), Celestina's changes of gait, Parmeno's "saltos" of relief at escaping danger (Act XII), Calisto's blind, deaf, and dumb raptures, and many others all complement the dialogue of words. Style, topic, and action join in conscious subservience to the first and second persons which conclude Rojas' artistic paradigm.

If, as we maintain, style in *La Celestina* is determined on the axis of spoken life that extends between *tú* and *yo,* it follows that we should be able to distinguish two more or less separate styles within the work, one based on one person, and the other on the other. We have already suggested the frequent alternation of question and exclamation as possibly representing a shift of expression from one end of the axis to the other. But even more than this, these two stylistic moments or modalities should be traceable in any given speech; that is to say, we should be able to judge stylistically any given speech insofar as it is intended either to touch the life of the listener or to express the life of the speaker. Those final remarks of Celestina to Melibea in Act IV, "Señora, que te acuerde la oración . . . ," would seem to belong to a style primarily directed to the *tú*. The facsimile of reason, the weighing of every word on a scale of effect, the underlining of the pronoun, all betray the predominant role of the second person. But what about the first person, the *yo* of the speaker which must play an inevitably equal part in all living dialogue? Must there not exist in *La Celestina* speeches and passages of this polar stylistic species? Let us take as an example one of the most splendid of the interpolations:

AREU.—Assí goze de mí, que es verdad, que estas, que siruen a señoras, ni gozan deleyte ni conocen los dulces premios de amor. *Nunca tratan con parientes, con yguales a quien pueden hablar tú por tú, con quien digan: ¿qué cenaste? ¿estás preñada? ¿quántas gallinas crías? lléuame a merendar a tu casa; muéstrame tu enamorado; ¿quánto ha que no te vido? ¿cómo te va con él? ¿quién son tus vezinas? e otras cosas de ygualdad semejantes. ¡O tía, qué duro nombre e qué graue e soberuio es señora contino en la boca!* Por esto me viuo sobre mi, desde que me sé conocer. Que jamás me precié de llamarme de otrie; sino mía. Mayormente destas señoras que agora se vsan. Gástase con ellas lo mejor del tiempo, e con una saya rota de las que ellas desechan pagan seruicio de diez años . . . Assí que esperan galardón, sacan baldón; esperan salir casadas, salen amenguadas; esperan vestidos e joyas de boda, salen desnudas e denostadas. Estos son sus premios, estos son sus beneficios e pagos. Oblíganseles a dar marido, quítanles el vestido. La mejor honrra que en sus casas tienen, es andar hechas callejeras, de dueña en dueña, con sus mensajes acuestas. Nunca oyen su nombre propio de la boca dellas; sino puta acá, puta acullá. ¿A dó vas; tiñosa? ¿Qué heziste, vellaca? ¿Porqué comiste esto, golosa? ¿Comó fregaste la sartén, puerca? ¿Porqué no limpiaste el manto, suzia? ¿Cómo dixiste esto, necia? ¿Quién perdió el plato, desaliñada? ¿Cómo faltó el paño de manos, ladrona? A tu rufián lo aurás dado. Ven acá, mala muger, la gallina hauada no paresce: pues búscala presto; si no, en la primera blanca de tu soldada la contaré. E tras esto mill chapinazos e pellizcos, palos e açotes. No ay quién las sepa contentar, no quién pueda sofrillas. Su plazer es dar bozes, su gloria es reñir. De lo mejor fecho menos contentamiento muestran. Por esto madre, he quesido más viuir en mi pequeña casa, esenta e señora, que no en sus ricos palacios sojuzgada e catiua. (IX, 40–43)

Formally, at least, this speech is addressed to Celestina ("O tía . . ." and

"Por esto madre . . ."), but, in reality and despite the abundant use of questions directed to the second person, it is addressed to no one. Rather it expresses Areusa's almost frantic sentiment of herself, the need for freedom not as an abstraction but as a living alternative to slavery. Stylistically this sentimental revelation of the self may be further broken down: there are moments of poetically elevated self-explanation ("he quesido más viuir en mi pequeña casa, esente e señora . . ."); there are also rapid antitheses ("esperan galardón, sacan baldón . . .") which, while still poetically arranged, reveal more closely Areusa's indignation on its own terms; finally, and most interesting of all, there are the two passages of rapid question and exclamation which represent as complete a breakdown of stylistic formality as was possible in Rojas' time. Here Areusa expresses her sentimental existence in terms immediate to itself, and all pretense to discourse, to intelligibility, or to poetic pattern, breaks down. It is a shotgun style which needs no specific target because it is dedicated to the force of its own explosion; it has been liberated from the demands of anyone else's point of view, and the *tú*＝*yo* relationship that as the grammatical requirement of the interrogative becomes a mere vestige of communication. Both the sequence of action and the particular existence of the listener are disintegrated stylistically by this eruption of the sentiment of self. Thus, just as in Celestina's persuasion of Melibea, the sentiments and desires of the *yo* were channeled by reason towards the *tú* and were completely redesigned for acceptance there, so here, having dispensed with channeling, Areusa's sentiments and desires have only a chaotic and superficial remnant of reasonable direction. In the one case, layers of calculated argument disguise the style; in the other, sentiment is covered by a transparent shred of grammar. It is between these two stylistic extremes, between *tú* and *yo*, between argument and sentiment, that Rojas practices his art of words. One is not necessarily less vital than the other; both are alive but in different ways and exist in calculated proportion in almost every line of *La Celestina*.[4]

Rojas' stylistic conquest of dialogue was, thus, made possible by his conscious combination and variation of two styles, a style of argument designed to impress the listener and a style of sentiment designed to express the speaker. Neither can be said to exist in an absolutely pure form (in the final argument to Melibea, far beneath the surface we detect Celestina's feelings of power and relief and in Areusa's outburst there remains a need for the second person). In most cases—for example, Celestina's answer to Sempronio's doubting—there is a vital fusion of the two. Nevertheless, such a division is supported by the interpolations as an adequate approach to Rojas' stylistic preoccupation on its own terms.

In affirming this conclusion, we must be particularly on guard against the temptation of accepting Rojas' mastery of dialogue, his ability to relate language and even gesture to two lives simultaneously, as a matter of course. Dialogue, as it is used in *La Celestina* was an extraordinary innovation both in Spanish literature and in European literature if we except certain passages of Dante. Perhaps the most serious objection to this statement might be made in connection not with previous attempts at drama but with such epics as the *Poema de Cid*. But even there, dialogue is intentionally exemplary and only occasionally surpasses the frame of heroism into an intuitive understanding of the two lives whose encounter it represents. In any case, however incredible it may seem in terms of a twentieth-century literature which rest upon the generic and stylistic discoveries of periods long past, Fernando de Rojas from out of the meager tradition that was available to him was among the first to develop techniques of writing a flexible and living dialogue. And, although stylistic analysis cannot in itself explain this achievement, the interpolations of 1502 testify to the fact that it was not accidental, partial, subconscious. It was the achievement of a great literary artist who knew exactly what he was doing, and who chose each of his words and sentences in terms of the living *tú* and *yo* who are the members of the "dialogic" situation.[5]

2. From Monologue to Dialogue: *La Celestina* and the *Corbacho*

At once a source for Rojas' style and a valuable point of contrast to it is the *Corbacho* of the Arcipreste de Talavera. The inspiration of Areusa's outburst and of other passages in the *Corbacho* has been pointed out many times. Nevertheless, in order to appreciate the stylistic innovation of *La Celestina*, it is convenient to recall a representative passage of the Arcipreste. Instead of that tirade following the loss of a chicken which is usually cited, I have chosen a moment reminiscent of the first garden scene and of Melibea's passive protest against Calisto's masculine activities. It is a fairer contrast, since for the Arcipreste it is less of an intentional caricature of popular speech and since we must imagine that it was addressed to a single person:

Talavera	*Rojas*
Yuy, dexadme, non quiero; yuy, qué porfiado; en buena fe yo me vaya, por Dios, pues yo dé vozes; estad en ora buena; dexadme agora estar, estad un poco quedo; ya, por Dios, non seades enojo; ay, paso, señor, que sodes descortés. Aved ora vergueña; ¿estáis en	MELIB.—Señor mío, pues me fié en tus manos, pues quise complir tu voluntad, no sea de peor condición, por ser piadosa, que si fuera esquiua e sin misericordia; no quieras perderme por tan breue deleyte e en tan poco espacio. Que las malfechas cosas, después de

vuestro seso?; anad, ora que vos miran; ¿non vedes que nos veen?, y estad para sin sabor. En buena fee que me ensañe, pues, en verdad, non me río yo; estad en ora mala. ¿Pues queréis que vos lo diga? En vuena fe, yo vos muerda las manos; líbreme Dios deste demonio, y andad allá si quieres. ¡O!, como soys pesado, mucho soys enojoso, ay de mí, guay de mí. Anad, que me quebráis el dedo; anad, que me apretáis la mano; el diablo lo troxo aquí. ¡O! mesquina; o, desaventurada, que noramala nascí!; mal punto vine aquí; dolores que vos maten, rabia que vos acabe, diablo, huerco, maldito; y piensa que tengo su fuerça, todos los huesos me ha quebrantado, todas las manos me ha molidas; rabia, señor, a osadas allá. ¿Y reía?; nunca jamás desta scré escarmentada; yuy, tomóme agora el diablo en venir acá: maldita sea mi vida agora; fuese yo muerta, ¡o, triste de mí! ¿Quién me engaño? Maldita sea la que jamás en hombre se fía, amen.[6]

cometidas, más presto se pueden reprehender que emendar. Goza de lo que yo gozo, que es ver e llegar a tu persona; no pidas ni tomes aquello que, tomado, no será en tu mano boluer. Guarte, señor, de dañar lo que con todos tesoros del mundo no se restaura.

CAL.—... ¿no quieres que me arrime al dulce puerto a descansar de mi passados trabajos?

MELIB.—Por mi vida, que avnque hable tu lengua quanto quisiere, no obren las manos quanto pueden. Está quedo, señor mío. *Bástete, pues ya soy tuya, gozar de lo esterior, desto que es propio fruto de amadores; no me quieras robar el mayor don que la natura me ha dado. Cata que del buen pastor es propio tresquillar das ouejas e ganado; pero no destruyrlo y estragarlo.*

CAL.—. . . Perdona, señora a mis desuergonçadas manos, que jamás pensaron de tocar tu ropa con su indignidad e poco merecer; agora gozan de llegar a tu gentil cuerpo e lindas e delicadas carnes.

MELIB.—Apártate allá, Lucrecia.

CAL.—¿Porqué, mi señora? Bien me huelgo que estén semejantes testigos de mi gloria.

MELIB.—Yo no los quiero de mi yerro. Si pensara que tan desmesuradamente te auías de hauer comigo, no fiara mi persona de tu cruel conuersación. (XIV, 116–18)

If we read these two passages superficially and for content, we are apt to conclude that the nameless woman of the *Corbacho* is more sincere in her protests than Melibea, who seems hypocritical and mealy-mouthed. The difference in pitch and tempo decisively confirms this impression. The Arcipreste's creation launches herself completely into a sequence of short protests and threats, into the sound and fury of her words. It is a style of pure exclamation in which each outburst has a minimum of relation to the next, and, although at the end there is the implication of some sort of concluded action (it is difficult to tell exactly what from the text), we might rearrange the separate parts without damage to any sense. The *yo* of the speaker, in other words, has lost all possible stylistic perspective; the *tú*, or in this case, *vos*, is in a very real sense nonexistent, a mere assumption of speech—like Areusa's neighbors. Melibea, on the other hand, is extremely conscious of Calisto's effective presence; she reasons with him, argues with him, and then surrenders, "Apártate allá Lucrecia," with little more than verbal reservations. And precisely because of this consciousness of the other, because of this awareness of what is happening to her, she betrays the weakness of her position. Her consent is revealed by her gentle effort to argue the matter from Calisto's point of view, a form of argument that is continued into the interpolation.

Yet despite this first impression, we learn by reading the next few lines of the *Corbacho* that the Arcipreste intended to portray feminine hypocrisy, the ultimate insincerity of the sex, at its worst: "Esto e otras cosas dizen por se honestar, mas Dios sabe la fuerça que ponen nin la femencia que dan a fuyr nin resistir, que dan vozes e están quedas, menean los braços, pero el cuerpo está quedo, gimen e non se mueven, fazen como que ponen toda su fuerça, mostrando aver dolor e aver enojo" (pp 279–80). We should not, however, dismiss the *Corbacho* as mere caricature or humorous exaggeration; rather it presents a kind of dichotomy of consciousness. We might well say that Melibea "doth protest too much," that she pretends what she does not intend, but for her counterpart there is no feigned reluctance. It is instead the typical double reaction of an irrational ego, the failure of the child mind to perceive the logical contradiction between "yes" and "no." Possessing no consciousness of the other, woman for the Arcipreste is an infrahuman being, hypocritical and insincere, illogical and obscure, not by intention but by nature: "gimen e non se mueven." Melibea, on the other hand, confronts her femininity with her humanity, that is to say she attempts to speak to Calisto on a plane removed from the complementary immediacies of pleasure and violence. You and I are human beings susceptible to reason, she implies, and we must face the peculiar situation of my sex from this point of view. She becomes a person (and a possible hypocrite) insofar as she is engaged in dialogue with the other; insofar as she urges Calisto to think of her as a *tú* as well as of his own passionate *yo*. It is not so much a question, then, of greater or lesser hypocrisy (both in the last analysis have no real objections to their fate) or of greater or lesser vitality as of the intricacies of dialogic interchange against the simplicity of a style corresponding only to the speaker. For one the lover is "diablo, huerco, maldito," a shadowy presence to be exclaimed away; for the other he is "señor mío," a human being who is loved and feared and to whom appeal can be made. Without the participation of the second person, both pretense and sincerity (and Melibea represents both) are impossible.

All of this is born out by Melibea's reactions after the act is concluded:

¡O mi vida e mi señor! ¿Cómo has quisido que pierda el nombre e corona de virgen por tan breue deleyte? ¡O pecadora de mi madre, si de tal cosa fueses sabidora, como tomarías de grado tu muerte e me la darías a mí por fuerça! ¡Cómo serías cruel verdugo de tu propia sangre! ¡Cómo sería yo fin quexosa de tus dias! ¡O mi padre honrado, cómo he dañado tu fama e dado causa e lugar a quebrantar tu casa! ¡O traydora de mi, como no miré primero el gran yerro que seguía de tu entrada, el gran peligro que esperaua! (XIV, 119)

She begins by addressing Calisto, but as her anguish and her remorse rise in her[7] his presence is forgotten. She thinks, instead, of her mother and father as incarnations of her broken obligation. At this point the style changes radically, becoming comparable to the remarks of the Arcipreste's lady after her friend has departed. There is the same continuity of exclamation and the same failure to integrate the discourse into any sort of sequence. Melibea, of course, recognizes clearly her own guilt and its consequences and so does not attack Calisto or lose all vestiges of reason. In the *Corbacho,* on the other hand, there is no such evident change of style with the departure of the *vos;* the outburst continues with him or without him until its force is exhausted. We may even imagine that after the final "amen" the lady forgets all about the whole thing and is quiescent until her next stimulus, a stimulus which she will have no means of evaluating. A loss of an egg is for the women of the *Corbacho* as great as the loss of honor, for lacking in dialogue they also lack a world which relates itself to them in terms of its greater or lesser value. Thus, the first tirade ends with the question (a question to be understood literally) "¿quién me engañó?" while Melibea turns from exclamation back to Calisto with a greater appreciation of his identity and of his meaning for her: "Señor, por Dios, pues ya todo queda por tí, pues ya soy tu dueña, pues ya no puedes negar mi amor, no me niegues tu vista de día, passando por mi puerta; de noche donde tú ordenares." (XIV, 120)

To sum up, the Arcipreste was unable to guide or control the style which his intuition of woman as vitally irrational had allowed him to discover. The unleashed ego of his words possessed no direction, no awareness of a *tú,* which might have converted them into dialogue. And barred from dialogue, he, somewhat like Rabelais, did not know how to tone the frenzy and impetus of his writing or to mould it into any sort of literary form. Each tirade, each outbreak of these torrents of feminine life, produced a style that is undeniably vital; but, lacking cellular genes and an inner pattern of growth, each dies when its initial momentum is exhausted. In contrast to that of *La Celestina,* the style of the *Corbacho* seems protoplasmic and formless, alive but confined to the present. It is a style without that internal past and future which might give it access both to duration and to form. Or to put the matter in another way, we may characterize it as a style without perspective, radiating from the sentiment of a single life, while Rojas, with his constant juxtaposition of two or more lives in their conversation, managed to control the vitality of his style and to build from it first a *Comedia* and afterwards a *Tragicomedia.* Essential to his mastery of dialogue was a stylistic perspective which his predecessor had not found.

The specific instruments of style which Rojas used to tame the floods of speech of his characters are not hard to find. They are clarity and logic, qualities noticeably and purposefully prohibited to the women of the Arcipreste de Talavera. By all rules of rhetoric, adherence to clarity and logic is the only effective means of converting language from expression to communication, and while this may not be a final linguistic truth, it is certainly true for Rojas. Almost any passage in *La Celestina* will testify to it; whenever, as in the case of Celestina's departing speech to Melibea, one individual tries to argue, persuade, or communicate with another, clarity and at least an appearance of logic become necessities. If the secret of Rojas style was, as we have said, his conscious mastery of dialogue, his ability to place a word, sentence, or speech within the perspective of two existences, it is not surprising that *La Celestina,* for all its profound intuition into life, should be one of the clearest and most logical works in Spanish literature. And, excepting certain passages in Act I, this is as true today as it was in 1500 when Rojas' style stood in such sharp contrast to those of the century preceding him.[8] It is also not surprising that in the revision of 1502 so many of the stylistic interpolations were intended to reinforce one or the other of these qualities. In spite of the apparently willed obscurities of the prefatory material, the quest for clarity and logic was one of Rojas' major stylistic efforts. We may measure his success by the most elementary comparison of the two foregoing passages.

At this point the objection may well be made: if all Rojas had to do was to brake the sentimental style of the *Corbacho* by obedience to the newly understood classical concepts of clarity and logic, why present the style of *La Celestina* as such an achievement? Why could not the Arcipreste, himself, or anyone else have done the same thing? Was it not, in other words, an inevitable result of what Menéndez Pidal calls (in the article cited in Chapter I) the shift from the rhetorical complications of fifteenth-century prose to the new humanistic styles of the reign of the Catholic kings? From one point of view this is true, but the suggestion that Rojas mixed together two antagonistic styles is an obvious oversimplification. As I tried to show in the preceding section, he achieves not a mixture but a compounding of sentiment and argument, a compounding which varies infinitely according to mood and circumstance. And to do this, he had to discover a clarity and logic that were not necessarily opposed to life, that were not mechanical rules or inert precepts, but which could combine with life in the creation of a new spoken style. In this sense, Rojas solved the problem which so preoccupied Cicero in his dialogues on oratory, the problem of rhetorical recipes versus natural and living effectiveness of speech.[9] As we shall see, Rojas' clarity and logic were not qualities abstracted intellectually and governing style in an *a priori* fashion; rather they were, to remake a famous phrase, "una claridad vital" and "una lógica vital." It was on these terms that Rojas was able to develop a scene from a sentence, an interchange from an outburst, that he could juxtapose *yo* and *tú* without destroying them.

3. The Quest for Clarity

With this introductory comparison of the stylistic artistries of the Arcipreste de Talavera and of Rojas, we are ready for the evidence of the interpolations. Let us begin with the matter of clarity and an example involving both a deletion and a substituted interpolation. Celestina in the course of her semifinal effort to obtain Pármeno's support remarks as follows in the *Comedia:*

Bién pensaua yo que, después que concediste en mi buen consejo, que no hauías de tornarte atrás. Todavía me parece que te quedan reliquias vanas, hablando por antojo, más que por razón. Desechas el prouecho por contentar la lengua. Oyeme, si no me has oydo, e mira que soy vieja e el buen consejo mora en los viejos e de los mancebos es propio el deleyte. Bien creo que de tu yerro sola la edad tiene culpa. Espero en Diós [que variarán tus costumbres, variando el cabello]; digo, hijo, cresciendo e viendo cosas nuevas cada día. Porque la mocedad en solo lo presente se impide e ocupa a mirar; mas la madura edad no dexa presente ni passado ni por venir. (VII, 232)[10]

The semiproverbial is suited to Celestina and to its context (the comparison of age and youth), but Rojas, upon rereading it, realized that it was wrongly directed, unclear from the dialogic point of view. In effect, "variarán tus costumbres variando el cabello" is inappropriately addressed to the adolescent Pármeno, a Pármeno who within the same act is to enjoy his first night of love. If Celestina is to wait until Pármeno's hair has turned gray she is going to wait a long time. As a result the text of the *Tragicomedia* is made to read: "Espero en Diós *que serás mejor para mí de aquí adelante, e mudarás el ruyn propósito con la tierna edad. Que como dizen, mudanse costumbres con la mudança del cabello e variación;* digo, hijo, cresciendo e viendo cosas nueuas cada dia." We may notice how the reference to Pármeno's age is introduced in terms of Rojas' evident awareness of the fault of the original and how the general nature of the proverb is underlined by the verb "dizen." The idea that Pármeno will sooner or later achieve a state of mature experience (an idea indispensable to Celestina's argument) has been kept and at the same time clarified in terms of his particular person and age. The clarification has been accomplished in terms of the dialogic direction.

The same thing is even more evident in one of the interpolations of Act V. Celestina is attempting to explain to Sempronio why he will not need an equal share of Calisto's bounty:

CEL.—¿Qué, hijo? ¡Una dozena de agujetas e vn torcé para el bonete e vn arco para andarte de casa en casa tirando a páxaros e aojando páxaras a las ventanas! *Mochachas digo, bouo, de las que no saben bolar, que bien me entiendes. Que no ay mejor alcahuete para ellas que vn arco, que se puede entrar cada vno hecho moxtrenco, como dizen; en achaque de trama etc.* ¡Mas ay, Sempronio, de quién tiene de mantener honrra e se va haziendo vieja como yo! (V, 197–98)

In this case, the original makes a certain amount of sense if the reader understands "páxaras" as a figurative parallel to "poule" or to the jazz age "chicken." But it is a sense which, even if admitted, does not exhaust the intention of the author. The real relation between "arco" and "páxaras" is not at all apparent and calls for a clarifying *glosa* to explain the hidden significance. This Rojas supplies, again in terms of dialogue. We must imagine that Sempronio looks puzzled at the mention of "páxaras," a look which causes Celestina to explain her reference not to us but to him: "Mochachas digo, bouo ..." She goes on to reveal that the search for an arrow lost through a window or over a wall is an ideal excuse for striking up an acquaintance; she has referred to "mochachas" as "páxaras" precisely because they can be hunted with a bow and arrow. Thus, Rojas has Celestina, with the implied assistance of Sempronio, clarify his thought for him, a very appropriate procedure since what is said refers both to Celestina's vocation (*alcahuetería*) and to Sempronio's aspirations to imitate his master. In terms of *La Celestina* as a whole, the arrow might be characterized as a kind of poor man's falcon.

Other examples of Rojas' preoccupation with clarity as indispensable to dialogue (and of its correction in terms of dialogue) involve not argument but sentiment. The quality of clarity is necessary not only for communication with the listener but also for sentimental expression of the self. In Act IV

Melibea's change from anger to consent furnishes an obvious interpolation of this sort:

> CEL.—... Que no es otro mi oficio, sino seruir a los semejantes: desto biuo e desto me arreo. Nunca fué mi voluntad enojar a vnos por agradar a otros, avnque ayan dicho a tu merced en mi absencia otra cosa. Al fin, señora, a la firme verdad el viento del vulgo no la empece. *Vna sola soy en este limpio trato. En toda la ciudad pocos tengo descontentos. Con todos, cumplo, los que algo me mandan, como si touiesse veynte pies e otras tantas manos.*
>
> MELIB.—*No me maravillo, que vn solo maestro de vicios dizen que basta para corromper vn gran pueblo.* Por cierto tantos e tales loores me han dicho de tus *falsas* mañas, que no sé si crea que pedías oración. (IV, 183–84)

Leaving aside the first interpolation having to do with Celestina's character, let us consider only the changes in Melibea's answer. The text of the *Comedia* expresses the dregs of her gradually subsiding fury in the form of sarcasm. Later Melibea will surrender, but at this point Rojas is concerned with her intermediate effort to hold on to a sentiment that already has been dissipated vitally. It is a delicate transition, and in 1502 he had obvious doubts as to its clarity. Might not "loor de tus mañas" be taken literally and lead to the belief that Melibea had already yielded? Hence, the insertion of the "No me maravillo ..." caustically directed to Celestina and of the word "falsas" which, along with the retention of "loores," gives a brutal clarity to the sarcasm.

We might further point out that with this interpolation, Rojas seems to feel that it is necessary to compensate for the missing intonation which would have made the meaning clear. Dialogue by its very nature depends on the human voice for its total clarification, and much of Rojas' effort toward clarity may be related ultimately to the aphony of his created lives. He must state in words what cannot be implied by enunciation. We are reminded, of course, of Alonso de Proaza's famous instructions for reading *La Celestina* aloud, instructions which were probably suggested to him by Rojas:

> *Dize el modo que se ha de tener leyendo esta tragicomedia*
>
> Si amas y quieres a mucha atención
> Leyendo a Calisto mouer los oyentes,
> Cumple que sepas hablar entre dientes,
> A vezes con gozo, esperança y passión,
> A vezes ayrado con gran turbación.
> Finge leyendo mil artes y modos,
> Pregunta y responde por boca de todos,
> Llorando y riyendo en tiempo y sazón.
> (II, 216–17)

There is here a note of regret at the theatrical impossibility of the work, a regret based on understanding of the problematical relationship of dialogue to style. But we might console Proaza by pointing out to him such passages as the above, passages which illustrate how Rojas achieved his marvellous and living clarity precisely because of this stylistic problem. If Rojas had been writing for actors, it is quite possible that the dialogue would have been neither so alive nor so clear. He might well have counted on—as so many dramatists do count on—acting and enunciation for the full communication of meaning.

There are, of course, many other instances of corrective clarification in the *Tragicomedia,* but the above are the most interesting stylistically.[11] In addition to testifying to the constancy of Rojas' search for clarity, they also show his fine perception of obscurities resulting from the lack of adequate relationship between the word and its speaker or listener. Each of the three is what we might call a vital obscurity and is corrected on its own terms with the greatest delicacy. But aside from these expected conclusions, conclusions which tend to support our authorship assumption, these examples (along with those noted) suggest the comparison of Rojas' whole notion of vital clarity with that implied by the word "clarté." A tentative understanding of his art of clarity can be developed from this evidence of its practice.

Even on this minimal level of stylistic self-correction, even for those obscurities, often more fancied than real, which can be overcome by minor word rearrangement, it is apparent that Rojas' guiding principle is quite distinct from that of *clarté.* Unlike Malherbe, Rojas' solution to any difficulty of language or significance is almost always additive. He respects his own creation to such an extent that he prefers to add words and even sentences of further explanation rather than to modify or delete. In every case, an effort is made to prevent the sentiment, image, or idea from being lost in the interests of clarity. He does not change the word "nouicios" (see note 11); he will not forsake the proverbial equation of wisdom and gray hair; he refuses to abandon the cynical reference to "páxaras"; and he further underlines Melibea's weakening sarcasm. In other words, for Rojas, clarity is a necessary ingredient of dialogue, but it is not an aesthetic principle or a controlling literary criterion.

Having said this, reference to Sempronio's well-known condemnation of stylistic extravagance is inevitable. The passage is as follows:

CAL.—... Ni comeré hasta entonce; avnque primero sean los cauallos de Febo apacentados en aquellos verdes prados, que suelen, quando han dado fin a su jornada.
SEMP.—Dexa, señor, essos rodeos, dexa essas poesías, que no es habla conueniente la que a todos no es común, la que todos no participan, la que pocos entien-

den. Di: avnque se ponga el sol, e sabrán todos lo que dizes. E come alguna conserua, con que tanto espacio de tiempo te sostengas. (VIII, 21–22)

It should first be noted that, while Rojas probably agrees with Sempronio, these remarks are by no means an independent stylistic manifesto which he has been waiting for a suitable opportunity to express. Instead it is integrated to Sempronio's larger reproof of Calisto's behavior (refusal to eat, failure to realize that the night has passed), a reproof which gives inner unity to the scene and which is characteristic of their mutual relationship. Rather than a completed statement of stylistic doctrine, it represents a recognition in passing of one aspect of Rojas' notion of clarity. Extrinsic adornment must be avoided precisely because it does not contribute to dialogue ("no es habla conueniente la que a todos no es común ...") because it is not organic to communication in language.[12]

Thus, while Rojas seems to favor the exile of superfluous decoration, in his own work this exile is a principle of dialogue which is applied before rather than after the fact. This doctrine of Sempronio's may help us to understand the radical distinction of Rojas' approach to prose from that of a Diego de San Pedro or of a Juan de Mena, but we must not demand that the textual changes of 1502 conform to it. In other words, it is possible to agree with Moratín, Foulché Delbosc, and Menéndez Pelayo who find passages in the *Tragicomedia* (and in the *Comedia*) which should have been deleted or simplified and, at the same time, admit that from Rojas' point of view what he writes is neither decorative nor superfluous. Anything that could so be described, Rojas might well have answered, he would not have written in the first place. Accordingly, his self-clarification does not cut the text but rather develops the meaning of the dialogue already written. While Rojas does not regard the *Comedia* as a sacred document unsusceptible of improvement, he tends to respect it as a whole and, in clarifying, to preserve its essential contours of significance. He does not choose to mutilate or foreshorten his text in the interest of either rational or rhetorical clarity. We must be careful, then, not to confuse a stylistic clarification which is in deep agreement with the nature of Rojas' art with concepts more appropriate to other nations and historical periods.

It is convenient to insist on this matter of clarity because it seems to be related to the whole process of revision in 1502. There are two observations to be made about the writing of the *Tragicomedia* which suggest a parallel with these examples of clarification of style. In the first place, we may notice the extent to which the few deletions are overwhelmed by the additions. Actually, only two or three of the deletions remove any substance or content from the

Comedia. In the second place, in view of the quantity of addition and interpolation, it is surprising to find only three or four changes designed to adjust or fit the new material to the original.[13] Not only does Rojas add rather than substract from his text but also all that is added (both acts and interpolations) seems to grow out of what was already there and so to require a minimum of change in it. There is, thus, a process of creative completion on the levels of character, structure, and theme which is reminiscent of the clarification by completion we have just witnessed. Or to put the matter in another way, the added acts clarify the whole in the same manner that the interpolations, large and small, clarify the parts. Unlike the sterile outbursts of the Arcipreste, Rojas' dialogic control over life permits and demands continuing vital clarification—a continuing growth to artistic maturity. The art of *La Celestina* is that of a vital dialectic guided skilfully towards a plenitude of meaning and on a scale ranging from stylistic clarity to thematic fulfillment.

Curiously enough, an image used in the often underestimated *Prólogo* provides an illustration of this larger concept of creative or vital clarity. The reference is to Heraclitus' "Omnia secundum litem fiunt," and reads as follows: "E como sea cierto que toda palabra del hombre sciente está preñada, desta se puede dezir que de muy hinchada y llena quiere rebentar, echando de sí tan crescidos ramos y hojas, que del menor pimpollo se sacaría harto fruto entre personas discretas." (I, 16–17)[14] This metaphor is quite different from the stale phrase, "a fruitful idea." Rojas visualizes the process of creative growth from the obscure potentiality of the seed idea through its germination and flowering in the human mind until new fruit is born from it. Clarity is in the fullest sense an evident plenitude; it is a final product, the result of a completed cycle of growth rather than a reduction to rational diagram. Such a definition admittedly goes far beyond our examples, far beyond stylistic practice as it can be studied in the interpolations, but, at the same time, for an authentic artist such as Rojas, the most insignificant choice of word necessarily implies the whole of his technique. A study of the style of *La Celestina* from the author's point of view cannot be isolated; it becomes instead an introduction to his artistry.

4. The Maintenance of Logic

The second ingredient of spoken language which distinguishes *La Celestina* from the *Corbacho* is logic. In theory a strict rhetorical frontier might be drawn between clarity and logic, but for the individual interpolation it is almost impossible to separate them stylistically. A practical distinction, however, may be developed from the observation that logical corrections are designed to strengthen the coherence of sentence or speech rather than to banish the obscure implications of a word or phrase. Logic is an instrument of communication insofar as its use reassures the listener that what is said is susceptible of proof and the speaker that it is coherent and complete. In this sense it organizes lesser units of clarity, and with these two functions it is one of the most characteristic and conscious aspects of Rojas' artistry of style. In the first place, insofar as the inhabitants of *La Celestina* (particularly Celestina, herself) continually attempt to persuade each other, continually combine sentiment with argument in their dialogue, logic is indispensable to them. We have already seen something of this in Celestina's final argument in Act IV, and that is an example that can be reproduced time and again from the work. In the second place, the extent of Rojas' conscious purpose in reinforcing the logic of his discourse is revealed by the number and importance of the interpolations included only for its sake. Among them, it is worth while pointing out, are many of those most severely criticized by Foulché Delbosc, Cejador, and Delpy.

The shorter interpolations, those intended to strengthen the coherence of individual sentences, will do little more than confirm Rojas' insistent preoccupation with the logic of his style. The following three examples need little explanation; they are mere grammatical corrections and lie close to that artificial boundary which we drew between clarity and logic:

PARM.—¿Qué sé yo si Melibea anda porque le pague nuestro amo su mucho atreuimiento desta manera? E *más,* avn no somos muy ciertos dezir verdad la vieja. (XII, 79)

CEL.—... Ya sabes tú, Pármeno amigo, lo que te prometí, e tú, hija mía lo que te tengo rogado. Dexada *aparte* la dificultad con que me lo has concedido, pocas razones son necessarias, porque el tiempo no lo padece. (VII, 257)

PARM.—¿Madre, mandas que te acompañe?
CEL.—Sería quitar a vn sancto para poner en otro. Acompáñeos Dios; que yo vieja soy, *que* no he temor que me fuercen en la calle. (VII, 260) [15]

Slightly less evident, perhaps, is this interpolation of two words (already reproduced for another purpose). "CEL.—Pocas vírgines, a Diós gracias, has tú visto en esta cibdad, que hayan abierto tienda a vender, de quién yo no aya sido corredora de su primer hilado. En nasciendo la mochacha, la hago escriuir en mi registro, *e esto* para saber quantas se me salen de la red." (III, 133) Here the correction shows Rojas' awareness of the lack of logical balance of the sentence as it appeared in the *Comedia*. Of the three parts of the whole, two are facts or actions (birth of the girl—entry in the register) and the third is a reason. Thus, *"e esto"* serves to set apart and underline the distinct category of the latter, to keep the reason from merging in the listener's mind with the second action. In other words, while the meaning of the original sentence was perfectly clear, because of its tripartite structure it failed to emphasize Celestina's reasoning, a reasoning which became a dependent tail to "la hago escriuir en mi registro." These minor interpolations, thus, illustrate Rojas' concern with grammar as a form of logic and his corresponding awareness of connectives and their adequacy.[16]

Going beyond the sentence to the paragraph, we find a number of interpolations which provide general conclusions to prior observations or reasons. There is, in fact, a tendency in *La Celestina* to finish each speech (or unit of argument) with a final statement—often proverbial—which serves to summarize and hold together all that has gone before. One example, from Sempronio's denial of the permanence of human sentiment and evaluation, should be enough:

> SEMP.—... Cada día vemos nouedades e las oymos e las passamos e dexamos atrás. Diminúyelas el tiempo, házelas contingibles. ¿Que tanto te marauillarías, si dixesen: la tierra tembló o otra semejante cosa, que no oluidases luego? Assí como: elado está el río, el ciego vee ya, muerto es tu padre, vn rayo cayó, ganada es Granada, el Rey entra oy, el turco es vencido, eclipse ay mañana, la puente es lleuada, aquel es ya obispo, a Pedro robaron, Ynés se ahorco, [Cristóbal fué borracho]. ¿Qué me dirás sino que a tres días passados o a la segunda vista, no ay quién dello se marauille? Todo es assí, todo passa desta manera, todo se oluida, todo queda atrás, Pués assí será este amor de mi amo: quanto mas fuere andando, tanto mas disminuyendo. *Que la costumbre luenga amansa los dolores, afloxa e deshaze los deleytes, desmengua las marauillas.* Procuremos prouecho, mientra pendiere la contienda. E si a pie enxuto le pudieremos remediar, lo mejor mejor es; e si no, poco a poco le soldaremos el reproche e menosprecio de Melibea contra él. Donde no, mas vale que pene el amo, que no que peligre el moço. (III, 129–32)

In the *Comedia* the conclusion might be restated as follows: "All sentiments and evaluations are passing. Therefore my master's love will pass. Since it will pass, let us try to take advantage of his suffering." And, finally, "even if this logic proves false, it does not matter." The general conclusion "Todo es assí ..." is drawn, and the particular applications follow automatically. What is missing is, then, not a conclusion but a summation of what has been said, a final résumé of content. And it is this that Rojas inserts after his last specific reference, the love of Calisto, and before the proposed applications.

Admitting the logical gap that is filled by Rojas in 1502, it is nevertheless evident that the interpolation breaks the flow of discourse. As a topic there may be need of summation, but for a speech the interruption is open to criticism.

Rojas seems in 1502 to be thinking more about what has been said than about who is saying it; his structure of logic has been allowed to show through the life of his dialogue. But it is precisely such excesses as these[17] which show off the full difficulty of the *lógica vital* which Rojas was attempting. His partial failure here underlines the usual unobtrusiveness of his logical intervention, his success in avoiding that dryness and conceptual difficulty which we ordinarily expect to find in a "logical" style. On the face of it, this success seems not only difficult but incredible, and the very phrase "lógica vital," somewhat of a paradox. The antithesis of logic and life has been too firmly engrained in our minds for us to imagine any genuine stylistic synthesis for them. Rojas may mix logic and life, he may use the one to restrain the other, but how can he compound them or even appear to have done so? Was not, in other words, the above failure an inevitability rather than an excess?

These questions may be answered by two of the longer logical interpolations, interpolations which, as in the case of clarity, give more than a glimpse of this aspect of Rojas' artistry of style. The first occurs in Act IV when Celestina, anticipating Melibea's anger, attempts to persuade her to pity and gentleness:

E pues como todas seamos humanos, nascidos para morir, sea cierto que no se puede dezir nacido el que para sí solo nasció. Porque sería semejante a los brutos animales, en los cuales avn ay algunos piadosos, como se dize del vnicornio, que se humilla a qualquiera donzella. *El perro con todo su ímpetu e braueza, quando viene a morder, si se echan en el suelo, no haze mal: esto de piedad.* ¿Pués las aues? Ninguna cosa el gallo come, que no participe e llame las gallinas a comer dello. *El pelícano rompe el pecho por dar a sus hijos a comer de sus entrañas. Las cigüeñas mantienen otro tanto tiempo a sus padres viejos en el nido, quanto ellos les dieron ceuo siendo pollitos.* ¿Pues *tal conoscimiento dió la natura a los animales e aues,* porqué los hombres hauemos de ser mas crueles? ¿Porqué no daremos parte de nuestras gracias e personas a los próximos ...? (IV, 175–77)

The most apparent reason for the added examples is the logical disparity of the two offered in the *Comedia,* the unicorn and the rooster; and the remedy was to add a domestic animal ("el perro") and an exotic bird ("el pelícano") under each heading. Thus, in the *Tragicomedia* the two classes, "animales" and "aues," are equally illustrated. And although they disarrange the symmetry of the above scheme, the "cigüeñas" also have their reason for entry into the text. They suggest again one of the underlying and essential motifs of this preliminary conversation with Melibea, the contrast between youth and age. Youth is here, just as Celestina hopes will very shortly be the case, distinguished for its kindly treatment of old age. The last interpolation is, of course, one more example of Rojas' effort to shore up the logic of his conclusions, an effort we have already witnessed.

The second example occurs in an ironically parallel scene, the persuasion of Areusa to accept Parmeno as an additional lover. But the terms and tone of the argument are quite different:

CEL.—... ¡Ay! ¡ay! hija, si viesses el saber de tu prima e qué tanto le ha aprouechado mi criança e consejos e qué gran maestra está. E avn ¡que no se halla ella mal con mis castigos! Que vno en la cama e otro en la puerta e otro, que sospira por ella en su casa, se precia de tener ... ¿E tú piensas que con dos, que tengas, que las tablas de la cama lo han de descobrir? ¿De una sola gotera te mantienes? ¡No te sobrarán muchos manjares! ¡No quiero arrendar tus excamochos! Nunca vno me agradó, nunca en vno puse toda mi afición. Más pueden dos e más quatro e más dan e más tienen e mas ay en que escoger. No ay cosa mas perdida, hija, que el mur, que no sabe sino vn horado. Si aquel le tapan, no haurá donde se esconda del gato. ¡Quien tiene sino vn ojo, mira a quanto peligro anda! Vna alma sola ni canta ni llora; [vn solo acto no haze hábito] vn frayle solo pocas vezes lo encontrarás por la calle; vna perdiz sola por marauilla buela [mayormente en verano]; *vn manjar solo continuo presto pone hastío; vna golondrina no haze verano; vn testigo solo no es entera fe; quien sola vna ropa tiene, presto la enuegece.* ¿Qué quieres, hija, deste numero de vno? Mas inconuenientes te diré dél, que años tengo acuestas. Ten siquiera dos, que es compañía loable [e tal qual es éste]: *como tienes dos orejas, dos pies e dos manos, dos sauanas en la cama; como dos camisas para remudar. E si más quisieres, mejor te yrá, que mientra mas moros, más ganancia; que honrra sin prouecho, no es sino como anillo en el dedo. E pues entrambos no caben en vn saco, acoge la ganancia.* Sube, hijo Pármeno. (VII, 254–56)

Although certain critics of *La Celestina* imply that most of the interpolations consist of such strings of proverbs, this is actually the only one of its kind.[18] Here Rojas, like Cervantes, seems to be aware of the stylistic tendency of proverbs to occur in series[19] and seems to display an equal enjoyment of the comic and popular exaggerations of this tendency. For both authors, humor is achieved not only by the length of the string but also by the disparity of the several proverbs (a disparity purposefully overcome in the persuasion of Melibea). In the *Comedia* and in the first interpolation the only requirement that a proverb need fulfill to gain entrance is to mention the number one. Even more, the only example in the original which corresponded to a more serious level of reasoning ("un solo acto no haze hábito") is deleted from the text. The second interpolation with its sudden and significant shift from parts of the body to bedclothes and "camisas" follows a similar pattern of disparity. Given the care in deletion as well as in interpolation,[20] there can be no doubt that Rojas was striving for a given stylistic effect and not just adding proverbs for their own sake.

With this in mind, it is interesting to observe the logical criteria which seem to direct Celestina's outburst of comic disparity. After presenting Elicia as a model of conduct, and after commenting on Areusa's relative poverty, Celestina opens the major phase of her argument with an introductory statement later to be supported by proverbial examples: "Nunca vno me agradó, nunca en vno puse toda mi afición. Más pueden dos e más quatro e más dan e más tienen e más ay en que escoger." Insofar as this is a plan or a statement to be justified, in the original it was not carried out; six proverbs denied value to the number one, but two and more were given no positive defense. The interpolations, however, complete the scheme. New proverbs increase the weight of the attack on "one" while "two and more" are developed, if not symmetrically, sufficiently to justify the introductory sentence. There follows a defense of even greater numbers with an epic reference, "mientra más moros más ganancia," and a conclusion (also missing in the *Comedia*) which gives a final touch to the cynical humor of the whole: "E pues entrambos no caben en vn saco acoge la ganancia." The argument is then finished, formalities have been satisfied, and Celestina does not need to wait for an answer. Pármeno is brought on to the scene without further ado: "Sube, hijo Pármeno."

This gross comedy, this apparent burlesque, so carefully completed in 1502, stands in sharp contrast to Celestina's serious briefing of Melibea on the pious customs of animals. In the one case, an effort is made to avoid disparity, while in the other all sorts of proverbial material is gathered to accentuate the quality. There is also a difference in tempo. The persuasion of Areusa begins with a rather long example of two sentences but then accelerates so rapidly that it leaves her no time to answer—or even think of an answer. By the time Celestina arrives at number two she uses a minimum of words for her five examples. For Melibea, on the contrary, the tempo is relatively slow; it is an invitation to meditate, not an attempt to overwhelm the listener with words. Nevertheless, in spite of these differences, the extreme care for logical composition in both passages indicates that Rojas was not just interested in producing contrasting reactions in the reader—on the one hand festive and on the other serious or didactic. Rather, through the mind of Celestina, he seems to be trying to invent arguments in terms of the listener and the situation. He seems to be concerned that both Melibea and Areusa be adequately prepared for what is coming. There must be recognizable appearance of logic—of convincing and coherent reasoning with introduction, precedents, and conclusion—for its own sake and not just because the content demands it. Logic, in other words, has the effect of directing the argument to the listener, while beneath its level the individual situation determines the tone, tempo, and decorum of what is said. In the one case Celestina is preparing for the mortally dangerous wrath of Melibea; in the other she is disposing of the patently false reluctance of Areusa. Each requires its own argumentative manner of solution but, at the same time, each as an argument requires a completed veneer of logic, a formal appearance of sincerity.

Thus, in Rojas' dialogic style we again see that the reader's reaction is secondary to the impression produced in the listener and the sentiments expressed by the speaker. For a comic situation there is a comic argument; for a potentially tragic situation there is a serious argument. If all Rojas wished to do had been to make us laugh or teach us about animals, he might have added many more examples than he did, he might have introduced *conceptismos* in the manner of a Quevedo, or he might have listed reputable authorities and precedents. Instead he interpolates within the logical terms of the argument itself and according to the living situation which the language represents. It is logic which, in a sense, keeps the dialogue from escaping from life, which limits the language within the boundaries of the situation. This vital function of logic may perhaps be clarified by pointing out that Rojas' use of it is just the opposite of that implied by the notion of instruction sugar-coated with entertainment, of a fictional invention designed to cover a hidden lesson. In *La Celestina* as a whole and particularly in the above two examples, the logical form of the lesson is used instead to cover the serious or jocose implications of the living situation. The characters seem to follow intuitively Cicero's advice that while the orator can really instruct, please, and move his listener, he can only pretend to be doing the first of the three. We, as mere spectators, have just seen Celestina as an independent orator under a careful guise of logic and instructions attempt to move Melibea and to please and overwhelm Areusa. The vital authenticity of the dialogue, the immediacy of speech to speaker and of tone and tempo to situation, is accomplished by placing logic and lesson where it belongs, on the surface of spoken language, rather than hiding it for the reader's benefit. There, on the surface, logic at once gives form to communication and helps restrict the living language to the matter at hand.

We may conclude, then, by pointing out that logical style in *La Celestina* is unobtrusive precisely because it is on the surface and that it is vital because instead of running counter to the living dialogue, it frames it and accentuates it. In these two interpolations Rojas carefully resolves the antagonism between logic and life by balancing them in the proper way. On the one hand, the logical veneer provides a level of contrast which allows us to see Celestina's fearful or humorous estimations of her situation. The very breaks or flaws in the logic bring out (as we saw in the final speech of Act IV) that intense juncture of two lives in words that is the great stylistic merit of the work. On the other hand, this same logic keeps sentiment from running away with itself, in the manner of the Arcipreste de Talavera; as a quality of argument, it continually reminds the *yo* both of the presence of the *tú* and of the purpose of their meeting. In a more flexible, and so less recognizable, manner the logical pretense serves Rojas' art of style in much the same manner that the alexandrine serves Racine's.

To return to our initial comparison of Rojas and the Arcipreste, we can now gauge the profound relationship between the former's interpolated insistence on clarity and logic and his mastery of dialogue. Neither quality governs the style on its own; neither is applied in an absolute fashion by the author for the benefit of the reader; rather, both become an integral part of the spoken language, elements of the dialogic situation. Clarity premised on *la habla común* is the result of Rojas' conscious effort to achieve a full ripeness of expression or persuasion—and so permits the meeting of the first and second persons in dialogue. Logic orders the expressed sentiments—or the direct appeal to the other's sentiments—within a necessary frame of argumentative technique: introductory statements, precedents, and adequate conclusions. And it is this ordering which allows the two lives to meet, not only with a common language, but with the realization on each part that the other is a thinking being who must understand and be convinced. The ever-varying individual lives and individual situations possess this common starting point for their dialogues; indeed their very individuality, their living spontaneity, is accentuated and given meaning by the balance wheel of logic. Thus, when Melibea says "Señor mío, pues me fié en tus manos, pues quise complir tu voluntad no sea de peor condición, por ser piadosa, que si fuera esquiua e sin misericordia; no quieras perderme por tan breue deleyte e en tan poco espacio ..." the clarity and logic of her gentle despair neither mutilate it nor destroy it. Her words become, instead, the substance of the meeting with Calisto. Conversation and communication have been built stylistically from the fresh yet sterile torrent of the Arcipreste de Talavera. Both *yo* and *tú* can now live together within the same sentence.

5. Balance and Decorum

A survey of all the interpolated passages reveals, I think, one very significant and conspicuous absence, the absence of that ordinary kind of correction which reveals the author's point of view towards his own style. By this I mean corrections having to do with the sound of words, unfortunate repetitions of the same word, the righting of the unbalanced sentences, etc. It is true, of course, that a few of the deletions reflect Rojas' consciousness of style as his own property, but in general the whole task of self-correction seems curiously remote, different from our customary notion of textual revision.[21] The very fact that there are only twenty-five individual deletions as against some eighty-seven interpolations[22] is perhaps, in itself, a sign that Rojas was relatively unpreoccupied with what we might call the objective balance or harmony of his style; and, at that, most of these deletions apply more to content than style. Rojas' whole concept of style seems to have been so profoundly dialogic, that he seldom judged his units of language from his own point of view (or at least from what we might expect his point of view to have been). Thus, corrections for clarity or logic, corrections contributing to the expressiveness and direction of the dialogue, far outnumber those applying to the style as such. Rojas' artistry of style is perhaps as far away from that of a Guevara or a Diego de San Pedro as we have seen it to be from that of the Arcipreste de Talavera.

The significance of this omission is not just that it confirms what we have already said about Rojas' artistry of style but that it draws our attention to what at first may seem to be a lack of over-all stylistic direction in the work. As far as we can tell from the interpolations, Rojas never writes according to what *he* considers to be a balanced or harmonious style, he imposes no stylistic control of his own on the work of art; rather he corrects and inserts from within the dialogue and according to the *tú* and *yo* who live in it.[23] And if this is true, how does he manage to accomplish the essential task of building scenes from speeches and acts from scenes? Such a problem is, of course, not confined to *La Celestina* but is general to all dialogue forms, that is to say forms which are built from a dialogue as authentic as that written by Rojas. The novelist achieves such control by narrative entrance into his own text whenever he sees fit, and by ironical distance on his part from what is said and done. He combines sympathy and judgment, narrative supervision and dialogic freedom, and becomes what Cervantes calls the "padrastro" of his creations. This was, of course, formally denied to Rojas. The dramatist must, on the other hand, arrange his characters in such a way that whatever it is necessary for them to say will result in a scene or an act. In both generic forms control is exercised by a creator who sees his creations not just as *tú* and *yo* in the immediacy of an encounter or a situation, but also, as *él* or *ella;* that is to say, in the third person as well as in the first and second. The usual result in dialogue is a typed or characterized language for each speaker, that kind of over-all control that we, as well as Juan de Valdés and previous authors of "poetics," might refer to as "decorum." It need not be that special kind of decorum which the nineteenth century knew as realism, but generic writing does seem to demand some sort of more or less fixed relation between the style of the speech and the character of the speaker, as it is known to the author. The existence of a stylistic artistry larger than that of the sentence or speech—and such an artistry is indispensable to achievement in literature— usually depends not on the first or second but on the third person.

I only mention these elementary conditions of literature in order to under- line what seems to me to be a fundamental peculiarity of Rojas' artistry as a whole—a peculiarity which affects not only style but character, structure, theme, and ultimately generic classification. It is the absence of an effective third person for the individuals inhabiting *La Celestina*. As far as style is con- cerned, this observation is hardly a new original discovery. The refusal of a Celestina to be limited to typical or low-class language and of a Melibea to re- frain from citing erudite precedents has long disturbed critics looking for a natural or hierarchical division of styles. Even Calisto, whose style seems some- what more consequential than that of the others, can, during his last fatal ren- dezvous, interrupt the language of love with a picaresque joke: "el que quiere comer el aue, quita primero las plumas." It is a striking example of what Rachel Frank has called the "paradoxes" of *La Celestina*.[24] Granting this freedom of the individual to "choose" his own style, it is all the more para- doxical in the sense that it would seem to prejudice Rojas' larger management of his artistry. While, on the one hand, the relative nonexistence of the third person may help give freedom and life to the dialogue, on the other, it would seem to be untenable artistically, an invitation to chaos. Yet this does not come to pass, for Rojas replaces third person control with a radically different variety of decorum. It is one which seems remotely related to that of oratory, the Ciceronian decorum of topic, but within *La Celestina* it receives a new basis which is peculiarly Rojas' own. Rather than ordering style rigidly by the per- son speaking or by what he talks about, Rojas at his best combines the two into a new decorum of situation. He sorts out a flexibility of styles in terms of the poetic elevation of the context and of the reaction to this elevation in the lives of the individuals concerned.

The existence of such an original pattern of stylistic control—a pattern al- most as alien to the literary past of *La Celestina* as it was to be to its future— is often camouflaged by the text itself. Since Pármeno, Sempronio, and their friends by the very nature of things are more likely to be involved in situa- tions and to mention topics of a lower poetic level than Calisto and Melibea, it frequently seems as if some more customary decorum were in charge of the style. More than one reader has been fooled by *La Celestina*'s realism, and the temptation to divide its dialogue by such categories, as "high" and "low," "sublime" and "simple," or even "living" and "conventional," is hard to resist. Only by a close study of certain interpolations can we reassure ourselves that exceptions are neither mistaken nor improper, that, instead of such oversimplified dualities, Rojas practices a wholly new sort of decorum. His is a dialogic decorum which guides the rise and fall of style without interfering with the autonomous *tú* and *yo* of the speakers. This subtlest achievement of his art of style is by its very nature well concealed.

Direct evidence of Rojas' preoccupation with the level of his style (a preoccupation which is basic to any sort of decorum) is furnished by several of the deletions. After rereading a series of phrases or clauses in the *Comedia,* he will delete any which seem to rupture the prevailing elevation. We have already noticed the removal of "un solo acto no hace hábito" from the series of disparate proverbs chosen by Celestina to destroy Areusa's questionable adherence to the number one. It was felt to be too scholastic, too serious for inclusion in a paragraph of logical illogic. A complementary example may be found in Pleberio's lament: "¡Ay, ay, noble muger! [Nuestro gozo en el pozo.] Nuestro bien todo es perdido. ¡No queramos más biuir! E porque el incogitado dolor te dé más pena, todo junto sin pensarle, porque más presto vayas al sepulcro, porque no llore yo solo la pérdida dolorida de entramos, ves allí a la que tú pariste e yo engendré, hecha pedaços." (XXI, 201) The deleted proverb was too colloquial for its elegiac circumstance, and, while we may perversely prefer the original sequence because of the ironical break in level, we must at the same time admit that it was indecorous. It is not that Pleberio might never be expected to say "Nuestro gozo en el pozo" but that the stylistic level of his grief will not support his saying it there. In the one case, a low level of comic argument is maintained by deletion; in the other, an high level of grief and final thematic mediation.[25]

If the deletions bring out a basic preoccupation with level of style, the interpolations illuminate the curious decorum which resulted from it. A possible relationship, of Rojas' stylistic practice to that of oratory is suggested by two interpolations so often criticized that they hardly need be reproduced. One is Celestina's invocation of Pluto with its added erudition: "Conjúrote, triste Plutón, señor de la profundidad infernal ... *regidor de las tres furias, Tesífone, Megara e Aleto, administrador de todas las cosas negras del reyno de Stigie e Dite, con todas sus lagunas e sombras infernales, e litigioso caos, mantenedor de las bolantes harpías, con toda la otra compañía de espantables e pauorosas ydras;* yo, Celestina, tu mas conocida clientula, te conjuro ..." (III, 148–50);

the other is Melibea's final soliloquy, a soliloquy which justifies cruelty to her parents with added classical precedents: "Buen tiempo terné para contar a Pleberio mi señor la causa de mi ya acordado fin. Gran sinrazón hago a sus canas, gran ofensa a su vegez. Gran fatiga le acarreo con mi falta. En gran soledad le dexo. Y *caso que por mi morir a mis queridos padres sus días se diminuyessen, ¿quién dubda que no aya auido otros más crueles contra sus padres? Bursia, rey de Bitinia, sin ninguna razón, no aquexándole pena como a mí, mató a su propio padre ...*" (XX, 192–93) In both of these cases, Rojas seems to feel that the situation requires appropriate stylistic recognition. The first represents the powers of darkness brought into play, a fearful invocation of final evil (even though Rojas, unlike Shakespeare, takes care not to introduce supernatural presences), and has a formidable mediaeval and classic tradition behind it. It is an announcement of tragic inevitability, a conventional introduction of fate. The second occurs at the other end of the same literary trajectory, at the moment of Melibea's final catastrophe, and there result such evident parallelisms as the complementary references to verticality (the depths of Hell and the high "açotea"). Furthermore, both are oratorical soliloquys which recognize in style the frame of literature which encloses the pulsating life of the whole. Thus, it hardly matters if Melibea cannot be expected to remember or even know about "Bursia, rey of Bitinia" or Celestina's necromancy is expressed in terms that transcend both her education and her native tradition. Each is at this point subordinated to a univalent, nondialogic situation. The climactic moment and its subject matter require an appropriate sublimity, a sublimity which, if not Ciceronian in its manner seems to possess a classical motivation. And Rojas, recognizing the oratorical rather than dialogical nature of these ultimate situations, reinforces them with appropriate interpolations. A third example, although uninterpolated, is Pleberio's final elegiac lament, again a topic which surpasses the life of the speaker and determines its own level of style.

But these three are exceptional cases within *La Celestina,* cases of extreme oratorical departure from that kind of decorum demanded by a Foulché Delbosc. In general, situation and style are dialogic; for even the monologues express arguments addressed to the self, along with the sentiments of the speaker. In these circumstances a decorum which originally was based on the topic is modified by the vital necessities of the speaker and listener. If Rojas is to use level of language as a means of managing his style artistically, he must do so in a manner more subtle and more influential than the above concept of decorum would allow.

An elementary decorum of living situation, of what we might call "dialogic decorum," is illustrated by two interpolations in Act VIII. Parmeno, returning from his night of love with Areusa meets Sempronio in a state of self-satisfaction and mental repletion; he is at that point engaged in savoring what he calls the "clear liquor of his thought." The style which corresponds to this sentiment is reaffirmed in 1502:

PARM.—No es, Sempronio, verdadera fuerça ni poderío dañar e empecer; mas aprouechar e guarecer e muy mayor, quererlo hazer. Yo siempre te tuue por hermano. No se cumpla, por Diós, en ti lo que se dize, que pequeña causa desparte conformes amigos. Muy mal me tratas. No sé donde nazca este rencor. *No me indignes, Sempronio, con tan lastimeras razones. Cata que es muy rara la paciencia que agudo baldón no penetre e traspasse.*

SEMP.—No digo mal en esto; sino que se eche otra sardina para el moço de cauallos, pues tú tienes amiga.

PARM.—Estás enojado. Quiérote sofrir, avnque más mal me trates, *pues dizen que ninguna humana pasión es perpetua ni durable.* (VIII, 11)

These two speeches of Parmeno had in the *Comedia* lacked the full elevation of phraseology typical of other parts of his dialogue (for example, the passages beginning "¡O plazer singular!" and "¡O Sempronio, amigo e más que hermano!"). And the interpolated material, with its preceding adjectives ("lastimeras razones," "agudo baldón," "humana pasíon"), and its uncommon words ("indignes," "penetre," "perpetua") and its decorative double conclusions, was apparently designed to remedy the defect. The two speeches have now been raised to the level of the whole.

The important thing, as usual, is not the appropriateness of these interpolations but their illustration of Rojas' art of style. We may notice how the high stylistic level corresponds not only to the topic, love, but also to Parmeno's sentimental experience of it. It is a state of mind which, in effect, spreads out beyond the frontiers of the topic and into the argument with Sempronio, and, as it does so, the style follows it. Unlike the oratorical erudition of Celestina and Melibea just seen, here Rojas uses a stylistic elevation designed to communicate the tranquil superiority, the annoyingly adolescent self-satisfaction, of the speaker. Along with this expression of Parmeno's contribution to the situation, there is the counterpoint of Sempronio's irritated reaction to him. The latter's style, with its sarcastic "que se eche otra sardina para el moço de cauallos," is as low in level as Parmeno's is high. Smugness and irritation, tranquility and impatience, love and hate, harmony and discord, result in a complex decorum of styles which gives an over-all perfection of artistry to the scene. Rojas, with an irony that is seemingly Cervantine but ultimately far more corrosive, plays one character against the other and rules their dialogic interchange not only with argument and sentiment but also with a decorum that is unique. Repetition is impossible, for in each case the level of style operates as a function of the unrelenting innovation of living dialogue.

Although such counterpoint of levels is frequent in *La Celestina* (particularly in the conversations of Calisto with the others), it is not Rojas' only means of stylistic management. There is also the possibility of variation within the same speech. In default of a conclusive interpolation, the following will serve for an example:

CEL.—... No pensé yo, hijo Sempronio, que assí me respondiera mi buena fortuna. De los discretos mensajeros es hazer lo que el tiempo quiere. Assí que la qualidad de lo fecho no puede encubrir tiempo dissimulado. E más que yo sé que tu amo, segun lo que dél sentí, es liberal e algo antojadizo. Más dará en vn día de buenas nueuas, que en ciento, que ande penado e yo yendo e viniendo. Que los acelerados e súpitos plazeres crían alteración, la mucha alteración estorua el deliberar. Pues ¿en qué podrá parar el bién, sino en bién e el alto mensaje, sino en luengas albricias? Calla, bouo, dexa fazer a tu vieja. (V, 199)

In this passage Celestina's elation at her unexpected success is expressed in a kind of stylistic complaisance. She patronizes Sempronio (who had previously questioned her competence) with a language that is comparable to Parmeno's after his success with Areusa. Preceding adjectives and *cultismos* reveal a smug Celestina who refuses to give Sempronio any details of the meeting with Melibea—because to do so would be to "desflorar su embaxada." But Celestina is too expert at managing the direction of her discourse to remain long on such a plane or to allow Sempronio a chance to undermine her linguistically. At the end she suddenly drops to a much lower and more comfortable level of style while retaining all of her satisfied superiority: "Calla, bouo, dexa fazer a tu vieja." The rather pompous "hijo Sempronio" becomes "bouo" as the juncture of sentiment and argument that is this speech is reincarnated on a new level. The whole encounter is, in fact, composed of "decorous" alternation of styles for Celestina, a series of "breaks" corresponding to her self-satisfaction, to her desire to punish Sempronio for his doubt in Act III, and to her need to retain his support. The first is a constant, but the last two vary and in so doing result in such sudden changes as the above.

Rojas does not always play one level of style against the other as in the preceding examples. At times a single style may last for pages of dialogue without a necessary sacrifice of subtlety. When Melibea finally surrenders her shame to Celestina in Act X, there is a special and unbroken elevation of language for both speakers—an elevation which Rojas took care not to betray in the following interpolation:

LUCR.—El seso tiene perdido mi señora. Gran mal es este. Catiuádola ha esta hechizera.

CEL.—Nunca me ha de faltar un diablo acá y acullá: escapóme Diós de Parmeno, tópome con Lucrecia.

MELIB.—¿Qué dizes, amada maestra? ¿Qué te fablaua esa moca?

CEL.—No le oy nada. *Pero diga lo que dixere, sabe que no ay cosa más contraria en las grandes curas delante los animosos çurujanos, que los flacos coraçones, los quales con su gran lástima, con sus doloriosas hablas, con sus sentibles meneos, ponen temor al enfermo, fazen que desconfíe de la salud e al médico enojan e turban e la turbación altera la mano, rige sin orden la aguja. Por donde se puede conocer claro,* que es muy necesario para tu salud que no esté persona delante e assí que la deues mandar salir. E tú, hija Lucrecia, perdona.

MELIB.—Salte fuera presto. (X, 57)

The semi-allegorical fiction of love's arrow wound in the heart, a wound which can only be stitched together by the "antigua maestra destas llagas," might seem stilted and artificial if it did not represent the long awaited stylistic agreement of the lives and purposes of Celestina and Melibea. An open declaration would have been false not only to this moment of love's capitulation but also to Melibea's sentimental existence. She can hardly say: "I now realize I love Calisto"; rather in collaboration with Celestina she must seek out a plane of style artificial enough to give her revelation of love all the inevitability of a ritual dance or ceremony. Thus, Melibea and Celestina change from antagonists in the battle of love (a battle which does not fail to have its own figurative tradition and style[26]) into accomplices. Each needs the other and a fabricated language of diplomacy as well, in order that the love's surrender may be negotiated. Only in this way can the virginal secret be brought to final and fainting admission.

The subtlety of Rojas' maintenance of this level of style is evident in the interpolation, an interpolation which arranges for Lucrecia's departure in words appropriate to the scene as a whole. The *Comedia* had read: "No le oy nada. Lo que digo es que es muy necessario para tu salud que no esté persona delante ..." and had seemed somewhat curt, given the new relation of Celestina to Melibea. The stylistic armistice with its elaborate protocol makes it improper for Celestina to remind Melibea so directly that secrecy was in both their interests. In effect, Lucrecia in this scene represents a possibility of counterpoint which is undesirable for the fiction of doctor and patient. The couple must play out their game alone, and Celestina's removal of the undesirable witness according to its rules is, to say the least, an effective instance of interpolation.

Thus, it is neither the person as a fixed character nor a topic of fixed or measured importance which determines the decorum of *La Celestina*. Rather it is the dialogue itself, the encounter of two or more lives in sentiment and argument, which occasions a decorum of its own. Topic and person (except in such oratorical moments as were mentioned) join together in the immediacy of a living situation. For example, what Celestina says about love to Pármeno at this time and in this circumstance is what matters and not the fact that it is Celestina or that it is love which concerns her. Stylistically *La Celestina* is a series of such units of dialogue, each of which joins all its component parts in a language which rises to a level corresponding to its density. This process may involve a counterpoint of levels between one speaker and another, a break of levels for a single speaker, or the maintenance of a single level when the war between the speakers is halted by mutual agreement. A study of the appropriate interpolations reveals Rojas' conscious and conscientious management of style on its own terms. The primordial nature of his dialogue results in a decorum specially suited to dialogic situations.

6. The Art of Style

In glancing back over this excursion through the style of *La Celestina* we may first record a general impression: that of the skill and consequence of Rojas' intervention into the text of the *Comedia*. Almost all the interpolations and deletions were made with the greatest attention to detail, with flexibility, and with precise adjustment of the new material to the significance of the old. It would seem, accordingly, that past attempts to classify the interpolations as interpolations, that is to say as varieties of padding (erudite, proverbial, repetitive, etc.), have not taken into account the individual circumstances of each change. Such classification passes over the particular flaws in logic, defects in decorum, and obscurities of expression or communication which Rojas hoped to correct and, at the same time, ignores or distorts the non-coöperative examples. Rojas' constant and successful effort is to join the new to the old in terms of an over-all surveillance of style. Thus, a more valid classification of the interpolations and deletions of 1502 is the one we have proposed here, a classification by the stylistic motivations of the author, himself. One of the most valuable by-products of this method of reading the interpolations is a substantial reinforcement of our preliminary assumption, the assumption that Fernando de Rojas was himself the author and corrector of 1502.

The stylistic criteria which provided the above reclassification should not be thought of as representing moments or phases of Rojas' creative process. We must not imagine, for example, that Rojas began by writing a passage purely on the basis of the living dialogic interchange and that he then checked it successively for clarity, logic, and appropriate decorum. Rather, at the moment of original creation all of these must have been joined together intuitively. Only afterwards in 1502 when it was a matter of self-correction can we begin to distinguish levels or kinds of stylistic preoccupation. The interpolations and deletions are in this sense an almost regal gift to the critic of *La Celestina*. They reveal what otherwise might have been hidden by the completed achievement: the manner in which Rojas, inspired by the New Comedy and out of a native tradition divided between fifteenth-century rhetoricism and the formless vitality of the Arcipreste de Talavera, created a style of dialogue without precedent in its time and hardly equaled afterwards in its literary authenticity. In times to come, dialogue was often to be a servant of characterization, a vehicle for poetry, or a device for dialect or presentation of ideas. Rarely has it been pursued so single-mindedly and so much for its own sake as in *La Celestina*—and it is this pursuit which we have just witnessed.

Rejecting, then, the mistaken notion that the dialogue of *La Celestina* was created in the same way that it was corrected, we may retrace briefly the path we have followed. Rojas' most elementary demand upon his style was that it possess direction, not only a point of departure in the life of the speaker but also a destination in the life of the listener. Every word, sentence, and paragraph exists dynamically, possessing what we might call a vital trajectory between a *yo* and a *tú*. Obviously these trajectories with their living beginnings and endings are not always (we might almost say, not ever) identical. At times the aim is precise, the trajectory is flat, and the *tú* is much more in control than the *yo*. This is the style we have referred to as argumentative. In the case of Areusa's sentimental outburst on the other hand, the *tú* is almost a fiction of grammar, the aim is wide, and the trajectory is steeply curved. It is a style designed to express the sentiments of the *yo*. Between these two extremes (and with an infinity of combinations) the style of *La Celestina* may be said to oscillate. What almost never occurs in the acts we have attributed to Rojas is either Rabelaisian expansion of style for its own sake (for example, the "puta vieja" passage in Act I) or those non-dialogic trajectories of joke or lesson which extend from the author to the reader. Insofar as *La Celestina* may be considered a drama, it is almost polar to the theatre of the Golden Age. Its dramatic basis in dialogue for its own sake renders it an extreme example of imitative or "glass-wall" drama, as distinguished from the "show" directed out to the audience.

The maintenance of this purely dialogic direction of style, its refinement and control, may be studied in relation to progressively larger units of language. For words, phrases, and sentences Rojas first requires full clarification of both argument and sentiment, a task which is accomplished in terms of the dialogue it serves. Rojas envisions each obscurity as an hindrance to communication or expression, as an obscurity belonging to the speaker or listener, and corrects it accordingly. Unlike Malherbe who is preoccupied by a kind of absolute clarity beneficial to the reader, Rojas does not excise the obscure word but explains it and expands on it in speech. It is a process of creative clarification which as we saw, suggests artistic corollaries far beyond the domain of style. Then, for sentences and paragraphs there is the further requirement of logic, an oratorical logic inconspicuous precisely because it is confined to the surface of the spoken style. In this position, logical coherence gives an impression of objectivity both to argument and sentiment, an objectivity which accentuates the inner and subjective significance of what is said. Logic, in *La Celestina,* helps convert living language into dialogue but is seldom allowed to convert it into discourse. Finally, for scene or situation the dialogue is allowed to find its appropriate decorum. According to the range of stylistic levels available at the time—as Anderson Imbert points out, the characters live within the literary language of the fifteenth century[27]—each encounter or situation rises or falls in style on its own terms. It is the momentary state of consciousness directed through the words of an argument (or a sentiment) which determines a vital decorum—and not character or topic abstracted from dialogue. For every aspect of language we may detect a consistent and consequential effort to mould style to the primordial needs of dialogue.

There are, as we said at the beginning of this chapter, many other ways to approach Rojas' style and many other important things to be said about it. We have not, for example, attempted to find out what is peculiar about this style in relation to the personality of the author or how the literary language of the fifteenth century was, in itself, changed by entrance into *La Celestina.* In studying the art of style it has been necessary to take both the literary raw material and the uniqueness of the artist more or less for granted and to limit ourselves to evidence of the techniques which relate the two on the level of conscious preoccupation. But no matter how limited this approach may be, it is not without value for Fernando de Rojas and his *Celestina.* The art that joins them is, we repeat, without real precedent or parallel. As an example of creative behavior, it is in itself highly unique and worthy of observation. Therein lies the excuse for what I have tried to do.

This self-justification may be supported by a brief comparison of Rojas' personal art of dialogue with those of the Spanish novel and theatre in the seventeenth century. (We have already seen its fundamental differences from the spurting monologue of the *Corbacho,* perhaps the least remote of its predecessors.[28]) In this comparison, in order to avoid generic difficulties, let us only consider the matter of decorum as it was practiced by Cervantes in the *Quixote* and by Lope in any of his *comedias*. At first glance, it might appear that Rojas' flexible stylistic levels and his use of dialogic counterpoint is distinctly Cervantine. Does not Don Quixote descend to vulgarity in given situations and cannot Sancho rise to chivalresque apostrophe when he needs to?[29] The whole process of "sanchificación" and "quijotización," first suggested by Madariaga seems, in fact, related to the dialogic decorum of *La Celestina*. Nevertheless, we should remember that this was a novelistic process, a culmination of experience by which the character adapts himself to his new circumstances. It was also one which Cervantes manipulated with conscious irony: freedom to transgress the frontiers of character is never absolute but is allowed by the author in terms of the genre he had invented. Thus, instead of *La Celestina*'s refusal to premise its decorum on the third person, instead of a dialogue with complete stylistic priority, in the *Quijote* there is an ironical control of speech in the first and second persons in terms of the novelist's changing vision of the third. The decorum of the "padrastro" with its controlled freedom (see Cervantes' remarks on Sancho's conversation with his wife) may be contrasted to the radically autonomous decorum of situation that was practiced and permitted by Rojas.[30]

The second term of comparison is the *comedia,* and again it presents us with a very different picture. In spite of the fact that changes in verse form— on a literary scale running from *redondillas* and *romançe* through *octavas reales* and sonnets, are specifically premised by Lope on given situations and attitudes—these seem more or less fixed and mechanical. It is not that the characters are severely decorous (although there is, of course, a fundamental difference in style between the *graciosos* and the rest of the cast) but that the repertoire of theatrically permissible situations has been reduced and ordered. The very reduction which gave full theatrical potentiality to this drama—and which corresponded in a sense to the French unities—resulted in an art of decorous versification that seems rigid when compared to varying levels of style of *La Celestina*. In the *comedia,* in other words, situation and appropriate verse are the given materials of the playwright's art, while for Rojas a comparable decorum is the end-product of his dialogic artistry. Thus, although *La Celestina* may be thought of in a sense as initiating the rupture of the classical division of styles in the Golden Age, its peculiar art was never repeated. Instead of balancing art against life (as in the novel) or creating a new life out of stabilized elements of art (as in the theatre), out of the very life of dialogue it created its own art of language. It is this that we have called "dialogic decorum."

Further pursuit of these comparisons would commit us to the problem of *La Celestina*'s genre, a problem which we are not at all ready to consider. At this point we have only sought to emphasize the uniqueness of the stylistic practice of Fernando de Rojas—to stress the peculiar nature of a literary art which is dependent solely upon dialogue.[31]

CHAPTER THREE

THE ART OF CHARACTER

ONE OF THE most effective and surprising conversations in *La Celestina* is that in which Areusa and Elicia comment with feminine malice on the physical appearance of Melibea. So used are we to that ecstatic vision of Melibea which emerges from Calisto's reverent description in Act I, that such expressions as "que assí goze de ni, vnas tetas tiene, para ser donzella, como si tres vezes houiesse parido: no parecen sino dos grandes calabaças" seem almost sacrilegious. It is a sardonic and ironical reminder that all evaluations in *La Celestina* are conditioned by their point of view—a forerunner of that perspectivism which Spitzer was to see as stylistically decisive in the *Quixote*. But aside from the humor and the novelistic possibilities inherent in this cattiness, the problem remains: what does Melibea look like? Does the author intend that we should think of her as beautiful or ugly—that we adopt the point of view of her lover or that of the envious prostitutes? Although we may suppose with reason that both parties exaggerate, exaggeration in itself is beside the point. The real truth is that Melibea has no fixed appearance, no objective reality apart from or beyond the dialogue. There is no determinable "she," no third-person Melibea known as such to author and reader, and it would distort the artistry of Rojas to try to discover one.

It is necessary to insist on this puzzling lack of fixed portraiture because it coincides with the curious decorum of *La Celestina,* the failure to maintain a recognizable language for each personage. If Celestina and Calisto can, as we have seen, use multiple levels of style and if Melibea's beauty is purposefully without determination, to what extent can we speak of an art of character at all? To what extent can we as critics speak of "characteristic" behavior or reactions? Does not the absence of the third person in style and in physical features apply as well to the zone of character? Is there, in other words, any point in writing a chapter entitled, "The Art of Character?"

By way of tentative answer to these questions, we may glance briefly at the especially convincing critical characterizations which have been made for

Calisto and Celestina. María Rosa Lida de Malkiel in her article entitled the "Originalidad de *La Celestina*"[1] asserts the gradual and living development of character in the work and exemplifies it in Calisto who is for her, "débil," "quejumbroso," "sentimental," "egoista." There can be little doubt of this; but at the same time, to what extent is Calisto permanently or characteristically anti-heroic because of these adjectives? At the door of Melibea's house and in a moment of apparent danger he cries out: "Cierto soy burlado: no era Melibea lo que me habló. Bullicio oygo, perdido soy! Pues viua o muera que no he de yr de aquí." (XII, 82) Here he suddenly fills his heroic role to the brim. The same thing is true in his final rush to defend Tristán in Act XIX. As for Celestina, Ramiro de Maeztu's interpretation of her as a genius of Satanic and hedonistic wisdom is well known.[2] Yet within this characterization, her fatal misjudgment of the state of mind of Pármeno and Sempronio is inexplicable. About all we can do is to conclude with María Rosa Lida de Malkiel, "Como las criaturas de Cervantes—y como el llamado *homo sapiens*— las de *La Celestina* observan en su desarrollo una unidad interna, una línea muy clara y, a la vez, variaciones libres que no impiden conocer un diseño coherente." The character of Celestina, Calisto, and the rest can only be judged or discovered after the fact of speech and action, as for living human beings. Under these circumstances it is hard to speak of an *art* of character.

Relinquishing, then, character conceived of as creation or vision of the individual in the third person (a full character such as Lear or Oedipus will exist in all three persons), we necessarily return to the *tú* and *yo* of dialogue. And it is this return which leads us to the real problem of this essay. If action and reaction in *La Celestina* can be explained only within the living circumstance of the moment, if they are indeed unforeseeable, how does Rojas make them humanly believable and knowable? What, in other words, can be an art of fictional existences without character? The very posing of the question in this manner hints at a method of solution: to study the individuals of *La Celestina* as they are related to each other in dialogue, and not apart from it. If we are correct in assuming that Rojas' art provides for no ultimate dramatic or novelistic definition of character—a definition which corresponds to the third person—there is little use in abstracting a "Celestina" or a "Calisto" from the dialogue in which they live. We may forego both symbolical interpretations and static portraitures and relate the speakers to what we already know of the art of their speech. Character in *La Celestina* exists, as we shall see, in intimate relationship to the style which provides for it, to the structure which it provides, and finally to the theme and genre which correspond to all three.[3]

To conclude, a study of Rojas' art of creating human lives in the first and second person may be pursued in two ways: first, by following each life through all its dialogic encounters and appearances, and, second, by considering the cast as an artistic whole bound together in dialogue—as Laocöon and his sons are bound by their serpent. Either of these ways taken by itself is necessarily incomplete; centering successive situations upon a single individual amounts to a distortion of the inherent plurality of dialogue, while a patterning of the cast as a joint creation ignores the authentic individuality of each of its members. And since we cannot investigate both of these perspectives into the life of *La Celestina* simultaneously—since by our very substitution of criticism for creation, we separate the one from the other—we must remember that each of them offers a limited and distorted view. Then, afterwards, we may strive for their integration and more faithful synthesis; together they may provide an adequate vision of this aspect of Rojas' art.

1. Patterns of Character

Let us begin with the cast as an artistic whole—a whole resting on that minimum of definition necessary to relate the individual members to each other. A cast of characters by its very nature involves a number of fixed relationships, father-son, servant-master, etc. It is not merely a list of the names of the persons involved; it is also preliminary explanation of how these names are joined together as a basis for dialogue and action. This, in turn, requires a certain amount of prior definition by the author, and even Rojas, for all his emphasis on dialogue, could not avoid this necessity. The cast of *La Celestina,* as a result, may be conveniently divided in terms of the three central dualities underlined by mediaeval critics of Terence: rich against poor (this includes social class, insofar as it exists, with its division of servants from masters and prostitutes from respectable ladies); old against young; and men against women. It is possible that in the world created by Rabelais, with its consistent refusal to admit human limitation, such prior notations have little artistic importance. But in *La Celestina,* as we shall see, the fact that Calisto is a young rich man and Celestina an old poor woman and that they meet each other as such is always taken into account. The elementary fact of cast with its least common denominator of human definition is converted by Rojas into the very backbone of his artistry of character.

Taken by themselves, these sexual, economic, and temporal elements of human definition (along with others, such as physical appearance, family relationship, or occupation, which apply only to the individual) seem too obvious in nature to possess the importance claimed for them. The point is

that they are more than definitions. Unlike the traditional and pernicious
division between courtly and picaresque characters, it is a matter of limiting
and conditioning life but never of arranging it ahead of time. No matter how
free the individual may be to speak or react in a manner suiting the situation
or encounter in which he finds himself, these things he cannot surpass.
Celestina must talk to Calisto, or Melibea, or Sempronio from her old age,
from her poverty, and from her sex, and she never fails to do so. Even more,
as well as limiting negatively the range of situations, these conditions of life
shape positively the sentiments and arguments which compose them. All along
La Celestina there occur and reoccur discussions of old age and youth, servitude and freedom, the opposing advantages of riches and poverty, and the
nature of men and women, discussions which are rooted in the preoccupation
of each individual with his conditioning. Thus, the cast of characters—an
imaginary one for the first editions—is more than a mere list tacked on for
the convenience of the reader: instead it impregnates and determines the very
substance of creation. In a work of dialogic freedom and without initial characterization, this minimum of prior definition acquires special artistic importance.

Let us consider only the condition of femininity, a condition which, like the
others (discussed in Chapter V), runs the course of *La Celestina* and originates
in Act I. In spite of our stand on the authorship question, we must not partition the work hermetically. Many if not all aspects of Rojas' artistry germinate
in the dialogue he attributes to his predecessor and should be studied accordingly. In Act I, then, discussions of femininity are at once reminiscent of a
mediaeval debate and, at the same time, echo the furious contemporary
polemic about women. Sempronio opens the question with a scholastic attack
based on such authorities as Aristotle and Saint Bernard and studded with
such commonplaces as "la imperfección de la flaca muger" and "Assí como
la materia apetece la forma, así la muger al varón." The artificiality of the
debate form is made evident by the fact that it is entirely against Sempronio's
interest to dissuade Calisto from his love. This is not the intense argumenta-
tion from *yo* to *tú* which we encounter in later acts—a conflict of two lives in
dialogue—but rather the restatement of a traditional argument for its own
sake. Nevertheless, along with this we find, on occasion, what seems to be
the expression of personal sentiment:

SEMP.—... Huye de sus engaños. ¿Sabes qué facen? Cosa es difícil entenderlas.
No tienen modo, no razón, no intención. Por rigor comiençan el ofrescimiento,
que de sí quieren hazer. A los que meten por los agujeros denuestan en la calle.
Combidan, despiden, llaman, niegan, señalan amor, pronuncian enemiga, en-

sáñanse presto, apacígüanse luego. Quieren que adeuinen lo que quieren. ¡O qué plaga! ¡O qué enojo! ¡O qué fastío es conferir con ellas, más de aquel breue tiempo, que son aparejadas a deleyte! (I, 51)

Thus, to the mediaeval debate, Sempronio adds a sentiment of his own and a very personal exception ("más de aquel breue tiempo ...") It is a series of bitter exclamations at his own experience, future as well as past. Indeed, a few pages further on we find him, justly suspicious of a rival but hopelessly out-maneuvered by the feminine talents of Celestina and Elicia. Their combined hypocrisy and violence so corner his reason that he prefers to abandon his masculine search for truth. Traditional argument has been authenticated first in sentiment and then in dialogic situation.

The opposite process is, of course, true for Calisto. Immersed in sentiment and its divinization of a single woman, he refuses to admit the authority of the topic: "¡Ve! Mientra más me dizes e más inconuenientes me pones, más la quiero. No sé qué s'es." (I, 51) Yet, in spite of this personal point of de-parture, Calisto ends by describing Melibea in terms of the impersonal mediae-val formulation of beauty. Each feature is considered separately in typical and ordered perfection: "Comienço por los cabellos ..."[4] If Sempronio begins with a *lugar común* and ends with a sentiment and an encounter, Calisto begins with an encounter and a sentiment and ends with a *lugar común*. His vision of Melibea can, as a result, be interpreted as a general defense of wom-ankind; the perfection of her beauty is sufficient for him to justify the sex. Sempronio's Aristotelian attack is fittingly met with a Platonic denial, and, as each presents his side of the debate, the other undermines him comically from his opposing point of view. The symmetry of the argument on these terms suggests that the fifteenth-century polemic it represents was based on the collision of two traditional attitudes: scholastic scorn of women and courtly exaltation, not of women, but of the woman. In any case, it would seem that with this initial exhaustion of the topic, it should now come to an end.

The author of Act I, however, was not yet satisfied. The inner relationships he had uncovered (perhaps in spite of himself) between topical debate and personal sentiment suggested that other masculine opinions of women might also be pertinent. The third man present in the act, Pármeno, had not yet expressed himself, and when Celestina mentions Areusa in their conversation, his reaction is alien to debate and polemic. He reveals, instead, that compound of personal desire and timidity which is the substance of his inexperience: "marauillosa cosa es." He goes on to speak somewhat puritanically of "lux-uria," "vicio," "pecado," and "deleyte." Unlike Sempronio and Calisto,

Pármeno in his immaturity sees women as neither divine nor subhuman but as a forbidden mystery. His sentiment is not of rational disgust nor of hopeless worship; it is rather of wondering sensuality, a sensuality which is appropriately disguised with pedantry. Thus, in Act I what begins as a more or less comic debate on women becomes at the end a display of three possible attitudes towards them—three apparently deliberate variations on a sentimental theme. The existence of this new human design is further confirmed by the underlying unity of its varieties of masculine feeling, a unity which satisfies the aesthetic requirement for patterned composition. For all three, for Sempronio, Calisto, and Pármeno, woman is what Simone de Beauvoir refers to as "l'autre," a creature apart from man, mysterious in her irrationality, her divinity, or in her incitation. She exists only in terms of man's desire—or abhorrence—and is not conceived of as sharing his finality as a human being. As an object, she awakens sentiments and holds values, but she is not thought of as a subject feeling and evaluating on her own part. From the moment it is premised on individual lives a suggestive new pattern begins to emerge from the conceptual, abstract debate.

Rojas was not content merely to continue or deepen the pattern he inherited from Act I. His artistry led him away from conversations *about* women, conversations which merely betray or allude to living sentiments; he preferred instead their direct expression in soliloquy or dialogue. As a result, he creates a complementary gallery of attitudes, not towards women or "woman," but towards femininity and by those who are most directly concerned with it as a condition of their own lives, by the women of *La Celestina*. It is curious to note that of the three men who spoke so convincingly in Act I, two (Sempronio, who is fascinated by Melibea, and Pármeno, who begins to surpass his adolescence after the achievement of love) modify their positions radically in the acts that follow. Changing situations are likely to change the sentiments they awaken; what remains more or less constant is the so-called *sentiment du moi,* and it is on this basis that Rojas resumes the previous pattern. The authenticity of his dialogic direction, from *yo* to *tú,* gives an equal and perhaps predominant importance to his feminine lives, an importance which the men of Act I would have found difficult to understand. Femininity is evaluated and felt from within, subjectively, as Rojas takes one more step away from the original debate.

Each of the four young women, Melibea, Elicia, Areusa, and Lucrecia (Celestina in a sense has discarded her femininity) is sentimentally preoccupied with her condition as a woman. And each proposes to herself more or less consciously an evaluation derived from this sentiment—an answer to femininity in the form of an evaluation of her own life and actions. In contemporary jargon, each of them formulates a "project of existence." We have already seen Areusa expressing her preference for independence, a preference based on a profound sentimental rejection of the legitimate paths of life offered by society to a woman of her station. Lucrecia, on the other hand, who has accepted servitude is timidly envious of the joys and irresponsibilities of prostitution: "Por cierto, ya se me hauía oluidado mi principal demanda e mensaje con la memoria de esse tan alegre tiempo como has contado e assí me estuuiera vn año sin comer, esuchándote e pensando en aquella vida buena, que aquellas moças gozarían, que me parece e semeja que estó yo agora en ella." (IX, 49) She rejects her own life but dares only in imagination to substitute another for it. Elicia creates a third position by purposefully limiting herself to the immediacy of impulse. Entirely dependent on Celestina for getting out of difficulties, she finds an answer to femininity in the violence and sensual delight which determine her dialogue from instant to instant. As Celestina realizes, Elicia's refusal to adopt a professional attitude toward her position (in this case, refusal of the disagreeable task of mending virgins) implies an almost willed lack of self-reliance:

> CEL.—Tú te lo dirás todo. Pobre vejez quieres. ¿Piensas que nunca has de salir de mi lado?
> ELIC.—Por Diós, dexemos enojo e al tiempo el consejo. Ayamos mucho plazer. Mientra oy touiéremos de comer, no pensemos en mañana. También se muere el que mucho allega como el que pobremente viue e el doctor como el pastor e el pápa como el sacristán e el señor como el sieruo e el de alto linaje como el baxo e tú con oficio como yo sin ninguno. No hauemos de viuir para siempre. Gozemos e holguemos, que la vejez pocos la veen e de los que la veen ninguno murió de hambre. (VIII, 262) [5]

Finally, there is Melibea who, when brought to a point from which she can view her life as a whole, rejects domesticity—that is to say matrimony or love within time and space—in favor of a love which, defined as "gloria," must necessarily exist outside them: "el amor no admite sino solo amor por paga." [6] Unlike Elicia who is in a sense domestic in her temporal dependence on Celestina, Melibea attempts to surpass dimensions with her passion, with her very femininity.

As in the case of Pármeno, Calisto, and Sempronio in Act I, there is a pattern-forming unity beneath these varying sentiments and evaluations. It is that all four of these young women—unlike Celestina who achieves an almost masculine vocation—in one way or another fail to provide for their feminine incompletion. Sempronio's repetition of Aristotle, "¿No as leydo el filósofo, do dize: Assí como la materia apetece a la forma, así la muger al varón?" is supported in a manner far more subtle than he might have predicted. Areusa erects an empty independence which constantly torments her with a need for companionship. She continually refers to her "vecinas"; she welcomes Pármeno not only as a lover but also as a person with whom she can speak about her "mal de la madre"; she begs Elicia to come and live with her; and, ultimately, for all her independence and skill at intrigue, she is victimized by Centurio, a *rufián* whose profession it is to prey upon women of her kind. Lucrecia, who never emerges from servitude and vicarious pleasure, is in the same way incomplete after the death of Melibea—after the loss of an experience of love which gave focus to her slightly sordid dreaming. It is on these terms that she attempts to embrace Calisto (like a motion picture devotee at a "personal appearance") and that Celestina gains her support by promising (with all the insight of an advertising agent) a remedy for halitosis. Elicia, in her perverted domesticity, is again incomplete without someone to think for her, without someone who knows how to turn her violence and pleasure to advantage. And when she is left alone, she, like the others, is faced with the failure of her existence. Thus, Rojas' use of the rhetoric and trappings of mourning for her reaction to Celestina's death; it is an ironic expression of her new and helpless "widowhood." Lastly, Melibea loses her *gloria* with the death of Calisto and is thrust forth fatally into the time and space she had previously denied.[7]

In commenting on the unity of this pattern, it is worth noting that these young women are never faced with a moral choice, a choice such as is offered to Calisto in Act I. The distinction between virtue, either in chastity or marriage, and vice is unimportant to them. Even Melibea's first resistance to love rests on sentiments of honor and, perhaps, of fear rather than on any principle of virtue. The possibility of marriage, significantly enough, occurs to her after the fact of love and not before. Being a woman, Rojas implies, is neither good nor bad in itself but rather a variety of existence enclosed by a single frame of limitation. It is not, therefore, a matter for debate or for virtuous correction from without. Femininity, old age, and poverty in *La Celestina* are, as we foresaw, intolerable and almost insurmountable dikes of conscious life, dikes common to many lives. And on this basis Rojas has patterned the dialogue of his cast, has joined his characters in mutual—yet variant—agonies and evaluations. Instead of a gallery of virtuous and vicious women or of predetermined roles, he presents us with four lives conditioned by femininity as a kind of incompletion. It is a pattern which emerges from the dialogue— from its authentic expression of sentiment—rather than being imposed on it.

Rojas' dialogic artistry, in other words, has resulted in a *cast of lives* rather than of *characters* in the usual sense of the term. It has enabled a new multivalent patterning of life in terms of its conditioning—a radically new approach to the creation of general significance from personal existence.

This change in creative direction—from within conscious life out to its common frontiers (rather than the other way around as in the Middle Ages with its exemplary heroes and saints in the third person)—must not be confused with an existentialist interpretation of *La Celestina*. It is almost axiomatic that human existence is the raw material of all great literature and that any authentic presentation of the human condition must in one way or another deal with both the essence and the existence of man. In this sense all occidental literature since Homer has been written by precursors of existentialism. And this is as true of Rojas as it is of Shakespeare, Racine, or the Arcipreste de Hita. It is not, therefore, that we are attempting a rigorously fashionable interpretation of *La Celestina,* but that Rojas' peculiar artistry of life as a continual dialogic innovation within corporal and social necessities allows us to use certain terms and concepts from contemporary philosophy for its better comprehension. Doctrinally, as we shall see, *La Celestina* is far more Stoic than it is existentialist (in the manner of a Sartre or a Heidegger). But since its creative substance is living speech (or, to reverse the phrase, spoken life), vocabulary taken from philosophies of life, value, and existence does not betray it. It would be anachronistic to claim that Rojas was a precursor of twentieth-century thought, but it is also true that a critical study of his (or any other) artistry is facilitated by that same thought. We can talk about life and its literary creation in *La Celestina* because we have now been given words for it.

2. Trajectories of Character

The charting of patterns of life in *La Celestina* is to a certain extent arbitrary. We have chosen from the larger dialogic interchange climactic moments of self-expression for several lives in order that their resemblances and variations might be commented upon and compared. Yet this was possible only because we assumed before hand that these patterns must exist, that the minimum of definition provided by the fact of cast must take on new artistic importance in the absence of the third person. Thus, our conclusion that Rojas' artistry resulted not in an arrangement of characters but rather in subtle patternings of life, while interesting in itself, has not been derived adequately from the substratum of dialogue. And it is there that it must ultimately stand or fall. In order to complete this task we must follow out the dialogic trajectory of a single life in its succession of encounters and situations. Each vital pattern is, in reality, composed of multiple strands of life, not at climax but in duration. In terms of Aristotle, final recognitions and catastrophes are built upon peripeties, and it is these we must examine. We are now, in short, to leave the exposition of finished patterns and penetrate into the dialogic studio where we may see the artist at work on life.

For this purpose I have chosen the life of Pármeno as a single example, if only because its trajectory is so explicitly traced by Rojas. We first meet Pármeno in Act I engaged in dialogue with Calisto—a dialogue which is more a description of Celestina and a preparation for her arrival than a genuine encounter of the two speakers. It is possible, of course, that Pármeno's incredibly detailed memories of Celestina and her malign establishment may correspond to that total recall which is appropriate to key experiences of childhood: "Pero de aquel poco tiempo que la seruí, recogía la nueua memoria lo que la vejez no had podido quitar." Nevertheless, this minute enumerative description does not reveal either the intimate *yo* or the intimate *tú* of the speakers. It is a passage lacking in inner direction, a passage not yet as fully dialogic as Rojas was later to demand. Only afterwards, when Calisto has insinuated interested motives for Pármeno's disapproval of Celestina ("Pero ruégote, Pármeno, la embidia de Sempronio, que en esto me sirue e complaze, no ponga impedimiento en el remedio de mi vida. Que, si para él houo jubón para tí no faltará sayo"), does he answer with a projection of himself: "Quéxome, señor, de la dubda de mi fidelidad e seruicio, por los prometimientos e amonestaciones tuyas. ¿Quándo me viste, señor, embidiar o por ningún interesse ni resabio tu prouecho estorcer?" (I, 87) This same vision of himself as a faithful and true servant reoccurs both in his exposé of Celestina's design to be overheard and in his comments on Calisto's obeisance to her: "Deshecho es, vencido es, caydo es: no es capaz de ninguna redención ni consejo ni esfuerço." Pármeno conversing with his master in his first dialogic situation seems sincerely wise and loyal—and to such an extent that it is not he but Calisto who suggests the envy of Sempronio.

In his second situation Pármeno finds himself faced with Celestina, a situation which she dominates and directs, just as he previously had dominated Calisto. She begins by a defense and illustration of love, and then, before Pármeno can answer her on this level, her speech drops in decorum and penetrates previously unexpressed strata of awareness. The interchange is well known but is so splendid that I cannot refrain from reproducing it:

Cel.—... y en lo vegetativo algunas plantas han este respeto, si sin interposición de otra cosa en poca distancia de tierra están puestas, en que ay determinación de heruolarios e agricultores, ser machos e hembras. ¿Qué dirás a esto, Pármeno ¡Neciuelo, loquito, angelico, perlica, simplezico! ¿Lobitos en tal gestico? Llégate acá, putico, que no sabes nada del mundo ni de sus deleytes. ¡Mas rauia mala me mate, si te llego a mí, avnque vieja! Que la voz tienes ronca, las barbas te apuntan. Mal sosegadilla deues tener la punta de la barriga.

    PAR.—¡Como cola de alacrán! (I, 95–96)

Pármeno's intellectual defenses are undermined by this sudden penetration, and he can recover his previous self-presentation only with difficulty:

Calla madre, no me culpes ni me tengas, avnque moço, por insipiente. Amo a Calisto, porque le deuo fidelidad, por criança, por beneficios, por ser dél honrrado e bien tratado, que es la mayor cadena, que el amor del seruidor al seruicio del señor prende, quanto lo contrario aparta. Véole perdido e no ay cosa peor que yr trás desseo sin esperança de buen fin e especial, pensando remediar su hecho tan arduo e dificil con vanos consejos e necias razones de aquel bruto Sempronio, que es pensar sacar aradores a pala e açadón. No lo puedo sufrir. ¡Dígolo e lloro! (I, 96)

Here, the Pármeno of the first situation manages to resurrect himself but on the verge of tears and without the self-righteous serenity of his reproof of Calisto. His envy of Sempronio, an envy which we saw him deny, manages to break through the seams of this weakening virtue. He is now ready for Celestina's major assaults. These are, in the first place, a provision of arguments for Pármeno's future rationalizations (cynical reflections on the master-servant relationship, on friendship, and on the nature of "deleyte") and in the second, the direct temptations of money and Areusa's love.

As the discussion goes on, Pármeno's weakening and indecision are the more evident as his counterarguments are the more pedantic. And when he at last says, "Todo me recelo, madre, de recebir dudoso consejo," it is a confession of final dilemma, and Celestina with the instinct of the bargainer realizes that she has only to withdraw in order to capture him: "E assí, Pármeno, me despido de ti e deste negocio." She is right, for in an aside Pármeno follows the first plan of rationalization so knowingly prepared for him, that of friendship: "Esta ¿qué me aconseja? Paz con Sempronio. La paz no se deue negar: que bién aventurados son los pacíficos, que fijos de Dios serán llamados. Amor no se deue rehuyr. Caridad a los hermanos, interesse pocos le apartan. Pues quiérola complazer e oyr." (I, 110) Thus, the Pármeno of the second situation ends by admitting his complete subjection. Instead of the stern judge of conduct, he is now an ignorant "discípulo" who says to his master: "manda, que a tu mandado mi consentimiento se humilla." It is not that Pármeno has made a rightabout-face from virtue to vice but that the defenses of his consciousness have been destroyed. Celestina's strategy of simultaneous attack on his intellectual self-awareness as virtuous and on his sentimental self-awareness (as nascently carnal) has left him spiritually naked, incapable of adopting any kind of firm attitude of his own. Thus, in the third situation—Pármeno's brief encounter with Sempronio at the end of the act— when the latter asks him, "¿Pues cómo estamos?" he answers: "Como quisieres; avnque estoy espantado." His adolescent pedantry, timidity, sensuality, and lack of emotional stability have been etched out by the acids of Celestina's dialogue; and he has been left stranded in anguished and fearful consciousness.

At this point Rojas takes over the trajectory of his life and in Act II presents us with a repetition of the first dialogic situation, a second meeting with Calisto. For those who have interpreted the surrender to Celestina in Act I as a revelation of hidden weakness and bad character, this fourth appearance of Pármeno must always be something of a surprise. For Pármeno reverts to his previous rectitude and reproves Calisto even more bitterly than in Act I. We must realize, however, that since Rojas' artistry of character is dialogic, dependent only on the first and second persons, any reunion of the same individuals must exhibit at least similar arguments and sentiments. Pármeno cannot suddenly turn to Calisto, proclaim a previous error, and advise him to place his confidence in Celestina, if only because he still is the *tú* he created for himself in Calisto's eyes. Unamuno's famous adaptation of Oliver Wendell Holmes's notion that every conversation between two friends involves at least six distinct speakers (A as he thinks he is, A as B thinks he is, A as he is ultimately from the point of view of God, and so on) would seem to apply here. Pármeno had presented himself in terms of a self-made characterization as virtuous, loyal, experienced, and severe, a characterization that was accepted by Calisto. In his second dialogic situation, it is true, this characterization was destroyed by Celestina, but it remains valid for Calisto who was not a witness to the destruction and who addresses Pármeno as if expecting a resumption of the earlier argument: "Tú, Pármeno, ¿qué te parece de lo que oy ha pasado? Mi pena es grande, Melibea alta, Celestina sabia y buena maestra destos negocios. No podemos errar. Tú me la has aprouado con toda tu enemistad. Yo te creo. Que tanta es la fuerça de la verdad, que las lenguas de los enemigos trae a sí." (II, 119) Pármeno is put into a position of having to reply in terms of a "second person" which is no longer authentically himself. Thus, while we may not have "characters" in *La Celestina*, Rojas knows well how to manage the characterizations furnished by the dialogue. Less complex than that proposed by Unamuno, in every conversation there are only four persons present, a first and second person for each life, but Rojas compensates for the missing absolute point of view by his dexterity in confronting those available to him.

Aside from this relative conservatism of the second person, it is also probable that Pármeno clings to the earlier opposition as a kind of cloak for his new nakedness of character. The open attack on Sempronio, the new bitterness of his feeling about Celestina ("E lo que más dello siento es venir a manos de aquella trotaconventos, despues de tres vezes emplumada"), the corrosive aside at the beginning, all indicate the lack of serene authenticity to Pármeno's virtue. The new violence is contingent on the internal destruction which it hides. The first situation is repeated but, as always in *La Celestina,* in terms of those situations which have intervened. This cumulation of dialogic situations within each living trajectory, this repetition of scenes framing the continual innovation of life, is brought out splendidly in Pármeno's closing monologue:

CAL.—... presto será mi buelta.
PARM.—¡Mas, nunca sea! ¡Allá yrás con el diablo! A estos locos dezildes lo que les cumple; no os podrán ver. *¡Por mi ánima, que si agora le diessen vna lançada en el calcañar, que saliessen más sesos que de la cabeça! Pues anda, que a mi cargo que Celestina e Sempronio te espulguen!* ¡O desdichado de mí! Por ser leal padezco mal. Otros se ganan por malos; yo me pierdo por bueno. ¡El mundo es tal! Quiero yrme al hilo de la gente, pues a los traydores llaman discretos, a los fieles nescios. Si creyera a Celestina con sus seys dozenas de años acuestas, no me maltratara Calisto. Mas esto me porná escarmiento d'aquí adelante con él. Que si dixiere comamos, yo también; si quisiere derrocar la casa, aprouarlo, si quemar su hazienda, yr por fuego. ¡Destruya, rompa, quiebre, dañe, dé a alcahuetas lo suyo, que mi parte me cabrá, pues dizen: a río buelto ganancia de pescadoes. ¡Nunca más perro a molino! (II, 125–26)

Here, Pármeno, driven from a previous interpretation of himself as virtuous and still without a new resting place in the "deleyte" offered by Celestina, is engaged in desperate and bitter rationalization. The second situation clearly has been superimposed over the first. Pármeno continues to recognize the paths of right and wrong, but to this recognition he adds the second rationalization suggested to him: "El mundo es tal." And by that he means that loyalty has gone out of style. Calisto has mistreated him as Celestina had predicted, so why should he suffer more for his principles? It is as if he had been waiting for a few harsh words and the petty indignity of being forced to act as a *moço d'espuelas* in order that Celestina might be confirmed and that an attitude which was no longer authentic might be rejected definitively. Once alone, once free of immediate encounter with Calisto, the *tú* which had maintained a facsimile of virtue is discarded by Pármeno.[8]

After Act II, Rojas has no further need of direct confrontation of Pármeno and his master, and he carefully avoids it. The gap between Calisto's second person for Pármeno and Pármeno's own first-person departure from it is now so wide that their encounter would be more painful than ironically revealing.[9] Hence, the next appearance of Pármeno is delayed until the splendid situation of Act VI, a situation which joins Calisto, Celestina, and both servants into a quartet of lives engaged in dissonant harmonies and counterpoints. Pármeno, we must admit, plays the smallest part in this reunion. His contribution seems relatively insignificant if compared to the triumph of Celestina, the enamoured ravings of Calisto, or even to the curiosity and fascination of Sempronio. Yet such as it is, Act VI resumes and confirms dialogically the state of mind that was so briefly revealed at the end of Act II. In the first interchange with Sempronio, Pármeno's desperate lack of self-definition, his negative anguish, is made explicit:

CEL.—... Mi vida diera por menor precio, que agora daría este manto raydo e viejo.
PARM.—Tú dirás lo tuyo: entre col y col lechuga. Sobido has vn escalón; más adelante te espero a la saya. Todo para ti e no nada de que puedas dar parte. Pelechar quiere la vieja. Tú me sacarás a mi verdadero e mi amo loco. No le pierdas palabra, Sempronio, e verás como no quiere pedir dinero, porque es diuisible.
SEMP.—Calla, hombre desesperado, que te matará Calisto si te oye. (VI, 203–4)

The next comment from Pármeno presents his continued opposition not just to Celestina but also to Sempronio.

SEMP.—... ¿No ternía este hombre sofrimiento para oyr lo que siempre ha deseado?
PARM.—¡E que calle yo, Sempronio! Pues, si nuestro amo te oye, tan bien te castigará a tí como a mí.
SEMP.—¡O mal fuego te abrase! Que tu fables en daño de todos e yo a ninguno ofendo. ¡O! ¡Intolerable pestilencia e mortal te consume, rixoso embidioso, maldito! ¿Toda esta es la amistad, que con Celestina e comigo hauías concertado? ¡Vete de aquí a la mala ventura! (VI, 207)

We may notice here and in the previous quotation how closely, Sempronio's (and Rojas') understanding of Pármeno corresponds to our own. The summation of his attitude in relation to the other three is given by Pármeno himself a few pages further on:

CAL.—Esso será de cuerpo, madre; pero no de gentileza, no de estado, no de gracia e discreción, no de linaje, no de presunción con merecimiento, no en virtud, no en habla.
PARM.—Ya escurre eslauones el perdido. Ya se desconciertan sus badajadas.

Nunca da menos de doze; siempre está hecho relox de mediodia. Cuenta, cuenta, Sempronio, que estás desbauando oyéndole a él locuras e a ella mentiras. (VI, 210)

At this necessary point of rest and résumé in the living trajectory of Pármeno, each of the preceding situations is implicit if only negatively. Loyalty to Calisto remains as distrust for Celestina; the blandishments of Celestina remain as scorn for Calisto; and, as for Sempronio, his continuing brutality affords a constancy of dislike.[10] The result is that a single sentence, "Cuenta, cuenta, Sempronio ... ," can harmonize all of Pármeno's past discords.[11]

Having, thus, reminded the reader of the state of Pármeno's consciousness, Rojas is now ready to continue the trajectory. The fifth stage or situation occupies the first half of Act VII and repeats the second (just as we saw the third to repeat the first). Pármeno is once more confronted with Celestina and with the same arguments she had used before: the advantages of friendship, the breakdown of the bonds between servants and masters, and the enticements of love. Nevertheless, it would again be wrong to equate the two situations. Rojas, for example, makes a great deal more of the Celestina-Claudina relationship than the author of Act I. Whereas before Celestina had merely said, "que tan puta vieja era tu madre como yo," now the demoniac friendship constitutes, in full detail, a final spiritual destruction for Pármeno.[12] He must be completely broken of virtue before his imminent reintegration.

More interesting from our point of view, however, is the apparent accumulation of awareness during the intervening situations (Acts II and VI) in both Celestina and Pármeno. Celestina opens her attack with the following remarks:

Pármeno, hijo, después de las passadas razones, no he hauido oportuno tiempo para te dezir e mostrar el mucho amor, que te tengo e asimismo como de mi boca todo el mundo ha oydo hasta agora en absencia bien de tí. La razón no es menester repetirla, porque yo te tenía por hijo, a lo menos quasi adotiuo e assí que imitavas a natural; e tú dasme el pago en mi presencia, paresciéndote mal quanto digo, susurrando e mumurando contra mí en presencia de Calisto. Bien pensaua yo que, después que concediste en mi buen consejo, que no hauías de tornarte atrás. Todavía me parece que te quedan reliquias vanas, hablando por antojo mas que por razón. Desechas el prouecho por contentar la lengua ... (VII, 231–32)

Celestina is perfectly conscious that Pármeno in Act VI no longer exercises an authentic opposition to her plans, that his remarks were *reliquias* of the first situation. Pármeno's answer is equally significant:

Madre, [para contigo digo que] mi segundo yerro te confiesso e, con perdón de lo passado, quiero que ordenes lo por venir. Pero con Sempronio me paresce que es imposible sostenerse mi amistad. El es desuariado, yo malsufrido: conciértame essos amigos. (VII, 234)

The speed of this surrender is evidently the result of defenselessness. Celestina's work in Act I was so well done that her second attack is immediately effective. Pármeno's only reservation is Sempronio, whose violence is fresh in his mind; but, aside from that, he can both explain and admit freely the lack of authenticity to his attitude:

Que, avnque oy veyas que aquello dezía, no era porque me paresciesse mal lo que tu fazías; pero porque veya que le consejaua yo lo cierto e me daua malas gracias. Pero de aquí adelante demos tras el. Faz de las tuyas, que yo callaré. Que ya tropecé en no te creer cerca deste negocio con el. (VII, 237)

Thus, we witness one further step in the accumulation of situations in Pármeno's mind. The individual trajectory is a growth of awareness from situation to situation, and if past encounters are repeated, it is only in terms of an unrelenting innovation in living dialogue.

Pármeno's second appearance in the same act (situation six) presents a wholly new encounter, an encounter which makes few dialogic demands upon him. His adolescent timidity in the presence of Areusa hardly permits of spoken expression, and we see him through the eyes of Celestina, sitting in the corner, a prey to comic embarrassment:

CEL.—... Sube, hijo Pármeno.
AREU.—¡No suba! ¡Landre me mato! que me fino de empacho, que no le conozco. Siempre houe verguënça dél.
CEL.—Aquí estoy yo que te la quitaré e cobriré e hablaré por entramos: que otro tan empachado es él.
PARM.—Señora, Diós salue tu graciosa presencia.
AREU.—Gentilhombre, buena sea tu venida.
CEL.—Llégate acá, asno. ¿Adónde te vas allá assentar al rincón? No seas empachado, que al hombre vergonçoso el diablo le traxo a palacio. Oydme entrambos lo que digo ... (VII, 256–57)

In this decisive situation, Pármeno's lack of participation in the dialogue corresponds to an appropriate clouding of consciousness in excitement and shame. The sentimental awareness of the moment—precisely because it represents only a segment of love—results in a shyness and muteness never shared by Calisto and Melibea. From this point of view, it is interesting to speculate on Rojas' reasons for the lengthy deletion in this scene:

AREU.—¿Qué te dize esse señor a la oreja? ¿Piensa que tengo de fazer nada de lo que pides?
CEL.—No dize, hija, sino que se huelga mucho con tu amistad, porque eres persona tan honrrada e en quien qualquier beneficio cabrá bien. [E assimismo que, pues que esto por mi intercessión se hace, que él me promete d'aquí adelante ser

muy amigo de Sempronio e venir en todo lo que quisiere contra su amo en un negocio, que traemos entre manos, ¿Es verdad, Pármeno? ¿Prometeslo assi como digo?
   Parm.—Sí prometo, sin dubda.
   Cel.—Ha, don ruyn, palabra te tengo, a buen tiempo te así.] Llégate acá, negligente, vergonçoso, que quiero ver para quánto eres, ante que me vaya. Retóçala en esta cama. (VII, 258)

The appearance here of preoccupations and dialogue inherited from previous situations must have seemed out of place to Rojas. The promise extracted from Pármeno is funny enough, but, at the same time, it is tangential to his living trajectory and ultimately unnecessary. Pármeno already has given his word not to interfere with Celestina and, as for friendship with Sempronio, it emerges naturally in the next act. The deletion is an element of plot possessing comic justification but alien to the life of the situation as such. The coyness of Areusa, the timidity of Pármeno, and the fierce carnality of Celestina are all, insofar as they are momentarily authentic, inimical to intrigue and to extraneous dialogue.

After Pármeno leaves Areusa the next morning, he finds himself in a state of euphoria and plenitude which is in direct contrast to his previous desperation. The mute shyness of the night before has also been transmuted into a serenity of elevated discourse (as we saw in the preceding essay) and a need for dialogue: "Bien me dezía la vieja que de ninguna prosperidad es buena la posesión sin compañía. El plazer no comunicado no es plazer. ¿Quién sentiría esta mi dicha como yo la siento?" This vital recognition of the truth of Celestina's third argument in Act I, that of "deleyte" and its dialogic awareness, constitutes the real end of Pármeno's trajectory as an independent life—as well as the new basis for his existence. The transformation of Pármeno is only completed when intellectual awareness and evaluation of himself (in terms of virtue) is replaced by a new sentimental awareness and evaluation: "¿Quién sentiría mi dicha como yo la siento?"

One result of this new situation and its corresponding state of being is that Pármeno is for the first time capable of overcoming the brutal and sarcastic rancor of Sempronio. He proposes the dinner of Act IX, and Sempronio's reply seals their friendship and the new identity of their lives:

¡O Diós! e cómo me has alegrado. Franco eres, nunca te faltaré. Como te tengo por hombre, como creo que Diós te ha de hazer bien, todo el enojo, que de tus passadas fablas tenía, se me ha tornado en amor. No dudo ya tu confederación con nosotros ser la que deue. Abraçarte quiero. Seamos como hermanos, ¡vaya el diablo para ruyn! Sea lo passado questión de Sant Juan e assí paz para todo el año. Que las

yras de los amigos siempre suelen ser reintegración del amor. Comamos e holguemos, que nuestro amo ayunará por todos. (VIII, 15–16)

As is here predicted—"Seamos como hermanos"—Pármeno's trajectory is from
now on identical to that of Sempronio, and even unto death do they never
part. For example, it is curious to note how small a part Pármeno is given in
the dialogue following this climactic situation. In the banquet scene of Act IX
he hardly opens his mouth; in Act XI, which brings together once more the
lives of Act VI, Pármeno's murmurings are a pale reflection of those which so
irritated Sempronio; and, at the first rendezvous of the two lovers, he and
Sempronio engage in a comically identical duet of cowardice. It is true, of
course, that in this last situation Pármeno's relief after evading the dangerous
approach to the door is the more vociferous as he is inexperienced, and, that
as a novice rascal, he continually follows the lead of Sempronio. Nevertheless,
it is evident that Rojas has lost interest in him for himself alone. He only
serves as a means to such Bergsonian repetition of gesture as the following:

> PARM.—... ¡O si me viesses, hermano, como estó, plazer haurías! A medio lado
> abiertas las piernas, el pie ysquierdo adelante puesto en huyda, las faldas en la
> cinta, la adarga arrollada e so el sobaco, porque no me empache. Que, por Dios,
> que creo corriesse como vn gamo, según el temor tengo d'estar aquí.
> SEMP.—Mejor estó yo, que tengo liado el broquel e el espada con las correas,
> porque no se me caygan al correr, e el caxquete en la capilla. (XII, 88–89)

Pármeno has, in effect, become a carbon copy of Sempronio, a reproduction
which can no longer serve as a guide to Rojas' artistry. It is almost symbolic
that his last words to Sempronio are "Salta, que tras tí voy."[13]

On glancing back over the biography of Pármeno, we may notice, first,
that it confirms the lack of characterization based on the third person. Just as
we deduced from our study of patterns of character, so the life of Pármeno
reassures us that, in effect, the *tú* and the *yo* meeting in one situation after
another are primarily responsible for what is done and said. Instead of fixed
characterizations directing dialogue *a priori*, we are made to follow an evolution of spoken life from one vital situation to another. This, in turn, provides
a new understanding of Rojas' artistry. Under such circumstances, it is (as it
must be) dedicated to the presentation of each life as a significant and easily
perceptible trajectory. Rojas is, thus, not just the creator of his characters but
even more the director, the skilled *metteur en scène* of their lives.

This artistic direction is, as we have seen, exercised in two ways: first by
calculated repetition and, second, by an equally calculated innovation. From
time to time, with full artistic purpose Rojas reunites the same speakers (Pármeno and Calisto in Acts I and II; Pármeno and Celestina in Acts I and VII;

Pármeno, Sempronio, Celestina, and Calisto in Acts VI and XI) in order to show off both the seeming paralysis of their relation to each other and, simultaneously, the profound dynamism of their inner lives. He balances the relative conservatism of the second person, with its intramural characterization, against the continuing free growth of the first person in experience. The repeated situation becomes, in this way, an index to the change of the individual, and at the same time a signpost to the direction of his trajectory. On other occasions, Rojas arranges the entrance of a single life into an utterly new situation and allows us to see innovations of behavior and speech in their immediate dialogic formation. Arrangement of situations, then, is Rojas' manner of organizing life into those trajectories which replace character and which are ultimately woven into the larger patterns we discussed previously. Like the style of dialogue managed by its own decorum, the individual lives of *La Celestina* organize themselves (or seem to do so) first into dialogic growth and, then, through repeated and variant situations, into significant trajectories—trajectories which become fully perceptible only after the work has been read. They are never predetermined and so never predictable.

This artistry of life without character might well have been premised on Bergson's doctrine that "la vida se hace viviendo." The growth and change of the individual from situation to situation—a growth which combines the living presence of past situations with an unrelenting originality in moment to moment dialogue—corresponds strikingly to the notion of creative evolution. Each life in *La Celestina* rather than following out a previous plan, constructs or creates itself in its course and, at the same time, is never free of past creations of itself. It must carry out in an original fashion what was begun in Act I. This is confirmed by our study of Pármeno, for when, as in his case, the individual life stops creating itself, Rojas immediately loses interest in it. Pármeno, after Act VIII, is limited to self-repetition and to a mechanical imitation of Sempronio which corresponds to the antivital concept of humor we find described in *Le rire*. The complementary example is that of Calisto and Melibea in the *Comedia*. Instead of coming to the end of their trajectories before the end of their lives, they are cut off in the very middle of their *proceso de amores,* and the result is the *Tragicomedia* dedicated to its completion before their death. Nevertheless, we must remember that no matter how enlightening the comparison with Bergson may be, it is also inexact; it is not life, as such, that is Rojas' raw material but spoken life, a life of mutual encounter in words. Trajectories of life are, after all, abstractions; within *La Celestina* it is perhaps more truthful to say that Melibea and Calisto are left with a great deal more to say to each other and about themselves.[14]

3. Modalities of Character

Thus, our two paths to Rojas' art of character have resulted in the very distortions we foresaw. Patterns based on the cast as a whole, while reflecting the dialogic mutuality of life in *La Celestina,* abstract it from the concrete situation. And the tracing of a single life from situation to situation results in a trajectory which in itself is an abstraction—which has an aspect of independence that is unreal for creation premised on dialogue. On the one hand, we saw Rojas primarily concerned with a cast of human consciousnesses engaged in evaluating themselves in terms of each other and of their living limitations; on the other, we saw him as an architect of life finding the best situations for the illustration of individual growth. Both of these points of view are valid; both Sartre and Bergson to a certain extent can illuminate this artistry; but, at the same time neither can explain it or suggest its full originality. We must, instead, attempt to combine them into a new synthesis which will capture the native peculiarity of the inhabitants of *La Celestina*—the way of being which permits their residence in the unique masterpiece. And to do it, we must forsake literary anthropology and biography for an excursion into literary psychology.

This excursion requires that we agree before starting out on one very simple assumption: that we cannot know more about the psychology of the characters than they are willing to tell us. Just as it would be impossible for us to make a composite portrait for Melibea out of the conflicting descriptions of Areusa and Calisto (or even to choose between them), so we may not aspire to an analysis of character outside of the first and second persons present in the text. It is clearly anachronistic to attempt Freudian explanations of Don Quijote's madness; and for *La Celestina,* with its lack of the third person, such attempts not only would be anachronistic but absolutely fatal. In other words, a psychology which is limited by definition to the first and second persons must of necessity be a psychology of consciousness. Although I, myself, have been on one occasion tempted in this direction,[15] it is contrary to the nature of the art we are studying to pretend to a possible knowledge of the subconscious life of the characters. The attention paid by psychologists to this level of the mind, implies, in effect, as rigorous an investigation of life in the third person as that of anatomists of character. And, if for *La Celestina* we reject the one, so also we must reject the other. We must, instead, cling to what the characters say to each other, *to what they can think and feel in words.* Vossler has pointed out the "humanism" of Racine's total artistic confidence in words; and in an even more radical fashion, the same thing is true for Rojas. What is not said in his text is simply not there.

We may be comforted in this assumption by observing that many shadings of psychological change—shadings which elsewhere might have corresponded to the omniscient observations of the author or which we might only be allowed to read between the lines—are fully known to the characters of *La Celestina*. We may recall, for example, Celestina's acute analysis of Pármeno's desperate asides in Act VI, "... te quedan reliquias vanas, hablando por antojo mas que por razón," as well as his own equally telling confirmation, "... veya que le consejaua lo cierto y me daua malas gracias." Even more unexpectedly conscious, is Melibea's well-known explanation to Calisto of the sudden crystallization of her love: "E avnque muchos días he pugnado por lo dissimular, no he podido tanto que, en tornándome aquella muger tu dulce nombre a la memoria, no descubriesse mi desseo ..." Instead of a deep-running accumulation of forces in the subconscious, Melibea is fully aware of her growing sentiment and of the catalytic function of Calisto's name in bringing it to expression. Along with love as a conscious presence, there is also lust. When Celestina mentions suddenly Pármeno's nascently vigorous sexuality in Act I, "Que la voz tienes ronca, las barbas te apuntan. Mal sosegadilla deues tener la punta de la barriga," his immediate answer, "¡Como cola de alacrán!" is as frank as the remark which stimulated it. For all his pretense to virtue, Pármeno makes no attempt to hide or sublimate this aspect of his life; it is as much a part of his awareness as Melibea's love is of hers. In *La Celestina* everything is said at least partially because everything can be said. To borrow a word and a concept from Castro, the "integralism" of Rojas' artistry can embrace in dialogue all levels of human existence, and, under these circumstances, a vertical division of the psyche would seem to be impossible. We must accept the fact that neither subtlety nor shame (in addition to the above sexual frankness, we may remember the full awareness of Pármeno and Sempronio of their own cowardice in Act XII) can limit verbal consciousness in *La Celestina*.[16]

If we establish our point of departure in the human consciousness, it is evident that here also must be found the axis of both the patterns and the trajectories already considered. Yet in both cases the thing seems difficult. Patterns of life in *La Celestina*, as we saw, rested not only on self-awareness in terms of physical and social limitations but also on sentimental reactions to them. Similarly, such trajectories as that of Pármeno, by their very growth from situation, would seem to depend on the participation of levels of existence not included in the phrase, "je pense, donc je suis." It would seem that there should be a direct relationship of the consciousness to realms of life exterior to itself for either pattern or trajectory to exist. The traditional interlocutor of reason is passion, and if we think of consciousness as necessarily rational, this duality would seem to hold for what we know of *La Celestina*—and to rule out a psychology exclusive of one of its terms. Thus, having eliminated the possibility of character based on the third person, we find ourselves faced with something which resembles it very much: a zone of unconscious and overwhelming passion, known to us and to the author, but hardly available to the minds and tongues of the individuals who must wrestle with it. Phèdre's dark surge behind the eyes of consciousness, her helpless realization of the passionate distortion of her vision, seems to be an inevitable model for the growth and counterpoint of life in *La Celestina*.

Nevertheless, in the very moment of drawing such a conclusion we know intuitively that it is false, that Rojas' artistry of character is dimensionally removed from that of Racine. The error seems to lie precisely in our unchallenged acceptance of a concept of consciousness that is far too limited, far too French (if we admit the customary equation of Cartesian thought with its nationality). Alongside rational consciousness, we must assume for *La Celestina* the effective existence of that sentimental consciousness expounded by Scheler and Heidegger. Celestina, herself, explains the importance of such a consciousness both vividly and convincingly to Pármeno in her discourse on "deleyte":

El deleyte es con los amigos en las cosas sensuales e especial en recontar las cosas de amor e comunicarlas: esto hize, esto otro me dixo, tal donayre passamos, de tal manera la tomé, assí la bese, assí me mordió assí la abracé, assí se allegó. ¡O qué fabla! ¡o qué gracia! ¡o qué juegos! ¡o qué besos! Vamos allá, boluamos acá, ande la musica, pintemos los motes, cantemos canciones, inuenciones, justemos, qué cimera sacaremos o qué letra. Ya va a la misa, mañana, saldrá, rondemos su calle, mira su carta, vamos de noche, tenme el escala, aguarda a la puerta. ¿Cómo te fué? Cata el cornudo; sola la dexa. Dale otra buelta, tornemos allá. E para esto, Pármeno, ¿ay deleyte sin compañía? Alahé, alahé: la que las sabe las tañe. Este es el deleyte; que lo al, mejor lo fazen los asnos en el prado. (I, 107–8)

"Deleyte" is here far removed from the blindness of sensual passion; it is hardly an obscure or overwhelming force antagonistic to the consciousness. Rather if we substitute the concepts of dialogue and spoken awareness for the word "compañía" above, we can appreciate the full distinction which Celestina is attempting to make between the conscious life of men and the instinctive life of beasts—or, on a higher level, between sentiment and passion. In his later vital acceptance of this doctrine, Pármeno confirms it with the question directed to no one: "¿Quién sentiría esta mi dicha como yo la siento?" In effect, in *La Celestina* we find neither Racinian passions nor Freudian instincts opposed to reason but rather a gallery of sentiments: love, "deleyte," fear, anguish, hatred, and many more. And all of them constitute a consciousness as real as that of their antagonist, reason. In Heidegger's vocabulary, the lives created by Rojas not only "feel" but also "feel themselves" to exist in dialogue.

Juan David García Bacca, whose splendid article, "Sobre el sentido de 'conciencia' en *La Celestina*,"[17] is to a certain extent responsible for these considerations, goes so far as to indicate that there is no other form of consciousness in the work—or at least for Celestina as its central figure. Referring primarily to her expression in Act IV, "assí goze desta alma pecadora," García Bacca suggests (although he does not so affirm) that this sinful "goce" is Rojas' fundamental sentimental discovery.[18] Be that as it may, the artistry of *La Celestina* as a whole requires the presence of both forms of consciousness in intimate cohabitation. Pármeno, on the one hand, observes himself intellectually and tries to fit his life into such general patterns as that of the virtuous servant. On the other, he feels himself sentimentally from situation to situation in terms of his anguish, his hatred, his "deleyte," or his fear. There is a continual effort, as we have seen, to convert the sentiment into a reasoned and defensible attitude, and to make the intellectual generalization correspond to the radical autonomy of sentiment. And this is true not only of Pármeno; each of the lives of *La Celestina* is engaged in a similar struggle of consciousnesses, in rationalization of sentiment and sentimentalization of reason. Calisto in his great monologue of Act XIII squirms helplessly between a consciousness of himself as a master and a gentleman of honor and his opposing consciousness of himself as in love. Elicia presents her sentimental anger and sensuality in terms of the most used of rational commonplaces; and even Celestina, before leaving for her first interview with Melibea, wavers between the sentiment of fear and her vocational self-vision. These simplified examples, admittedly foreshorten Rojas' artistry, for in the agonic embrace of these two consciousnesses there is frequent transposition of terms from one to the other: Pármeno's reasoned virtue, for instance, remaining as a hatred from Celestina after Act VIII. Nevertheless, the reader of *La Celestina* cannot fail to recognize the validity of an approach which allows him to explain Rojas' art of character for what it is, an art of conscious life.

The full significance of this juncture of sentimental and rational consciousnesses in *La Celestina* will become clear if we relate it back to the primacy of dialogue, a primacy from which it was originally derived. On these terms, sentimental consciousness may be identified with consciousness in the first person while rational consciousness belongs to the second person. Alive only through his dialogue, each individual sees himself, on the one hand, as others see him or as he imagines they see him. In terms of the conditions of his life—young, old, servant, master, man, woman, etc.—he attempts to fit himself and to know himself within generally recognizable classifications. And it is in relation to this *tú* that the style of argument, with its superficial logic and its fifteenth-century commonplaces, runs all through the work. On the other hand, this same individual "feels himself" as a *yo* and expresses that feeling in a style which we have already referred to as sentimental. On this level according to García Bacca's presentation of Heidegger, he becomes real, authentically himself. Unlike Racine's creations caught in a destiny of passion alien to self and to consciousness, these lives are their sentiments, at least as much as they are their thoughts. Thus, life in dialogue is not only (and by definition) conscious or spoken life but also is divided into two modalities of consciousness corresponding to the first and second persons of that same dialogue. The *tú* and the *yo* in addition to their function as grammatical signs, represent respectively transcendent and immanent, rational and sentimental, manners of being aware. And unless we recognize this dialogic duality, a dialogic duality which is the psychological passport to residence in *La Celestina,* we must inevitably distort Rojas' artistry of character.

Having presented this psychological theory for what it may be worth, we may now return to those patterns and trajectories which gave artistic cohesion to life in *La Celestina,* despite the absence of the third person. It is in their explanation that this psychology must stand or fall, for they represent the evidence of the text. In the case of Pármeno, what we have called his trajectory is obviously a progression in dialogue from one intellectual self-portrait to another—from one *tú* to another. Celestina began the process by stimulating his nascent sentimental awareness and by providing means for future rationalization. And afterwards from situation to situation we witness the change as a desperate lack of accord between his two consciousnesses—until his sentimental repletion in Act VIII brings about a new stasis. Reason then becomes the servant of feeling. Other trajectories (except for that of Melibea) are perhaps not as meticulously followed nor so clear in outline: Sempronio's growing sentimental incitement by Melibea, for example, can hardly overthrow his stable combination of a cynical self-vision with fear and sensuality. Nonetheless, insofar as each life reacts differently in different situations—in the complex give and take of multiple first and second persons—its two modalities of consciousness must modify their diplomacy. For every person and every sentence in *La Celestina* there is at least a potentiality of trajectory.

As for patterns, they depend on moments of conscious plentitude, moments in which the *yo* and the *tú* of a given life provide a maximum of mutual consciousness. Conditioning is then perceived most sharply by the intellect; this in turn awakens a profound "sentiment of self" and finally a more or less reasoned statement of position. Areusa's outburst on freedom with its initial realization of femininity (the comparison with Lucrecia), its sentimental outbursts (imaginative evocation of the independent life and the misdeeds of mistresses) and its final summation in a total vision of her own life ("Por esto, madre, he quesido vivir ...") is probably the best illustration of such a moment. Then, given the fact that the same conditioning is necessarily shared by other members of the cast, a patterning of several conscious lives is to be expected. Thus, even though trajectories depend on the shifting opposition of the first and second person modalities of each conscious life, such opposition of conflict is not inevitable. There are also moments of deep and authentic collaboration between the two kinds of consciousness, moments comparable in a way to Sophoclean self-recognition, and it is on these that patterns of character rest. Since Rojas' artistry is rooted in dialogic duality, each of the two possible forms of duality—conflict and collaboration—produces its own artistic ordering.

Paradoxically Rojas' faith in his peculiar creation of character, his refusal to adulterate it with elements of personality, personal appearance, or anything else that might suggest the third person, gives an exemplary quality to *La Celestina*. Exemplary characters in literature are, almost by definition, confined to the third person. If they must speak, they do so in a rigid and representative fashion. We might, therefore, expect to classify Pármeno and Sempronio, Calisto and Melibea, Areusa and Elicia, and the others as polar to such beings. Representing only themselves, how can they possess a significance which extends beyond the limited frontiers of what they think and feel in dialogue? It is a final question which involves not just the discovery of techniques but the value of those techniques once discovered. For any art which aspires to greatness must surpass believability and lifelike maneuver and achieve total human connotations. A complete answer must await the essay on theme, but, for now we may point out that the very consequence of Rojas' self-restriction to *tú* and *yo* gives exemplary overtones to the conscious life of *La Celestina*. Just as Berceo restricting himself to *él*, knew how to create the saint as an exemplary *man*, so Rojas creates exemplary *lives* in the other two persons. The divorce of his art from anecdote, from superfluous details of description, and from external reality (except as reflected in the consciousness) results in an almost classic purity of life. Melibea's living of love, her self-dedication to it, can in this way become as exemplary as that of Iseult, even though the artistries responsible for them are so far apart from each other.

The patterns and trajectories of conscious life in *La Celestina* extend beyond their dialogic *modo e manera de lauor* into realms of universal recognition.

4. Interpolations of Character

There is in *La Celestina* one central human creation whose being and life imply an art worth treating apart and for its own sake. This creation can, of course, be only Celestina herself. A hasty review of her relationship to the two terms here employed—pattern and trajectory—will illustrate the peculiarity of her position. In the first place, unlike the servants, the lovers, and the prostitutes, Celestina is not naturally paired with anyone else. In spite of her necessary sharing of the conditionalities of cast, her reactions to femininity, poverty, and age seem, somehow, removed dimensionally from those of the others. She is heterogenous and resistant to patterning.[19] In the second place, rather than possessing a clear trajectory of her own, Celestina's role is to generate those of the others, particularly those of Pármeno and Melibea. She is a mistress of trajectories as, out of her own living stability, she directs the lives which surround her. It is true, of course, that the greed responsible for her death and the desperate resolution responsible for her success with Melibea result from Rojas' mastery of living growth. But, aside from these moments, her life rests more or less immobile in its completion and serves as an axis around which everything else revolves. The picture of Celestina in Act I as surrounded by a hundred women and dominating their insults without a change of expression ("con alegre cara") is never betrayed by Rojas.

This central position is possible only because Celestina's rational and sentimental consciousnesses, her *tú* and her *yo*, are at most times joined integrally and seem to be almost indistinct. Rather than tormented by internal division and self-debate or arriving upon a single moment of clear vision in both the first and second persons, Celestina possesses a constant and integral awareness in terms of her vocation. The tremendous Spanish assertion, "Soy quien soy" or "Yo sé quién soy," while never formulated as rigidly as in later centuries, is the source of her individuality. Phrases such as "Soy una vieja qual Dios me hizo, no peor que todas" and "Viuo de mi oficio como cada qual oficial del suyo, muy limpiamente" found her consciousness upon the rock of her vocation.

As a result of these differences, Rojas seems to feel that he can afford to distinguish Celestina with a variety of personal details. Unlike the rest of the cast, her age makes possible a memory redolent with a vicious savor of incidents and atmospheres forgotten by the city. Her scarred face, her house, her occupations, her vices are known to all and contribute to a possibility of characterization that is systematically denied to others. Celestina, insofar as she is vocationally "solid," need not fear the third person. Or to put the matter in another way, Celestina's *tú* and *yo* are so identical that they presume an *ella*. Unlike Melibea, we know how Celestina looks; we can imagine her. It is as simple as that. Hence, the changes we are about to observe in Rojas' artistry of character.

The major effort at characterization of Celestina took place, of course, in Act I. There is the initial presentation in action (the deception of Sempronio in what almost corresponds to an *entremés*), then the long description, and finally her full entrance into dialogue with the persuasion of Pármeno. It is only in Act I that we are informed of her house and its contents, her face and its decorations, her vocation and its deceits. The resulting character is so complete than on some occasions we suspect that her dialogue may have been tailored to its measure. An example is the insulting aside half-overheard by Calisto, "Sempronio, de aquellas viuo yo ... ," a speech she would hardly have risked in later acts (as in Act VI) and which she probably would have replaced by hints of her desire for money. Instead of being premised on the situation, the outburst confirms a fixed characterization in the third person—as does the whole contrast of the kneeling and flowery Calisto to the degenerate object of his adoration.

Now, when Rojas inherited Celestina, he submitted her to an artistry which by its very nature forbade such tableaux; and from Act II on, she like all the others, begins her life in dialogue, rather than merely representing it or showing it off. But at the same time because of Celestina's unique role, Rojas does not hesitate to recall from time to time those details from Act I which may be related to her consciousness. In Act III, for example, Celestina shows off her sinister collection in dialogue: "Pues sube presto al sobrado alto de la solana e baxa acá el bote de azeyte serpentino que hallarás colgado del pedaço de la soga, que traxe del campo la otra noche, quando llouía e hazía escuro ..." Again, Celestina's scar is recalled when Lucrecia attempts shamefacedly to identify her to Alisa: "ALISA.—¿Con quién hablas, Lucrecia? LUCR. —Señora, con aquella vieja de la cuchillada, que solía viuir en las tenerías, a la cuesta del río." (IV, 159–60) Thus, while Rojas does not repeat the previous characterization, he uses some of its details within the terms of his own artistry.

The result of this discrete continuation of Celestina as a full character is her living domination of the work. Rojas' reinforcement with appropriate and even typical dialogue of Celestina's key position in pattern and trajectory —the underlining in this way of her integrated consciousness (in contrast to the purified divisions and agonies of the others) has allowed her to capture the sensibilities of many generations of readers. Because of these calculated reliques of characterization, Celestina has impressed the Unamunian "carne y hueso" of her living reality not only on the other characters but also on those who, by reading, once again give life to her. Hence, the popular change in title from *Tragicomedia de Calisto y Melibea* to simply *La Celestina*. It is precisely on these terms that we must study the interpolations for Celestina. In making them, Rojas added to his artistry a new experience, that of being a reader of his own work. And as such a reader, he was (like other readers) inevitably entranced and conquered by Celestina. Of the ninety-five separate deletions and interpolations in Acts I through XII, some fifty-one occur in her speeches as against only forty-four for all the rest of the cast. It is a figure which indicates the extent to which even for Rojas Calisto and Melibea had been supplanted by Celestina as the maximum life of his creation.

Naturally, not all of these fifty-one changes are related directly to the character of Celestina. Most of them have to do with style, while others may be best explained in terms of structure or theme. There are, however, a number of significant and relatively long interpolations which betray Rojas' heightened interest in and preoccupation with Celestina. It is these which we propose to consider here. They will illustrate better than anything else both the special artistry of character which he reserved for her and the special importance which she had come to possess.

A first kind of interpolation presents the attribute upon which Rojas insisted most, Celestina's Rabelaisian fondness and capacity for wine. In the *Comedia* this weakness (inherited, according to Menéndez Pelayo, from such classic go-betweens as Ovid's Dipsas) appears in the banquet of Act IX where it serves as a substitute for Celestina's lost ability to love:

CEL.—Assentaos vosotros, mis hijos, que harto lugar ay para todos, a Dios gracias: tanto nos diessen del parayso, quando allá vamos. Poneos en órden, cada vno cabe la suya; yo, que estoy sola, porné cabo mí este jarro e taça, que no es más mi vida de quanto con ello hablo. Después que me fuy faziendo vieja, no sé mejor oficio a la mesa, que escanciar.[20] (IX, 28)

Here the situation itself (sitting down to the table) extracts this sentiment from Celestina, and the same thing is true of the later listing of the varieties of wine delivered to her by the clergy. Nevertheless, when Rojas reread these passages, he seemed to interpret them apart from their context—as an appropriate and amusing characteristic which ought to be stressed. (It was also one belonging entirely to him, for there is no reference to wine in Act I.) As a result, he enlarged two of the three original passages[21] and even inserted a new discourse on wine where there had been none before:

CEL.—... Su madre e yo, vña e carne. Della aprendí todo lo mejor que sé de mi oficio. Juntas comíamos, juntas dormíamos, juntas auíamos nuestros solazes, nuestros consejos e conciertos ... ¡O muerte, muerte! ¡A quántos priuas de agradable compañía! ¡A quántos desconsuela tu enojosa visitación! Por vno, que comes con tiempo, cortas mil en agraz. Que siendo ella viua, no fueran estos mis passos desacompañados. ¡Buen siglo aya, que leal amiga e buena compañera me fué! *Que jamás me dexó hazer cosa en mi cabo, estando ella presente. Si yo traya el pan, ella la carne. Si yo ponía la mesa, ella los manteles. No loca, no fantástica ni presumptuosa como las de agora. En mi ánima, descubierta se yua hasta el cabo de la ciudad con su jarro en la mano, que en todo el camino no oya peor de: Señora Claudina. E aosadas que otra conoscía peor el vino e qualquier mercaduría. . .Que jamás boluía sin ocho o diez gostaduras, vn açumbre en el jarro e otro en el cuerpo. Ansí le fiauan dos o tres arrobas en vezes, como sobre vna taça de plata. Su palabra era prenda de oro en quantos bodegones auía. Si yuamos por la calle, donde quiera que ouiessemos sed, entráuamos en la primera tauerna y luego mandaua echar medio açumbre para mojar la boca. Mas a mi cargo que no le quitaron la toca por éllo, sino quanto la rayauan en su taja, e andar adelante. Si tal fuesse agora* su hijo ... (III, 134–36)

Here, a finished conception of Celestina as a winebibber is inserted into a situation and an act in which originally she had not been so revealed. The taste for wine that in the *Comedia* was the living product of its own circumstances (the banquet scene) seems to have become a now fixed, "characteristic," a possession of the author. Nevertheless, it would be unfair to consider this interpolation as a total betrayal of Rojas' dialogic artistry. Celestina does not regale us, for example, with a topical discourse on wine nor one completely dissociated from her context of preoccupation. Indeed, the added material is hardly comparable to the later "Esto quita la tristeza del coraçón ...; esto da esfuerço al moço e al viejo fuerça, pone color al descolorido, coraje al cobarde, al floxo diligencia ..." It is in reality, not a discussion of wine as such but rather of the drunken companionship of Celestina and Claudina—a companionship which becomes a part of the larger reminiscence. Rojas may have felt, on rereading the passage in its original form, that it was too abstractly elegiac, too much a repetition, no matter how ironical, of the current commonplaces on friendship and death. Accordingly, he joins to the intellectual consciousness of the *Comedia* a sentimental consciousness which can revive in poignant (and bitingly comic) detail the living experience of the past. To memory Rojas has added recollection; to the past, as such, he has added the sentimental recapture of old times—drunken old times.

The interpolation just considered exemplifies one aspect of the special artistry of character which Rojas reserved for Celestina. It integrates, intellectual to sentimental consciousness, and, in the course of so doing, makes use of elements of characterization denied to the cast as a whole. Just as there was no complete abandonment of the well-characterized Celestina of Act I, so here the love of wine which had grown from the circumstances of Act IX is brought back as the point of departure for a sordid but authentic reminiscence. If Celestina by role and by definition is relatively changeless in the midst of trajectory, if she is unique in the midst of pattern, then—provided always that they are introduced in terms of dialogue—such attributes as the above may be transplanted freely from one situation to another. The joining of her *tú* to her *yo* gives her, as we pointed out, a facsimile of character, a facsimile of which Rojas takes full advantage in his interpolations.[22] It is significant that such interpolations of character are limited to Celestina. When, for example, Pármeno's utterances are corrected, it can only be in terms of the surrounding dialogue. Unlike Celestina he has neither the age nor the firm vocational self-awareness that are necessary to surpass the needs of his immediate situation.[23]

Of the other interpolations demonstrating Rojas' special characterization of Celestina, we may notice two which accentuate her canniness and foresight. Sentimental recollection of the thirsty past is here balanced with intellectual foresight into the future:

ELIC.—¿Cómo vienes tan tarde? No lo deues hazer, que eres vieja; tropeçarás donde caygas e mueras.

CEL.—No temo esso, que de día me auiso por donde venga de noche. *Que jamás me subo por poyo ni calçada, sino por medio de la calle. Porque como dizen: no da passo seguro quien corre por el muro e que aquel va más sano que anda por llano. Más quiero ensuziar mis zapatos con el lodo que ensangrentar las tocas e los cantos.* Pero no te duele a ti en esse lugar. (XI, 74–75)[24]

The second is placed not in Celestina's mouth but in Sempronio's—during a conversation with Pármeno already discussed:

SEMP.—Avnque ella te crió, mejor conozco yo sus propriedades que tú. Lo que en sus cuentas reza es los virgos que tiene a cargo e quántos enamorados ay en la cibdad e quántas moças tiene encomendadas e qué despenseros *le dan ración e quál lo mejor e cómo les llaman por nombre, porque quando los encontrare no hable como estraña* e qué canónigo es más moço e franco. Quando menea los labios es fengir mentíras, ordenar cautelas para hauer dinero: por aquí le entraré, esto me responderá, estotro replicaré. Assí viue ésta, que nosotros mucho honrramos. (IX, 25)

Celestina's diabolical prudence becomes a function of dialogue, and it is on these terms that the interpolation illustrates her further.

Finally there are interpolations which underline neither sentimental nor intellectual continuities of awareness (neither perverse comradeship nor shrewdness) but rather their union in a vocational consciousness of self. The most striking example is the long addition in Act VII:

Cel.—... Retóçala en esta cama. ...

Areu.—*Ay señor mío, no me trates de tal manera; ten mesura por cortesía; mira las canas de aquella vieja honrrada, que están presentes; ... Assí goze de mí, de casa me salga, si fasta que Celestina mi tía sea yda a mi ropa tocas.*

Cel.—*¿Qué es eso, Areusa? ¿Qué son estas estrañezas y esquiuedad, estas nouedades e retraymiento? Paresce, hija, que no sé yo qué cosa es esto. que nunca ví estar vn hombre con una muger juntos e que jamás passé por ello ni gozé de lo que gozas e que no sé lo que passan e lo que dizen e hazen. ¡Guay de quien tal oye como yo! Pues auísote, de tanto, que fuy errada como tú e tuue amigos; pero nunca el viejo ni la vieja echaua de mi lado ni su consejo en público ni en mis secretos. Para la muerte que a Dios deuo, mas quisiera vna gran bofetada en mitad de mi cara. Paresce que ayer nascí, según tu encubrimiento. Por hazerte a tí honesta, me hazes a mí necia e vergonçosa e de poco secreto e sin esperiencia o me amenguas en mi officio por alçar a tí en el tuyo. Pues de cossario a cossario no se pierden sino los barriles. Mas te alabo yo detrás, que tú te estimas delante.*

Areu.—*Madre si erré aya perdón e llégate mas acá y él haga lo que quisiere. Que mas quiero tener a tí contenta que no a mí; antes me quebraré vn ojo que enojarte.*

Cel.—*No tengo ya enojo; pero dígotelo para adelante.* Quedaos adios *que voyme* solo *porque me hazés dentera con vuestro besar e retoçar.* (VII, 258–60)

The sudden violence of Celestina's reaction, a violence which Areusa (as well as the reader) may hardly have expected, is not merely due to disgust with the false display of coyness. It is rather the violence of an offended honor. As Celestina proclaims, she would rather have been given "una gran bofetada en mitad de la cara" than be so ejected and humiliated. It does not matter that Rojas wrote this passage with an almost ferocious irony or that the whole value of honor is shattered by the obscenity of its context. For Celestina (and the very existence of the irony depends on this) both the violence and the value are authentic. This is the honor of the *officio* which with age and experience has come to represent Celestina's life. As a *yo* she feels herself to exist in terms of a deep sense of honor; as a *tú* she portrays herself as honorable and demands that others see and treat her appropriately. Celestina has formed for herself a vocational *ser* which is true in the midst of all her deceits and lies. And a vocational *ser*, as a gentleman, a wife, or as an *alcahueta,* is merely another way of explaining honor—with its simultaneous internality as a sentiment and externality as intellectual conformance to a code or system of opinion.[25]

Thus, both in the *Comedia* and in its interpolations, Rojas removes Celestina (or shows how she removes herself) from the category of a mere *alcahueta* dedicated to her own self-interest and to the deceit and destruction of others. Unlike Trotaconventos, her uncharacterized predecessor of an infinity of names, and Gerarda, her overcharacterized successor of an infinity of proverbs, Celestina asserts intellectually and sentimentally her own independent being. In her famous soliloquy of doubt she constructs her vocation in two words: "Yr quiero," and after this moment of self-definition, she is inescapably the artistic center of the work. It would be tempting at this point to speak of the relationship of this Celestina to Spanish forms of life (a relationship which indicates that Rojas, for all his desperate and ironical cynicism in the years of Spain's greatest hope and glory and for all his Judaism, was radically Spanish) or to the tradition of the epic hero (supernatural help, belief in *agüeros, mocedades* with Claudina, etc.) But these things would lead us into the profundities of Rojas' creative intent and away from the conscious art of character which is our only concern. It is enough for us to have seen how Rojas reinforces by interpolation the integration of *tú* and *yo* in the life of Celestina—and how this integration results in a vocation and in an inherent honor which he is equally careful to strengthen. Celestina's special consciousness within the realm of this dialogic artistry has been consciously specialized.[26]

CHAPTER FOUR

THE ART OF STRUCTURE

----

1. Structure in Acts

WHEN CRITICS—from Aristotle to the present day—discuss the art of the dramatist, they tend to see it primarily as an art of structure. What the dramatist makes is, above all, a plot, and a successful plot is, above all, a suitable arrangement of happening in time. Hence, even though the greatest achievement of the dramatist may be his character creation or his poetic style, as an artist he must first be praised or blamed for the effectiveness of his temporal structure, for his ability to arrange scenes, acts, discoveries, climaxes, etc. It is in terms of structure that his artistic success may be judged with greatest justice, because it is precisely in terms of structure that he works most conscientiously and most purposefully.

Yet if we accord this same primacy to the art of structure in the making of *La Celestina,* disappointment is inevitable. Taken by itself—apart from other aspects of Rojas' art—the whole division into acts seems capricious and absurd, the afterthought of an author impressed by a classic tradition that was alien to his comprehension. The number of acts (sixteen in one version and twenty-one in another) is not only unheard of but also hardly seems to correspond to any internal structure of action. Furthermore, comparison of the individual acts reveals puzzling divergencies in length and importance. Act XI, for example, containing only the briefest sort of report to Calisto by Celestina is followed by the enormity of Act XII with its first confession of love and its multiple deaths. From the point of view of structure, *La Celestina* seems anything but well made. It seems to be a monstrous freak, the appropriate creature of a period that was no longer the Middle Ages and not yet the Renaissance.

Naturally, a point of view which yields such a distorted and foreshortened vision of *La Celestina* is inacceptable. In his own way, Rojas was a great artist of structure, and each of his acts is, in its own way, the result of calculated arrangement. Each has a hidden structural significance which can be found once we bring ourselves to understand that structure is never an isolated aspect of Rojas' art—that it is joined organically to all that we now know about the arts of character and style. Primarily and specifically, this means that what is divided by acts in *La Celestina* is not action, as we ordinarily think of it, but rather a continuum of consciousness in dialogue, of spoken consciousness. It is almost superfluous at this point to insist that Rojas was hardly concerned with plot—even though he does praise in the *Carta* the "principal hystoria o fición toda junta" of Act I. The rejection of the third person in favor of the first and second, the rejection of types and even of characters in the usual sense of the word, necessarily results in individuals whose lives, thoughts, and speeches are artistically more significant than their actions or deeds. It results in a work in which the conscious spoken reaction to the plot is far more important than the plot itself.

Under these circumstances, the brief "Argumento de toda la obra" can reduce all that happens in *La Celestina* to a few lines without difficulty, and Rojas, himself, can borrow this same basic happening from his several sources without the slightest loss of originality. It would indeed be hard to write a paragraph that would tell us less about *La Celestina,* that would furnish less insight into its artistic peculiarity, than this "Argumento de toda la obra," and the same thing is true for the *argumentos* to each of the acts. Rojas would not—and probably could not—have written them as they appear in the *Comedia;* and it is significant that he openly disclaims responsibility for them. Instead of the flesh and blood of spoken consciousness, these *argumentos* present merely the skeleton of movement or plot, an anatomical abstraction which not only kills the work but also subverts its meaning. Admittedly, *La Celestina* must have an argument, a minimum line of action which encloses seduction with love and death, just as it must have a cast with a minimum of definition. But, at the same time, we must recognize that Rojas uses both creatively for other purposes. When adapted for the theater (Paul Achard's version is a spectacular example), how much can and must be eliminated! From the point of view of plot, act after act is reduced to mere subplot. The seduction of Pármeno, for instance, makes no real contribution to that of Melibea and is easily cut out. We must, therefore, relinquish the usual connotation of the word, "act." We must try to imagine a kind of act which will not correspond to pre-arranged manipulation of the characters in the third person.

This proposed redefinition of the act in *La Celestina* returns us to that notion of dialogic situation or encounter—the decorous units of dialogue which went to make up such living trajectories as that of Pármeno. If Rojas had seen fit to isolate formally each of these dialogic situations, to present *La Celestina* merely as a sequence of scenes, our structural problem would have solved itself automatically. Indeed, his very failure to signify temporal breaks in action (we except here the month of time provided by the additions) might seem consistent with such an ordering. Temporally, of course, the *Comedia,* and even the *Tragicomedia,* can be thought of as one enormous act divided into a multitude of scenes.

But Rojas' structural artistry does not take the form of easy segmentation of these stylistic and characteristic units. Instead of isolating each dialogic situation Rojas joins them together in acts, each of which emphasizes and frames its particular state of spoken consciousness. Out of units of dialogue he builds a superstructure in twenty-one calculated acts—a pattern for the whole which, as we shall see, gives visible order to the patterns and trajectories we have already traced. In other words, having rejected the traditional concepts of plot and action, we may further circumscribe our task by proposing to analyze each act as an intentional grouping of the dialogic situations it contains. People speaking, or rather the conversations of people, are the units of meaning of *La Celestina,* the building blocks of its remarkable and very consequential structure.

We may begin, then, by an over-all listing of Rojas' twenty acts in terms of their component situations. The list, with Act I bracketed, is on page 91. Glancing over this list we may notice that (with a few exceptions) the several situations of a given act possess at least one speaker common to all of them. It is an observation which suggests that in each case the life of one individual serves as a structural axis around which the others are placed—and that we may, accordingly, explain the act as a framing device. In the second place, the list suggests that this key individual tends to be given an initial or closing soliloquy for further reinforcement of his position (Acts II, III, IV, V, X, XIII, XVII, XVIII). Or if this is not the case the termination may be a brief dialogue of two persons—a dialogue which is used to accent the phase or state of consciousness which the act presents (Acts VII, VIII, XI, XIV, XVI, XX). In both cases, whether soliloquy or closing dialogue, we may notice that the structure repeats on a larger scale the discursive logic of the style— the logic of introduction and conclusion, of presentation and summary.

These observations are, of course, merely tentative, but they do suggest that our task may be made more easy by examining the beginnings and endings of acts along with the part played in each by the central individual.

[I - 1 Calisto Melibea
2 Calisto Sempronio
3 Sempronio Celestina Elicia
4 Sempronio Celestina
5 Pármeno Calisto
6 Pármeno Calisto Sempronio
Celestina
7 Pármeno Celestina
8 Pármeno Calisto Sempronio
Celestina]
II - 1 Pármeno Calisto Sempronio
2 Pármeno Calisto
3 Pármeno
III - 1 Celestina Sempronio
2 Celestina Elicia Sempronio
3 Celestina
IV - 1 Celestina
2 Celestina Lucrecia
3 Celestina Lucrecia Alisa
4 Celestina Lucrecia Alisa
Melibea
5 Celestina Lucrecia Melibea
V - 1 Celestina
2 Celestina Sempronio
3 Celestina Pármeno Calisto
Sempronio
VI - 1 Pármeno Calisto Sempronio
Celestina
VII - 1 Celestina Pármeno
2 Celestina Pármeno Areusa
3 Celestina Elicia
VIII - 1 Pármeno Areusa
2 Pármeno Sempronio
3 Pármeno Sempronio Calisto
IX - 1 Sempronio Pármeno
2 Sempronio Pármeno Celestina
Elicia Areusa
3 Sempronio Pármeno Celestina
Elicia Areusa Lucrecia
4 Celestina Lucrecia
X - 1 Melibea
2 Melibea Lucrecia Celestina
3 Melibea Lucrecia
4 Alisa Celestina
5 Melibea Alisa Lucrecia

XI - 1 Celestina
2 Calisto Sempronio
3 Calestina Calisto Sempronio
Pármeno
4 Celestina Elicia
XII - 1 Sempronio Pármeno Calisto
2 Sempronio Pármeno Calisto
Melibea Lucrecia
3 Sempronio Pármeno Calisto
4 Sempronio Pármeno
Celestina Elicia
XIII - 1 Calisto
2 Calisto Tristán
3 Tristán Sosia
4 Calisto Tristán Sosia
5 Calisto
XIV - 1 Melibea Lucrecia
2 Sosia Tristán Calisto Melibea
Lucrecia
3 Melibea Lucrecia
4 Sosia Tristán Calisto
5 Calisto
6 Sosia Tristán
XV - 1 Elicia Areusa Centurio
2 Elicia Areusa
XVI - 1 Pleberio Alisa
2 Melibea Lucrecia
3 Melibea Lucrecia Pleberio
Alisa
XVII - 1 Elicia
2 Elicia Areusa
3 Elicia Areusa Sosia
4 Elicia Areusa
XVIII - 1 Centurio Elicia Areusa
2 Centurio
XIX - 1 Tristán Sosia Calisto
2 Melibea Lucrecia Calisto
Tristán Sosia
3 Melibea Lucrecia Tristán
Sosia
XX - 1 Pleberio Lucrecia
2 Pleberio Lucrecia Melibea
3 Melibea
4 Melibea Pleberio
XXI - 1 Pleberio Alisa[1]

It is in these things that Rojas' structural preoccupation, his intentional ordering of consciousness, will be most clearly revealed. Also in accordance with our usual method, attention to the interpolations (particularly to those inserted for the single speaker present in all the scenes or situations) may be helpful. In the absence of plot, we must have recourse to such secondary indications as recurrent appearance, location of soliloquies, and interpolated emphasis in order to glimpse the intended structure of *La Celestina*.

Act II is an almost perfect example of the utility of all these three criteria for structure. There is one individual, Pármeno, who is present in all its situations; he is given a closing monologue which makes explicit his state of mind; and in that monologue there is an interpolation which, as we have seen, contributes substantially to our understanding of the despair, the rationalization, and the weakness framed by the act. Let us see the matter in some detail. The author of the *argumento,* evidently believed, in spite of Calisto's opening "Hermanos mios ..." that Pármeno was absent from the first dialogue: "Partida Celestina de Calisto para su casa, queda Calisto hablando con Sempronio, criado suyo; al qual, como quien en alguna esperança puesto está, todo aguijar le parece tardança. Embía de sí a Sempronio a solicitar a Celestina para el concebido negocio. Quedan entretanto Calisto e Pármeno juntos razonando." (II, 113) Yet in spite of this, if we read carefully, it becomes apparent that the whole conversation of Calisto and Sempronio was designed in order that Pármeno might overhear it. Sempronio's cynical pretense to virtue in his discourse on honor and Calisto's exaggerated praise of him ("Sabido eres, fiel te siento, por buen criado te tengo") are exactly the remarks which might best shatter Pármeno's weakened portrayal of himself in this same light—and so provoke the reactions foreseen by Celestina. The concluding interchange is decisive:

> CEL.—Sempronio amigo, pues tanto sientes mi soledad, llama a Pármeno e quedará comigo e de aquí adelante sey, como sueles, leal, que en el seruicio del criado está el galardón del señor.
> PARM.—Aquí estoy, señor.
> CAL.—Yo no pues no te veya. No te partas della, Sempronio, ni me oluides a mí e vé con Dios. (II, 119)

Here the final adulation of Sempronio rubs further salt in Pármeno's mental wounds—as must Calisto's failure even to be aware of his presence. Aside from the fact that Sempronio's virtuous double-talk and Calisto's lovelorn acceptance of it may be read for their own sake, structurally we must read what they say in terms of Pármeno and his experience. His is the silent, resentful awareness which makes the conversation contribute to the act.

The second situation opens with an almost visual confirmation of what we previously had imagined. Calisto comments on the sulky sadness that is evident on Pármeno's face: "Pues pido tu parecer, seyme agradable, Pármeno. No abaxes la cabeça al responder. Mas como la embidia es triste, la tristeza sin lengua, puede más contigo su voluntad, que mi temor. ¿Qué dixiste, enojoso?" (II, 120) In the following interchange, the lack of authenticity to Pármeno's virtue becomes increasingly evident. The saddling scene is an ultimate humiliation, and it results in the closing soliloquy. But what is important for us now is the way the whole is built structurally in terms of an accelerating evidence. First, we, as readers, are led to imagine Pármeno's state of mind; then, we intuit it from the conversation with Calisto; and at last, it is openly revealed in a speech to no one. Pármeno proceeds from the *tú* of the silent listener, through the *tú* and *yo* of dialogue, to the last feeling of himself as a *yo*. Thus, this stage in Pármeno's trajectory of consciousness becomes an artistic unity, an act of an appropriately dialogic structure. From the point of view of plot, it is the hero Calisto's predicament around which the act should turn—and it is into this fallacy which the writer of the *argumento* is led. But the real significance of the act is, as we predicted, otherwise. The real significance is that of having organized and so accentuated Pármeno's consciousness as revealed in dialogue. And this was dismissed in the *argumento* with a single sentence: "Quedan entretanto Calisto e Pármeno juntos razonando"! The subtlety and consequence of Rojas' artistry of structure is apparent in the first of his acts.

Referring again to the list of situations, we may deduce that the next three acts, as acts, are dedicated to the conscious life of Celestina. Corresponding to the sequence of before, during, and after the encounter with Melibea, the three acts are closely interrelated. Rojas seems to want to make sure that Act IV with its dramatic confrontation and its strong element of suspense will not overshadow his major artistic preoccupation—the full self-revelation of Celestina in speech. Hence, he places the action of Act IV between two acts which have no other reason for being than to show Celestina off. Act III, in effect, returns for a moment to situation 4 of Act I (Celestina-Sempronio) and reminds us of her previous attitude of cynicism and trickery: "CEL.—... Digo que me alegro destas nuevas, como los cirujanos de los descalabrados. E como aquellos dañan en los principios las llagas e encarecen el prometimiento de la salud, assí entiendo yo facer a Calisto." (I, 65) Nevertheless, in spite of this initial intention, Sempronio's misgivings (¿... nos puede venir a nosotros daño deste negocio?") bring out by dialogic reaction Celestina's vocational pride, "¡Avn si quisiesses auisar a Celestina en su oficio!" The result is not a picaresque trick but the terrible conjuration of "Plutón" by his "más conocida clientula." We are given an almost official presentation of a diabolical efficiency and a vocation which up until now had been confined to hearsay.

Terrible as this conjuration is, its ritualistic formalism is pale alongside the monologue which begins Act IV. Here no Satanic second person and no cringing Sempronio are present to draw Celestina into rhetoric or prideful self-assertion; rather we are alone with her and are allowed to witness the awful authenticity of her *yo* in its crisis and decision. It is in this passage that Celestina's reason and her sentiment arrive at their vocational integration and that her "character" is fully formed. Indeed, the conjunction of fear and resolution, of self-projection as a *tú* ("Tú, puta vieja, ¿porqué acrescentaste mis passiones con tus promessas?") and self-assertion as a *yo* ("Yr quiero"), is so powerful and frightening that it almost overshadows the interview with Melibea. The opening monologue of Act IV stands as a central moment of consciousness between the seemingly vain boasting of Act III and the real accomplishment of the seduction. It displays and emphasizes with fearful candor the new Celestina with whom we are to live for the rest of the act.

Even the *agüeros,* original and interpolated, which repeat the supernatural conjuration of Act III on a plane more appropriate to Celestina's individual experience, add to the impetus of this soliloquy. Far from being the comical or poverty-stricken superstitions of a frightened old lady, they seem somehow even more impressive, more fatal, than the elaborate classic horror which preceded them. The very contrast between the literary invocation of the one act and experienced superstition of the other emphasizes in its own way the new diabolic consciousness (as against the demoniac type) of Celestina.[2] Before dialogue can be made from the incredible good fortune of being left alone with Melibea, from the perverse Stoicism of self-presentation, from the courage in the face of Melibea's wrath, or from the low cunning of excuse and final domination, we must be made to know their protagonist from within. We must be made to know Celestina as she is to herself. To sum up, Rojas is more interested in his intermediary than in his heroine precisely because his structure is one of spoken consciousness and not one of action. On these terms, Celestina's willed transition from fear to completed vocation is more significant than Melibea's manageable anger and surrender. The victor is more important than the vanquished, and her initial soliloquy is the structural keystone of the act.

This same general scheme is repeated in Act V. It begins with Celestina again alone in the street and expressing the perverse glee of her triumph—a state of mind contingent on, yet opposite to that of the fearful resolution of the soliloquy just discussed.[3] There follows a repetition of the encounter with

Sempronio (which had been the first situation of Act III) but the roles are now significantly varied. Sempronio has lost all traces of his cynicism and is now eager—almost as eager as his master—to learn the results of the visit. As Celestina shrewdly remarks, "ya lo veo en ti, que querrías más estar al sabor, que al olor deste negocio." She, on the other hand, has replaced the wordy boasting of Act III with a jubilant and lofty reserve, a refusal to "desflorar mi embaxada comunicándola con muchos." Her haste to tell all to Calisto is also quite different from her previous plan to dole out news by bits and pieces in order to collect as much as possible. The act—an act subsequent to action— is thus, dedicated to consciousness of victory, to an awareness of a confirmed and successful vocation that is the more sweet to Celestina as it is rooted in her previous fear. The final touch of structural emphasis is masterful. Rojas repeats briefly the door scene of the first act (the whole act is designed as a repetition and variation of earlier situations); and, upon hearing the approach of Calisto and Pármeno, Sempronio urges Celestina that she invent as before a deceitful speech for their ears. But Celestina, true to her new consciousness, refuses: "Calla, Sempronio, que avnque aya auenturado mi vida, más merece Calisto e su ruego e tuyo e más mercedes espero yo dél." The structure, in a sense, confirms our belief that the final "vocational" Celestina is ultimately much more sinister than the greedy trickstress of Act I or the latter-day sibyl of Act III.

Up to now (through Act V) Rojas' structural technique has been, first, varied repetition of previous situations; and, second, calculated alternation of monologue and dialogue. We may conclude roughly, in connection with the second point, that the monologue or soliloquy begins the act when the central speaker is on the offensive and is to dominate what is to come (Celestina in Acts IV and V) but ends the act when he is on the defensive and is changed or affected by the dialogue (Pármeno in Act II and Celestina in Act III).[4] In Act VI, however, Rojas presents us with a new structural pattern, one based only on dialogue and involving a single situation. On these terms, it is impossible to say whether Calisto, Celestina, Sempronio, or Pármeno is the central consciousness of the act. As we pointed out in the previous essay, it was precisely this that Rojas intended: a dialogic quartet of consciousnesses, each reacting in its own way to the tale of the meeting with Melibea. Certainly Celestina who tells what has happened and Calisto to whom the telling is directed are respectively the major *yo* and the major *tú* of the act. But even so, Rojas makes no effort to bring out any new insight into their states of mind; they are merely the leading voices in the discordant yet somehow harmonious polyphony of the act. Celestina's jubilant triumph and cunning self-display, Calisto's displaced reason and rampant passion, Sempronio's brutality and half-curious love for Melibea, and Pármeno's envious desperation and continuing disgust with Celestina—all are forms of consciousness that have been revealed in the preceding acts. And they are all equally significant. Here in Act VI the reader and the author rest briefly in their fascinating yet terrible journey through the paths of consciousness of *La Celestina*. And as they rest they realize more sharply the appalling nature of what they have witnessed.

Hence, when Rojas reread the act in 1502, he was careful to stress in new interpolation those attitudes, to the repetition and confirmation of which it was dedicated. Celestina reveals her jubilance and calculated exaggeration (the prevailing sentiment and argument of the moment) by fabricating a grotesque caricature of the wrath of Melibea:

> ... *E empós desto mill amortescimientos e desmayos, mill milagros e espantos, turbado el sentido, bulliendo fuertemente los miembros todos a vna parte e a otra, herida de aquella dorada frecha, que del sonido de tu nombre le tocó, retorciendo el cuerpo, las manos enclauijadas, como quien se despereza, que parecía que las despedaçaua, mirando con los ojos a todas partes, acoceando con los piés el suelo duro. E yo a todo esto arrinconada, encogida, callando, muy gozosa con su ferocidad. Mientra más vasqueaua, más yo me alegraua, porque más cerca estaua el rendirse e su cayda ...*[5] (VI, 213–14)

Calisto, in another interpolation, is made to misinterpret Pármeno's disgusted gestures and so to re-emphasize his own distraught self-centered eagerness:

> *Mira, señora, qué fablar trae Pármeno, cómo se viene santiguando de oyr lo que has hecho con tu gran diligencia. Espantado está, por mi fe, señora Celestina. Otra vez se santigua. Sube, sube sube y asientate, señora, que de rodillas quiero escuchar tu suaue respuesta.* (VI, 209–10)

Finally Pármeno reaffirms his disgust with his master's senseless exaltation. Most of Pármeno's asides in the act are directed against the greed and perversity of Celestina, and in 1502 Rojas apparently felt it necessary to retouch this complementary phase of his desperation:

> *¡O sancta María! ¡Y qué rodeos busca este loco por huyr de nosotros, para poder llorar a su plazer con Celestina de gozo y por descubrirle mill secretos de su liuiano e desuariado apetito, por preguntar y responder seys vezes cada cosa, sin que esté presente quien le pueda dezir que es prólixo! Pues mándote yo, desatinado, que tras tí vamos.* (VI, 209)

Only Sempronio is left without interpolated accentuation of his dialogic part in this four-way encounter of consciousness.

Act VII returns to Celestina (as the speaker present in its three situations) and combines a repetition of her previous persuasion of Pármeno, significantly

varied, with the seduction of Areusa. This second situation parallels the seduction of Melibea in Act IV and, as we saw, brings out not only the corrosive
similarity of the two varieties of feminine reluctance but also Celestina's skill
in adapting her techniques of domination to the lessened tension of the second
encounter. In Celestina's last major act, the repertory of her consciousness is
completely displayed in a kind of re-exploration of her previous triumphs and
self-revelations. It is here, of course, that her friendship with Claudina and her
perverted yet authentic sense of honor are explored most deeply. The concluding scene, a brief conversation with Elicia, illustrates the continuing structural
pre-eminence of spoken consciousness over action—in this case over Pármeno's
attainment of Areusa. It brings out Celestina's devotion to a phase of her
vocation mentioned in Act I but not yet given its place in dialogue by Rojas,
that of mending virgins:

> CEL.—... Que la mocedad ociosa acarrea la vejez arrepentida e trabajosa. Hazíalo
> yo mejor, quando tu abuela, que Dios aya, me mostraua este oficio: que a cabo de
> vn año, sabía mas que ella.
> ELIC.—No me marauillo, que muchas vezes como dizen, al maestro sobrepuja
> el buen discípulo. E no va esto, sino en la gana con que se aprende. Ninguna
> sciencia es bienempleada en el que no le tiene afición. Yo le tengo a este oficio
> odio; tú mueres tras ello. (VII, 262)

This last suggestion of a deep-rooted perverse enjoyment, at once obscene and
professional, is in deep accord with Celestina's previous desire to witness the
relations of Pármeno and Areusa and with her chortling delight at the display
of the latter's charms. By means of variation and ironic parallel, we are led
at last to the depths of Rojas' excavation of "la conscience dans le mal." The
trajectory has been completed in structure, and from this point onwards
Celestina is never again to dominate an act. We now know as much about her
as it is possible to know through dialogue.

Act VIII, of course, is Pármeno's and leads to that new identity with
Sempronio which is to be his until their death. It again ends a trajectory. Act
IX, on the other hand turns in a completely new direction in order to find and
outline its unity of spoken consciousness. At first it might appear that Sempronio and Pármeno together are the object of Rojas' attention (they appear
in all situations but the last), but a close reading of the act will not support
this hypothesis. The table of acts and situations should not be understood as
presenting an infallible rule of structure but as an indication—an indication
which is inexact in this case. For in Act IX, it is not the servants who direct
the conversation or who are revealed by it. Rather the assembly is successively dominated by Elicia, Areusa, and Lucrecia with their respective senti-

ments and femininities. Somewhat as in Act VI, Rojas offers us a pattern of
conscious variations—even though here the structure is that of a suite and not
simultaneous or choral. I cannot deny, of course, that the external shape of the
act is that of the perverse banquet with Celestina at the head of the table
directing its alternation of orgy and quarrel. Nevertheless, the scenic circumstance and even Celestina, herself—with her eulogies of wine and memories
of past prosperity—really serve as a point of departure, a springboard, for
feminine awareness fully revealed for the first time. It is only necessary to
imagine how such a banquet might have been presented in a picaresque novel
or, perhaps, by Rabelais or Boccaccio to recognize again Rojas' characteristic
accentuation of spoken consciousness. The violent domesticity of Elicia (in
an interchange with Sempronio reminiscent of their meeting in Act I), the
sterile independence of Areusa, and the wistful imaginings of Lucrecia are
the three columns of the act and mark the individuality of its structure.[6]

The presentation in Act IX of these three young feminine consciousnesses
(a character pattern which, as we saw, was made possible by the fact of cast
and its minimum of definition) is preparatory in nature. It prepares for
Melibea's major self-revelation in Act X. On the level of linguistic and circumstantial decorum the contrast between these two acts could not be more calculated; but beneath this superficial contrast, the mental disrobing of Areusa,
Elicia, and Lucrecia leads to that of Melibea in ironical yet fecund parallelism.
Not only is Melibea the principal topic of conversation, the major preoccupation of the prostitutes, at the picaresque dinner, but also her surrender and
servitude to love are, by their examples, cunningly readied for our acceptance.
Rojas saves this pattern of feminine lives for the moment of its full structural
service. He uses it to build a bitter, ironical, and profound portico for our long
awaited entrance into the temple of Melibea's virginity.

All of this does not mean that Melibea is to be considered hierarchically
more important (as a heroine or principal character) than, let us say, Elicia.
On the contrary, it would seem that the structural relationship of these two
acts was designed to quit her of any prestige by definition. The point is that
Melibea is for the first time to meet a situation which she will dominate. Previously Melibea had existed in the second person, in a state of violent defense
and retreat, and now—with the customary initial monologue and with full
revelation of her sentimental consciousness—she is to manage rather than be
managed. (It is, by the way, to the credit of Celestina that she knows so well
how to adapt herself to the change.) In other words, it is not the person or
character of Melibea as such that is prepared for in Act IX but a metamorphosis of earlier situations—exactly the sort of metamorphosis which is

so typical of *La Celestina* and which is so often marked in its structure. Thus, the elevation in decorum to an almost courtly ritual, the preliminary revelations of sentimental consciousness in a monologue given to Melibea and not to Celestina, and the closing note of nascent feminine guile[7] take on heightened meaning in terms of the infamous decorum, the violent sentiments, and the too experienced, defeated femininities of the banquet. Rojas' use of structure to strengthen and develop spoken consciousness is once again masterful.

Act XI is less readily defensible from the point of view of structure. It seems to be composed of fragments of preceding acts that have been foreshortened and accelerated—fragments within which Rojas makes no strenuous effort to exhaust an accumulation or charge of awareness. The first speech, "¡Ay Dios, si llegasse a mi casa con mi mucha alegría acuestas ...!" is a one-line résumé of Celestina's monologue in Act V. The reuniting of the two servants, Celestina, and Calisto briefly recalls the structural fireworks of Act VI but without a parallel intensity of display. And the final home-coming scene with Elicia reveals the same perverse domesticity as the one in Act VII, even though the lurid vocational suggestiveness has been removed. The truth is that Celestina's successful completion of her mission has become by this time an almost foregone conclusion and can excite neither her nor her listeners (nor, for that matter, the reader) to the same pitch as before.[8] As a result, each of the previous situations is repeated in a state of lessened tension; the engagement of *tú* and *yo* has lost the violence and the strain of earlier encounters. That this difference was known to Rojas, that it was for him a moment of necessary relaxation rather than a decline of creative energy, is made evident in a deletion and substituted interpolation at the beginning of the act: "Cel.— ... Pero todo vaya en buena hora, pues tan buen recabdo traygo. *E óyeme, que en pocas palabras te lo diré, que soy corta de razón: a Melibea* dexo a tu servicio."[9] (XI, 68) The striking contrast of this purposeful abbreviation to Celestina's long preambles and descriptions of Act VI suggests that the fall of the dialogue pressure is precisely Rojas' structural point—his intention in isolating the act.

As we pointed out at the beginning of this essay, Act XII is apparently the most puzzling and inexplicable of all the twenty-one. Its sheer accumulation of events puts quite a strain on the writer of the *argumentos*:

Llegando la media noche, Calisto, Sempronio e Pármeno armados van para casa de Melibea. Lucrecia e Melibea están cabe la puerta, aguardando a Calisto. Viene Calisto. Háblale primero Lucrecia. Llama a Melibea. Apártase Lucrecia. Háblanse por entre las puertas Melibea e Calisto. Pármeno e Sempronio de su cabo departen ... (XII, 76)

He goes on for some 108 words more and still is forced to omit significant details of happening. And fundamentally the same problem faces us. How can we hope to demonstrate structural order or intention for an act which builds climax upon climax and weaves multiple strands of movement around two or three widely divided centers of interest? A superficial solution might be to decide which of the two major events (the meeting with Melibea or the murder of Celestina) deserves primacy and then attempt to find a meaningful relationship between them on these terms. The courtly rendezvous, for example, might be thought of as an ironical elevation which prepares by contrast the grim sordidness of the last scene. Or, on the other hand, if the reader concedes a greater importance to the love interest, what happens to Celestina might appear as a ferocious and ironical anticlimax.

There is possibly some truth to these suppositions. But, if we admit them fully, we betray our initial concept of the act as a unit of dialogic consciousness—as designed without dependence on the third person. Let us, instead, return to the table and ask ourselves again if there is not one speaker who turns up in the several situations. There are, in effect, not one but two: Pármeno and Sempronio who have been joined in trajectory and consciousness since Act VIII.[10] But such a discovery poses a more difficult problem than it solves. How can we possibly explain these two as centering the act, particularly at the beginning when they are present as mere onlookers, as tangential *graciosos* to the meeting of the lovers? My only reply to this is outright denial. They are neither onlookers nor *graciosos* and their conversation in the street, rather than providing comic relief, is in itself structurally significant. It is precisely their consciousness that Rojas is framing with his usual subtlety. Pármeno and Sempronio, together and in a situation of imminent danger, are at last brought face to face with their human indignity, with their absolute lack of nobility or virtue. To be specific, they are faced with the shame and misery of their cowardice. This, of course, had been prepared for in the preceding act both in its original version and in careful interpolation:

SEMP.—Cata madre, que assí se suelen dar las çaraças en pan embueltas, porque no las sienta el gusto.
PARM.—Nunca te oy dezir mejor cosa. Mucha sospecha me pone el presto conceder de aquella señora ... *Pues alahé, madre, con dulces palabras están muchas injurias vengadas ... Assí como corderica mansa que mama su madre e la ajena, ella con su segurar tomará la vengança de Calisto en todos nosotros, de manera que, con la mucha gente que tiene, podrá caçar a padres e hijos en vna nidada e tú estarte has rascando a tu fuego, diziendo: a saluo está el que repica.* (XI, 72–73)

But it is in Act XII that this shared cowardice and hysterical suspicion is converted into a state of mind—a total self-awareness which centers the structural unity of whole.

Let us not hasten past this matter. We have already noticed the comic Bergsonian identification of Pármeno and Sempronio in external gestures of cowardice: their nervous glancing and listening in the dark, their foot-racer's crouch, their rolled up clothes, and the rest. But these are mere accessories, by-products of an internal anguish of self-recognition. For in their dialogue each sees himself in the other and knows the shameful truth, even though he may attempt to rephrase it:

SEMP.—¡O Pármeno amigo! ¡Quán alegre e prouechosa es la conformidad en los compañeros! Avnque por otra cosa no nos fuera buena Celestina, era harta la vtilidad que por su causa nos ha venido.

PÁRM.—Ninguno podrá negar lo que por sí se muestra. Manifiesto es que con vergüença el vno del otro, por no ser odiosamente acusado de couarde esperáramos aquí la muerte con nuestro amo, no siendo más de él merecedor della. (XII, 81)

In 1502 Rojas reinforces by repeated interpolations the pain and unspoken shame of this least common denominator of friendship. He inserts, for example, an almost pathetic anecdote in the mouth of Sempronio—an anecdote of past daring which betrays the teller by its minimum of exploit. This is the same Sempronio who carried rocks in his helmet to throw at Pleberio's servants and who later emptied them out in order to run faster:

SEMP.—¿E yo no seruí al cura de Sant Miguel *e al mesonero de la plaça e a Mollejar, el ortelano? E también yo tenía mis questiones con los que tirauan piedras a los páxaros, que assentauan en vn álamo grande que tenía, porque dañauan la ortaliza.* Pero guárdete Diós de verte con armas, que aquel es el verdadero temor. No en balde dizen: cargado de hierro e cargado de miedo ... (XII, 90) [11]

But even more significant than this is an interpolation given to Pármeno in which he recognizes his cowardice by the very use of the word:

SEMP.—... En sintiendo bullicio, el buen huyr nos ha de valer ...

PÁRM.—Bien hablas, en mi coraçón estás. Assí se haga. Huygamos la muerte, que somos moços. *Que no querer morir ni matar no es couardía, sino buen natural. Estos escuderos de Pleberio son locos: no desean tanto comer ni dormir como questiones e ruydos. Pues más locura sería esperar pelea con enemigo, que no ama tanto la vitoria e vencimiento como la continua guerra e contienda.* (XII, 88)

Thus, both in the original and in the interpolations Pármeno and Sempronio not only feel fear but also realize it rationally as cowardice. Sentiment and reason at the end of the long trajectory have joined in a conscious definition of the self. Like those of the three women in Act IX, it is the revelation of this final consciousness which justifies the act.

But what about Calisto and Melibea? What relation can their hesitant and affected rendezvous have with all this? In the first place, it must be noted that Calisto participates in the darkness and uncertainty—in the same fearful situation which dredges self-recognition from the servants. That is to say, he participates in it up until the time he recognizes the voice of Melibea through the door. He accepts readily Pármeno's initial suggestion that he arm himself against all dangers and, when Lucrecia first speaks to him instead of Melibea, he recalls Sempronio's suspicion that he may have been lured into a snare. But his reaction, as we have seen, is significantly different: "Cierto soy burlado: no era Melibea la que me habló. ¡Bullicio oygo, perdido soy! Pues viua o muera, que no he de yr de aquí." In this way, Rojas allows the valor of the hero to accentuate the cowardice of the servants. He reverses structurally the expected relationship between the two planes—in that Calisto's show of courage, a courage that is authentic at the moment, is much less developed than the negative sentiment of Pármeno and Sempronio. That this reversal of normal emphasis was fully intentional on the part of Rojas is shown by the fact that he continues and sustains it with interpolation later in the amorous dialogue. Calisto has boasted of the prowess of his servants at some length, and Melibea replies: "Bienempleado es el pan que tan esforçados siruientes comen ... *E quando sus osadías e atreuimientos les corregieres, a buelta del castigo mezcla fauor. Porque los ánimos esforçados no sean con encogimiento diminutos e yrritados en el osar a sus tiempos."* (XII, 91) The intention is clear. There is no reason why this particular sentence of the first tremulous meeting should be so underlined, unless it is to continue to etch out the consciousness of the servants with ironic acids. The juxtaposition of these two dialogic situations (Pármeno, Sempronio and Calisto, Melibea) results in a vicious backspin or undertow which subordinates, at least in part, the major event (from the point of view of plot and hierarchy) to Rojas' own structural practice. The balance of planar awarenesses, of disparate hesitancies, is masterful precisely because it is so precarious.

So much, then, for the first two situations. But a major problem remains— that of the relationship of this plenitude of rational and sentimental consciousness, of this vile anagnorisis, with the second major climax of the act—the murder of Celestina. It is here that the fullness of Rojas' structural intention in Act XII becomes evident. On the face of it, it is puzzling that Celestina with her knowledge of human conduct, with her mastery of strategy and tactics in dialogic warfare, should have allowed her last conversational skirmish with Pármeno and Sempronio to deteriorate so fatally. There is certainly some truth to the explanation that she was blinded by avarice as predicted in Act XI: "*Semp.*—No es esta la primera vez que yo he dicho quánto en los viejos reyna este vicio de cobdicia." (XII, 99–100) But Rojas is never content with such elemental motivations. Celestina's efforts to find a compromise solution to the dispute—promises of more women, offer of clothes, etc.—fail to placate the servants because she has badly misjudged their state of mind. When Sempronio and Pármeno enter her house, they begin by bragging of a fictional battle in which they have been engaged. In part, this is designed to frighten Celestina and to furnish an excuse for the request for money (the need to repair and replace the damaged arms), but, even more essentially, it reflects a weak attempt to bandage the gaping wounds in their self-esteem. Read rightly (that is to say, in reference to himself), there is ironical truth to this proclamation of Pármeno: "Que cierto te digo que no quería ya topar hombre que paz quisiesse. Mi gloria sería agora hallar en quién vengar la yra que no pude en los que nos la causaron, por su mucho huyr." (XII, 96) Celestina, however, unaware of the significance of this ranting, justifies keeping the chain as a reward for her own bravery, "... dos vezes he puesto ... mi vida al tablero." And when they threaten her, she signs her own death warrant by accusing them openly of cowardice:

¿Qué es esto? ¿Qué quieren dezir tales amenazas en mi casa? ¿Con una oueja mansa tenés vosotros manos e braueza? ¿Con vna gallina atada? ¿Con vna vieja de sesenta años? ¡Allá, allá, con los hombres como vosotros, contra los que ciñen espada, mostrá vuestras yras; no contra mi flaca rueca! *Señal es de gran couardía acometer a los menores e a los que poco pueden* ... (XII, 102–3)

The assassination follows almost immediately, for it is this accusation (even more explicit in the interpolation than in the original) that neither Pármeno nor Sempronio can now tolerate. Paradoxically, the whole wretched experience of Act XII is necessary for the servants' one intrepid act; dramatic action has once again been premised on consciousness in dialogue.[12]

Thus, in Act XII, for all its sustained tension and double climax, Rojas returns in interpolation to insist again and again on the dolorous consciousness of Pármeno and Sempronio. And he does so not only in their own speeches but also in those of the others: Calisto, Celestina, and even Melibea. His intention, in these latter instances, is not to reveal the awareness of fear but to accentuate it and so to relate it structurally to the meeting of the lovers and the murder of Celestina. In the one case, this is achieved by parallel juxtaposition and uses the hero and heroine as ironic foils for the cringing servants; in the other, there is a similar reversal of expected emphasis in that the victim is deprived of tragic consciousness in comparison to her murderers. Celestina's is—and intentionally so, despite all the power of her being—a comic death: she is structurally, at least, one more foil. The result is that the twelfth, far from being a monstrosity or an accident, is perhaps the most delicately consequential of all Rojas' twenty acts. It is in it that he meets and conquers the climax of his action.

Having said so much of these eleven distinct yet dialogically faithful structures, it is unnecessary to continue with detailed analysis. Act XIII frames Calisto's reaction to the swarming events which precede it and ends with his monologue of well-rationalized despair. Acts XIV and XIX suffer structurally the intervention of the added acts—but, in the *Comedia* along with Act XX, were entirely Melibea's. And Act XXI, intended as a thematic epilogue, is spoken by Pleberio in a speech which, according to R. F. Giusti, "hace las veces del coro en las tragedias de Esquilo."[13] His is the consciousness of the survivor, the survivor against his will, and in his words are gathered all the broken perspectives of sentiment and reason with which he remains. He surpasses his own grief and its rational consolation and harmonizes the voices of the dead in the traditional measures of *fortuna, mundo,* and *amor.* The dialogue is at the last absorbed structurally into a transcendental monologue. Of this and of the new structure of the added acts we shall have more to say later. For a major portion of the *Comedia,* at least, the point has been made that the structure in acts, far from being arbitrary or careless, was calculated to accentuate and unify the over-all progression of the dialogue. It serves, like the logic of the paragraph and the decorum of the situation, to give form without restraint to the vital growth of Rojas' art. Without this subtle structural training, *La Celestina*'s "tan crescidos ramos y hojas" might have run wild and never yielded the "harto fruto" of their consummate art.

2. Structure in Scenes

The customary partitions of dialogue submitted to a theatrical ordering include not only a conventional number of acts but also a varying number of separate scenes within each of them. These scenes are usually determined in either of two ways: on the one hand, by the entrance or departure of any of the characters, or, on the other, by a change of physical location or setting. Now, as far as *La Celestina* is concerned, the first of these varieties of scene— that used, for example, by Racine—is roughly parallel to our division of the act into dialogic situations. These are, as we have seen, structurally bounded by the range of desires, attitudes, and arguments of the speakers (the range of spoken consciousness in the first and second persons) in such a way that a new situation seems to be produced by the arrival or departure of any individual. Furthermore, and here style, character, and structure converge, each situation tends to possess its own dialogic decorum—a decorum which, by its recognizable counterpoint or harmony of stylistic levels, establishes the situation as the minimum unit of structure. All of this has been discussed at some length. But the question remains: what about the second theatrical definition of scene? What relation does physical location or setting have to Rojas' use of dialogic situations? According to Nicoll, any vital situation is premised not only on "who" but also on "where" and "when," among other pertinent interrogatives. And in order to complete our understanding of *La Celestina*'s scenic structure, we must consider it from this point of view. Since Rojas' whole artistry is radically non-theatrical or a-theatrical, it is likely that his situations will embrace in a new way elements from both definitions of "scene"—rather than adhere strictly to either of them.

From the first moment after his return home when Calisto calls for Sempronio and then contradicts the latter's claim to have been caring for the horses by asking, "Pues, ¿cómo sales de la sala?" we know that we are in a realm of physical space, a realm of rooms, houses, and the streets around and between them. After the indefinite "lugar" of the first meeting (we learn in Act II that it was Melibea's garden), we are never lost for a moment in the world of *La Celestina*. The dialogue compensates for the lack of inserted stage directions, in terms of each speaker's preoccupation with where he is and with where the others are in relation to him—a preoccupation that is ever present in the work. We should take care, accordingly, not to confuse this method of revealing the scene of dialogue with an artifice or mannerism on the part of the author. Nor should we consider those bits of dialogue which refer to place as purposefully substituted for marginal indications. As we shall see, these references are integrated fully to the individual situation and its participants. The characters do not announce hollowly to the reader, "Here we are at Celestina's house"; rather, that fact occupies a sector of their awareness and emerges from it naturally in the course of their conversation.[14]

It is on this basis that we can explain best two of the most striking characteristics of space in *La Celestina:* its three dimensional quality and the absolute freedom of movement it permits. In connection with the first of these, Rojas, as usual disobedient to Aristotle (in this case to the advice that the "tragic poet" while writing "put the actual scenes before his eyes"), does not place his characters on any sort of imaginary stage. Rather than projecting an *él* or an *ella* against a two-dimensional background, he leads the reader to intuit the long perspectives of a street through the speaker's own awareness of distance:

"Párm.—¡Señor, señor! Cal.—¿Qué quieres, loco? Párm.—A Sempronio e a
Celestina veo venir cerca de casa, haziendo paradillas de rato en rato ..." (V,
200) Similarly we are led to imagine the shadowy contours of a room:
"Lucr.—Señor, apresúrate mucho, si la quieres ver viua, que ni su mal conozco
de fuerte ni a ella ya de desfigurada. Pleb.—*Vamos presto, anda allá, entra
adelante, alça essa antepuerta e abre bien essa ventana, porque le pueda ver el
gesto con claridad.* ¿Qué es esto, hija mia?" (XX, 188–89) It is precisely this
subjective point of view which converts scene into space and, despite the
scarcity of specific reference, gives such a strong illusion of reality to the implicit city. As I pointed out in another place, "Así como la casa de Calisto
surge ante nosotros tal como se refleja en los ojos y en la mente de los que viven
en ella, así también se presenta una ciudad entera de tamaño natural, una
ciudad por lo visto tan natural que los eruditos han intentado muchas veces
identificarla historicamente."[15] The language here may be a bit too strong
(Calisto's house hardly "surge ante nosotros"), but it nevertheless represents
the truth. In his own way, Rojas reverses the Shakespearian focus and makes
of all the stage a world.

As for freedom of movement, it is in fact absolute, seemingly (as I pointed
out in the article mentioned above) cinematographic. Referring to the end of
Act II when Pármeno saddles a horse for Calisto and then curses him as he
rides off down the street, I remarked:

No hay en este fragmento de diálogo geometría estática de escena; lo que hay es
un cálculo dinámico, pues la acción mueve sus puntos, sin traba alguna, del cuarto
de Calisto a la cuadra, luego al portón de un patio, y, por fin, calle abajo. No hay
necesidad de cambios formales de escenario o de apartes artificiosos; la conversación
viva emerge con una libertad tan natural que no atrae atención hacia si misma.
Las convenciones dramáticas de escena y acto, el método racional y jerárquico de la
presentación del dialogo, pierden su función, pues en la *Celestina* la circunstancia
exterior emana del diálogo, de las percepciones de los personajes y no es nunca un
agregado adjetivo o formal.[16]

This holds true not only for limited movements through a room or a house
but also for the long walks through the streets and plazas of *La Celestina*.
And when Rojas wishes to transfer our attention from one dialogue to another
in a different location, he does so without the slightest fear that we shall be
lost or confused. The priority of dialogue is so complete that it can move
through space instantaneously without hesitancy of marginal annotation.[17]

This three-dimensional quality and its resultant freedom of movement,
taken by themselves, would seem to make unlikely any structural use of location in *La Celestina*. Is not freedom by its very nature antithetical to structure?

Yet, as we shall see, there is in *La Celestina* an internal or scenic structure based on space. To understand how this is possible we must remind ourselves once again that the scene is not primarily a scene of action but a scene of spoken consciousness—a scene we do not see (or imagine seeing) but of which we are aware. This will explain, in the first place, the incredible vacancy of space in the work. As the inhabitants of *La Celestina* walk to and from their houses, there is little indication in the text that they meet with a living soul, a recognizable place, or anything at all. The same thing is true to a great extent of the interiors of the houses with only the barest indication of furniture and rooms. So intent are these people on the immediate dialogic (or monologic) situation, so involved in the interlocking *tú* and *yo* of human conversation, that they usually fail to notice the external artifacts of urban and domestic existence. Space almost seems to have been purified of content in a world schematically limited to a minimum of contour. In a different way from that of Racine, Rojas achieves the barrenness of the classical anteroom or temple chamber. He eliminates everything that does not of its own weight penetrate to the consciousness of the speaker.

The necessary result of this is that whatever things *are* mentioned have a charge of significance, an implication of structural importance, which is frequently lost in the realistic novel or in other such imitations of existence in the world. When in moods of reminiscence Celestina dwells on scenes from her past life, the everyday utensils which she uses to recapture their texture— jugs of wine, talley sticks, dead men's teeth, and the rest—achieve an almost symbolic value. And the same thing is true for the multitude of cosmetics, clothes, bagatelles, and household objects which typify in conversation the activities of lovers, housemaids, and other human types. In contrast to the immediate physical emptiness of *La Celestina*'s space, these images of dialogue carry the full impetus of their illustrative intention. In a similar way, certain real objects are brought into high relief—for example, Celestina's ragged cloak, Sempronio's armor, Melibea's girdle, Areusa's white bed, or the snake oil and goat beard of the incantation—because of their special evaluation by members of the situation. These, in particular, have meaning for the structure. Within their vacant circumstance they tend to center the dialogue on themselves, to become the nuclei for frequently divergent preoccupations. In a scene of consciousness, those things which are not just seen but noticed are of high artistic potency. They are no longer just "things"; rather they have been absorbed into living structure of each situation. Rojas, in other words, often seems to compensate for his lack of description of things by their use in calculated structural play.

We must not pass by this matter without some reference to the role of color and light in *La Celestina*. Perhaps entranced by Calisto's reverent and traditional description in Act I of the golden hair, red lips, white teeth, and ruby nails of Melibea, most readers fail to realize the incredible parsimony of color references in the work. Aside from this description and several suggested notes of color in the inventory of Celestina's sinister warehouse, a few glimpses of black, white, and gold complete the spectrum of Rojas' artistry.[18] The significance of the choice is apparent; all three of these colors rather than describe the object, subject it to a catagorical evaluation, a linguistically prescribed attitude. For example, when Celestina sees Areusa in bed, she remarks with undisguised sensuality:

¡Ay cómo huele toda la ropa en bulléndote! ¡A osadas que está todo a punto! Siempre me pagué de tus cosas e hechos, de tu limpieza e atauío. ¡Fresca que estas! ¡Bendígate Dios! ¡Qué sáuanas e colcha! ¡Qué almohadas! ¡E qué blancura! ¡Tal sea mi vejez, qual todo me parece perla de oro! (VII, 248–49)

Here the word, "blancura," refers at once to the color of the sheets and to a vivid awareness of quality. More than a description, it is a part of the larger exclamation. As for the phrase, "perla de oro" (used on other occasions by Celestina), the color gold has been completely transformed into a superlative of value.[19] And the same thing is true for black which expresses negative connotations of mourning and evil: "... los sombrosos árboles del huerto se sequen con vuestra vista, sus flores olorosas se tornen de negra color."[20] (XV, 139) In a world which is made of spoken consciousness and not just described in dialogue, color is not seen. It is, instead, assimilated to the mind and to the tongue.

Realization of the lack of color in *La Celestina* leads us to examine Rojas' corresponding use of light and darkness—a use which is frequently structural. Aside from the assimilated colors of conversation, there is no color in the work precisely because there are no things or surfaces to be colored, no props, no backdrops, nor even characters. It is an absence which must also affect the lighting of the work, for under such circumstances Rojas is denied artistic access to the realm of chiaroscuro; that is to say, he is denied the artistry of reflected light. It would be wrong, therefore, to think of *La Celestina* as a work, if not in color, in black and white. Darkness and light are present but as consciously experienced, experienced in relation to the dialogic obligations of each situation. Act XII, for example, is a dark act, but its darkness is manifest in the nervousness, the constant listening, of the servants and in the uncertainty of the lovers' first encounter. And when the darkness of the act is punctuated by the torches of the watch, it is not their direct glare which we perceive but the fear and subsequent relief of the servants as well as the annoyance of Calisto. Similarly, in the balanced first and last scenes of Act VIII in which light filters through the shutters of darkened rooms, the mental rather than the visual impact is accented:

> PÁRM.—¿Amanesce o qué es esto, que tanta claridad está en esta cámara?
> AREU.—¿Qué amanecer? Duerme, señor, que avn agora nos acostamos. No he yo pegado bien los ojos, ¿ya hauía de ser de día? Abre, por Dios, essa ventana de tu cabecera e verlo has.
> PÁRM.—En mi seso estó yo, señora, que es de día claro, en ver entrar luz entre las puertas. ¡O traydor de mí! ¡En qué gran falta he caydo con mi amo! De mucha pena soy digno. ¡O qué tarde que es! (VIII, 7)

The same thing is true of Act VII with its first dark street scene and its later transition to the lighted chamber of Areusa. We are left with an impression of brilliance—of bright appeal—in the latter scene, precisely because its light has become a part of Celestina's excitement, Pármeno's timidity, and Areusa's coyness. Thus, certain scenes are framed structurally by the presence or absence of light, but that light can never be reflected and so is never visible. It is, instead, refracted through the first- and second-person consciousnesses of the situation—integrated to their dialogue. Like that created by centering a situation around an object, the vividness of this illusion of light is hardly a paradox. Light as conscious experience is of potentially greater candle power than light as sensation or impression.

To return to space as a path of movement rather than as a path of vision, we may suppose that Rojas will use it structurally whenever it is, like light, contributory to the dialogic situation. But the word, "whenever," is slightly misleading; Rojas, in spite of his reputation, is not given to wasting words or to introducing needless sentences in his dialogue. Rather we suspect that if location and movement are mentioned at all in the dialogue, it is because they have a dialogic function—a function which on one level, at any rate, may be structural. At first glance, the numerous references of this sort may appear casual, accessory, and related only to action. If we are told in Act I, for example, that Sempronio is in the "sala" when Calisto comes in, it is only in order to provide an initial spark for the latter's explosion of anger and despair. But these cases are, I believe, outnumbered and outweighed by those which enter directly into the structure of the situation, those in which movement and location are seen in terms of the space *between* the speakers. As the physical medium of each person's isolation, space cannot help but enter as a mould-

ing and directing force into what he says. It becomes consubstantial with the
tú and *yo* of dialogue, a structural element of situation.

This is not meant to imply that Rojas was primarily concerned with such
subtleties of spatial experience as the tone of conversation at a distance compared, let us say, to the murmurings of an embraced couple or to the quiet
talk of a pair sitting side by side. Neither does he experiment consistently with
what might be called spatial atmospheres, that is to say, the more or less in-
definable qualities of space: chilly, warm, shut in, heavy, charged, etc. These
things which were to be developed to the full in the nineteenth-century novel
are still rudimentary in *La Celestina*—not necessarily because of its primitive
nature, but rather because the characters are too intent upon the immediacies
of sentiment and argument, to notice them. In accord with Rojas' art of character, insofar as such differences do affect the dialogue,[21] it is only through
consciousness of them.[22] This is, of course, quite unlike the novel which tends
to portray atmospheres and distances as more or less subconscious factors
which contribute to experience in a manner unknown to its subject. Characteristically it is Zola and the naturalists in general who have used this technique as one of the bases of their narrative art. But in *La Celestina* space can
seldom, if ever, be described as environmental.

Thus, if the distance between speakers is to be given structural emphasis
in *La Celestina,* it must be done in a manner which more directly involves
spoken consciousness than do the above intangibles. Space must be defined in
elemental terms, with inescapable self-assertion, and must provide not so
much a private experience (although that may be suggested from time to
time) as a sharp awareness for all the dialogic persons. This Rojas achieves
in two sorts of situations: first, those in which one or more speakers can hear
but not see the others; and, second, those in which one or more speakers can
see but not hear the others. Or to put the matter in another way, space in *La
Celestina* is structurally either a barrier or a distance. Only in these two forms
is it immediately relevant to that complex unit of consciousnesses which we
have called the dialogic situation, and only in these two forms can it accentuate
the unity of the dialogic situation as the least common denominator of structure. Since Rojas rejects formal and explicit separation of scenes within each
act, this spatial demarcation of situations is the necessary substitute. Or perhaps
it would be better to say that barriers and distances entering directly into the
group consciousness allow Rojas to avoid the mechanical artifice of scene.
They allow him to de-emphasize the dramatic concept of scene (as the mere
setting or location of action) in favor of a variety more appropriate to his
own art.

Let us consider first those situations in which the participants can hear each other but cannot see each other. The primordial example occurs in Act I when Sempronio and Celestina feign diligent discourse outside of Calisto's door and when, Pármeno, warning his master of the stratagem from within, is, in his turn, overheard. This, it would seem, is a purely comic barrier, relatively simple, and premised on the typification of the four speakers. It can even be imagined scenically in terms of the multiple stage of the Middle Ages. Yet it does set a pattern for situation structure in the rest of *La Celestina* in that it establishes the personal relationships to be developed in succeeding dialogues and serves as an effective means of initial emphasis for the encounters to follow. The spatial barrier acts almost as a signpost to the exploitation of Calisto and the necessity of tempting Pármeno.[23] It does not constitute a full-fledged situation in itself but rather prepares and pre-defines the situation it initiates.

In later acts of the *Comedia* Rojas learns to manage barrier in a much more subtle manner (the refusal in Act V to repeat the door device is meaningful in this connection). Typical of his scenic practice, in this sense, is the delicious dialogue between Lucrecia and Alisa at the beginning of Act IV in which the former announces Celestina's arrival but is reluctant to pronounce the fatal name of the visitor. The situation at the entrance involves a triple location of persons: Celestina just inside (since Lucrecia says "Entra e espera aquí ..."); Lucrecia probably half-way up the stairs (since Alisa questions her from a distance, "¿Con quién hablas?"); and Alisa on an upper floor (since Celestina is told, "Sube, tía"). Instead of underlining exaggerated postures of deceit as in Act I, space here serves to introduce three varieties of indiscretion and discretion: Celestina's purposeful silence, Alisa's reckless talkativeness, and Lucrecia's ridiculously self-conscious diplomacy. The point is that each of these attitudes is an almost indispensable introduction to the dialogue which follows—and each could not have been expressed so freely if the speakers had been brought face to face. In the first place, their spontaneous reactions, both discrete and indiscrete, are placed in ironical counterpoint to the formal greetings which follow—the barrier to vision providing for social hypocrisy rather than the intentional deception of Act I. But this is less important than the provision of an off-guard moment in which we may estimate vividly Alisa's unawareness of the danger entering her house. The striking contrast of Alisa's superficial forgetfulness with Celestina's conscious determination in the preceding monologue not only prepares for her heedless departure (leaving Melibea alone with Celestina) but also marks the entrance from without to within, from *a* street to *this* house. Celestina is now in Melibea's house and there, for the rest of the act, the one's life and the other's honor are to be at stake. In other words, Rojas insists on the moment of entrance to such an extent because he wishes to integrate what is said by all speakers during the rest of the act to the fact of place. Here, Alisa speaks carelessly from within her own house and her own life; Celestina says nothing for she is outside both; and Lucrecia stammers bashfully from somewhere in between. And from this moment on scene unit and speech unit are as they must be: structurally one. The dialogic situation has been introduced.

Admittedly there are in *La Celestina* few other instances of dialogue without vision used with this telling structural intuition. Rojas is often content to bring out location with such casual but direct remarks as Pármeno's "Bien has dicho. Calla que está abierta la puerta. En casa está." (IX, 26) And still more frequently, he employs vision at a distance to provide a spatial frame for the individual situation. On one occasion after another, one speaker will see another in the street as he approaches or leaves the close skirmish of consciousness. The above entry into Melibea's house is introduced by a typical example:

CEL.—... Ni perro me ha ladrado ni aue negra he visto, tordo ni cueruo ni otras noturnas. E lo mejor de todo es que veo a Lucrecia a la puerta de Melibea. Prima es de Elicia: no me será contraria.
LUCR.—¿Quién es esta vieja, que viene haldeando?
CEL.—Paz sea en esta casa.
LUCR.—Celestina, madre, seas bienvenida. (IV, 158–59)

Here, awareness of distance is translated into speech as awareness of a person at a distance; a *tú* with whom each speaker is shortly to be engaged. Unlike barriers, these distances traversed in vision stress not so much the location as the spatial rapprochement (or process of enmeshment) of the dialogic situation. They remind us not of this place or that but of place itself as a necessity of human encounter. They remind us, in short, that the words we are about to hear (or have just heard) emerge from spatially finite human beings, human beings who are fully susceptible to perspective. Since each dialogic situation is dedicated to the crossing of living points of view, it is fitting that Rojas should set them apart in structure by moments of perspective in space —that is to say by moments in which the point of view is physical rather than mental.

Rojas frequently refines this scenic technique by including distant glimpses not only of an identified person but also of the same person in a significant attitude. How central to our recollection of *La Celestina* are Sempronio seen lounging by Calisto's door, Sosia dishevelled and crying as he comes home with the news of the execution, or Elicia in tearful mourning trudging along toward Areusa's house! Indeed, the changing gait of Celestina in her comings and goings about the city often furnishes an effective transition between the situation left behind and the situation to come. Visually noted by the others, her flying skirts or doubtful pace provide both a point of departure for the next conversation and a sure index to the carry-over of a state of consciousness from one unit of dialogue to another. An even better example is an interpolation in Act V—an interpolation which increases appreciation of the situation we have just heard and, at the same time, infects us with Calisto's anxiety to know the meaning of what he sees:

PÁRM.—¡Señor, señor!

CAL.—¿Qué quieres, loco?

PÁRM.—A Sempronio e a Celestina veo venir cerca de casa, haziendo paradillas de rato en rato *e, quando están quedos, hazen rayas en el suelo con el espada. No sé que sea.*

CAL.—¡O desuariado, negligente! Veslos venir: ¿no puedes decir corriendo a abrir la puerta? ¡O alto Dios! ¡O soberana deidad! ¿Con qué vienen? ¿Qué nueuas traen? (V, 200)

Sempronio's absent-minded, nervous gesturing with the sword (as noticed by Pármeno) confirms with visual precision his anxious curiosity—his borrowed love for Melibea—in the preceding situation. By concluding the dialogue of Sempronio and Celestina with a distant glimpse of the two speakers, Rojas has converted a more or less amorphous succession of speeches into a meaningful unit of consciousness. Thanks to this single sentence of Pármeno's and especially to its interpolation, we end with a crystallized structural whole, a completed scene of dialogue. The physical point of view, the revealing attitude seen in perspective, is here fully joined to the points of view—to the living perspectives of the speakers. The dialogic situation is, thus, not a critical abstraction but a real literary presence; space has been structurally integrated to spoken consciousness. Dialogue has been "situated."

Having considered such a striking example there is little need to insist upon others. We should, however, point out that sudden and telling glimpses of one speaker or another are by no means confined to moments of scenic transition. At times, they are also granted us within the situation and serve as a reminder of the physical humanity of the speakers. They constitute that dialogue of gesture and expression which we have already seen complementing the dialogue or words and compensating for the relative lack of facial or physical description.[24] Very frequently too the union of attitude and word is further cemented by ironical misunderstanding on the part of the observer. We remember the interpolation from Act VI in which Calisto assimilates Pármeno's desperate and derisive gesturing to his own expectant delight:

CAL.—... ya he perdido temor, ya tengo alegría. Subamos, si mandas, arriba. En mi cámara me dirás por estenso lo que aquí he sabido en suma.

CEL.—Subamos, señor.

PÁRM.—*¡O sancta María! ¡Y qué rodeos busca este loco por huyr de nosotros, para poder llorar a su plazer con Celestina de gozo y por descubrirle mill secretos de su liuiano e desuariado apetito, por preguntar y responder seys vezes cada cosa, sin que esté presente quien le pueda dezir que es prolixo! Pues mándote yo, desatinado, que tras tí vamos.*

CAL.—*Mirá, señora, qué fablar trae Pármeno, cómo se viene santiguando de oyr lo que has hecho con tu gran diligencia. Espantado está, por mi fe, señora Celestina. Otra vez se santigua. Sube, sube, sube y* asiéntate, señora que de rodillas quiero escuchar tu suaue respuesta.[25] (VI, 209–10)

Here again we are afforded a glimpse—a glimpse all the more effective because it is misinterpreted—of the physical accompaniment of the dialogue just read. It is by such devices as these that Rojas continually reminds us of the scene we cannot see. Instead of betraying his dialogue by adjusting it to non-dialogic artifices of structure, marginal directions, descriptive insertions, etc., he allows the situation to notify us on its own terms of its necessary dimensionality. In this way, we retain the illusion (in a deeper sense, the fact) that we are reading not words, sentences, and paragraphs but speech. And in retaining this illusion, we are all the more prepared for the spoken structures with which we have been concerned.

Logically, we should now go on to investigate the structural use of time as well as space, the function of "when" as well as "where" in defining situations. But to do so would be to encounter the underlying temporal paradox of the work; the apparent existence of two separate varieties of time as we read from act to act. This we shall not be ready to discuss until we can relate it to Rojas' deepest level of artistry, his art of theme. For now, it will be enough to note that he often employs the speaker's immediate preoccupation with the hour (as well as its darkness or light) in order to situate the flow of conversation. In this sense, references to the time of day are comparable in function to the glimpses through space which we have just considered. This final situation of Act XII, for example, is opened by Celestina's question: "¡O locos trauiessos! Entrad, entrad. ¿Cómo venís a tal hora que ya amanesce?" And there is a good deal more evidence to show that such temporal specification tends to mark the transition from one scene to another.[26] It is in this position that time references can best contribute to the setting apart of those structural units we have here called dialogic situations. For a situation to be in fact a situation (and not just conversation about a given topic) it must be integrated, through the living consciousness of the participants, with both space and time.

We may conclude our discussion of the several means used to establish scenic structure in *La Celestina* with the reservation that they are not mutually exclusive. Having enumerated them separately, we must deny the implication that they are in fact separate. Rojas, in fact, tends to join consciousness of distance or barrier, object or light, hour or place, in such varying composition as may be appropriate. Let us take the first two situations of Act XII as typical examples. The act opens with Calisto's question, "¿Moços, qué hora da el relox?" and this is followed by mention of that same armor which is to worry the servants later in the act: "Descuelga, *Pármeno,* mis coraças *e armaos vosotros e assí yremos a buen recaudo."* There is also a brief suggestion of the dark and vacant perspective of the street, a darkness and a vacancy at once frightening and reassuring: "Cal.—... Mira tú Sempronio, si parece alguno por la calle. Semp.—Señor, ninguna gente parece e, avnque la houiesse, la mucha escuridad priuaría el viso e conoscimiento a los que nos encontrasen." (XII, 78) After a second mention of hour and place and after significant glimpses of Pármeno through the eyes of Sempronio ("No saltes ni hagas esse bollicio de plazer") and through his own ("Calças traygo e avn borzeguíes de essos ligeros que tú dizes para mejor huyr que otro"), the first situation approaches its end. The wide variety of physical, spatial, and temporal reference is not just possible but aesthetically necessary because of the nature of the situation. Preoccupied as all three participants are with the dangerous interview to come, they can have little dialogue beyond hushed and at times irritable comment on the immediate circumstance. It is for this reason one of the least dialogic—the least determined by the sheer encounter of first and second persons—and the most "situated" of all the situations of *La Celestina.*

The beginning of the second situation is marked only by Sempronio's comment: "Salido deue auer Melibea. Escucha que hablan quedito"; for, as usual, the enmeshment is almost imperceptible. What follows is a novel yet very effective combination of both distance and barrier—each of which is made to contribute its own complementary brand of spatial definition. Sempronio and Pármeno are stationed in the street somewhat apart from the house while the lovers, like Pyramus and Thisbe, are separated by the unyielding portal. Thus, each pair, while talking easily between themselves, can partially overhear the other. (Calisto and Melibea, more intent upon each other, only hear the noises of flight while the servants seem to catch whole fragments of amorous murmuring.) And it is on these terms that Rojas ironically weaves a single situation out of what might otherwise have been theatrical parallelism. Aside from the spatial preoccupation, consciousness is also crystallized scenically by each group's awareness of those material objects which in ironical counterpoint interfere with motion: the armor and the door itself. And finally, the situation is ended by the torches of the watch, the one flare of light in its total darkness. It is not that Rojas emphasizes this skeleton of structure; the reader is, in fact, hardly aware of the delicately balanced geometry of space, object, and light which orders the disparate consciousness of the speakers. Yet in this climactic example of scene construction—precisely because of the priority of living dialogue—sentiment and argument grow naturally upon a trellice of physical circumstance. Unlike the preceding scene with its anarchic awareness of time and space and unlike the topical debate between Sempronio and Calisto in Act I (because topical, so unsituated), here we are offered a four-dimensional scene of consciousness, the free structure of the dialogically vital situation.

3. The Art of Structure

Continued meditation on the unique and surprising structure of *La Celestina* must inevitably involve the problem of genre. Our very use of the terms, "act" and "scene," directs us towards an implicit comparison with the structural practices of the drama. At the same time, insofar as Rojas diverges from these practices, we are tempted to approximate him to the novelist—to novelistic organization of experience by chapters. But, for all the inevitability of these comparisons, they are also premature. Although we tend at times to equate form with genre, to interpret generic distinction as the distinction of verse, narrative, and dialogue structures, such equation can be misleading. Genre is more than form or structure; in its deepest sense it is a means of classifying the theme or creative vision of life. And it is precisely in this deepest sense that we shall return to it in the final essay. Lacking such precaution, we might well find ourselves confronted here with that awkward and confusing generic hybrid, the "dialogue novel."

In spite of this apparent difficulty, the very ambivalence of our notion of genre—on the one hand, purely formal such as the narrative or sonnet and, on the other, thematic embracing such concepts as dramatic, tragic, or comic— leads to a possible conclusion for an essay on Rojas' art of structure. It is only necessary to isolate a term for the normal structures of dialogue, a generic term, but one which makes no open commitment to intent or theme. The answer, I think, is to be found in the formal demands of the theater. The adjective "theatrical" describes the necessary structures of scene and act when designed for actors and audience but implies little or nothing about the meaning of the dialogue which they shape. From such a point of reference, then, we may attempt to estimate the peculiar nature of Rojas' art of structure and, at the same time, avoid those ultimate generic problems which we are not yet ready to face. In other words, we shall now try to forget the deeper implications of the adjective, "dramatic," and view what we have seen of the structure of La Celestina from the perspective of the theater and its direct physical representation.

To begin with, when dialogue is ordered theatrically, the structure in acts is internal in nature—that is to say, it represents certain natural divisions in the skeleton of action. Each act is a step in the movement from initial event to ultimate resolution. The scene, on the other hand (at least insofar as it is scenic), is an external division, a segment of what Aristotle calls the "spectacle." It is usually designed to ornament and accentuate the action from without, to provide background and new possibilities of movement for the actors. In La Celestina, however, this order of interiority and exteriority is clearly reversed. It is the scene as a situation (with all the spatial, temporal, and physical circumstance implied in the word) that is built from within. Place, consciousness, and spoken word are identified in it, as we have seen, and so constructed intuitively. Or to say the same thing in another way, Rojas does not write his dialogue or visualize his characters against a scene; rather he seems to imagine creatively the situation as a unit with all its parts suitably organized. The act, again in direct contrast to theatrical expectations, is structurally external. It is a gathering of several situations in such a way as to underline (even to "ornament and accentuate") by appropriate juxtaposition the inherent significance of each. By means of the act, Rojas exercises artistic control of presentation and effect from without and, at the same time, avoids any sort of direct intervention. He can even communicate irony structurally and so without the need of audience participation. In Act II, for example, we have seen how the formal juxtaposition of three situations allows us to grasp the full meaning of each of them. Apart from the act, the ironic significance of Pármeno's silent presence at the beginning might have been entirely lost.

Granting this inversion of traditional theatrical practice in La Celestina, we must also concede that it hardly corresponds to a fully intentional change on the part of Rojas. Even if he had wished, Rojas probably could not have reduced his structural practice to a "poetics" issued in defiance of Aristotle. As we said at the outset of this essay, creative awareness must be distinguished from critical awareness, and perhaps the most evident sign of this is the failure to delimit each situation externally. Precisely because Rojas knows intuitively how to relate dimensional reference to each change of speakers—because, in short, he is gifted at "situating" spoken consciousness from within—the resulting situations are vital units which do not need formal recognition. Instead each seems to grow out of the other in accord with the deepest matrices of their continuing creation. Once again we are reminded of that significant image of the *Prólogo:* "E como sea cierto que toda palabra del hombre sciente está preñada, desta se puede dezir que de muy hinchada y llena quiere rebentar, echando de si tan crescidos ramos y hojas ..." There is, in effect, within *La Celestina* a vital inner structure of dialogic growth from situation to situation. It is a structure far removed from geometry, winding through reoccurrent situations with that same inexplicable unity of innovation and repetition which characterizes life itself. It would be tempting to compare this structure to that of a spiral—in view of the fact that Rojas is seldom contented with a single situation but inevitably returns to it for purposes of living contrast and comparison. The two seductions of Pármeno, the two interviews with Melibea, the two reports to Calisto, and above all the two garden scenes would be a few of the many examples. But this scheme, in spite of its suggestiveness, only substitutes solid for plane geometry; it can hardly account for all the ivy-like windings of the growth of the work. We must be careful not to demand geometrical perfection of the tentative symmetries of life. About all we can say with safety is that Rojas employs with consummate artistry the trellice of dimensional and physical circumstance which upholds—and in a sense combines with—his dialogue of consciousness.

Complementary to this vital structure integrating dialogue to the temporal and spatial frame of *La Celestina,* there is the formal structure in acts. These are, we maintain, designed to accentuate by appropriate partition the inherent significance of the situations they include. If each situation, as well as the total sequence of situations, is supported on an inner trellice of awareness of place and time, the act corresponds to the calculated arrangement of the landscape gardener who trains the vine in order to illustrate this or that feature of its growing beauty. There is, of course, no pruning, no simulated geometry, but rather a delicate collaboration of inner and outer necessities—a collaboration of structures enabling both completed growth and completed expression. Vitality and formality coincide as the living innovation and repetition of the one are framed with successive effectiveness from act to act. We are as far removed from the purposeful disorder of Romanticism (or the rioting uncultivated growth of Rabelais and the Arcipreste de Talavera) as we are from the artificial symmetries of neoclassicism. There is, indeed, something prodigious about the adequateness and adequation of Rojas' artistry of structure. Without generic parallel and without historical parallel, he has found a counterpart over the span of the whole for that intimate union of sentiment and argument, of vital clarity and formal logic, which characterizes the dialogic prodigy of his style.

CHAPTER FIVE

THE ART OF THEME - CREATION

STRICTLY speaking, an "art of theme" is both an impossibility and a contradiction in terms. The usual critical distinction between "theme" and "thesis" will bear this out. If a thesis be taken to mean the intentional idea which directs a work of art, a theme must, on the other hand, live in the work in a much more radical and pervasive manner. It permeates and informs the work as the soul in the body and, as a result, is elusive and resistant to definition. It can never be completely known either to the author or the critic. Salinas describes the theme—in his book on Rubén Darío—as a "vital preoccupation," an obsession, which constitutes the matrix of poetic creation and which evolves from poem to poem and year to year. Hence, for Salinas a discriminating and sensitive survey of the whole work of an author is the best means for its capture. Ortega y Gasset recommending the stylistic approach sees the theme as an "individual postura ante ... la vida" which is betrayed in the minimal peculiarities of writing. And again in fundamental agreement, Augusto Centeno speaks of a unique "livingness," "a sense of life, deep and intense, arising out of spiritual relationships and to be apprehended only by the intuition."[1] In each case, the critic recognizes the theme as profoundly vital, as a "sense of life" clearly distinguishable from those specific intentions, ideas, or lessons which, being consciously proposed, may fairly be called theses.[2] In other words, if we accept this definition of theme, have we not surpassed the domain of art? An "art of thesis" would be entirely possible but the theme of *La Celestina* can hardly be studied in the same way we have studied style, character, and structure.

There is, of course, no real answer to this objection. I cannot and ought not disguise the process of intuitive revelation which is ultimately responsible for my understanding of what *La Celestina* is about—that is to say, of its theme. Without this prior intuition, an intuition emerging from love and the possession of many readings, I could never possibly have deduced a theme from analysis of interpolations or from other evidence of Rojas' artistic practice. Nevertheless—and this is one of the special advantages offered by *La Celestina* to its critics—it is possible to illustrate its deepest "postura ante la vida" in terms of the dialogic artistry which gave it form. A theme must not only be intuited; it must also be explained and rationalized, and it is for these tasks that our artistic criteria may be useful. It is unlikely that Salinas, Ortega, Centeno, or anyone else would rule out this possibility.

1. The Art of Thesis

To continue our theoretical discussion, we may point out that the above definitions of "theme" and "thesis" are not mutually exclusive. It is not only possible but highly probable that both will coexist in any given work. According to the *incipit* the thesis of *La Celestina* is to be the "reprehensión de los locos enamorados, que, vencidos en su desordenado apetito, a sus amigas llaman e dizen ser su dios"; and the guiding presence of this proposition is evident not only in Act I but also from time to time later on.[3] Yet, at the same time, even in Act I it is evident that beneath the level of exemplary transgression there is a creative posture, a possession of life, impossible to encompass in didactic formulae. There it was intuited by that self-proclaimed "first reader" Fernando de Rojas—who described it as a "fuerte e claro metal," to be shaped by subsequent artistries of style, structure, characterization, and thesis.[4]

Admitting, then, the likelihood that theme and thesis must together direct literary creation, we may further assume that they are closely related. The one is frequently the conscious formulation of the other, its reduced and rationalized counterpart, and so may serve as a springboard for the reader's intuitive leap into the darkness. If we were concerned, for example, with the explanation of Calderón's personal, yet profoundly baroque, theme, where better might we begin than with such titular theses as "La vida es sueño" or "El gran teatro del mundo"? For *La Celestina,* in any case, it is from the art of the thesis that we may most conveniently rationalize an intuition of the theme. The emphasis which Rojas accords to the thesis in the prologue material and in Act XXI as well as the apparent evolution of the thesis through the three stages of writing (Act I, the *Comedia,* the *Tragicomedia*) are significant in this connection. Just as for the *Quijote* an understanding of the Cervantine theme may be achieved by using the repeated assertion that exile of the romances of chivalry was the only intention as a point of departure, so for *La Celestina* it may be profitable to retrace Rojas' artistic footsteps.

Mention of the prologue material reminds us of a preliminary difficulty to be overcome: that of the innumerable minor theses found by Rojas in

Act I and praised by him as being instructive and entertaining. These, are, of course, the "deleytables fontezicas de filosofía" referred to in the *Carta* and presumably imitated and continued in the *Comedia* and *Tragicomedia*. It is true that much of what is actually said in the work consists of the familiar topics and commonplaces of the late Middle Ages. Observations on wine, women, the clergy and its immorality, riches and poverty, love and heresy, old age and youth, servitude, witchcraft, fortune, death, friendship, and other such matters occur and reoccur in passage after passage. Castro Guisasola, in fact, converts his source study into a vision of *La Celestina* as a breviary of fifteenth-century doctrine. The fundamental deceit of such a listing, however, is that it abstracts what is listed from its context. And, if we have learned anything at all from our consideration of Rojas' art, it is that for *La Celestina* this is an exceptionally hazardous thing to do. Apart from the dialogue of its pronouncement, apart from the *yo* and the *tú* who give it birth, each such topic tends to set itself up as a minor thesis, a message to the reader copied from a wise source. The inevitable result is the artistic dismemberment of the work. We must not be misled by the *Carta* (or by the desirability of identifying sources) into confusing received ideology with creative intentions. If we do so, we shall never understand *La Celestina*.

Actually our discussion of Rojas' art of character indicates the way most of these commonplaces are integrated to the dialogue. Almost all the topics on the above list are related to the patterns of character which we saw emerging from the elementary conditioning of the cast. These limits or frontiers of life by their very nature determine the possible topics of conversation. As barriers they catch or channel the attention of the speakers. Thus, the servants are preoccupied with servitude, Celestina with old age, wealth, and the comfort of wine, the men with the nature of women, the women with surpassing their femininity. And each expresses his preoccupation in the only terms available to him: the commonplaces which abounded in the atmosphere and literature of the time. Instead of being merely appended to dialogue, such phrases as "la vejez no es sino mesón de enfermedades, posada de pensamientos ..." emerge from it and from the conscious life it expresses. The fact (noticed by Castro Guisasola) that Rojas often referred to an index of "principalium sententiarum" first included in the Basle, 1496, edition of Petrarch's Latin works shows adaptation for a purpose, not mere copying.[5] He seems to have looked up material appropriate for a particular person or a given situation.

If the selection of certain commonplaces is based on those patterns of character implicit in *La Celestina,* others seem to follow along the trajectories of individual lives. A typical example is the topic of friendship first introduced during Celestina's argument with Pármeno in Act I:

E por tanto, en los infortunios el remedio es a los amigos. ¿E a dónde puedes ganar mejor este debdo, que donde las tres maneras de amistad concurren, conuiene a saber, por bien e prouecho e deleyte? Por bien: mira la voluntad de Sempronio conforme a la tuya e la gran similitud, que tú y el en la virtud teneys. Por prouecho: en la mano está, si soys concordes. Por deleyte: semejable es, como seays en edad dispuestos para todo linaje de plazer ...[6] (I, 104–5.)

And as we follow Pármeno from situation to situation, his relation with Sempronio demonstrates the efficacy of the commonplace. At first, their collaboration is reluctant and based only on "prouecho"; after Act VII "deleyte" offers its own variety of companionship; and, finally, in Act XII the friendship is firmly and ironically cemented in terms of "bien." Alone in the street the two dwell almost lyrically on "la conformidad en los compañeros," never realizing that the sharing of cowardice (the "bien" in this case) will ultimately result in the sharing of death. Thus, at each stage of Parmeno's trajectory, the commonplace is continued and, at the same time, corroded by the circumstances of its utterance. Pármeno and Sempronio are not friends in any authentic sense; instead they have been paired off in life. They are partially aware of this, aware of their joint degradation if not of its consequences, and still must speak in the customary terms of friendship because they have no others.

It is necessary to insist so much on the functionalism of these received commonplaces in *La Celestina* in order to correct past misinterpretations. But for a better understanding of Rojas' particular combination of tradition with originality (Salinas suggests that the combination was fundamental to any sort of fifteenth-century literary greatness) we must distinguish what happens in *La Celestina* from Elizabethan revitalization of mediaeval topics, especially those relating to death.[7] Rojas does not attempt poetic transfusion; indeed in most cases there is little more than literal translation or repetition. For every commonplace—and the discussion of friendship above is only one of innumerable examples—the particular context of sentiment or argument provides a new dimension of significance. The general precedent (which is what most of these commonplaces are) is placed in fecund counterpoint with the particular living application. In this, as we shall see, lies the deepest source of Rojas' distance from his own creation, that creative distance which Ortega y Gasset describes in a brilliant image: "Los que viven junto a una catarata no perciben su estruendo; es necesario que pongamos una distancia entre lo que nos rodea inmediatamente y nosotros, para que a nuestros ojos adquiera sentido." [8]

In any case, Act I aside, there is no consistent comic or satirical intention in this counterpoint, for Celestina does not betray any more than she confirms the inherited truths she utters. Rather the effect is one of irony, of simultaneous ironical vision of two kinds of truth, spontaneous and traditional, living and canonized, particular and general. And since simultaneous vision of two aspects of a situation or object is really another way of saying perspective, it is, I believe, fair to speak of Rojas' ironical separation from his work in much the same sense that we speak of Cervantes'. It may well be that certain types of commonplace perform the same artistic task for *La Celestina* as the romances of chivalry (once the thesis of satire is surpassed) do for the *Quijote*.

We shall return to this central aspect of Rojas' art later on when we have prepared the necessary background. For now I ask acceptance of the supposition that the large amount of thesis material in *La Celestina* is not to be isolated from the living texture of sentiment and argument. Rather than multiple theses (or multiple jests), the primary use of the mediaeval commonplace is as a vehicle of consciousness. As such it serves to furnish both the author and the reader with an ironical perspective into conscious life. Only in a few cases do we seem to be faced with an opinion of Rojas rather than of the speakers. We must remind ourselves once again to read from the situation—just as "Apenas el rubicundo Apolo ..." must be read from its situation and not isolated as an autonomous gem of style. Unlike the *Roman de la rose* or in a different way the *Libro de buen amor* it is not a crazy-quilt arrangement of "fontezicas de filosofiá"; these fountains rise to the surface in calculated accord with the underlying streams of Rojas' art. [9]

Having rejected as effective theses for *La Celestina,* its misleading array of traditional commonplaces, where, then, should we look? The most likely place, of course, is Pleberio's hopeless valedictory in Act XXI with its castigation of Fortune, the World, and Love as responsible for Melibea's suicide. From the point of view of thesis it is significant that Pleberio, for all the singlemindedness of his grief, should refer to the other deaths:

Si amor fuesses, amarías a tus siruientes. Si los amasses, no les darías pena. Si alegres viuiessen, no se matarían, como agora mi amada hija. ¿En qué pararon tus siruientes e sus ministros? La falsa alcahueta Celestina murió a manos de los mas fieles compañeros que ella para su seruicio emponçoñado jamás halló. Ellos murieron degollados. Calisto, despeñado. Mi triste hija quiso tomar la misma muerte por seguirle. Esto todo causas. (XXI, 210)

Thus, in Pleberio's epilogue of lament we are confronted not with commonplaces relevant only to this situation or that state of consciousness but rather with a general relevance to all the personages and to the whole of the history. Fortune, the World, and Love are determinants of life in a more radical way than those which patterned character and which were implicit in the fact of cast. They apply, or at least Pleberio seems to make them apply, to all the lives in the work. In this sense, it is fair to speak of them as constituting a résumé, a final agreement of author and character as to the meaning of what has happened.

Admitting that Act XXI represents a thesis (and in a far more developed form than the warning against blasphemy in the *incipit*), we are still faced with a major problem: to what extent are *fortuna flutuosa, mundo falso,* and *amor* actually responsible for *La Celestina?* To what extent are its style, characters, and structure of occurrence determined by such explicit and transcendental factors? Or to rephrase these questions, to what extent is the thesis creatively efficient? Now, we cannot attempt even a tentative resolution of these doubts without understanding clearly that none of the above three traditional antagonists to successful living should be considered a single entity operating in a single direction. Instead all three are dual in nature, and they function in two distinct realms. On the one hand, they are cosmic forces besetting man from without, tormenting and destroying him with all the inevitability of Nemesis. On the other, they are the expressions of a series of evaluations, false evaluations, for which each individual is morally and subjectively responsible. Fortune is an allegorical figure spinning a relentless wheel and at the same time an attitude or mode of directing behavior. In this latter sense we might call it trusting to luck, or confiding in oneself far too much. Again, but in a different way, *el mundo* is at once the world of time, space, objects, and human society which surrounds and limits man, and the deceitful evaluations—honor, wealth, rank, etc.—which make it important. Finally, love is a little god, the tyrant of mythology, and also a sentiment or discovery of value in the beloved. When Rojas copies Juan de Mena in the acrostic verses, "A otro que amores dad vuestros cuidados," he asserts the belief that love as an inner sentiment can be controlled by the will.

An evident reason for insisting on the dual nature of these commonplaces is that their inner division is related to our stylistic (or dialogic) division between sentiment and argument. Just as the commonplace of servitude and liberty could be used by Areusa to express an authentic evaluation of her own position and by Celestina to persuade Pármeno to a course of action, so Fortune, the World, and Love may either be imposed on man in the second person or joined by him in the first. With this in mind the significance of the fact that Pleberio's exegesis closes *La Celestina* becomes apparent. After the action is over and consciousness extinguished, at least two of these three entities are seen only from the outside—only as personified opponents of human life to be castigated and feared. And in the third case, that of the *mundo,* even though Pleberio's reference is primarily to false evaluation, "Ceuasnos ... con el manjar de tus deleytes," the portrait is more or less objectified:

Yo pensaua en mi mas tierna edad que eras y eran tus hechos regidos por alguna orden; agora, visto el pro e la contra de tus bienandanças, me pareces vn laberinto de errores, vn desierto espantable, vna morada de fieras, juego de hombres que andan en corro, laguna llena de cieno, región llena de espinas ... (XXI, 204)

In other words, Act XXI is a statement of the thesis precisely because it is limited to the aspect of argument. And it is no more than a statement of thesis because it cannot by its very nature embrace that complex of sentiment and argument which describes the conscious life of the work. As a thesis for *La Celestina,* it is evidently incomplete.

This denial of the efficacy of the thesis must stand or fall on the evidence of the other twenty acts. And there—at least as far as love and fortune are concerned—Pleberio's estimate of what has occurred seems to be upheld. Certainly if we were asked to choose a single motivating force for the inhabitants of *La Celestina,* that force would be love. This is not only true of the titular protagonists but also of the servants and even Celestina, who holds love's ministry for all of them. Other motives (such as the greed or vanity which correspond to *el mundo*) are present but are deeply overshadowed by the erotic compulsion which dominates the work. Then too, there is the testimony of the prologue material which insists again and again that Rojas' intention was to provide defensive armor against the arrows of love. As for Fortune, it is clearly the paramount limitation of human life and is emphasized much more than its traditional companions, Time and Death, unmentioned by Pleberio but not absent from the text.[10] Not only is Fortune repeatedly blamed by the speakers for all their misadventures[11] but also it fits very neatly the artistically inevitable (yet metaphysically casual) nature of the catastrophes. The falling which contributes to the deaths of Parmeno and Sempronio as well as to those of Calisto and Melibea reflects, as we shall see, the fall from Fortune's wheel. And if we add to this the fact that the major source for so many of the commonplaces of the text (as well as of the *Prólogo*) is the *De remediis utriusque fortunae,* Pleberio would seem to be confirmed in his estimate. The co-operation of Love and Fortune for the destruction of the vulnerable individual has all the appearances of an efficient thesis.

Such is the seemingly strong argument which can be made for *La Celestina*'s being governed decisively by its thesis.[12] But when we realize that the admission of such a thesis as creatively valid, immediately identifies Rojas' art with a tradition reaching from the Alexandrine novel through the Middle Ages and into the seventeenth-century,[13] we return instinctively to our previous denial. The very nature of our reading experience will not allow us to equate *La Celestina* to such works as Machaut's *Remède de Fortune,* appropriate episodes of the *De casibus,* or even Chaucer's *Troilus and Cressida.* Although Love and Fortune are the prime movers in all these works they seem somehow different—dimensionally withdrawn—from the Love and Fortune that are active in *La Celestina.* What has happened, as I hope to show, is that in accord with Rojas' art both of them have been transferred from the status of thesis to that of theme. And in this transferral they undergo inevitable and profound metamorphosis.

A brief comparison with the *Troilus and Cressida* will illustrate the problem. There, in spite of the delicacy and psychological penetration of the dialogue, Chaucer sets within the foreordained future of Troy the necessary failure of a prince's love (a love imposed from without) at the hands of Fortune. In passage after passage he exercises his privilege as narrator to intervene and, by stressing the hopelessness of Troilus' situation, to contradict the go-between, Pander, who lamely defends freedom of will and action. Fortune has become a kind of destiny for Chaucer, a destiny which he feels called upon to advocate, even though, as Farnham points out, "The more alive Troilus and Cressida are, the more they act as though not wholly enchained by an external necessity."[14] Thus, transcendent Fortune, the goddess Fortune, offers an ever-present temptation to thesis in spite of the fact that Chaucer "comes to distill his actual experience of life into this . . . poem" and is able to make his creatures "act vitally, that is, purposefully and hopefully."[15] And much the same could be said about love in the work.[16] In *La Celestina,* on the other hand, the dialogic form in and of itself (discounting the possibility of allegorical speakers) prevents this kind of intervention. Fortune and Love may or may not be transcendent and irresistible forces, but they are subordinated to the situation of the dialogue at the moment, to its complex of interlocking sentiment and argument. And even when they are mentioned explicitly by the speakers, they serve, like other commonplaces, for the communication of particular experiences or desires. They are integrated with rather than opposed to conscious life.

Rojas' artistry of thesis, then, is clearly an ex post facto artistry, an artistry of prologue and epilogue. He and his characters may deduce the efficient domination of a traditional concept of love and a traditional concept of fortune after meditating on the whole;[17] but in the sequence of particular situations in dialogue which make up that whole, tradition gives way to artistic innovation. Let us conclude with a single example. When Celestina remembers her past prosperity in Act XII, she whines:

Yo ví, mi amor, a esta mesa, donde agora están tus primas assentadas, nueue moças de tus días, que la mayor no passaba de dieziocho años e ninguna hauía menor de quatorze. Mundo es, passe, ande su rueda, rodee sus alcaduzes, vnos llenos, otros vazíos. La ley es de fortuna que ninguna cosa en vn ser mucho tiempo permanesce: su orden es mudanças. No puedo dezir sin lágrimas la mucha honrra que entonces tenía ... (IX, 43–44)

Aside from that ironic juncture of commonplace and context already considered (here, the irony relates as much to "honrra" as to fortune, or more, we may notice how Fortune is mentioned in passing by Celestina, and only in terms of the sadness and resignation of the moment. There is no underlining by Rojas, no assertion comparable to that of Calderón when Segismundo reminds us that "la vida es sueño—y los sueños sueños son." There is not even an implication of agreement between author and speaker such as we find in Act XXI or when Sempronio denounces stylistic adornment in Act VIII. But, having relegated the artistry of thesis to such a secondary position, the major question remains: in what way do Fortune and Love (as well as other familiar theses of the time) function in *La Celestina?* They are undeniably present, even if they are not to be identified with their occasional mention by the speakers. And if they are there, if Fortune and Love are indeed significant, how and in what new form?

2. From Thesis to Theme - Fortune

Our suspicion that fortune and love are not now either conventionally or actually divine, that in *La Celestina* the goddess with her wheel and Cupid with his bow have been surpassed artistically, is an invitation to return to the text. Let us begin with fortune and try to find out not what is said about it (we have already rejected this approach) but exactly how it functions in determining or limiting the lives of the work. For this the death of Calisto will be of decisive importance. The reader is led to expect his death both by the prologue material (particularly the *incipit* with its moral *reprehensión*) and by certain premonitions included in Act I. Sempronio, for example, specifically predicts the retribution to which Calisto exposes himself: "Lee los ystoriales, estudia los filósofos, mira los poetas. Llenos están los libros de sus viles e malos exemplos e de las caydas que leuaron los que en algo, como tú, las reputaron." (I, 47) Nevertheless, in the end Rojas does not stress punishment so much as accident—that is to say naked chance stripped of all moral purpose. This is true of the *Comedia* with its sudden misstep from the ladder, but it is even more true of the *Tragicomedia*. For in the added acts he seems intentionally to avoid the denouement of violent revenge made possible by Areusa's intrigue. He complicates the death with a new chain of circumstances and, in doing so, clarifies even more its accidental antecedents, its absence of fatality. Sempronio's "caydas," traditionally the result of pride and high position (for example, Alexander and Nimrod with their mediaeval *hubris* both compared in the same sentence of Act I to Calisto), are thus converted into a dark night, a high ladder, and a moment of carelessness. The allegorical fall from fortune's wheel becomes an actual fall in which gravity plays the leading part. And Fortune, herself, is reduced to the inescapable hazard of man's existence in alien space. As thesis is replaced by theme, death becomes independent of transgression.[18]

If we tentatively replace the word "fortune" with the word "space"— remembering that the individual speakers are not inclined to confirm the substitution in their use of commonplaces—there results an immediate illumination of *La Celestina* from within. Our initial remarks on the nature of theme begin to be justified, as all sorts of aspects demand attention and comment at the same time. For the moment, however, let us not abandon the notion of "la cayda" which serves as a bridge between the two concepts and which is certainly one key to the singularity of the work. The four deaths by falling (although the servants officially are executed, it is significant that Rojas chooses to make a fall the efficient cause of their demise) are prepared for by a continuing preoccupation with both levels of significance of the word. Sempronio's traditional and semi-allegorical use of "cayda" reoccurs in half a dozen ironical contexts: for example, Parmeno's "Riqueza desseo; pero quien torpemente sube a lo alto, mas ayna cae que subió" (I, 103); Celestina's "No sé como puedo viuir, cayendo de tal estado" (IX, 47); or Sosia's warning to Calisto, "Recuerda e leuanta, que si tu no buelues por los tuyos, de cayda vamos" (XIII, 109). In these sentences the fall in space is semantically absorbed by the commonplace of fortune with its inevitable transfer of man from high to low estate.

In Sempronio's "Que primero, que cayga del todo, dará señal, como casa que se acuesta" (III, 129), however, the allegorical implication is reinforced with an image of gravity and acceleration. Space and spatial disintegration, "casa que se acuesta" have been injected unconsciously into fortune's moral hierarchy. But beyond this we must note the purely physical preoccupation with falling which appears and reappers in the work. Elicia warns Celestina: "¿Cómo vienes tan tarde? No lo deues hazer, que eres vieja; tropeçarás donde caygas e mueras." But Celestina is a mistress of space as well as of the human soul, and she replies: No temo esso, que de día me auiso por donde venga de noche. *Que jamás me subo por poyo ni calçada, sino por medio de la calle. Porque, como dizen: no da passo seguro quien corre por el muro e que aquel va más sano que anda por llano.* (XI, 74-75). Or again when Melibea, waiting for Calisto, imagines the dangers of the alien night, among which is the following: *"O si ha caydo en alguna calçada o hoyo, donde algún daño le viniesse?"* (XIV, 115) Thus, these two vertigoes joined in a single word illustrate the transition from thesis to theme, from fortune to space. The moral limitations of man (ironically reduced from situation to situation) have been replaced by the ultimate dimensional limitations of human life.[19] It is only these latter limitations which are now capable of producing catastrophe.

Given the importance of "la cayda" as an indication of the thematic metamorphosis of fortune, we might expect to find reference to it in the prologue material—alongside attempts to assert the thesis. In fact, in the acrostic verses there is mention of the myth of Daedalus and Icarus: "No hizo Dédalo cierto a mi ver—Alguna mas prima entretalladura," and in the *Prólogo* a reference to the fabulous bird of the *Arabian Nights:*

De una ave llamada rocho, que nace en el índico mar de oriente, se dize ser de grandeza jamas oyda e que lleva sobre su pico fasta las nuues, no solo un hombre o diez, pero un nauío cargado de todas sus xarcias e gente. E como los miseros navegantes estén assí suspensos en el ayre, con el meneo de su buelo caen e reciben crueles muertes.[20] (22)

Although it would be misleading to claim in either case that Rojas intended to refer to his theme, both "Dédalo" and the "rocho" may well betray the same preoccupation continuing beyond the actual process of creation. Furthermore, it is significant that both references raise "la cayda" to the level of mythological illustration (and so give it a finality of meaning unavailable to the particular catastrophes of the text) and that both are the result of flying. We are also reminded of Rojas' comparison in the acrostic verses of his creative act to the ant who grows wings, takes to the air, and is devoured by birds. The phrase "el ayre ... ageno y estraño" is an expression of that hazardous thematic space which surrounds and destroys the individual with his "alas ... nublosas nascidas de ogaño."[21] Again space in its pure dimensionality is made to bring out the insignificance and vulnerability of its inhabitants.

This aspect of the theme of *La Celestina* is reminiscent of Breughel's wellknown *Fall of Icarus* (1554), another illustration of the unconcern of the spatial universe to man's fall. Breughel and Rojas, who were roughly contemporary, seem to coincide in their bitter recognition of a world beyond human bounds which becomes thematically a final determinant of the frailty of life. Thus, Icarus' melted wings in the far distance and Calisto's brains scattered over the "cantos" are both results of the metamorphosis of fortune. Possible thematic resemblance to the *Icarus* of Breughel is further confirmed by a certain circumstance of the death of Melibea. Without revealing to Pleberio her intention to commit suicide, she explains her desire to climb to the "açotea" in the following manner: "Subamos señor, al açotea alta, porque desde allí goze de la deleytosa vista de los nauíos ..." (XX [Vol. II], 190–91) It is a sentence which suggests that the "açotea" is not only an instrument of death but also a point of view (in the primary sense of the phrase) embracing long perspectives of land and sea. But it is the mention of "nauios," a perplexing problem for those scholars who have tried to locate the city of *La Celestina*,[22] that is particularly clarified by the painting. For Breughel and other painters of the time, the sea and ships, the seascape from the land, is a customary background. It portrays in accepted fashion the uncertainties and attractions of sheer distance, the alien fascination of space. The allegorical figure or emblem of the "fortune of the seas" commented on by Patch[23] has, in a sense, been replaced by extensions of sea and lonely ships. It is, therefore, significant that Rojas should at the moment of Melibea's "cayda" indicate a similar view. Like the description of Gloucester's mock suicide in *King Lear,* both Breughel and Rojas represent Fortune's new dimensionality with a fall and far off ships—that is to say, height and distance together. Melibea mentions "navios" in accord with the graphic language of her time just as she strings together classical precedents in accord with the literary language.[24]

The thematic space of *La Celestina* is, thus, fully dimensional—horizontally as well as vertically "ageno y estraño" to life and its concerns. As a result its role is not limited to climactic falling. Rather, as we saw in the analysis of structure, most of the dialogic situations are both defined and brought to full significance by spatial determination. Space is a continuing and effective condition of life as well as a cause of death. The structural delimitation is a thematic limitation as well. This is, of course, particularly evident in that undercurrent of spatial preoccupation which may be detected beneath the

THE FALL OF ICARUS

From a painting by Pieter Breughel

surface of selected commonplaces and which wells up through the most unlikely contexts and the most casual remarks. In Act I, for example, Sempronio defines in a significantly off-hand way the nature of spatial perception: "La vista a quien objeto no se interpone cansa. E quando aquel es cerca agúzase." (I, 38) In other words, it is not space as such that is the circumstance of consciousness but rather barrier and distance—precisely as in the case of the art of structure. Space is the medium of movement and vision and so exists in immediate partnership with feelings and motives—with fear, love, pride, and any number of others. It is the final arbiter of possibility and impossibility. In this sense, Celestina's remarks on the cunning of women in love give an almost choral elevation to that intimate warfare of sentiment and space already noticed:

Catíuanse del primer abraço, ruegan a quien rogó, penan por el penado, házense sieruas de quien eran señoras, dexan el mando y son mandadas, rompen paredes, abren ventanas, fingen enfermedades, a los cherriadores quicios de las puertas hazen con azeytes usar su oficio sin ruydo. (III, 138)

Here the idea of barrier surpasses the particular barriers of the action and, with diction that reaches the frontier of poetry, takes on the generality of theme. The thematic pregnancy of doors, walls, and windows has raised them from mere elements of scenic structure to poetic mention for their own sake.

In other places a lack of barrier, the availability of distance, results in similar expressiveness. We may notice, for example, how freedom of movement is interpreted as supernatural by Celestina:

Quatro hombres, que he topado, a los tres llaman Juanes e los dos son cornudos. La primera palabra que oy por la calle, fue de achaque de amores. Nunca he tropeçado como otras vezes. *Las piedras parece que se apartan e me fazen lugar que passe. Ni me estoruan las haldas ni siento cansancio en andar. Todos me saludan.* Ni perro me ha ladrado, ni aue negra he visto ... E lo mejor de todo es que veo a Lucrecia a la puerta de Melibea. (IV, 156–58)

The difference between this skillfully interpolated moment of consciousness and the sentence which follows—"... veo a Lucrecia a la puerta ..."—is exactly the difference between merely structural use of space and its thematic exaltation. In the one case there is transition and evident preparation of scene; in the other, there is a conscious and verbal realization of liberated movement. Space—as we phrased it previously—is here the thematic partner of Celestina's vocation, and again achieves an almost poetic description.

Of this direct yet casual correlation of spatial freedom or impediment to consciousness, *La Celestina* offers an embarrassment of riches, and there is no need to accumulate examples here. The naked minds of the characters are faced with a naked world, a world of dizzy heights, far perspectives, and silhouetted obstacles. Just to live in this alien space with its "dañosos y hondos barrancos" requires a maximum of cunning. As Celestina—who "de día se auisa por donde venga de noche"—says, "¡Quién no tiene sino vn ojo, mira a quanto peligro anda!" (VII, 255) But mere living with its incessantly necessary calculation of perspective is insufficient. It is, as we have seen and shall see again, the hopeless task of those ·who dwell within such radical inhospitality to create human values and find human consolation—in short, to war against it with their lives.

3. From Thesis to Theme - Death and Time

Realization that the role of space in the scenic structure of *La Celestina* may correspond to its thematic replacement of fortune, reminds us of that other dimensional component of the dialogic situation: time. And time, in its turn, reminds us of death, that same death which goes hand in hand with time and fortune through the didactic writing of the late Middle Ages. Salinas remarks as follows of their community:

Ya están completos los tres sirvientes más fieles de esa empresa de menosprecio del mundo, los tres incansables. Porque si el tiempo no para, si la muerte no descansa, tampoco se esta quieta un segundo la rueda de la Fortuna. De seguro que en algunas atribuladas imaginaciones de la Edad Media, atormentadas por la cogitación sobre el destino humano, esas tres grandes figuras simbólicas de otras tantas tremendas realidades debieron aparecer al modo de tres gigantescos pastores, que empujaban a la grey de los humanos hacia el desengaño de todo lo terrenal; tres fantasmas invisibles y siempre al lado, cuya voz se sentía amenazadora, aun en los momentos esos en que las apariencias del mundo fingen las formas mas engañosas de la alegria y la confianza.[25]

Thus, we seem to be confronted with two problems: not only the thematic role of time in *La Celestina* but also the fate of both Time and Death as theses—as didactic commonplaces on the same transcendental plane as Fortune. But, as we shall see, they are problems which converge on a single solution.

To begin with, Death in *La Celestina* seems to have lost much of the significance seen for it by Salinas. It appears to have been reduced almost to a mere termination of life, a mere *dejar de existir,* to use the contemporary formula of journalism. One of the most convincing signs of this change is Rojas' disinterest in the traditional thesis of the *Danza de la muerte.* He fails consistently and it would seem purposefully to underline the so-called democratic death of his time—to notice Death's unrelenting equalization of rich and poor, fair and plain, proud and humble, foolish and wise.[26] Even more, in Pleberio's lament, instead of personification and castigation of Death (as of Fortune, Love, and the World) we find the following:

... yo no lloro a ella muerta, pero la causa desastrada de su morir. Agora perderé contigo, mi desdichada hija, los miedos e temores que cada dia me espauorecían: sola tu muerte es la que a mí me haze seguro de sospecha.

¿Qué haré, quando entre en tu camara e retraymiento e la halle sola? ¿Qué haré de que no me respondas, si te llamo? (XXI, 207–8)

Thus it is not Death which grieves Pleberio but its causes and results in life. In *La Celestina*, unlike the *Libro de buen amor*, Death no longer seems to be a valid generalization.[27]

This loss of validity may best be understood by reconsidering the thematic metamorphosis of fortune. Fortune and its fall had been in preceding centuries an aspect of man's condition or, as Salinas phrased it, of "el destino humano." The falls in *La Celestina*, on the other hand, are not generic but personal. They result not from the condition of man as man but from each individual's enforced and solitary existence in space. One is preoccupied by Fortune because he is a man and subject to human weakness; by space, because he personally is alive. Thus, a delayed and personified threat of retribution has been replaced by a continuing dimensional presence, an antagonist to life utterly without regard for human misconduct. But Death, unlike Fortune, is incapable of such particularization. It cannot be transformed from a condition of the genus man to a condition of the individual life, precisely because it is a negation of that life. Death may loom over man as the grim reaper, a fit companion for perverse Fortune, but from within life itself it is so alien as to be almost unimaginable.[28] Even when it does descend, and in a moment life is gone, nothing remains but an incident and an absence. This loss of significance, apparent in Pleberio's lament, is cynically confirmed when Sempronio includes "muerto es tu padre" and "Ynés se ahorcó" in his list of easily forgotten incidents. Life goes on, and in their turn the atrocious deaths of Act XII will be forgotten: first by Areusa ("... verás con quanta paciencia lo çuffro y passo ...") and then by Elicia. There are as a result five casualties in *La Celestina* but no Death in the traditional sense of the word. It cannot exist for the living consciousness of an authentic dialogue.

One might be tempted to point to the works of Quevedo and Heidegger in order to refute the above propositions.[29] But for each of these thinkers the presence of death in life is discovered and described by a process of logical interpolation that is foreign to the sentiment of self. In any case, whether ascetic, conceptistic, or existentialist, the evidence necessary for consciousness of growth towards death can only be obtained from aging and sickness—

neither of which is effective thematically in *La Celestina*. Rather than linger-ing demise, we find that in its world death is sudden and violent: "¡O muerte muerte! ... Por uno que comes con tiempo, cortas mil en agraz." (III, 135) It is also significant that when Celestina does illustrate in detail the physical decline of old age—"aquel hundimiento de boca, aquel caer de dientes, aquel carecer de fuerça"—all of which would have been exploited by a Quevedo, she prefaces her remarks with "Todo por viuir." (IV, 165) In other words, even though death may not be as radically inconceivable from within life as is sometimes claimed, for *La Celestina* and its thematic vision, the opposition of the two is significant. As a result the very absence of death commonplaces may be thought of as an aspect of the theme.[30]

Such a hindrance to thematic contribution is not at all effective in the case of time. Time is a preoccupation of man primarily because he is alive and so has no specifically moral implications. Without the need of a new discovery like space, it is an immediate condition of all life. Petrarch may, for example, deny the concept of fortune to the animal world; doctrine may affirm that the death of animals is of a different order from that of men (as Calisto says, "si el purgatorio es tal, mas querría que mi espíritu fuese con los de los brutos animales"); but, by the very fact of being alive, animals share space and, above all, time with man. As a result time can pass from tradi-tional thesis to thematic preoccupation—from malign personification to haz-ardous dimension—without difficulty or startling metamorphosis. Sempronio's discourse on the temporality of human concerns (a discourse which Madariaga terms the "most significant" of the whole work) renovates the age-old com-monplace with contemporary reminiscence but does not change it basically:

Que no ay cosa tan dificile de çofrir en sus principios, que el tiempo no la ablande e faga comportable. Ninguna llaga tanto se sintió, que por luengo tiempo no afloxase su tormento, ni plazer tan alegre fué, que no le amengüe su antiguedad. El mal e el bién, la prosperidad e aduersidad, la gloria e pena, todo pierde con el tiempo la fuerça de su acelerado principio. Pues los casos de admiración e venidos con gran desseo, tan presto como passados, oluidados. Cada día vemos nouedades e las oymos e las passamos e dexamos atras. Diminúyelas el tiempo, házelas con-tingibles. ¿Que tanto te marauillarías si dixesen: la tierra tembló o otra semejante cosa, que no oluidases luego? Assí como: elado esta el río, el ciego vee ya, muerto es tu padre, vn rayo cayó, ganada es Granada, el Rey entra oy, el turco es vencido, eclipse ay mañana, la puente es lleuada, aquel es ya obispo, a Pedro robaron ... Cristóbal fué borracho. ¿Qué me dirás, sino que a tres dias passados o a la segunda vista, no ay quien dello se marauille? Todo es assí, todo passa desta manera, todo se oluida, todo queda atrás ... *Que la costumbre luenga amansa los dolores, afloxa e deshaze los deleytes, desmengua las marauillas.* Procuremos prouecho mientra pendiere la contienda. (III, 129–32)

There is only one significant difference between this presentation of time and that of the "ubi sunt" commonplace of previous years. In the latter, time passes by objects, atmospheres, and men, while for Sempronio time joins life from within causing the individual to forget past evaluations and excitements. Preoccupation with time joins preoccupation with space at the roots of the consciousness of being alive. Otherwise Sempronio's assertions are not unlike those describing Father Time in the preceding century.

It was necessary to reproduce this passage again not only because it offers key testimony to the thematic role of time but also because as a commonplace it is open to the suspicion of irony. Yet it is clear that Rojas does not intend here to emphasize his usual counterpoint of vital context with traditional doctrine. Sempronio's conclusion, "assí será este amor de mi amo," and his proposed course of action, "Procuremos provecho," are perhaps unworthy of his doctrine. They may even seem artistically out of balance when compared to the lengthy discourse which preceded them. But their cynicism is in fundamental accord with the corrosive nature of Sempronio's understanding of time. Sempronio is perversely delighted with temporality rather than sadder and wiser, and he concludes not with "menosprecio del mundo" but with "menosprecio de la persona," that very same "persona" whose life is thematically subject to dimensionality.[31] Lacking irony, then, we may conclude tentatively that time and space are given equal thematic roles because they are both dimensions. Obliteration by falling or obliteration by the passage of days and years are major hazards of life in a universe which no longer demands "menosprecio del mundo" as the correct moral response but which is instead radically "ageno e estrano" to body and mind. The nature of Rojas' innovation in theme begins to be clear: he has reduced Fortune from an allegorical personage to its temporal and spatial media of operation. And in doing so, he substitutes human lives for literature's previous didactic and exemplary concern with man.

A curious corollary to this thematic "sea-change" is Rojas' new kind of animal illustration. All along La Celestina's continuing argument, precedents are chosen not just from antiquity but also from the world of animals. We may remember Celestina's calculated pedantry when she tries to persuade Pármeno to tolerance of his master's love:

... el que verdaderamente ama es necesario que se turbe con la dulçura del soberano deleyte, que por el hazedor de las cosas fue puesto, porque el linaje de los hombres perpetuase, sin lo qual perescería. E no solo en la humana especie; mas en los pesces, en las bestias, en las aues, en las reptilias y en lo vegetatiuo algunas plantas han este respeto, si sin interposición de otra cosa en poca distancia de tierra están puestas, en que ay determinación de heruolarios e agricultores, ser machos e hembras. (I, 95)

Later she informs Melibea of the "piedad" of "los brutos animales" with further lessons from natural history, and there are other examples aside from those of the *Prólogo*. The significance of these excursions outside the world of men resides in Rojas' treatment of animals as animals—as sharing certain traits of human life in their own way. Unlike Trotaconventos, Celestina is not interested in animals who are facsimiles of men; she rejects the fable with its incarnation of human characteristics in exemplary lions, foxes, and mice. The fable, after all, finds its thesis in man's behavior, while Rojas, preoccupied thematically by dimensions which condition life, can go beyond the "humana especie" and introduce the lives and habits of other orders of creation.[32]

If not anthropomorphic in his animal references, Rojas is fully and purposefully anthropocentric. The lives of animals only serve as passing or picturesque comparison to the lives of men—lives which possess the almost divine capacity of consciousness, self-awareness. In saying this we are reminded of Celestina's explanation of "deleyte" with its despective conclusion: "lo al, mejor lo fazen los asnos en el prado." But it is not only "lo al" which the individual transforms and intensifies with consciousness and speech; it is also space and time. It was in conjunction with consciousness, in intimate warfare with it, that we saw space receiving its full thematic charge. And the same thing is true of time. Already in Sempronio's discourse we noted the change from the external passage of time to its internal effects on consciousness. Nevertheless, that discourse was still doctrinal in nature and the time it presented still an abstraction, a device of argument. It was merely the starting point of Rojas' elaboration of time in thematic *rapprochement* to human—that is to say conscious—life. Sempronio was primarily concerned with the opposition of time to love, the decline of passion as it recedes into the past. And by examining other and more vital encounters of the same two antagonists, we may gauge the full significance of time as an element of theme. Just as in given situations spatial awareness was sharpened by the demands of love, so with time. It is precisely within such situations that this aspect of the theme is fulfilled.

Love, Celestina informs us on several occasions, in its passionate impetus chafes at the inexorable passage of time and alternately demands acceleration or deceleration. The lover waiting for his beloved is, beyond all other mortals, impatient: "No es cosa mas propia del que ama que la impaciencia. Toda tardança les es tormento. Ninguna dilación les agrada. En vn momento quer-

rían poner en efeto sus cogitaciones." (III, 128) On the other hand, when he
is with her (or she with him), he wishes that the heedless minutes would
pass as hours: "Si de noche caminan, nunca querrían que amaneciese: mal-
dizen los gallos porque anuncian el día e el relox porque da tan apriessa."
(III, 138) Whatever remains of doctrine in these statements is soon confirmed in life. Calisto, for example, sees Celestina coming towards his house
after her first interview with Melibea and murmurs in anguish:

¡O! ¡si en sueño se passasse este poco tiempo, hasta ver el principio e fin de su
habla! Agora tengo por cierto que es mas penoso al delinquente esperar la cruda
e capital sentencia, que el acto de la ya sabida muerte. ¡O espacioso Parmeno,
manos de muerto! Quita ya essa enojosa aldaua: entrará essa honrrada duena,
en cuya lengua esta mi vida. (V, 201)

Apart from whatever confirmation of death's loss of validity these statements
may offer, the desire to sleep and the comparison with a condemned man
reveal a consciousness rubbed raw by time, a consciousness caught in acute
thematic crisis.

The opposite conflict emerges in one of Calisto's last speeches, a speech
not without some implication of amorous satisfaction: "Jamás querría, señora,
que amaneciesse, según la gloria e descanso que mi sentido recibe de la
noble conversación de tus delicados miembros." (XIX, 182) Sempronio had
looked at love from the point of view of time and found it subject to
spiritual erosion and forgetfulness;[33] here time, seen from the point of
view of love, does not decrease but rather sharpens the awareness. Like an
intervening door in space, time's very unconcern with love is a stimulus to
consciousness. Hence, the preoccupation with clocks and hours which betrays
this aspect of the theme in all parts of La Celestina. There is probably no cast
of characters in western literature which is more aware, not of Time as the
mournful accomplice of Death and Fortune, but of the particular time of the
night or day. Hence, too, the structural utility of time in the internal definition of scenes. In these, as we have seen, time and space (often joined visually as light and darkness) co-operate in the maintenance of authentic dialogue and consciousness. When they are missing as in certain passages of
Act I, there is an inevitable tendency to comic interchange or Corbacho-like
expansion of style.[34]

The opposition of time and love is not, however, limited to pessimistic
predictions of time's ultimate victory or to those moments of intensified
awareness when the conflict is at its sharpest. Rojas also allows love, if only
briefly, to gain the upper hand. Either in moments of satisfaction or in the
long hours of despair, love is often capable of shutting out time and space—

of offering an illusory antidote to awareness of dimensions. We have already seen the way Rojas balanced the first and last situations of Act VIII by having the window thrown open and allowing daylight to enter. It is there that the defenses of love against the onslaught of time are most strikingly emphasized:

> PARM.—¿Amanesce o qué es esto, que tanta claridad está en esta camara?
> AREU.—¿Qué amanecer? Duerme, señor, que avn agora nos acostamos. No he yo pegado bien los ojos, ¿ya hauía de ser de dia? (VIII, 7)

> CAL.—¿Es muy noche? ¿Es hora de acostar?
> PARM.—¡Mas ya es, señor, tarde para leuantàr!
> CAL.—¿Qué dizes, loco? ¿Toda la noche es passada?
> PARM.—E avn harta parte del día. (VIII, 19)

Areusa recalled from delight and Calisto recalled from the morbid pleasures of despair ("Coraçón bien se te emplea—Que penes e viuas triste ...") cannot believe the evidence of morning. As each returns to space and time, there is something of caricature—of purposeful exaggeration and distortion—in his previous blindness. Independence of time is more a delusion than a possibility, a lack of awareness rather than a new sort of awareness. But, in any case, the intentional symmetry of structure illustrates Rojas' progressive exploration of the conflict of time and love. He seems to be on the verge of discovering a variety of time which, as we shall see, he had known intuitively all along: duration, or "psychological" time.

Calisto's great soliloquy in Act XIV brings final issue to time's alternate victories and defeats in its war with love. Added in 1502, it seems to express Rojas' full possession of this aspect of his theme and so will serve as a conclusion to our comments. Calisto begins by recalling the traditional relationship of time and human life:

¡O mísera suauidad desta breuíssima vida! ¿Quién es de ti tan cobdicioso que no quiera mas morir luego que gozar un año de vida denostado e prorogarle con deshonrra, corrompiendo la buena fama de los passados? Mayormente que no ay hora cierta ni limitada, ni avn un solo momento. Deudores somos sin tiempo, contino estamos obligados a pagar luego ... ¡O breue deleyte mundano! ¡Cómo duran poco y cuestan mucho tus dulçores! (XIV, 123)

Time as a commonplace wins the first round by default, but a few moments later love returns to the attack. The battle is rejoined in anguished awareness when, forgetting honor, Calisto reveals his impatience for the next rendezvous with Melibea:

¡O luziente Febo, date priessa a tu acostumbrado camino! ¡O deleytosas estrellas, apareceos ante de la continua orden! ¡O espacioso relox, avn te vea yo arder en biuo fuego de amor! Que si tú esperasses lo que yo, quando des doze, jamás estarías arrendado a la voluntad del maestro que te compuso. (XIV, 128)

After this culmination of anguish, Calisto envisions love itself as a rest in the struggle with time. He sees it as a temporary check to awareness:

Pues ¡vosotros, invernales meses, que agora estays escondidos!: ¡viniessedes con vuestras muy complidas noches a trocarlas por estos prólixos dias! Ya me paresce hauer vn año que no he visto aquel suaue descanso, aquel *deleytoso refrigerio de mis trabajos* [italics mine]. (XIV, 128)

Against this recollection of love's release from dimensionality (the same release that was found by Pármeno and Areusa), time returns not as a commonplace or as an annoying clock but with all the prestige of its universal ordering:

¿Pero qué es lo que demando? ¿Qué pido, loco, sin sufrimiento? Lo que jamas fué ni puede ser. No aprenden los cursos naturales a rodearse sin orden, que a todos es vn ygual curso, a todos vn mesmo espacio para muerte y vida, vn limitado término a los secretos mouimientos del alto firmamento celestial de los planetas, y norte de los crescimientos e mengua de la menstrua luna. Todo se rige con vn freno ygual, todo se mueue con igual espuela: cielo, tierra, mar, fuego, viento, calor, frío. ¿Qué me aprouecha a mí que dé doze horas el relox de hierro, si no las ha dado el del cielo? Pues, por mucho que madrugue, no amanesce mas ayna. (XIV, 128–29)

Thus, time has joined alien space explicitly and as a full partner. At the end of its thematic evolution (and we may notice how the stages of the evolution have been retraced in this soliloquy), it is given dimensional status. It is an "ygual curso," a condition of life that is both "ageno e estraño"—as is brought out in the final proverb. The thematic circumstance is now complete and transcendent Fortune reduced to its dimensional media. It is even suggestive to wonder whether Pleberio's special emphasis on "el mundo" in Act XXI as an active cause of life's defeat may not correspond in some way to the time and space of the theme. After all, time and space are both the dimensions and the only efficient reality of Rojas' version of "hac lachrymarum valle."

But to return to time as presented in Calisto's soliloquy, its victory would now appear to be complete. For what can Calisto or any of the others oppose to an antagonist at once so unconcerned and so cosmic? A possible answer is given in the first sentence of the final paragraph: "Pero tú, dulce ymaginación, tú que puedes, me acorre ..." Before we can realize the full meaning of such an answer to time, however, we must understand better the nature of love in

La Celestina. If Fortune has become in Rojas' hands the dimensions of time and space, what will he do with the blessing or curse of love?

4. From Thesis to Theme - Love

Often when the inhabitants of *La Celestina* speak of love, they do so with the language of mythology—presenting themselves as naked and defenseless against the love god's golden arrows. Calisto remarks to Pármeno in Act II: "Si tu sintiesses mi dolor, con otra agua rociarías aquella ardiente llaga, que la cruel frecha de Cupido me ha causado." (II, 122) Act X is constructed, as we have seen, around the conceit of Melibea's wound and Celestina's surgery. And even the moral justification of the work in the *Carta's* "defensivas armas para resistir sus fuegos" seems to confirm this interpretation of love. Again and again, love is explained as caused by an arrow and accompanied by an intolerable fire of the spirit.[35] Hence, Menéndez Pelayo finds abundant textual support for his belief that love "es, para Rojas, una deidad misteriosa y terrible cuyo maléfico influjo emponzoña y corrompe la vida humana."[36] His words are figurative, of course; there is no allegorical pretense (as in the *Roman de la rose*) of divine sponsorship. But, even so, if we are to believe Menéndez Pelayo, who in turn believes Calisto, Melibea, and above all, Pleberio, we must conclude that love is a transcendent imposition upon man's intimacy, a fatal passion to which he must submit, no matter what betide. Love is a fit companion for the goddess, Fortuna, and if not actually personified, it might as well be.

We have, however, seen enough of Rojas' art of theme to realize that it is not safe to take such statements by the characters at their face value. Although Calisto and Melibea feel themselves to be in the grip of blinding and exemplary passions, although Celestina invokes demoniac assistance in awakening passion, and although Pleberio castigates "amor" as responsible for his catastrophe, it is still licit to wonder to what extent *La Celestina* incorporates this traditional explanation of love. We ask once again: ought *La Celestina* be assimilated in thesis to Chaucer's *Troilus* and to a thousand and one other works which celebrate or chastise love as an ungovernable passion? Our answer, of course, has already been given. Love in *La Celestina* surpasses the concept of blind passion and becomes a kind of awareness—the dialogic, sentimental awareness which we have seen contributing to the patterns and trajectories of Rojas' art of character. Just as Fortune is reduced to consciousness sharpened (and ultimately extinguished) by the dimensional conditioning of life, so love is converted from mythological inevitability to the intimate "percibir sentimental" described by Max Scheler. And it is in this role that it takes thematic priority in that gallery of sentiments which endow with their inherent authenticity the dialogue of *La Celestina*. More than hate, desire, fear, anger and all the rest, it is the sentiment of love which joins the cast in mutual awareness. On these terms, love, no longer an exemplary thesis, becomes a primary aspect of theme.

To illustrate the difference between passionate and sentimental love we do not need to reread Scheler or to interpret such definitions as "el acto de amor ... juega el papel de autentico *descubridor* en nuestra aprehensión del valor—y solamente él representa ese papel; igualmente representa un *movimiento* en cuyo *proceso* irradian y se iluminan para el ser respectivos valores hasta entonces totalmente desconocidos."[37] Instead *La Celestina* offers its own unmistakably clear presentation of the matter. We have already seen Celestina's startling explanation of "deleyte" as a dialogic consciousness, and now we may look higher than this lowest rung of love's sentimental hierarchy. Sempronio in Act I presents the case for passion:

O soberano Dios, ¡quán altos son tus misterios! ¡Quánta premia pusiste en el amor, que es necessaria turbación en el amante! ... Todos passan, todos rompen, pungidos e esgarrochados como ligeros toros. Sin freno saltan por las barreras. Mandaste al hombre por la muger dexar el padre e la madre; agora no solo aquello, mas a ti e a tu ley desamparan, como agora Calisto. Del qual no me marauillo, pues los sabios, los santos, los profetas por él te oluidaron. (I, 42–43)

Blind impetus, compulsion from without, unpredictable danger even to the wisest, all characterize love as a passion and as a possibility of thesis. But when in an act far removed from this Calisto hears Melibea singing, his reaction is hardly that of a man (or a beast) driven helplessly by elemental forces:

Vencido me tiene el dulçor de tu suaue canto; no puedo mas suffrir tu penado esperar. ¡O mi señora e mi bien todo! ¿Quál muger podía auer nascida, que despriuasse tu gran merecimiento? ¡O salteada melodía! ¡O gozoso rato! ¡O coraçón mío! ¿E cómo no podiste mas tiempo sufrir sin interrumper tu gozo e complir el desseo de entrambos? (XIX, 179)

Neither timeless nor elementally blind, love exists within a "gozoso rato" of consciousness—a "rato" which sharpens almost intolerably Calisto's appreciation of his beloved. It is a sentiment in sentimental climax, an appropriate opening for the completed awareness of the second garden scene.[38]

As we have already indicated, the thematic import of sentimental love does not at all eliminate the opposing interpretation from the dialogue. Thus, love (in the same manner as Fortune and dimensions) is usually talked about as a traditional passion and lived as a sentiment—or perhaps it would be better to say as a number of possible sentiments ranging imperceptibly from "deleyte" to "gloria." It might almost be said that while for Calisto love begins as a passion (in lengthy discourse) and ends as a sentiment, for Melibea it begins as a slowly growing sentiment and ends passionately. Her climax of suicidal heroism is the result of months of sentimental evolution and is accompanied by an outburst of oratory which is in appropriate contrast with her previous reticence. On this basis, we may question severely the thematic authenticity of both their passions—particularly that of Calisto. Even the author of Act I takes good care to insist that for all his verbal anguish, he is driven neither to heroic action nor to final despair. Unlike Leriano, the hero of the *Cárcel de Amor,* Calisto allows us to suspect that Sempronio's prediction of the effects of time on his love might—in other circumstances— have been correct. It is, as we shall see, only after the success of his love and from within its engendered sentiment that Calisto becomes thematically central to *La Celestina.* In the early acts his so-called passion is so ineffective as to be derided by all who witness it. It is a mere excess of emotion, the very stuff not only of weakness but of insignificance.

But what about Melibea? Surely her *Liebestod* is sufficiently desperate and sufficiently heroic to justify passionate love as a major element of the theme (or thesis). In her own discourses and in that of Pleberio passion is explicit, and in her suicide it is certainly efficient. Yet at the same time, as Menéndez Pelayo himself points out, the end of *La Celestina* is not to be identified with that of the *Tristán.* The death of Melibea is hardly, he says, a "verdadera y triunfante apoteosis del amor libre." There is in fact no apotheosis at all, for Melibea never emerges from the emotion of grief except to excuse the effects of her action on her mother and father—that is it say, except for a purely family preoccupation. Her first reaction to Calisto's fall, "¿Qué es esto? ¿Qué oygo? ¡amarga de mí!" sets the tone for what is to follow. She goes on to bewail not so much her lover's fate as her own private loss. We may notice the dominance of the first person in these typical fragments:

¡O desconsolada de mí! ¿Qué ese esto? . . . ¡Mi bien e plazer todo es ydo en humo! ¡Mi alegría es perdida! ¡Consumióse mi gloria!

¡O la más de las tristes triste! ¡Tan tarde alcançado el plazer, tan presto venido el dolor!

¿Oyes lo que aquellos moços van hablando? ¿Oyes sus tristes cantares? ¡Rezando lleuan con responso mi bien todo! ¡Muerta lleuan mi alegria! ¡No es tiempo de yo viuir! ¿Cómo no gozé mas del gozo? ¿Cómo tuue en tan poco la gloria que entre mis manos toue? ¡O ingratos mortales! ¡Jamas conocés vuestros bienes, sino quando dellos caresceys! (XIX, 185–86)

Later on, of course, when alone on the "açotea" or when speaking to her father, Melibea attains a deceptive calmness. By the very fact of dialogue, her reason is partially detached from her grief, and she is able both to plan her death and to realize its effect on others. It is in this connection that she avails herself of the excuse of passion:

Tú, Senor, que de mi habla eres testigo, ves mi poco poder, ves quan cautiva tengo mi libertad, quan presos mis sentidos de tan poderoso amor del muerto caballero, que priua al que tengo con los viuos padres. (XX, 194)

This same point is made as a warning in the final speech to Pleberio, "Porque, quando el coraçón esta embargado de passión ..., las fructuosas palabras en lugar de amansar, acrecientan la saña." Nevertheless, in spite of these references to passion and in spite of the seeming objectivity of her discourse, Melibea, unlike Phèdre, never makes of reason a point of view and prefers to speak of such states of consciousness as "deleyte," "gozo," and "gloria" than of love in capital letters. Rather than a sacrificial victim to passion, she is in a state of shock and violent emotional upset, and it is precisely for this reason that the introduction of "Bursia, rey de Bitinia" and the others has always sounded so artificial. No one would think of criticizing similar passages in the *Fiammetta* or in the passionate novels it inspired. But for Melibea who speaks from within her love, the elevated style of the passionate apotheosis seems not so much unreal as it does alien. As she herself says a moment later, "Algunas consolatorias palabras te diría ... sino que ya la dañada memoria con la grand turbación me las ha perdido ..."

After the first outburst of purely personal emotion and the subsequent calm with its dubious rationalization, there is a third phase to Melibea's valedictory: that of sentimental awareness—of truly thematic résumé. By this I mean the evocation of Calisto and the sentimental history of their love, consciously and appropriately recollected. It is a sentiment which dwells on the value and person of the beloved, a sentiment which cannot bring itself to admit the effective death of the beloved, and accordingly Melibea hurls herself down half believing that Calisto is waiting for her: "¡O mi amor e señor Calisto! Espérame, ya voy ..." This is subtly different from the end of the *Tristán* whose lovers, according to Denis de Rougement, are more in love with love than with each other as persons.[39] Accordingly both Tristán and Iseult give death a positive significance that is quite out of the question for *La Celestina*. Death in the *Tristán* is a voluntary offering to passion, and the history leading up to this culmination only a means to an end (just as the potion is a means to a love that is thereby a passion). In *La Celestina*, on the other hand, it is only Pleberio looking back over past events who can echo the phrase, "Amour par force nous demène." But no briar will grow from the graves of Calisto and Melibea.

Granting this thematic change from traditional passion to personal sentiment, we are now ready to return to Calisto's soliloquy and to its attempted answer to the conditioning of life by time and space. Having understood at last the terrible inexorability of the physical universe, Calisto reacts in a way which reveals the central thematic conflict of *La Celestina:*

Pero tú, dulce ymaginación, tú que puedes me acorre. Trae a mi fantasía la presencia angélica de aquella ymagen luziente; buelue a mis oydos el suaue son de sus palabras, aquellos desuíos sin gana, aquel apártate alla, señor, no llegues a mí; aquel no seas descortés, que con sus rubicundos labrios vía sonar; aquel no quieras mi perdición, que de rato en rato proponía; aquellos amorosos abraços entre palabra e palabra, aquel soltarme y prenderme, aquel huir e llegarse, aquellos açucarados besos, aquella final salutación con que se me despidió. ¡Con quánta pena salio por su boca! ¡Con quántos desperezos! ¡Con quántas lágrimas, que parescían granos de aljofar, que sin sentir se le cayan de aquellos claros e resplandecientes ojos! (XIV, 129)

In this brief "recherche des temps perdus" Calisto—like Proust for Albertine —recreates from memory and imagination a segment of existence more gratifying than the agonizing exposure to dimensions of an instant before. Love, as a sentiment, has furnished him with its own duration—a duration into which he may retreat from the bleak perspectives of the cosmos. The answer is now clear: if physical space and time are conditions of human life, that life has in turn its own variety of time and space. And it is a variety which is neither "ageno" nor "estraño." Furthermore, this second space and time (space-time actually) is one of which the individual is sentimentally aware, precisely because it is replete not with facts but with sheer value. It may readily be related to Bergson's "durée."[40]

In commenting on the style of the above passage we may notice its basic resemblance to that already designated as sentimental—to that of Areusa in her imaginative expression of the experiences of freedom and servitude. There is the same lack of logical sequence and the same substitution of an evaluative ordering, a mounting of sentiment to its own climax. There is even a similar use of fragments of imaginary dialogue as well as expansion of single references into repetitive pluralities. But there is also one major difference: Areusa imagines her two situations for life in the present tense, while Calisto remembers his experience in the imperfect, the classic tense of duration. The rendezvous with Melibea exists neither in an irrevocable past

nor in an imaginary present but rather in the time of experience and continuing value—a time which is at once (and neither) present and past. As Proust
says in his extraordinary discussion of Flaubert's style,

Cet imparfait si nouveau dans la littérature change entièrement l'aspect des choses
et des êtres. ... Cet imparfait sert à rapporter non seulement les paroles mais toute
la vie des gens. *L'éducation sentimentale* est un long rapport de toute une vie,
sans que les personnages prennent pour ainsi dire une part active à l'action.[41]

It is not love, in and of itself, which Calisto opposes to dimensions but love
as a sentiment and as an authentic experience in its own duration. As the
major sentiment of the work—as the primary experience of almost all the
characters—it can furnish its own inner defense against a Fortune which has
become time and space. Thus, although *La Celestina* is more a *faillite sentimentale* than an *éducation sentimentale,* Calisto and the others can at times
take refuge in an imperfect comparable to that of Flaubert and Proust.[42]

To sum up, in *La Celestina* there is not only a quantitative justification
for the thematic importance of love but also a qualitative justification. As a
sentiment, love endows the individual life with something more than the
transitory and pointless violence which accompanies the outbursts of Elicia
and Areusa. At least for Calisto and Melibea, it possesses the additional
authenticity of experience, of an experience which is neither rationalized nor
imaginary but profoundly lived. But I must hasten to add that these two are
not the only ones to oppose the duration of sentimental awareness to dimensions. Calisto's monologue merely makes explicit a fundamental thematic
opposition which has been implicit all along. Of the major characters, we
may notice Celestina in particular as living in the presence of the past. Characteristically she uses her memory not so much for reminiscence as for evaluative recall—not so much to spin out the isolated scenes or adventures usual to
old people, as for re-creation of a whole mode of sentimental experience. We
may notice the inner resemblance of this evocation of Claudina to Calisto's
sentimental evocation of Melibea:

SEMP.—¿Tantos días ha que le conoces, madre?
CEL.—Aquí está Celestina, que le vido nascer e le ayudó a criar. Su madre e
yo, vña e carne. Della aprendí todo lo mejor que sé de mi oficio. Juntas comíamos,
juntas dormíamos, juntas auíamos nuestros solazes, nuestros plazeres, nuestros
consejos e conciertos. En casa e fuera como dos hermanas. Nunca blanca gané en
que no touiesse su meytad. Pero no viuía yo engañada, si mi fortuna quisiera que
ella me durara ...

And the likeness is even more evident in the interpolation (already discussed
from a somewhat different point of view) which follows:

*Que jamás me dexó hazer cosa en mi cabo, estando ella presente. Si yo traya el
pan, ella la carne. Si yo ponía la mesa, ella los manteles. No loca, no fantástica,
ni presumptuosa, como las de agora. En mi ánima, descubierta se yua hasta el
cabo de la ciudad con su jarro en la mano, que en todo el camino no oya peor de:
Señora Claudina. E aosadas que otra conoscía peor el vino e qualquiar mercaduría.
Quando pensaua que no era llegada, era de buelta. Alla la combidauan, segun el
amor todos le tenían...* Si tal fuesse *agora* su hijo, a mi cargo que tu amo quedasse
sin pluma e nosotros sin quexa. (III, 134–36)

All irony aside, Claudina is remembered with the same imperfect tense,
the same use of the plural, and the same duration as Melibea. An authentic
experience has imparted to the sentiment of friendship (a sentiment perverse
in this case but not far from that of love) a special thematic resonance—a
density of living central to the whole meaning of the work. Again the individual life shows itself in duration to be far larger than its configuration or
character in the external present, larger than a repulsive old woman named
Celestina who professes *alcahuetería* with typical cunning. It is in such
passages as these that the *yo* overflows the *ella* and the *tú* which attempt to
limit it and to categorize it. In saying this, however, we must not forget that
(as in Calisto's case) these two modalities of life and of time are interde-
pendent. It is only such a Celestina who can be so acutely aware of time
passed and time passing as problematical or of the need to dominate with
cunning the space she traverses. For it is consciousness itself which joins
the durative space-time of sentimental recall to that other space and time
which condition life from without. Even more, these two *create* consciousness
in their unrelenting opposition. Symptomatic of this in the above passage are
the initial and closing references to past and present, the mention of fortune,
and, above all, the reduced evaluation of "agora" which emerges inevitably
from the freshened values of "entonces." Other examples may not be quite so
graphic as this one, but it is nevertheless true that each of the characters of
La Celestina lives consciously within his own individual juncture of duration
and dimension, of sentiment and argument, of experience and necessity. This
is what happens to Fortune and Love when submitted to a dialogic art; this
is the very core of Rojas' theme.

A curious betrayal of this central conflict is Rojas' failure to equate the
duration of the individual life with external time—with what Thibaudet
calls the "durée commune," measurable by the church bells and darkness
noticed in the dialogue.[43] As early as Act II when the sequence of speech
and event is still unbroken by nightfall, Parmeno speaks of Calisto's encounter
with Melibea as occurring "el otro día."[44] And by Act X, when just one day
has been registered in action, Melibea remembers "muchos e muchos días"

as having gone by since "esse noble caballero me habló en amor." Just as
Calisto in his soliloquy converts one or two sentences of Melibea (as tran-
scribed in the dialogue of Act XIV) into an almost limitless duration of
delightful hesitancy, so a little more than twenty-four hours may correspond
to an experience so timeless that it only can be expressed as "many days."
There are a number of other examples and (as I tried to point out in the
article mentioned in note 43) almost all of them refer to the lovers and to the
interval between their meeting and their satisfaction. In spite of all the clocks
in the world, love as a sentimental experience both requires and makes possible its own independent duration. It is true, of course, in this case that Rojas
was hardly aware of the thematic conflict—that such anomalies exist precisely because the theme has not yet reached the level of artistry. A repeated
"error" of composition, it is all the more significant for that very reason.[45]

Thus, love, like fortune, has been reduced thematically from a passion in
allegorical trappings—a passion which blesses or afflicts man from the outside—to a sentiment intimately joined to his living consciousness. The traditional presentation of Love and Fortune in mythological conflict with man
as the only loser (or else joining forces for his destruction) has become the
intramural opposition of time and space as conditions of life against time and
space as sentimental experience. These two, otherwise known as duration and
dimension, continue the roles of their predecessors in a new way and in terms
of a new definition of the human being. When traditional thesis is replaced
with personal theme (personal to Rojas) there is appropriate metamorphosis
of its members. And that of love is from blind passion to perceptive sentiment. Subjection to passion is the fate of man in general but the amorous
experience is the dangerous privilege of purely personal existence. It is dangerous, even more dangerous than Cupid's arrow, because in its inevitable
conflict with the alien universe it leads to the phenomenon of acute self-
awareness.

5. A Definition of the Theme

The fundamental thematic opposition of duration and dimension which
has just been insinuated reminds us of the living duality which we first discovered in Rojas' art of dialogue. In the chapter on style and in those that
followed we saw each life in *La Celestina* as a complex of first- and second-
person modes of consciousness, of a *tú* and a *yo* inextricably interwoven
through successive situations. And it is on these terms that we may best relate
the theme to other levels of Rojas' art. Sentimental experience and its duration are, of course, the capacities of life as an autonomous *yo*—a *yo* which

according to Unamuno strives to encompass the world in itself. Alien time and space, on the other hand, condition life as a *tú*—a victim helplessly bound to earth and to the moment. Consciousness in the second person is necessarily receptive, in the position of being set upon by others, appealed to, persuaded, convinced, bracketed in one category or another. It is, accordingly, in this tense that dimensions must afflict and destroy the inhabitants of *La Celestina*. In the deepest sense Rojas' theme, like his style, characterization, and structure is dialogic—the thematic dialogue of living itself.

The objection may be made that time and space cannot speak, that indeed full realization of their inorganic power can only occur in a moment of solitude. Are they not instead the ultimate criteria of life's loneliness, the final victors over dialogue? Yet we have already seen how even at the moment of ultimate issue, even when the solitary Calisto at last becomes fully aware of chains of his dimensional conditioning, he must do so from a point of view external to himself. He must argue with himself from without as a *tú*. After all, the second person, actual or implied, is almost a law of the tragic soliloquy. But it is Celestina herself who most strikingly illustrates the necessity of time's aggression in the second person:

Señora, ten tú el tiempo que no ande; terné yo mi forma, que no se mude. ¿No has leydo que dizen: verná el día que en el espejo no te conozcas? Pero también yo encanecí temprano e parezco de doblada edad. Que assí goze desta alma pecadora e tu desse cuerpo gracioso, que de quatro hijas que parió mi madre, yo fué la menor. Mira como no soy vieja como me juzgan. (IV, 171–72)

Here the effects of time on life are clearly defined as mirrored effects, effects which can only be realized when the self is put in the second person. Even Celestina, for all her acuteness, cannot accept the temporal conditioning of her age in the first person: "... que no soy vieja ..." Just as one imagines one's own death by thinking of oneself as another person, so time and space in their war against life must encounter it as a *tú*.

Within *La Celestina*, of course, such a rigid duality is an abstraction; the expressive modalities of the *yo* and the *tú* are for each life and for all the lives too intertwined for schematic separation. But the identification just made of the metamorphosis of love and fortune with Rojas' dialogic art does enable us to grasp the theme as a whole, to integrate its several aspects into a tentative definition. Thus, while it would be pitifully insufficient to claim that the matching of duration against dimension is *the* theme of the work, we can now understand these two as providing an axis for *the larger conflict in dialogue of conscious life struggling to assert its power, desires, and values against all the limitations, arguments, and facts which are imposed on it from without.* At this point I must stress again that Rojas is not interested in persuading his reader that life is struggle in the same sense that Calderón and Strindberg would like to persuade him that life is a dream. Rojas has no prior definition to deny and, indeed, formulates no such phrasing on his own initiative. Unconcerned with truism or thesis, he creates from a thematic intuition of life and so dwells more on the phases of its struggle than on the fact of struggle itself. Spoken awareness is the battleground, and across the dialogue surge such varied antagonists as we have seen: values and arguments, sentiments and bleak perspectives, emotions of desire or fear and physical barriers to their expression. The first and second persons which together constitute conscious life prevent the assertion of a single direction— as in Juan Ruiz or Rabelais—and bring about the undefined but inherent theme of struggle.

This combination—a customary combination—of the author's intuitive faithfulness to theme with a lack of formal and conscious definition is most apparent in the *Prólogo*. A piece that was probably Rojas' final contribution to *La Celestina,* we may assume the *Prólogo* to have been written with a maximum of critical perspective.[46] Hence, the use of material from the prologue to the *De remediis* is significant. The first lines confirm our theme of struggle:

Todas las cosas ser criadas a manera de contienda o batalla, dize aquel gran sabio Eráclito ... E como sea cierto que toda palabra del hombre sciente está preñada, desta se puede dezir que de muy hinchada y llena quiere rebentar, echando de si tan crescidos ramos y hojas, que del menor pimpollo se sacaría harto fruto entre personas discretas (15-17)

Here the initial quotation with its clear reference not only to "contienda" but also to "la contienda" as the very essence of life ("ser criadas"), is followed by an implication of the thematic function. The notion of "contienda" as a "palabra del hombre sciente" is depicted as pervading creative growth and final form. We have already mentioned this metaphor in connection with Rojas' stylistic clarification of the *Comedia;*[47] now we may extend this to the notion of a deeper thematic clarification. A seed intuition of struggle is shown as growing into a finished creation. Then, after mentioning the inorganic conflict of the universe as well as the dumb struggling of the animal kingdom, Rojas continues:

Pues ¿qué diremos entre los hombres a quien todo lo sobredicho es subjeto? ¿Quién explanará sus guerras, sus enemistades, sus embidias, sus aceleramientos e mouimientos e descontentamientos? ¿Aquel mudar de trajes, aquel derribar e renouar edificios, e otros muchos affectos diuersos e variedades que desta nuestra flaca humanidad nos prouienen? (22)

This is indeed the world of *La Celestina* with its multiple and intimate "guerras, embidias, aceleramientos," etc. linked to the fact of existence in time. (Space has just been referred to with the example of the "rocho" in the preceding paragraph.)

The curious thing, however, is that Rojas does not go on to apply this notion of universal and human warfare to the dialogic struggle of the work he had just finished. Instead, the whole adaptation from Petrarch with its newly ordered imagery and its careful sequence of illustrative material[48] only leads to an anticlimactic discussion of the conflicting reactions provoked by the *Comedia*:

E pues es antigua querella e uisitada de largos tiempos, no quiero marauillarme si esta presente obra ha seydo instrumento de lid o contienda a sus lectores para ponerlos en differencias, dando cada vno sentencia sobre ella a sabor de su voluntad. (22–23)

Thus, Rojas' choice of prologue reveals his thematic "postura ante la vida," yet at the same time fails to make it explicit.[49] It is as if he were on the verge of announcing the theme of the expanded work but then drew back and refused to finish the task of self-discovery. The reader, as a result, is left with that feeling of intellectual dissatisfaction—of stimulation without fulfillment —which is common to so many prologues and essays in autocriticism (including those of Cervantes). A brief and incompletely focussed glimpse of the theme has left him all the more uncertain of its possible statement and significance.

The best defense for this attempt to define the theme in terms of the *Prólogo* is that such a definition seems to work. Since Rojas does not permit any direct invocation of his authority, we must be consoled by the fact that the shopworn quotation from Heraclitus almost invites us to return to the text in a final attempt to summarize and integrate our several aspects of thematic art. In the first place, if the battleground is the spoken awareness of dialogue, the two major antagonists and causes are the alien universe which limits and destroys life and the sentiment of love which attempts to create from life autonomous significance. As we have seen, the unfeeling external dimensions of time and space are pitted in the consciousness against duration, that sentimental time and space which is lived and impregnated with value. This battle, of course, is in its own way a continuation of the older battle of commonplaces—of the forces of Fortune, Time, Death, and Love against man. Alliances have been rearranged and the contestants have lost their mythological armor, but it is apparent that the traditions of an older enmity contribute to the relentless pursuit and issue of the struggle. Dimension and duration being the principal enemies, it is to be expected that they should direct the course of action from initial encounter to final catastrophe. As the major thematic opponents, their conflict underlies the innumerable offensives and skirmishings of the dialogue.

In the second place, there is what might be called the strategic order of battle. It is not enough to say that the battleground is spoken awareness; we must also remember that it is the spoken awareness of individuals who are conditioned not only by existence in time and space but also by their youth or age, their richness or poverty, their masculinity or femininity. These lesser conditions of life provide coexisting patterns of conflict which channel in human terms the deeper opposition. In a sense we might term them subsidiary themes. In any case, it is on this level that the cast of characters is determined and that act and situation are integrated into the action as a whole. Without it the battle could never have taken place. Life, for all its sentimental striving against time and space, would ultimately have been as impersonal as it was for a Berceo. The final issue is neither disguised nor confused but rather given human immediacy by this necessary individuation with its accompanying patterns. Although masculinity and femininity are most directly related to love's aspiration and impossibility, the others also define lives which share the defeat of Calisto and Melibea. Man or woman, high or low, young or old, each individual lives the battle in terms of his own predefined conditioning and contributes to *La Celestina* his particular variety of military terrain.

In the third place, we may call attention neither to the issue nor to the order of the thematic battle but to its continuous and intimate engagement within the successive situations. The texture of the work is one of strife, of bickering and dispute on all sorts of subjects deriving more or less remotely from the central dilemma. Momentary desires, emotions, and attitudes are being constantly checked by arguments, precedents, and persuasive reasoning. Or, to put the matter in a different light, accepted values expressed as commonplaces meet that other realm of personally lived and discovered values in a continuing skirmish line. Friendship, honor, charity, peace, freedom, and the like are broken into ironical dichotomies. Thus, as values they provide successive moments of awareness for the individual but no "humanistic" salvation. In one way or another all these values are doomed by their predication on human existence. To sum up, *La Celestina,* being what it is, integrates its major thematic conflict to an infinity of minor engagements and encounters. It is on this level, far beneath climax and catastrophe, that the dialogue spins out the ultimate anomaly of life in successive phases of consciousness. It is on this level that comedy can coexist with tragedy.

Finally, and apart from the immediate struggle of life, *La Celestina* frequently offers panoramic views of social discord and decay. These suggested panoramas constitute a kind of background for war—insofar as the individual projects his life against them and understands it on their terms. Specifically I am referring not just to Sempronio's sardonic listing of natural cataclysms, historical events, and minor excitements (a list which echoes the *Prólogo*) but also to the corruption of the clergy, the irresponsibility and egotism of the nobility, and the disloyalty and bestiality of the lower classes. It is a broad thematic background which reminds us of the vivid evocation of Menéndez Pelayo's *Cuadro de la cultura en la corte de don Juan II*. Rojas, in fact, seems old-fashioned, little attracted by that spiritual renaissance which, guided and stimulated by Isabel la Católica, led to the conquest of so much more than Granada. Instead, he prefers to underline the gradual decay of the mediaeval community—if only because it was that decay which corresponded to and made possible his thematic metamorphosis from man to life.[50] By definition a society in a state of disintegration can no longer provide meaningful varieties of existence in the third person: as a servant, as a master, as a hero, or, ultimately, as a man. A person living in such a society finds himself, instead, more and more aware in the first and second persons singular—in the intimacy of his own life and in the struggle of that life with other lives.[51] Thus, exposure to the cosmos, reduction of character to a minimum of conditioning, and the ironical relativization of accepted values possess a social and historical dimension, a dimension which is continually presented by Rojas as a corollary of his theme of vital conflict.

In conclusion, we may note that this thematic transition from man to life is more profitable for understanding *La Celestina* than Burckhardt's classic formulation of Renaissance individualism:

In the Middle Ages both sides of human consciousness—that which was turned within as that which was turned without—lay half dreaming and half awake beneath a common veil. The veil was woven of faith, illusion, and childish prepossession, through which the world and history were seen clad in strange hues. Man was conscious of himself only as a member of a race, people, party, family, or corporation—only through some general category. In Italy this veil was first melted into air; an *objective* treatment of the world and consideration of the state and all the things of this world became possible. The *subjective* side at the same time asserted itself with corresponding emphasis; man became a spiritual individual and recognized himself as such.[52]

This opposition of species, party, family, or corporation to the individual tends to place the Middle Ages at a disadvantage. Interpreted in this way, mediaeval man appears semiconscious or sleeping, a man who has not even begun to realize his possibilities of existence. Indeed Burckhardt seems to identify himself so completely to the period and tradition he studies that all before it seems naively infantile, childishly charming. But *La Celestina,* for all its maturity and all its thematic preoccupation with consciousness will hardly support such a judgment. We must remember that Rojas invokes not just consciousness but a new kind of consciousness, a desperate spoken consciousness existing at the very battle line of external dimensions and internal sentiment. It is not so much that the individual has waked up happily to the world as that that world has waked up to him and proceeds to block all his possibilities of evasion. A mediaeval consciousness of the toils and salvation of man has become the biting, hopeless, and perspective-ridden consciousness not of potent individuality but of a lonely life.

It must be admitted, of course, that the self-awareness which arises as each life attempts to master its dimensional, social, and corporal necessities does correspond to increased individuation. Areusa in the freedom of her sentimental life is no longer a carbon copy of Elicia; she is not even equal unto herself as she proceeds from one situation to another. But this individuality is a mere by-product of the theme. Rojas in the long run is more interested in patterning the comparable offensives (and defeats) of his characters' lives than in stressing individual differences for their own sake. Thus, the lack of specific styles for each speaker and the use of impersonal names. In this lies the major difference between Burckhardt's Renaissance men and the fictional entities of *La Celestina:* the ones, bound by the rules of historical progress, wake up and go on to conquer the world and themselves as individuals; the others, representing a thematic intuition of life, are caught in a literary nightmare, the purified and hopeless clash of dimensional universe and sentimental selves. It is important to remember that the substitution of "life" for "man" in *La Celestina* is not an historical evolution but a metamorphosis of theme; it may have an historical background but it is not historical in itself. It does not, therefore, reflect a sudden discovery and application of the sense of individuality. Instead it represents a change in self-understanding—a change from man's conscious acceptance of destiny (Fortune, Love, Time and Death as in the *Coplas*) in terms of salvation to the conscious rebellion of life against its conditioning. And at the end it is a doomed consciousness, a consciousness of total and final perdition.[53]

CHAPTER SIX

THE ART OF THEME - TRADITION

1. The *De remediis utriusque fortunae*

THE RELATIONSHIP, so hesitantly indicated, between Rojas' theme and the period in which he lived is meaningful only insofar as *La Celestina* presents from within its own interpretation of history. From the point of view of literature, an historical period is an aspect of theme rather than the reverse, and it is necessary to beware of the tempting suggestion of causation of such terms as "pre-Renaissance." Other works such as Mena's *Laberinto*, the *Chronicle of Álvaro de Luna*, the satirical *Coplas de Mingo Revulgo*, and even the *Cárcel de amor* are all premised on a Spain lying between the Middle Ages and the Renaissance. Yet each of them provides its own vision of history, drawing upon the period in terms of its own theme or thesis. To attempt to account historically for these several works would be as fatal to each of them as would equation with their sources. They do not so much reflect as create their times.

It is necessary to insist once more on this doctrine of thematic priority (a doctrine which by this time has become almost axiomatic) not only because of the continuing superstitions of "race, milieu, et moment" but also because of the need to place *La Celestina* within some sort of larger context. Having tried to define my intuition of the theme, it would now be well to view it not from within but from without, not just as a matrix of artistic creation but as a human preoccupation possible in Spain at the end of the fifteenth century. How could such a thematic metamorphosis come about? How is *La Celestina* related thematically to the European literature of its time? These are questions which pose themselves inevitably and which, at the same time, put us on guard against the too facile answers offered by the concept of historical periods and the evidence of sources and influences.

T. S. Eliot's famous essay, *Tradition and the Individual Talent* (an essay which in 1917 began what might almost be described as a critical revolution in the understanding of literary relationships), suggests an approach to our problem. I refer, of course, to the notion of literary tradition further developed and applied to Spanish literature by Pedro Salinas in his *Jorge Manrique*. As Salinas explains it, we must substitute for historical and literary causality an understanding of the "poetic habitat," that is to say of the habitat of poetry within which the poet spiritually lives and breathes. Just as the *Quixote* would be artistically inconceivable without the *Lazarillo, La Celestina,* and *Orlando furioso,* so *La Celestina* in its turn emerges from the *Libro de buen amor,* the *Corbacho,* the *Historia de dos amantes,* and others. These are not sources nor yet are they comparable expressions of an historical epoch; rather they constitute the living literary history, the lived tradition, which contributes to the originality of both masterpieces. And only by departing from them may we approach Rojas' art externally.

Our particular problem, however, is slightly different from that encountered by Salinas in his essays on the *Coplas.* Unlike that of a poem, the theme of *La Celestina* is subject to a gradual change and clarification through Act I, the remaining fifteen acts of the *Comedia,* and the additions of 1502. It is a preoccupation which becomes more and more sharply outlined (in a sense more isolated and so more "visible") as certain paths are taken and others rejected, as the first theses are surpassed and the final shape in twenty-one acts grows to maturity. Inspiration and contemplation, "criticism and creation," as Diderot was the first to point out, necessarily accompany each other in the process of artistic elaboration. As a result in each of the three stages of *La Celestina,* we may detect an increasing depth of thematic understanding, a keener insight into its artistic planning, as well as further profundities of sheer creation. Now then, if we apply this doctrine of Diderot to Rojas' art of theme, it follows that tradition will affect primarily the aspect of continuing self-criticism and thematic meditation. It is there that Rojas' art joins itself to the spiritual life of his time—to the "habitat of poetry" which shapes his self-understanding. Or, to put the matter in another way, the theme which is, on the one hand, an ultimately personal posture towards life can, on the other, be expressed by an author or become known to an author only in terms of a tradition. Precisely because the theme is so personally authentic, a critical understanding of it involves an exploration by the poet of his tradition. It can only be seen through the mirrors of other works. In any case, as *La Celestina* from act to act becomes more and more what it is, more and more Celestinesque, it does so in terms of an increasing grasp of its own tradition—a tradition which provides words for its comprehension of itself. For such a work as this, the "tradición y originalidad" of Salinas come very close to meaning the same thing as Diderot's "criticism and creation."[1]

In the *Prólogo,* as we have seen, Rojas offers Petrarch's *De remediis* as the major contibutor to his theme and, through Petrarch, Heraclitus.[2] Not only was the hesitant utilization in the *Prólogo* of the borrowings from Petrarch made meaningful by its accord with the dialogic theme, but also in that same dialogue Petrarch's Latin is the major source. As Castro Guisasola makes clear, passage after passage is lifted with a minimum of restyling from the *De remediis,* the *Rerum memorandum,* the *Epistolae* and others.[3] Admittedly mere identification of these borrowings—erudite citations, maxims, and commonplaces—would by itself hardly establish Petrarch's claim to thematic contribution. We have already seen how such commonplaces achieve refreshened significance in their literary context. Nevertheless, the very extent of quotation and re-estimation of Petrarch reveals a constant concern with his portrayal of life. It is as if Petrarch were found to be especially adaptable to Rojas' thematic art. Even though Cervantes' concept of heroism far surpasses in depth the stilted heroism of the romances of chivalry, chivalric reference is not only grateful but continually necessary to the creation of the *Quixote.* What I now propose to do is precisely this: to elaborate on my suggestion that the *De remediis* and *La Celestina* have something of the same relationship.

In spite of the *Prólogo* and in spite of the rejuvenation of Stoic commonplaces from the *De remediis* in the dialogue, Petrarch's thematic contribution has been ignored or denied by most critics. Menéndez Pelayo is explicit on the subject:

A los grandes escritores suele resistírseles más la correspondencia familiar o la redacción de un documento de oficio, que la composición de un libro entero. Uno de esos apuros debió de pasar el bachiller Fernando de Rojas, y para salir de él apeló al extravagante recurso de echar mano del primer libro que sobre la mesa tenía y traducir de él unas cuantas páginas, que lo mismo podían servir de introducción a cualquier libro que a la *Celestina.*

Por los trozos transcriptos se ve claro que la lectura del Petrarca no sirvió al bachiller Rojas para nada bueno, sino para alardear de un saber pedantesco; pero valga lo que valiere esta influencia, es de las que pueden documentarse de un modo mas auténtico e irrefutable.[4]

And Menéndez Pelayo is not alone in this belief. Only Farinelli, referring to the *Prólogo* in his *Sulla fortuna del Petrarca in Ispagna nel Quattrocento,* seems to have glimpsed the significance of Petrarch to *La Celestina:*

E nel *De remediis*—chi lo crederebbe?—è un primer germe del dramma umano che tragicamente ed originalissimamente svolgeva, negli anni estremi del '400, la storia d'amore e morte di due giovani amanti: *La Celestina.* Poteva l'autor suo

metter in testa al dramma il motto di Giobbe: Militia est (vita) hominis super
terram: ma di maggior peso sembravagli l'analoga sentenza espressa dal Petrarca
nel suo trattato morale dove la natura tutta è considerata come un campo di
contínuo travaglio e combattimento e l'ardua lotta dicevasi estendersi dalla som-
mita del cielo sino all'infimo centro della terra.[5]

Unfortunately Farinelli refrained from further pursuit of this thematic intuition (he was perhaps impeded by the word "fortuna" in his title with its
implications of influence). In any case, his observations remain isolated and
are easily questioned by anyone who may choose to insist on Rojas' apparently nonthematic, anecdotal use of Petrarch in the *Prólogo*.[6]

To sum up, Menéndez Pelayo, seemingly perturbed at the extent of borrowing, tries to protect Rojas' originality by winnowing out personal creation
from added "saber pedantesco." Farinelli, on the other hand, perhaps too
eager to document Petrarch's importance in Spain did not surpass the notion
of influence. In neither case did the critic re-examine the suppositions of his
criticism in terms of the work of literature facing him—and neither is for
that reason completely convincing. For my own part—and with the enormous
advantage of writing at the middle rather than at the beginning of this
century—I propose to reverse the terms of the problem: to ask not to what
extent Petrarch influenced Rojas but rather why and how Rojas was interested
in Petrarch. Castro Guisasola has recorded what was taken from the *De
remediis* and other treatises; it is now time to inquire into the sense—the
implications of interpretation and utilization—of the taking.

Our unique concern with *La Celestina* makes it unnecessary to embark
upon a general survey of Petrarch and his works or even of all the *Latin*
treatises. The *De remediis* with its adapted and adaptable prologue and with
its major contribution of commonplaces will suffice. As the most widely
circulated (both in Latin and in numerous translations) compendium of
Petrarch's doctrine,[7] its particular significance to Rojas is part of a larger
problem, that of its general significance to fifteenth- and sixteenth-century
Europe. In other words, the role of the *De remediis* in *La Celestina*—its
crystallization of a prior thematic preoccupation—depends to a certain extent
on the terms of its acceptance by men who, like Rojas and his characters
were engaged in living fifteenth-century lives. In order to get at Rojas' art of
theme, we must first understand the *De remediis* as a statement of the "theme
of its time"—or in the words of Menéndez Pelayo, as a "breviario moral del
siglo xv." [8]

But at this point we must forsake Menéndez Pelayo along with his
unsympathetic evaluation of the *De remediis:* "Aunque hoy nos parezca tan

vulgar el contraste entre una y otra fortuna ... nuestro siglo XV ... aplicaba
a todos los momentos de la vida sus pocos originales sentencias diluídas en
un mar de palabrería ociosa."[9] Rather Salinas' splendid defense of the *lugar
comun* and his poetic reliving of the *Secretum meum* suggests if not the literary salvation of the *De remediis* at least a new comprehension of its forgotten
vitality:

Para nuestro objeto [the tradition and originality of the *Coplas*] el valor del
Secretum es altísimo ... La oposición entre sensualidad y ascetismo, entre valores
del mundo y valor del trasmundo, el consejo incesante de la doctrina cristiana
de despreciar los unos por el otro, no eran un texto muerto, fórmula repetida de
púlpito en púlpito, de tratado en tratado; eran vida pura. En ese conflicto el
hombre vivía tragicamente. ... Y es que las verdades existen, como la materia, en
muchas formas: petrificadas, inermes, en el mineral; fluídas y corredoras, como
en el arroyo; o invisibles y alentadoras, como el aire que se nos entra por los
pulmones y da respiro, mas alla del cuerpo, a las potencias del alma.[10]

Thus, Salinas warns us to suspect the misleading criterion of originality and
proposes instead that we admit once again a living truth that is beyond
personal invention. Farnham too is dissatisfied with the out-of-hand rejection of the *Secretum* and the *De remediis* by post-Romantic sensibilities. He
sees in the former that vital juxtaposition of love and scorn which was to
characterize treatment of the world long after Petrarch's time.[11] Both critics
have realized that in considering the themes of other times it is necessary to
recapture—as Dilthey prescribes—their living urgency. In this sense, their
work is very encouraging to us.

The *De remediis,* however, is not as easy to defend as the *Secretum.*
Although both share contempt for the world and although both propose the
usual meditation on death as an antidote to false values, the *De remediis*
can hardly be said to present Petrarch's private drama of salvation. Forsaking
the appeal of personal reference, it deals instead with doctrine—with the
relationship of human life to that external causality known as fortune. The
debate with St. Augustine in the *Secretum* (a debate with Petrarch's second
self, according to Farnham) centers on the immediate dilemma and the
immediate need to choose or compromise. But in the *De remediis* the discussion of fortune—favorable or adverse to all men—directs attention to the
prior conditions of the same dilemma. It is a treatise rather than a confession
of intimacy, a doctrinal prescription rather than a secret. And precisely for
that reason—although all the more alien to post-Romantic generations—it
appealed to an age preoccupied with certitude. Furthermore, as Huizinga
and so many others have observed, fortune was described and depicted,

denied, and invoked with increasing fervor as the time of the Middle Ages ran out.[12] It was an increase which seems to have corresponded to a heightened concern with life on earth and with its corollaries of uncontrollable happening, of chance, and of inexplicable destiny. In spite of Boethius, St. Thomas, and Dante, the word and image of fortune along with the imprecise concept they represented were used and needed more and more. The success of the *De remediis* must certainly be understood within the frame of reference of its time, its treatment, and its topic.

Admitting these historical generalizations, it is all the more apparent that Petrarch must have presented fortune and its antidotes in a special way—in a way particularly suited to the consciousness of his contemporaries. While it is undeniable that there are few ideas in the *De remediis* that are not inherited from Seneca, Boethius, or later predecessors, the structure and sensibility of what Petrarch had to say must have been particularly grateful to his readers. The long trajectory of fortune from antiquity to modern times has usually been traced as a part of the history of ideas or motifs. As a result fortune seems increasingly worn away—dulled and corroded as a coin over the centuries—as it is treated by one writer after another. Nevertheless, beneath the level of traditional idea or convenient emblem, it is also an intuition into the nature of life—a means of expressing those arbitrary and mysterious aspects of success and failure which each generation, society, and individual must learn to explain to itself and himself. And it was Petrarch who—for all his lack of originality—found doctrinal form and lyric expression for the intuition of fortune of his own and succeeding generations. He reminted the time-worn coin and gave sharp contour and new lustre to the inherited metal. It was in this condition that the theme of fortunte reached the hands of Rojas; and it was in this condition of greatly increased vital purchasing power that it was spent on *La Celestina*.

The structure of the *De remediis* is its most perceptible innovation.[13] Doctrinal dialogue in the Middle Ages was usually vertical, that is to say it was a dialogue between a narrator and an allegorical personage who comes to him from above and who instructs him on the basis of admitted infallibility. This personage may be Philosophy (in the *Philosophiae consolationis,* a prototype of doctrinal verticality), Hope (in Machaut's *Remede de la fortune*), Reason (in the *Roman de la rose*), or any one of a host of others, and he may hold forth on many matters unrelated to fortune and its remedies. Yet despite the vogue of this pattern, Petrarch rejects it and finds in Seneca's *De remediis fortuitorum*[14] a structure which we may term, in contrast to that of Boethius, "horizontal." The dialogue takes place between two parts of the soul, Reason against the four traditional passions of Joy, Hope, Sorrow, and Fear. Speech for the first time emerges from a point of view and is rapid and trenchant rather than lengthy and educational. Like the *Secretum* (in spite of its partial retention of verticality), the *De remediis* does not insist on the overwhelming didactic superiority of one speaker over another and so avoids endless monologues of instruction and persuasion.[15] Instead, and even though Reason is usually given the last word, there is a very convincing pretense of discussion, a dialogic direction of style (from *yo* to *tú*) as one topic after another is taken up and discarded.

Let us take as an example one of those not infrequent instances in which Reason is forced to make at least verbal concessions to its interlocutors:

Temor—Temo mucho el terremoto.
Razón—Yo te digo que el temblor de la tierra es un gran daño de la natura nuestra madre y no sin causa temido de nuestros passados más que otra cosa alguna. Porque cierto es más grave que todos los otros daños. Verdad es que acaece menos veces y esto parece alguna manera de remedio. Muchas veces la tristeza del aire y su oscuridad os anuncian que quiere atronar. Mas el terremoto ninguna señal da de si antes que venga ...
Temor—No me das remedio como sueles; antes me haces mayor peligro.
Razón—Ya yo pensaba que esto te había de parecer y en la verdad es así ... esto de que hablamos; es de calidad que con su fuerza desecha y sacude todos los argumentos de palabras que los hombres pueden hacer. Solo un consuelo tiene ... que este mal acaece pocas veces. (*De terremotu*, F. Madrid, fol. CXXXIX.)

How much more appealing to Rojas and to men like him must have been this animated dialectic than long vertical disquisitions in the mediaeval pattern! The revival of the *De remediis fortuitorum* as a model gave the age-old doctrine a structural novelty, a change of tempo, and a dialogic conviction which, if not comparable to that of *La Celestina,* was nonetheless effective. Petrarch's conclusions are thereby made to seem neither predigested nor foregone.

Petrarch, however, did more than just borrow a structure and style which suited him. Seeming to realize the inherent advantages of the horizontal ordering, he not only continued but expanded upon it. For his *De remediis* (two books each longer than its model) does not limit its discussion to the usual benefits of reliance upon the goddess: treasures, jewels, and fugitive glories. Instead of this traditional résumé of fortune's offerings, Petrarch gives a brilliant and at the same time specific panorama of mundanity in all its aspects. He dwells, often lyrically, on beautiful women, on the delights of love, on military triumph, on dancing and music, on furniture, on paintings, on libraries, on blooded horses, and, in one splendid passage, on the pleasures of landscape lost with blindness.[16] The world is, in effect, provided with its best weapons for the contest with reason—that is to say, it is presented as an immensely attractive circumstance for life. No longer are worldly goods deceptive and vacant by the very terms of their presentation; rather the newly vocal passions unfold a splendidly heterogenous world and in chapter after chapter seem to revel in freshly discovered values—values that are aesthetic, vital, and even spiritual in kind. In their very intensity, in the very force of their attraction, they bring to the debate of the *De remediis* something of that quality of vital fluidity seen by Salinas in the *Secretum*. The horizontal structure, thus, allowed Petrarch to match reason, virtue, and contempt of the world with worthy opponents and, in so doing, to give renewed interest to the doctrinal struggle. In the language of sports promotion the *De remediis* presents more of a drawing card.[17]

This revival of Senecan Stoicism along with its rejuvenation of dialogue could not help but give a new complexion to fortune's role in the affairs of mankind. To begin with, Petrarch no longer has to feign a fortune that is even conventionally anthropomorphic. The Goddess Fortuna had always been more or less of a convenient fiction to be castigated allegorically by such equally emblematic personages as Philosophy or Reason. Nevertheless, as Salinas points out,[18] this representation did correspond to a belief (denied with suspicious frequency) that fortune, like time and death, was an external and somehow conscious entity—an entity with a grim purpose. It might be resisted or placated, but it still waited relentlessly overhead for a chance to destroy man and his endeavors. But in the *De remediis* this vision of fortune (along with the goddess) disappears. Fortune is a convenient word but one which no longer implies a vertical or transcendent interpretation of the human condition.[19] As a result, in the prologue to the first part Petrarch insists repeatedly that the home of fortune is in ourselves. Just as the dialogue is carried on between opposing elements of the psyche, so fortune is the responsibility of our inner lives:

Y que esto sea verdad, cualquiera con agudo juicio considerare el curso de su vida, lo conociera. Sino dime (yo te ruego) ¿qué día pasa de tanto plazer o tranquilidad que no tenga mas de traba? ¿Qué mañana vimos tan serena que solicitud y lloro no la turbase antes que fuese noche? Y puesto que deste mal alguna causa sea la mudanza de las cosas [*sic*]; pero si afición no nos ciega la culpa de nosotros procede. (". . . in nobis est." (*Epistolaris praefatio*, F. Madrid, fol. 1)

The reason for this change in fortune's habitat (a change which fits the horizontal structure perfectly) is clear. Petrarch's interest in Seneca revives a variety of consciousness that was hardly conspicuous in the *Roman de la rose* or even in the *Libro de buen amor* and the *Divine Comedy*. It is the consciousness of Stoicism, a consciousness which rests on a strict division of the interior world from the exterior, of the subject from the object, and which presupposes a necessary war between these realms.[20] We are reminded, of course, of the thematic warfare of *La Celestina* with its unrelenting struggle between an universe which is "ageno e estraño" and the subjective self-awareness. In any case, fortune is not to be found on the objective side of this duality; it cannot exist objectively because as a concept it is necessarily so human.[21] It must therefore be a property, a condition, of the subject. Or to put the matter in another way, since one cannot (as both Calisto and the Stoics recognize) change or placate the dimensional universe and since fortune may be remedied by definition, it must be subjective. It must reside within an area of controllability, within the realm of opinion, to use Stoic terminology.

Just what is fortune then? What new form does it take for the Stoic revival? It is precisely this: a failure of adjustment to the universe inherent in the very fact of consciousness, a failure which can only be corrected from within by the reason. The reader of the *De remediis* is, thus, subject to fortune when the world perceived sentimentally (Seneca and Petrarch would say passionately, a difference in nomenclature to which we shall return shortly) appears as a series of tempting and tormenting values. For example —and the *De remediis* consists of nothing but examples— a wife may be beautiful for her husband, a value in her that is discovered by his love; but, at the same time, that very discovery torments him with jealousy and with dependence on corroding time. The husband has become subjected to fortune insofar as recognition of beauty contributed to the victory of the world over the self. Awareness of mundane values, no matter how spiritual or irreproachable they may be, has betrayed him.

One result of this definition of fortune as the penalty of being aware is the absolution of the animal kingdom (a kingdom which interested the Stoics in much the same way as Rojas[22]) from tribute to it:

Quando yo pienso los súbitos e inciertos movimientos de las cosas humanas, casi ninguna cosa mas flaca, ninguna de menos reposo, hallo que la vida de los mortales. Viendo que a todos los otros animales, por la simpleza o ignorancia suya, la natura proveyó de maravilloso género de remedio; y a nosotros solos dando memoria, entendimiento, y prudencia, clarísimas y divinas partes del alma, ser tornados ya en nuestra destrucción y trabajo ... (*Epistolaris Praefatio*, F. Madrid, fol. i)

In the same way for man himself, those things which reduce him to animal existence—sleep, death, imprisonment—are often blessings in disguise. Each of them in its own way cuts consciousness off from the world, acts as a barricade between the object and the subject, and so limits the power of fortune.

Such remedies as these, however, are artificial and can hardly be advocated for an individual alive to the world, in full possession of his faculties, and so the natural prey to its enchantments and accidents.[23] How can such a one resist fortune? This is, of course, the question the *De remediis* was designed to answer: the reader must with his reason (as well as his faith) forge a defensive armor of virtue (we may recall the reflection of this in the *Carta*) against a world not only full of temptation and evil but also totally at war against his interiority. Only in this way can he see through the deceptive values which subject him to fortune. Virtue is at once Christian and something approaching *ataraxia,* the freedom to accept rationally the human condition. It is a supreme exercise in self-control. This in substance is the Christian Stoicism of Petrarch and the particular contempt of the world which it advocates.

It must be admitted that Petrarch neither sought out nor resolved the ultimate contradictions of Christianity and Stoicism, and that the *De remediis* is more of a compromise of the two traditions than an original outgrowth of their meeting. Nevertheless the way Petrarch goes about his compromise is quite original. In Boethius, for example, almost all Petrarch's ideas are present or implied, and they come from similar sources.[24] Yet in Boethius we find that the vertical structure discussed previously corresponds to a vertical preoccupation. Boethius and the centuries and generations which followed him were far more concerned with the relation of the soul to God than with the opposition of consciousness to the mundane circumstance. As a result, reminiscences of Stoicism occur above all in the early books of the *Consolations* when Philosophy is still preparing Boethius for her final revelations and antidotes—revelations and antidotes somewhat different from those offered by Petrarch, Seneca, or the author of the *De remediis fortuitorum.* Book V, in effect, denies fortune not internally but externally—that is to say in terms of providence, a providence that does not prohibit the freedom of the will. Arbitrary fortune, Boethius tells us, is a mere appearance, a failure to understand the mysterious workings of the divine scheme. The work as a whole is, thus, a philosophical preparation for a Christianity that is never mentioned explicitly: "Superata tellus sidera donat." In spite of many identical ideas, the structures and inherent preoccupations of the *De remediis* and the *Philo-*

sophiae consolationis reveal quite distinct intuitions of fortune and its cure.

The newness of Petrarch's compromise of Stoicism with Christianity results from the fact that Boethius' work was a key presentation of fortune during most of the Middle Ages. Almost 800 years after the publication of the *Philosophiae consolationis,* Chaucer, as we have seen, was still concerned vertically with the same fortune, providence, and free will.[25] It was almost in spite of Boethius that he achieved so much creative insight into the lives and consciousnesses of his characters and that these seem to surpass the patterns of fate and punishment. Farnham not only supports this interpretation but even goes so far as to imply that because of Chaucer's mediaeval definition of fortune he could not integrate the Troilus thematically—that he allowed an explicit thesis to contradict an implicit theme. And if this is true, we might in our turn suggest that Chaucer was, in a sense, ready for the *De remediis* with its internal fortune and horizontal structure of dialogue. Thus, Chaucer's apparent need of a thematic tradition at least similar to that found by Rojas illustrates the originality of the *De remediis* as well as its acceptance as a *"breviario moral* by the century following its writing. It presents and explains a new intuition of fortune, an intuition for which the lives of that century seem to have been waiting.

It would be incomplete, however, to limit our remarks on the success of the *De remediis* to the vital accord of its definition of fortune with the changing conscience and consciousness of Europe—that is to say to the fact that it was a precursor of the fifteenth-century surrender to Stoicism.[26] As we saw in Petrarch's detailed and at times affectionate panorama of the world he scorns, the *De remediis* does more than it sets out to do. Like so many works of the Renaissance or pre-Renaissance (*La Celestina,* itself, is a striking example) the intentional imitation of older forms and doctrines is subtly innoculated with the new *Erlebnis* of its author and time. It joins an original intent to an inherited intention.[27] This as we shall see, is manifest at both ends of what we have called Petrarch's "axis of preoccupation": in the object and the subject—in the world and in the consciousness which the world surrounds and attacks.

As for the latter—the subject and its awareness—we may begin by noticing the almost intolerable sensitivity displayed by Petrarch (we are reminded of his complementary vocation as a poet) to certain sights and sounds. The following goes deeper than the usual Stoic version of the warfare of universe and mind. It reveals a more intimate horror, a feeling which it would be interesting to compare to Sartre's best-known contribution to the twentieth century, "la nausée":

¿... quién no padece las guerras de las aves nocturnas, de los buhos y lechuzas, y el demasiado velar de los perros que ladran a la luna, y los gatos que entre las tejas con espantosos miados hazen sus tratos y con infernales voces rompen los sosegados reposos, y el enojoso chirriar y roer de los ratones, y todo aquello que de noche haze ruydo enojoso ..., y sobre todo el grunir de los puercos, el clamor y voces del pueblo, las risas de los locos ..., y el cantar de los borrachos y su placer, que ninguna cosa puede ser mas triste, y las querrellas de los litigantes, y el reñir de las viejas y sus gritos, y las questiones y el llorar de los ninos, y los regocijados conbites de las bodas y sus danzas, y las alegres lágrimas de las mujeres que fingidamente a sus maridos lloran, y los verdaderos lloros de los padres en las muertes de sus hijos ...?[28] (*Epistolaris praefatio,* F. Madrid, fol. LXXXI)

In Seneca's tragedies the messages of the senses are often atrocious in their exaggeration, but Seneca does not attempt to communicate horror in terms of a naked sensibility—a sensibility which can make the recognition and evaluation of the slightest sound a torment for the soul. What has happened is that in the *De remediis* the Stoic scheme of aggression and resistance has been inoculated with a new awareness, an awareness that is not rational but sentimental. Although Petrarch speaks of the adversaries of reason with the terminology of the past, actually his passions (or vices) function more often than not as sentiments. By the very fact that Joy, Hope, Fear, and Sorrow are allowed to speak so persuasively from their several points of view they are no blinding bestial passions. Instead they uncover unsuspected realms of positive and negative value, not in the world of man as a whole, but in the immediate circumstance of life. Here are the real enemies of reason—enemies all the more dangerous in that they unexpectedly, imperceptibly, and fatally infiltrate the horizontal Stoic structure revived for them by Petrarch. Acute sentimental awareness is perhaps the fundamental innovation of the *De remediis;* and, in its anguished confrontation with rational awareness, we may begin to understand not just its importance to the fifteenth century but also its thematic role in *La Celestina.*

But what about the other pole of the Stoic axis, not the subjective consciousness but the objective universe? Here occurs precisely that innovation which Rojas chose to continue and to reinforce in his adapted *Prólogo:* the notion or intuition of universal struggle. One of the best-known tenets of Stoicism in its original form was the government of the cosmos by a law at once natural and rational. The objective world, in other words, was not so much an alien realm of space and time as it was rigid and inflexible to those who could not or would not adjust their minds to its order. Precisely for that reason, fortune was thought to be a failure of the consciousness and not a condition or entity beyond the control of man. As a result it was traditional for the Stoics to explain conflicts and contradictions as emerging from the distorted point of view of the individual. Above the level of apparent struggle, there was an inherent unity of purpose or, at worst, a harmony of opposites.

Now it must be admitted that in the *De remediis* Petrarch did not tamper openly with this doctrine. In his second prologue (to the remedies for adverse fortune) he speaks of harmony and order, but there is a perceptible change of emphasis. Petrarch stresses far more than Zeno, Seneca, or the author of the *De remediis fortuitorum* might have thought wise the apparent struggle and only mentions in passing the ultimate reconciliation. The dynamism, the incessant collision of opposites, the warfare relentlessly pursued on every scale from the insects to the stars, indeed the whole vision of the universe which we know from Rojas' *Prólogo,* is substantially that of Petrarch. Thus, although Rojas consistently eliminates from his adaptation Petrarch's philosophical commitment to harmony, in doing so he only continues a transition that was already apparent in the *De remediis.*

We may go on to a tentative assertion. An internal battle between sentimental and rational forms of awareness and an external battle of elements and animals are integrally joined aspects of the new intuition of life which informs the Stoic frame of Petrarch's thought. To the extent that universal struggle replaces natural law, the universe of that struggle surpasses mere opposition to the peace of mind of the refractory individual and becomes radically alien to his life. The gap between the subject and the object which Stoicism proposed to bridge is for Petrarch—at least implicitly—unbridgeable. At the same time, the internal struggle between reason and sentiment not only sharpens consciousness but also prevents either from finding meaningful unity with its circumstance. As we have seen in *La Celestina,* sentiment (in a manner more subtly indomitable than passion) prevents any stable intellection of the world, while reason argues against lasting and positive sentimental union with any part of it. Thus, both phases of the struggle work for the divorce of the two realms concerned, and each is, in a sense, the cause of the other. An individual torn between feelings and conclusions tends to see the world as disjointed and anarchical, and a world newly perceived in this condition tends to sink the mind deeper into its doubt and confusion. An alien universe and a lonely self are the inevitable results.

Now, as far as the *De remediis* is concerned, the complementary nature of these two varieties of struggle seems to prevent any sort of comforting solution to the problem of fortune. The essays of Petrarch—particularly the second prologue—are much more unsettling than the relatively tranquil discourses of Seneca and Epictetus. Indeed the horrors of existence as presented by Petrarch are the more horrible as they are the more intimate. The result is, of course, that as we read the *De remediis* we become increasingly dissatisfied with the Stoic answers. We become more and more despairing of any ultimate peace, for its battles, interior and exterior, offer no hope of ever coming to an end. In spite of the title, external harmony and internal serenity seem more remote than when we opened the book. Beneath the intention and the borrowed ideology, there is a long half-muted cry of desperation: "Morta fra l'onde é la ragion e l'arte,—Tal ch'i' 'ncomincio a desperar del porto."

Along with the emphasis on the ceaseless struggle of the universe, there is a new realization of space and time as dimensions. Insofar as man (in this case Petrarch) finds himself alive in an inscrutable universe of conflict—a universe for that reason all the more alien to himself—he becomes acutely aware of its dimensions. To paraphrase Kant somewhat inaccurately, space and time are the forms of man's recognition of the alien quality of his surroundings, the products of a consciousness confronted with an estranged world. In the *De remediis,* however, this version of the Copernican revolution is, by itself, insufficient to explain continual and anguished reference to these forms of human isolation. Returning to the internal war (characterized in such essays as *De discordia animi fluctuantis* and *De ambiguo statu* as the most destructive and fearful of all), we must not forget that consciousness for Petrarch comes in two varieties, rational and sentimental, and that the very pretension of the sentiments to discover the world as a circumstance of value sharpens rational awareness of it as indifferent and dimensional. The failure of the sentiments—an alternation of illusion and disillusion stressed over and over again by Petrarch—leaves a recurrent vacancy in the world, a vacancy to be filled by the reason with space and time. Or to see the matter from another point of view, the only possible weapons of reason faced with sentimental rather than passionate attack are these same dimensions.[29]

Corresponding to this rational and argumentative utilization of dimensions, the notion of natural warfare, in itself, seems to unfold them like a chart before the eyes of the reader. Astral phenomena, the birds in the middle reaches of the air, the insects and animals which share the earth, and even the fish under the surface of the sea locate themselves spatially as their struggles appall and impress. And in the same way, the very movement of battle as well as the incessant and meaningless change which accompanies its shifting fortunes is the constituent of time. It is unnecessary to demonstrate the counterproposition that belief in universal order and natural law tends to collapse time and space (we are in the world of Heraclitus, not that of

Parmenides), if only because it is apparent that universal conflict emphasizes and punctuates dimensions with a multitude of warring entities. Thus, the external struggle provides a frame or structure for a time and space produced by the self-conscious isolation of the inner struggle. We are reminded that Petrarch is famous, among other things, for being the first man to climb a mountain to see the view—a view that must have been at once beautiful for the sentiments and depressingly distant for the reason.[30]

To conclude, the *De remediis* is something more than an anthology of stale commonplaces and moralities. To think of it in this limited way obscures not only the thematic tradition which Rojas found in it but also its vital significance for the centuries and generations following Petrarch. It compensates, as we have seen, for its lack of original ideas with substantial innovations in structure and sensibility. In the first place, we pointed out the way in which Petrarch's revival of Stoicism and his use of the *De remediis fortuitorum* as a model renovated his dialogue, his tempo, and—by separating subject from object—his understanding of the human condition. In the second place, within the Stoic framework we found signs of a new sensibility, of a new sense of living in the world.

At this point I must insist again that it does not matter to what extent Petrarch may have been conscious of his innovations (Dilthey is sure that he was quite aware of what he had done) or how much of this discussion he might have admitted. Aspects which are occasional or even under the surface of the *De remediis* become more and more significant as the fourteenth passes into the fifteenth and the fifteenth into the sixteenth century. Preoccupation with universal struggle and anguished internal creation of time and space are remarkable not so much in terms of Petrarch's intentions as in the light of their relevant afterlife. Of this the Breughels and Hieronymus Bosch furnish pictorial illustration while the works of Boccaccio, Rabelais, and even Marlowe contribute literary testimony. Mention of these painters and writers does not mean, of course, that they found in the *De remediis* the same sort of direct thematic enlightenment as Rojas. Rather the whole period as we saw it reflected in *La Celestina* and as it is portrayed by Menéndez Pelayo, Huizinga, and so many others was one of conflict, disruption, and social and spiritual demoralization. And it is that period which is implied and to a certain extent predicted in Petrarch's variations on Stoicism. In attempting to provide spiritual help for the harassed and frightened individual alive in such a world, Petrarch reveals unwittingly its intimate texture and sensibility, the peculiar quality of its experience. It is on these terms that the *De remediis* seemed so meaningful to Rojas (and so meaningless to

Menéndez Pelayo) and was able to help guide the thematic evolution of *La Celestina.*

2. *La Celestina* and the *De remediis*

Insofar as the *De remediis* is considered to be a source or influence among other sources or influences, it does not particularly matter where its traces are to be found in *La Celestina* or how they may contribute to the meaning of its situations. A factual listing of appearances is sufficient. But if we begin to speak of such concepts as thematic tradition, *where* and *how* become extremely pertinent questions. The *De remediis* is for us a functional element of Rojas' art, and it may be expected to function differently in each of its three artistic phases. Without the least implication of organic disunity, the phases were listed as follows: Act I, Acts II–XVI of the *Comedia,* and the added acts and interpolations of the *Tragicomedia.* The authorship question aside, these phases suggested not so much increasing maturity in itself as they did the ripening of Rojas' creative self-knowledge—the ripening of the thematic criticism inherent in his creation. It is in this process that we shall see the *De remediis* taking so decisive a part.

To begin with, we may notice that in Act I incompleted projects of thesis—blasphemy and its punishment—coincide with an absence of reference to Petrarch. This is, of course, explained by Castro Guisasola as due to the ignorance of the first author (an ignorance which becomes evidence for separate authorship). And, indeed, if there were no signs at all of familiarity with the *De remediis* in Act I, we should hardly be able to conjecture further. Fortunately, however, Castro Guisasola overlooked one very definite reminiscence. It is an oversight which allows us to attribute Petrarch's usual absence in the act to lack of thematic need rather than to mere lack of knowledge.[31] Unquestionably the author of Act I had read Petrarch but found no special reason to cite him.

But instead of trying first to explain why Petrarch is missing, let us approach the matter through those authors and works which are present and which fail to reappear to any extent in the following acts: Aristotle, Boethius, and Seneca.[32] Aristotle, perhaps the most significant of the three, gives scholastic and at the same time comic overtones to Sempronio's castigation of women and to Pármeno's defense of virtue. The following two examples are typical:

SEMP.—... por ser tú hombre eres mas digno.
CAL.—¿En qué?
SEMP.—En que ella es imperfecta, por el qual defeto desea e apetece a ti e a

otro menor que tú. ¿No as leydo el filósofo, do dize: Assí como la materia apetece la forma, así la mujer al varón?

    Cal.—¡O triste, e quando veré yo esso entre mi e Melibea! (I, 56–57)

    Parm.—No curo de lo que dizes, porque en los bienes mejor es el acto que la potencia e en los males mejor la potencia que el acto. Assí que mejor es ser sano que poderlo ser, e mejor es poder ser doliente que ser enfermo por acto e, por tanto, es mejor tener la potencia en el mal que el acto.

    Cel.—¡O malvado! ¡Cómo, que no se te entiende! (I, 97)

In both passages we may notice a similarity to that integration of moral commonplaces to dialogue discussed at the beginning of Chapter V. Instead of being taken seriously or importing doctrine for its own sake, these reminiscences of Aristotelian thought are received comically as the replies of Calisto and Celestina demonstrate.

    Yet in spite of the apparent similarity in absorption of borrowed material, we may notice that the kind of argument which avails itself of Aristotle is quite different from the kind which avails itself of Petrarch. The arguments of Act I are not only longer but also involve the defense of points of view by Pármeno and Sempronio quite opposed to their later inclinations. Sempronio actually tries to dissuade Calisto from love (a fire it is in his interest to fan) while Pármeno attempts a virtue he does not possess. It is as if the author were not yet sure which interested him more, portrayal of character or the topic being discussed.[33] On the one hand, these conversations seem to burlesque the mediaeval debate and on the other they furnish fixed characterizations—the mature cynic and the pedantic adolescent—for their speakers. Neither Pármeno nor Sempronio have as yet been touched vitally, and neither, in the Celestinesque sense, has arrived at full self-consciousness. As a result they can argue questions intellectually and employ a scholastic logic that is laughable in its mechanical, non-vital assertiveness—that is to say, laughable by Bergsonian definition. Later on neither of the two will have time or inclination for such debate and Aristotle will be forgotten.

    Thus, the presence of Aristotle and the absence of Petrarch in Act I coincide not only with tentative theses but also with characters who are not yet fully engaged in conflict, not yet involved vitally in dialogic situations. An exception to this rule is, of course, Calisto who, in his passionate blasphemy, has little occasion to remember Aristotle or Seneca (although even he briefly recalls erudite precedents and compares such abstractions as Appearance and Existence).[34] It is above all the lives of the others which have not yet reached that mutually intense awareness, that interlocking combat of reason and sentiment, which we are to witness later on.[35] Instead they are kept apart by barriers of scholastic argumentation, by verbal display and runaway rationalization. It is undeniable that already in Act I there are abundant indications that such isolated, nonsituated postures will be more and more difficult to maintain. Sempronio quickly forgets his opinions about women in terms of future gain, and when Celestina says, "Mal sosegadilla deues tener la punta de la barriga," it is the beginning of the end of Pármeno's pedantry. It is precisely these indications of vital struggle which Rojas continues and develops in the rest of the *Comedia,* but until then in the long first act Aristotle contributes more than Petrarch.

To sum up, the *De remediis* was hardly needed in that part of *La Celestina* which was only beginning to find its thematic unity of character, structure, dialogue, and style. The state of total war referred to in the Petrarchist *Prólogo* had not yet been reached; the characters were still occupied with preliminary skirmishings and reconnaissance; and the issues of the struggle were still subject to diplomacy, to debate on their merits. When Rojas took over they had not yet merged with what we have seen to be a full thematic vision of verbal *contienda o batalla.* The debate of issues had not yet become a dialectic of lives.

As we begin to read into Act II, Sempronio's opening remarks on nobility, honor, and generosity, if not taken directly from Petrarch,[36] do demonstrate clearly Rojas' way of using him. It is a first example of ironical integration of commonplace to speaker and situation:

> CAL.—Hermanos mios, cient monedas dí a la madre. ¿Fize bien?
> SEMP.—¡Hay! ¡si fiziste bien! Allende de remediar tu vida, ganaste muy gran honrra ... ¿Qué aprouccha tener lo que se niega aprouechar? Sin dubda te digo que mejor es el vso de las riquezas, que la possesión dellas. ¡O qué glorioso es el dar! ¡O qué miserable es el recebir! Quanto es mejor el acto que la possesión, tanto es mas noble el dante qu'el recibiente ... E dizen algunos que la nobleza es vna alabanza que prouiene de los merecimientos e antiguedad de los padres; yo digo que la agena luz nunca te hará claro, si la propia no tienes. E por tanto no te estimes en la claridad de tu padre, que tan magnífico fué; sino en la tuya. E assí se gana la honrra, que es el mayor bien de los que son fuera del hombre ... Por ende goza de haber seydo assí tan magnífico e liberal. (II, 113–14)

This reunion of commonplaces is irreproachable in its truth. No one can deny the virtue of Sempronio's arguments. Yet because of their virtue and merit, the sordid occasion of the speech (the money given to Celestina) and its unscrupulous motivation (Sempronio's desire to milk his master dry) is all the more apparent and even vivid. Rojas has stepped back and allowed his speaker to betray himself—to show off his rascality in his own words.

It is worth noticing, of course, that this passage is longer and far more obvious than comparable examples in later acts. It is clearly a first experiment in ironical technique (even though there are a few premature and undeveloped examples in Act I). A general statement of truth has been linked dialogically to the particular human circumstances of its utterance. In Act I preliminary experiments towards integration of commonplace and dialogue—semi-comic debate, cynical asides, description of the vices of women followed by exemplification at Celestina's house—were not wholly successful because the speakers were not fully revealed and engaged. In each case, the topic could still pretend to exist for its own sake. Thus, this first speech of Act II with its full interdependence of speaker and speech may be considered a signpost indicating the direction of Rojas' new artistry. Honor and nobility have—typically—become contingent upon the living consciousness of a rascal.

Granting this art of ironical integration, an art which we now see really beginning in Act II, we may inquire into its relation to Petrarch. Why is it that the *De remediis* was able to contribute so much to this special kind of utilization of commonplaces? How was it adapted by Rojas to the possibilities and necessities of his intensified irony? Among the borrowings from Petrarch in Act II (as listed by Castro Guisasola), the following may help provide an answer:

CAL.—¿Quánto descanso traen consigo los quebrantados sospiros? ¿Quánto relieuan e disminuyen los lagrimosos gemidos el dolor? Quantos escriuieron consuelos no dizen otra cosa.

SEMP.—Lee mas adelante, buelue la hoja: fallarás que dizen *que fiar en lo temporal e buscar materia de tristeza, que es ygual género de locura* ... En el contemplar esta la pena de amor, en el oluidar el descanso. Huye de tirar cozes al aguijón. *Finge alegria y serlo ha. Que muchas vezes la opinión trae las cosas donde quiere, no para que mude la verdad; pero para moderar nuestro sentido e regir nuestro juyzio.* [The italics here indicate not interpolation but borrowings.] (II, 116–19)

CAL.—Tú Pármeno, ¿qué te parece de lo que oy ha pasado? Mi pena es grande, Melibea alta, Celestina sabia y buena maestra destos negocios. No podemos errar. Tú me la has aprobado con toda tu enemistad. Yo te creo. *Que tanta es la fuerça de la verdad, que las lenguas de los enemigos trae a si.* (II, 119)

It is not necessary to compare these fragments to the original Latin (they are surprisingly faithful translations) in order to notice that in all three cases the horizontal axis of Stoic structure and preoccupation is explicit. "Opinión" and "verdad," "lo temporal" and "tristeza," clearly divide the subject from the object and internal from external reality. Even more, each of the borrowed sentences has to do with human consciousness, with its government and its relation to truth. Unlike the previous Aristotelian classification and explanation of such matters as sex, friendship, or moral conduct, now consciousness has become an operating factor in the discussion. Awareness of truth seems as important as truth itself. Sempronio, speaking as an apt student of Stoicism, no longer argues scholastically, "Women are this way or that way, and therefore you, Calisto, should conduct yourself accordingly"; rather he urges, "The state of your mind in relation to women is what is wrong with you, but, since it is yours, you may reform it."[37] And then—as begins to be evident even in these cases—after the Stoic concept of consciousness has made its doctrinaire appearance, it invokes immediate reference to the particular consciousnesses of the speaker and listener. At this point that kind of irony we have seen as so typical of *La Celestina,* with its juxtaposition of general and particular, becomes possible.

It may well be argued that in none of these three passages is Rojas' art fully ironical. His intentions are nowhere near as unmistakable (if only because the commonplaces pass so rapidly before the reader's eye) as in Sempronio's long and evidently hypocritical discourse on noble generosity and personal honor. Nevertheless the potentiality, the implication, of irony is present. That Sempronio should advise Calisto to cheer up is not surprising. But that Sempronio, given his own personal surrender to "lo temporal" (his successive domination by fear, sensuality, greed, and anger), should prescribe Stoic medicine for Calisto's "enfermedad de alma" is not so much comic hypocrisy as an ironical personal contradiction. Again, when Calisto remarks to Pármeno, "Yo te creo. Que tanto es la fuerza de la verdad que las lenguas de los enemigos trae a si," there is a similar divergence between what he intends to say and his unrecognized admission that Celestina is exactly as bad as she was painted. The commonplace has been confirmed all unwittingly by the consciousness.[38] In other words, the horizontal commonplaces of the *De remediis*—commonplaces involving the conduct of consciousness—are by their very nature adjusted to the needs of dialogic engagement, to situations involving the enmeshment of spoken consciousnesses. The debate is over. Living conversation has begun. And insofar as, in its course, Calisto and Sempronio reveal the distance of what they feel from what they say—of intended meaning from true meaning—irony has been born.

Thus, after Act I, the entry of the *De remediis* into *La Celestina* coincides with a new possibility of irony and with the engagement of consciousness in dialogue on a level more profound than that of mere argumentative discussion. The Stoicism of Petrarch helps invoke ironically the anguished (or cynical) anti-Stoic awarenesses of the speakers.

It would be both possible and helpful to discuss the other borrowings from the *De remediis* and to see how each is related ironically to its dialogic circumstance. But since it is the art of Rojas that is our concern and not a complete critical survey of *La Celestina* two more examples will suffice. Menéndez Pelayo offers a ready-made test of what has been said when he illustrates his denial of the importance of Petrarch's contribution as follows:

Más interés tiene este plagio directo [the prologue] que las vagas reflexiones morales sobre la próspera o adversa fortuna que hay en varios pasos de la *Tragicomedia,* registrados ya por Arturo Farinelli:

"¡O fortuna (exclama Calisto en el aucto XIII) quánto e por quántas partes me has combatido! Pues por más que sigas mi morada, e seas contraria a mi persona, las adversidades con ygual ánimo se han de sufrir, e en ellas se prueba el corazon rezio o flaco."

Y antes había dicho Celestina (Aucto XI) convirtiéndose en eco de las palabras del Petrarca:

"Siempre lo oí dezir, que es más dificil de suffrir la próspera fortuna que la adversa; que la una no tiene sossiego e la otra tiene consuelo."[39]

Menéndez Pelayo's first example is an excerpt from Calisto's soliloquy immediately after the death of the servants and Celestina. And, although it is not directly reminiscent of the *De remediis* (or of Petrarch's other Latin treatises according to Castro Guisasola), it does express the Stoic reaction to fortune.[40] In its context, however, there is an ironic multiplication of meaning; for it is precisely in this monologue that Calisto reveals the full extent of his moral weakness, of his "corazón flaco" and his "ánimo desigual." In it he makes the shameful decision (or rather lets his love make it for him) to overlook honor and the death of his servants and to continue his affair with Melibea from in hiding. His rationalization of the death of Celestina is caustically underlined: "La vieja era mala e falsa, según parece que hazía trato con ellos, e assí que riñieron sobre la capa del justo. Permissión fue diuina que assi acabasse en pago de muchos adulterios que por su intercessión o causa son cometidos." (XIII, 112–13) Then, as a final excuse for his irresolution and failure to act, Calisto offers to himself the following plan, a plan which even he must have known would never be accomplished: "Mañana haré que vengo de fuera, si pudiere vengar estas muertes; sino pagaré mi inocencia con mi fingida absencia."[41] Thus, by presenting the noble doctrine of Stoic resistance to fortune at this point of maximum surrender to it, Rojas keeps—and knows he is keeping—the promise of irony which was implicit in those first borrowings from Petrarch in Act II.

Menéndez Pelayo's second example (this time directly from the *De remediis*) involves not the above irony of vital contradiction but one of unwitting confirmation. We may remember that both kinds were potentially present in Act II, the first in Sempronio's advice and the second in Calisto's interpretation of the description of Celestina. In this particular case the confirmation—the full reach of the truth present in the commonplace but unrealized by the speaker—depends on the fact that Celestina's remarks on the dangers of good fortune are made immediately after receiving the gold chain. Celestina intends to refer to Calisto and to his overwrought reception of the good news from Melibea. But we must not forget that we are in Act XI, the evening of the night which will be so fatal to Celestina. It is the night when her own unexpected good fortune will turn on her and destroy her; and it cannot but be assumed that Rojas allows her to speak these words from Petrarch on the dangers of "la próspera fortuna" with full ironical enjoyment. Rather than illustrating Petrarch's lack of influence on *La Celestina,* these two examples and many others like them show the extent of his penetration into its thematic art.[42]

We must not dismiss this aspect of Rojas' interest in the *De remediis* without again observing that in none of the above examples is Petrarch's Stoicism made fun of or burlesqued. The art of humorous take-off which at times seems to have such a central role in Act I, with its scholastic pedantry and its coarse asides, seems to have lost much of its importance. The humorist or satirist tends to identify himself with one version of truth and to deride deviation from it in conduct or belief, but the ironist, such as Rojas, cannot allow himself such open partisanship. He must and does see both life and doctrine, both private intimacy and public standards of judgment, both the particular and the general, simultaneously. He works from a perspective and with distant vision; and, as a result, he can explore human beings not merely in their misconduct or mechanical self-distortion but in their living depths. Thus it was (as we suggested tentatively in Chapter V) that the *De remediis* came to play much the same role in Rojas' art as the *Amadís* in Cervantes'. The *De remediis* furnishes commonplaces of anxious and struggling consciousness just as the *Amadís* furnishes commonplaces of heroism. In both cases a plane of generality is provided from which living particularities may be effectively explored, and in both cases an initial phase of satire or humor is surpassed as the new ironical perspective results in an increasing gravity of creative preoccupation. We have all followed this trajectory in the *Quijote,* but all too few of us have understood literally enough this sentence from the *Prólogo:*

Otros han litigado sobre el nombre, diziendo que no se auía de llamar comedia, pues acabaua en tristeza, sino que se llamase tragedia. El primer auctor quiso darle denominación del principio, que fué plazer, e llamóla comedia. Yo viendo estas discordias, entre estos extremos partí agora por medio la porfía, e llaméla tragicomedia. (p. 25)

It is to the credit of the *De remediis* that, with its horizontal structure and with its Stoic introduction of consciousness into the didactic commonplace, it proved to be such an ideal vehicle for the ironic art of Fernando de Rojas.

The remark of Celestina just cited, "es mas facil sufrir la próspera que la adversa fortuna" (with its implied reference to her own death through greed), along with the fact that Rojas seldom turned against Petrarch in satire or humor, suggests that the *De remediis* may be present not only in individual fragments of irony but also in what we have called patterns of character. These were, we remember, outlined by certain fundamental determinants of consciousness—age, sex, social position—and consisted of the projects or definitions of life advanced by different individuals confronted with them. Furthermore, each of these determinants seemed to have its own axis of discussion, of sentimental and argumentative preoccupation, all along the dialogic course of *La Celestina*. Thus, these patterns of character involve the same two factors that are so decisive in Petrarch, the inner consciousness and the general pattern or commonplace of doctrine.

It should not, therefore, be surprising that character design in *La Celestina* should so often bear the stamp of Stoic inspiration or origin, that patterns of character so often seem to become patterns of exposure to fortune. A ready example is that of the women—Areusa, Elicia, Lucrecia, Melibea—as it was worked out in Chapter III. The consciousness of each of them, we remember, is confronted with the determinant of a very lusty femininity, an imposed, seemingly objective limitation. And each of them reacts against this determinant or condition with fatal self-exposure. Elicia's sensuality and violence (twin indices of unreason), Lucrecia's vicarious titillation, Areusa's precarious independence (independence for no purpose except surrender), and Melibea's dedication to love are all, in effect, false remedies, the antitheses of reasonable self-control. The only possible result is the one we have seen: that each is victimized by fortune—abandonment, discovery, servitude, and death —in terms of her particular disarmament.

But however interesting this example may be, Petrarch's presence in *La Celestina*'s patterns of character seems much more convincing when we turn to the two individuals, Pleberio and Celestina, whose major preoccupation is old age. Pleberio, in spite of all the virtue we may at first suppose for him, has (and this is clearly emphasized by Rojas) far too much confidence in material security. He has bolstered up his old age with riches and provisions, and, up to the death of Melibea, has enjoyed that deceitful comfort described by Petrarch in the essay entitled, *De tranquillo statu:*

Gozo—Abundantemente son proveídas todas mis cosas.
Razón—Debe ser llegada la nave que deseabas cargadas de mercadurías; edificaste casa ... hiciste acequias ... hiciste palomares; pusiste ganado en sus pastos, las abejas en sus colmenares, la simiente en sus surcos, nuevas mercaderías en mar, en lugar seguro tu usura; tienes el arca llena, rica la casa, ataviada la cámara, llenos los graneros, rellena la dispensa, proveýdo el dote de la hija y el casamiento para el hijo, comprada la gracia del pueblo ..." (F, Madrid, fol. LIX)

It is this illusion of security which makes Pleberio all the more unprepared for catastrophe, for assault against that part of himself which possessions cannot protect. I refer, of course, to the loss of Melibea, the manner of whose death is mentioned specifically in *De infantis filii caso misero* with its similar conversion of fortune's fall into a dimensional fall. The lengthy Petrarchist reaction to all this in Act XXI hardly needs more emphasis than Rojas himself gives it. But we might notice from among the numerous borrowings the following doctrinaire "consolation" (taken from the dialogue preceeding *De infantis filii, De amisso filio*): "Agora perderé contigo, mi desdichada hija, los miedos y temores que cada dia me espauorecían: sola tu muerte es la que a mi me haze seguro de sospecha." (XXI, 208)

Unlike Pleberio, Celestina is irreproachable in her Stoic response to old age. In the course of her literary existence she can and does utter the correct commonplaces with all sincerity; and, according to that definition from Petrarch which so becomes her, she is truly "el verdadero viejo." It is a human equation which not only explains her strength in the work but also shows us the deepest corrosion of Rojas' irony. Yet in the end Celestina too opens herself up to fortune and succumbs. Her fatal blindness to the state of mind of Pármeno and Sempronio—a blindness inexplicable, given her usual intuition —begins to make sense in terms of the phrase of the *De remediis* to the effect that treasures are the unexpected "engaños y asechazas de la fortuna." Furthermore, as both Sempronio and Petrarch point out, old people with their characteristic passion of avarice are particularly susceptible to treasure, to chains of gold which bind them, in this instance both literally and figuratively, to the traditional wheel. If Pleberio builds his doom with lifelong accumulation of riches, Celestina finds hers in a windfall, a windfall which invalidates a lifelong picture of "virtue." It would be hard to refute Petrarch's contribution to these two patterned *casos* of old age, wealth, and fortune.[43]

At this point it would be well to insist again on the lack of fixed character in *La Celestina*. Patterns of femininity or old age are based solely on the encounter between first- and second-person modes of consciousness and should not be confused with any sort of imposed characterization. In this Stoicism plays its part. One of the fundamental tenets of Stoic doctrine is, of course, freedom: freedom to attain rational virtue, freedom to control one's own mind, and, as a result, freedom to choose even the slavery of passions. Calisto, we pointed out, is not a weak character in spite of his manifest weakness. Rather he is enslaved by love and so has relinquished the strength of freedom. Petrarch points this out:

> *Gozo*—Di lo que te plaze que yo tengo por cosa noble amar.
> *Razón*—Cada uno habla como siente; pues yo la tengo por cosa muy vil y muy flaca; y tal que aun a los muy fuertes varones amollenta y enflaquece. (*De gratis amoribus,* F. Madrid, fol. L.)

Thus, Rojas' free dialogic portrayal of conscious life as a *yo* and at the same time as a limiting *tú* corresponds to the basic Stoic opposition of reason and sentiment, an opposition which, being real, is never of predetermined outcome. We should understand the role of the *De remediis* in these characterless patterns of character at least partly in terms of the unrestrained freedom of being conscious which it proposed. Petrarch might in this way be considered the Burton of *La Celestina,* a sort of Burton in reverse.

To sum up, in the fifteen acts of the *Comedia* the *De remediis* may be detected not just as a series of dispersed borrowings but more importantly in the elaboration of irony and the patterning of character. Its presence accompanies Rojas' first relinquishment of thesis in favor of full thematic expression. As the speakers and what they say become more and more integrated to each other—more and more independent of traditional verticality and imposed opinion—there is an increasing need of Petrarch. His horizontal structure and his doctrinal emphasis on the free consciousness of the subject help Rojas to build in irony the several consciousnesses of his characters and to order them artistically in terms of a few elementary determinants. In this sense, the *Comedia* is a bitter and subtle comedy of errors—a comedy, ironically underscored but hardly funny, of sentimental evaluation and mistaken conduct from the Stoic point of view. As a result, Pleberio's lament which closes it and the *Carta* which introduces it are both appropriately dedicated to furnishing the reader with defensive armor. It is a comedy of doctrine and amorous error.

Now—and I would be the first to affirm it—it is true that this severely Stoic interpretation of the theme foreshortens and misrepresents not only

La Celestina as a whole but also these same fifteen acts of the *Comedia*. Even in Act I it is already possible to intuit a thematic preoccupation, a radical posture towards life, which it would be hard to define as doctrinaire misbehavior. Insofar as the inhabitants of *La Celestina* encounter not merely determinants of age, sex, and class but the dimensional conditioning of all life—insofar as each is aware of time, space, and love as sentimental discovery of value—the deepest theme, the tragic predicament of human life struggling for meaning in an alien universe, is already effective. This is the authentic theme of the *Comedia* (as well as of the *Tragicomedia*), but it is not as fully recognized, as fully processed by Rojas' "creative criticism," as it was to be in Calisto's second soliloquy or in the second garden rendezvous. It was precisely in order to overtake the theme that the added acts were written and that a month of love was inserted between seduction and death. But we need not now retrace a path that has already been explored. Rather we must go on to estimate Petrarch's participation in this last phase of thematic art—a phase without which *La Celestina* would have been as incomplete as the *Quixote* without its second part. To what extent and in what form was the *De remediis* effectively available for Rojas in 1502?

To begin with, we may notice that according to Castro Guisasola's tabulation, there is a substantial reduction of borrowings from Petrarch in the added acts. The *De remediis* seems to have been forgotten, and there are only eight short sentences from the other Latin writings (as compared to some seventy, many of considerable length, in the *Comedia* and its interpolations).[44] Furthermore, none of these eight can make a valid claim to thematic contribution. Instead, they seem to be used as mere reinforcement—as learned buttressing—for discussions larger than themselves. Rather than enabling irony or expressing cohesive attitudes towards life (as in the case of Celestina prior to her catastrophe and Pleberio posterior to his), these fragments seem only to accomodate the turn of the conversation. We may, in other words, consider Petrarch as a source for the added acts no more important quantitatively or qualitatively than any other. Insofar as he is still present in the text, it is not now as a purveyor of the theme.

What has happened is that Rojas has forsaken the Stoic doctrine of the *Comedia* and launched himself into a creation of awareness that is at once self-justifying and more hopeless of remedy than supposedly correctable behavior or attitude.[45] Hence, he no longer needs Petrarch textually to the same extent as before. On the one hand, he concentrates the struggle of duration and dimension into Calisto's soliloquy (with its recognition of dimensionality as a function of the inner conflict) and into the last night of love. On the other, he fills the interstices between these thematic situations with an intrigue derived from Roman comedy, and so more humorous than ironical. In neither case does he need the previous web of commonplaces, of complementary generalities and particularities. A rapid census of commonplaces from Act XIV to Act XIX (and it can be rapid because they are relatively sparse) will reveal to what extent the vital polemic, the intricate sentimental and argumentative alternation of points of view that was the texture of the *Comedia* has given way to a more or less superficial plot enfolding scenes of maximum thematic density.

This change is further illustrated by the new complexion of the prologue material. Rojas is no longer concerned, as he was in the *Carta,* with doctrinal armor borrowed from the introduction to Part One of the *De remediis*. Instead for his new *Prólogo* he turns to the introduction of the second part (adverse fortune), an introduction probably written at a later date than the first and revealing Petrarch's new intuition of life with greater frankness. It is in this introduction that Petrarch sketches with rapid disorder—and something like surprise at his own sensibility—his desperate innovations within the frame of inherited Stoicism. He seemed even to feel that this introduction was, somehow, the book he would have liked to write:

Mas ya yo veo que he comenzado gran obra y con gran ímpetu en breve tiempo y en pequeño espacio, y que tuve para ello mas corazón que fuerzas, y que ni a mí ni a otro alguno que bien quisiese hacerlo sería facil declarar cada cosa por si, para que se viese como en todas las cosas hay discordia—pues sin duda la hay y no sin gran maravilla, ahora sean grandes ahora pequeñas. (F. Madrid, fols. LXXXI–LXXXII)

Thus, it was here that Rojas found more or less clearly set forth the thematic struggle towards which he had been working all along. And he incorporated it with numerous changes, eliminations, and rearrangements into the last pages written for the *Tragicomedia*. Fascinated as Rojas must have been with the suggestiveness of this essay on conflict, he hardly could have imagined that later critics might charge him with plagiarism or demand an explicit manifesto. He presumed only to explain the changes he had made in the final version and to use for this purpose those passages from Petrarch which had come to mean the most to him. Rojas in the added acts—like Petrarch in his second introduction—almost realized the extent of his transformation of Stoic doctrine into a tragic sense of life.

These, then, are the three phases of Petrarch's thematic contribution to *La Celestina*. In Act I beneath an appearance of thesis, vertical didacticism, and comic debate, we can feel the stirring of a new consciousness, a new life, not yet fully engaged in dialogue and lacking an art completely adequate for its revelation. Petrarch has not yet been used to any extent, but if Rojas is to explore these creative possibilities further, his introduction will be indispensable. In the *Comedia,* accordingly, a new artistry availing itself of the Stoic commonplaces and doctrine of the *De remediis* comes into being. Patterns of awareness and of confrontation of life and wisdom create an anti-Stoic comedy, more alive, more subtle, and more anguished than the antisocial comedy of Moliére. It is an ironical comedy of conscious life—a comedy already containing within itself an intuition of the tragedy of conscious life, that same tragedy that was to be found again in the *Quixote* and ultimately in the agony of Unamuno. Finally, in the added acts—acts in which the aspect of tragedy is isolated into key situations—references to Petrarch again diminish. It would seem that by this time Rojas is less concerned with what is said in the *De remediis* than with what is implied by it. Hence, the thematic adaptation of the *Prólogo.*

In none of these phases is the notion of influence applicable. The *De remediis* should above all not be thought of as affecting, or radiating its doctrine into, *La Celestina.* Rather it was sought out—as, according to T. S. Eliot, all tradition must be sought out—in order that the theme might be expressed more effectively. Only such an understanding of the thematic tradition of *La Celestina* will enable us to grasp the creative relationship of Fernando de Rojas with his age. Or to say the same thing in another way, it is by assimilating the revelations and implications of the *De remediis* that Rojas creates his century, his original version of the theme of his time.

3. *La Celestina, Tamburlaine,* and *Fiammetta*

In order to place the theme of *La Celestina* within its tradition, it is not enough to estimate the role of the *De remediis* in the three phases of its writing. We must also compare it briefly to other works sharing, directly or indirectly, the same tradition. Insofar as Petrarch both continues and revitalizes a tradition (and does not act as a mere influence), it should be possible to compare significantly the themes of the various writers whose originality was stimulated by him. Influence and imitation are closed problems, problems confined to the two works involved. There would be little point or profit in comparing *La Dorotea* to Salas Barbadillo's *Hija de Celestina,* for Rojas' creation, in a sense, ceases to exist in both of them. A tradition, on the other hand, does not die at birth; it is by definition alive and possesses at any given moment a plurality of original futures. I now propose to leave the thematic roots of *La Celestina* and to speak of the choices it refused: its parallel thematic branches or bifurcations.

Accepting this tentative comparison between tradition and a growing plant, it is clear that *La Celestina* in relation to the *De remediis* is the central thematic trunk or stem. There is, as far as I know, no other work in Occidental literature in which the *De remediis* plays so open a part or in which its stimulating presence offers so little room for discussion or denial. In contrast to this, my assertion that Petrarch contributes thematically to the two works chosen for comparison with *La Celestina*—*Fiammetta* and *Tamburlaine*— is likely to provoke questioning from the specialists. This, of course, is probably more true in the case of Marlowe than in that of Boccaccio, intimately joined to his predecessor both in life and ideas. In Marlowe's extensive bibliography there is little or no mention of Petrarch, and, even though he might well have read Twyne's translation of the *De remediis* (1579), it has never been mentioned even as a source. Instead, most what we shall here project against the theme of *La Celestina* is explained by historians of English literature as Machiavellianism or the hard to define atheism of the time (although the latter seems to be a matter of some discussion).[46] Nevertheless, the effective presence of a theme does not necessarily demand an accompanying portion of influence. Whether the *De remediis* came to *Tamburlaine* deviously and indirectly—perhaps bracketed by Machiavelli and Seneca— or whether students of Marlowe have, indeed, overlooked a reasonable possibility of investigation, our comparison of themes remains unperturbed.[47] The thematic preoccupation of Marlowe as revealed in the *Tamburlaine* and that of Boccaccio in the *Fiammetta* effectively serve our Celestinesque purposes. And on that, if we do not pretend to the rigors of comparative literature, we may rest our case.

Opening the *Tamburlaine* in either of its parts, the reader is inevitably impressed by the texture of violence. This is true of Marlowe's works as a whole, as well as those of many other Elizabethan dramatists, but in the *Tamburlaine* this violence far surpasses dramatic, not to speak of theatrical, needs and possibilities. It is a play without climax because it is all climax, without plot because it is all action—a play of innumerable battles, triumphs, treacheries suicides, and murders. But, above all, there are battles and the continual mobilization, conflict, and destruction of armies. The world of *Tamburlaine* is, thus, one of flux and torment, a world shown not as a spectacle (which would be both intolerable and impossible) but reflected in the "tragic glass" or mirror of language. Now by this I mean not only reflection in the violent content of the language (the blasphemy and horror that is so continually uttered) but also and more importantly in its violent struggle for meaning.

Indeed, a great part of the shock experienced by the reader of Marlowe is the shock of watching words and sentences struggle to dominate a horror previously inexpressable, to master in bloody semantic warfare new sectors of meaninglessness. Bajazet, for example, a moment before braining himself on the bars of his cage, cries out:

> Then let the stony dart of senseless cold
> Pierce through the center of my withered heart
> And make a passage for my loathed life.[48]

This image, "stony dart of senseless cold," is evidently an attempt to capture, to dominate, death in words. To Marlowe's intuition, death is inorganic, aggressive, a meaningless lack of vital warmth. Yet each of these words piled up poetically not in the hope of solving the mystery but of scaling the senseless inaccessibility of death is a confession of failure—a confession that language, no matter how forcefully ordered, cannot do the impossible. Death so besieged is still death. But even more surprising than the failure is the direct battering violence of the assault.

Thus, although the happening of the *Tamburlaine* is more or less historical, its art, like that of *La Celestina,* is purely linguistic. With a few exceptions (such as the crown symbol) historical violence is transformed into even more violent expression. And Marlowe, quite aware of the axis between his writhing excess of action—all of the *Tamburlaine* seems to correspond to the classically unstageable death of Hippolytus mentioned at the end—and his poetry, begins his prologue as follows:

> From jigging veins of rhyming mother wits,
> And such conceits as clownage keeps in pay,
> We'll lead you to the stately tent of war,
> Where you shall *hear* the Scythian Tamburlaine
> Threatening the world with *high astounding* terms. . . .

Thus, the *Tamburlaine* is a play, or perhaps a dialogue novel in which war is heard in a fashion astounding for its violence. Accordingly, rhyme and conceits (both of them plays on the known meanings and forms of language) must be suppressed in this new expression of war and war for expression.

This close correspondence of word and deed will help us conjecture as to the theme. In the above verses, Marlowe announces war as his subject, but we realize at once that he gives the word a much more literal and restricted sense than do the prologues to the *De remediis* and *La Celestina.* Marlowe is primarily interested in warfare as conducted by the warrior Tamburlaine and only secondarily or not at all in the wars of "todas las cosas." We may

further restrict his concept of war—and this by a mere reading—to the clash
and shock inherent in it, to that same violence which first impressed us.
Here is the problem, then: to understand and rephrase our theme of war in
a work which reduces it to elemental violence. In search of a solution, let us
return to the diction of the *Tamburlaine* and consider a few of Marlowe's
most characteristic images. Violence on its own terms seems beyond definition
—it is just violence—but when translated into poetry, into language and
poetic description, we may hope for a critical purchase, an intellectual foot-
hold into its autonomy.

Let us begin with three images, images which have nothing directly to do
with the violence of the action. They describe successively a rainstorm, human
hair, and an infinite number:

> . . . the drops which fall
> When Boreas *rents* a thousand swelling clouds;
>
> (p. 70)

> Their hair as white as milk, and soft as down,
> Which should be like the *quills* of porcupines . . .
>
> (p. 67)

> In number more than are the quivering leaves
> Of Ida's forest, where your highness' hounds
> With open cry pursue the wounded stag . . .
>
> (p. 90)

In these fragments we begin to see the ever varying sharpness of point and
edge which punctuates the style—which rends, penetrates, and pursues from
image to image. On these terms it is appropriate that Cupid should "wound
the world" with his darts, that Bellona should throw "naked swords . . .
upon the heads of all our enemies," that Tamburlaine's foes should fly from
his glove "as from a scorpion," that the razor-edged bits of the captive kings
should "break through the hedges of their hateful mouths," and that the
weak-kneed inhabitants of Babylon should be told to "fall to the earth and
pierce the pit of Hell."

There are innumerable other examples, some more evident and others
more elusive, but these should suffice for our limited purposes.[49] Together
they show a sustained stylistic insistence on needle sharpness, on entry into
the flesh or bodies resembling the flesh. It is this wounding, piercing, biting,
breaching, darting, cleaving, rending, breaking through, and other sinister
present participles which define Marlowe's intuition of violence. Violence is
for him essentially violation, violation of the spirit and the body. As a result
the primary thematic symbol of both plays is not the crown but Tamburlaine's

sword, its point and its "slicing edge" where "sits imperial Death." War as violation, with Tamburlaine himself as the greatest violator of history, is the theme of these plays, a theme equally present on its two major planes of action and language.[50]

In terms of this intuition of the theme, it seems rather pointless to continue past discussion of Marlowe's moral intentions or lack of them, of the qualifications of Tamburlaine for the role of tragic hero, or of the work as a compromise between the author's abnormal psychology and the theatrical demands of the audience. How the plays begin and end, how the contestants fit into generic patterns, and how acts and scenes are put together, all seem of subsidiary importance when confronted with this thematic primacy of violence as violation—a violence so aesthetically purified that it no longer appears atrocious or repulsive. It is just the way things are in this world. We, as readers or listeners, are so far removed from the realm of our lives and from our usual paths of evaluation, that pity, terror, and moral or psychological explanation are meaningless. As in the case of *La Celestina,* the *Tamburlaine* is ultimately self-justifying in its thematic artistry of war:

> View but his picture in this tragic glass,
> And then applaud his fortunes as you please.
> (p. 1)

Between the two planes of action and language there are, of course, human beings, but, exactly as in *La Celestina,* they are not characters in the usual sense of the word. Instead they are combatants eternally engaged with sword and tongue—combatants in the long run more important in their combat than in their beings, in what they do and say *to* each other than in what they are. Tamburlaine, his allies, and his enemies either violate or are violated. There is no other choice for them. And while this in a sense approximates them to the lives of *La Celestina,* it is also the sign of a fundamental difference. The rigid division between those who violate and those who are violated prevents the effective integration of first- and second-person consciousness into a single life. In the *Tamburlaine* one is forced into the second person and usually dies in spirit or flesh as a result (both in the case of Bajazet). And one can live only in the first person. Life is an explosion of the ego; there is no intimate recognition of any vital limitation of any kind and, least of all, of another's point of view. The captive kings continue to insult Tamburlaine without regard for the retaliation to which their insults may provoke him, and they can only be made to stop by the completed violation of the bits in their mouths. Hence, although whatever is done or thought in the *Tamburlaine* finds immediate expression in language, there is no dialogue as we know it in *La Celestina*. Deed, thought, and word are joined in the ego and in its effort to violate other egos. Neither argument nor communication is possible since the second person has no positive existence. What is left is a monologue of poetic violence sustained for its own sake or, at best, an interchange of insults and blasphemies.

This refusal to admit limitation of the self or even the independent existence of the selves of others (the sons of Tamburlaine are permitted to live only insofar as they are projections of himself) prevents that internal conflict of reason and sentiment which was thematically so important to Rojas. Here reason has been reduced to a mere body-servant of the will, a body servant who is never given the impertinent privilege of suggesting restrictions or impossibilities. It has lost its Celestinesque role as psychic second person. And the will, now in complete control, seldom indulges itself in sentimental awareness or value discovery. Rather it is dedicated to its own blindly passionate expression and to the violation—the value destruction—of others. Passion has become its way of being. Thus, although in the *Tamburlaine* as in *La Celestina,* the theme of war leads from man to life and prevents characterization in the third person, Marlowe's particular vision of war also eliminates the second person as a participant in life. The result is not only a recession of genuine dialogue but also the subordination of the univalent person to his own language and outrageous activities.[51]

But what about the world in which Tamburlaine and the others live and in which they practice violation? Defining it, as we did for *La Celestina,* as the realm of life's external conditioning, we may notice that while both parts of the *Tamburlaine* refer frequently to time, space, fortune, and death, only the last is thematically efficient. In contrast to the *Faustus,* time here is not considered a force for retribution. We are in the midst of action as atrocity, that is to say as atrociously present and lacking in past or future. And from such self-sufficient violence it is difficult to abstract those causative and evaluative sequences which suggest time—so difficult, in fact that none of the speakers does more than threaten Tamburlaine with what will happen "some day." It is the time of children, a "non-time" or "some time," a time which does not and cannot condition the living instant of violence. In this sense it is Elicia who, rejecting temporal conditioning, is closest to the inhabitants of the *Tamburlaine.*

As for space, it too is frequently mentioned but usually with geographical rather than vital reference. By this I mean all the exotic place names which contribute so much to the astounding effect of the language. It is the space of a map (an artifact introduced by Marlowe on more than one occasion), a space which Tamburlaine can dominate or violate at will and which is incapable of limiting him or providing him with perspective.[52] He often seems to play with the whole world with the same ease as Chaplin in *The Great Dictator*. Vertically, too, the same situation prevails. Ranging rhetorically from heaven to hell, height is an invitation to ultimate conquest rather than a hazardous dimension. There is none of the implicit vertigo of *La Celestina* and, of course, none of the danger of falling.

Nevertheless, in spite of this lack of thematic need for dimensions, the *Tamburlaine* does not return to the mediaeval supremacy of fortune. As a goddess, she is continually violated by Tamburlaine and to such an extent that her unimportance may almost be considered a thesis. The following boast from Act I of the first play is upheld by Marlowe to the end:

> I hold the Fates bound fast in iron chains,
> And with my hand turn Fortune's wheel about;
> And sooner shall the sun fall from its sphere
> Than Tamburlaine be slain or overcome.
>
> (p. 11)

Marlowe, with these remarks, has left Chaucer's intellectual preoccupation with fortune quite as far behind as Rojas. Since violence depends on force and since Tamburlaine is, by thematic definition, the ultimate in forcefulness, he is beyond any transcendental retribution. Fortune has not been transmuted into something else. Marlowe, instead, actually proposes its conquest by life!

Thus, of all the constituent commonplaces of the world, only death is left as a condition of life. Bajazet's "stony dart of senseless cold" is the unanswerable violation and one to which even Tamburlaine is subject. But death is not a punishment or a reward, for Marlowe (like Rojas and even Petrarch, whether he knew it or not) has dispensed with the moral order of the Middle Ages.[53] It is instead a senseless phenomenon, and in this very senselessness it attains a thematic function which we saw it to lack in *La Celestina*. Insofar as life in the *Tamburlaine* may be defined as a process of violation, it is dedicated to death, to the creation of senselessness in the destruction of value. Life needs death thematically precisely because life is a killer, because it too is senseless in its self-expression. In *La Celestina* we saw death as the mere end-product of a complex internal and external war, a war involving such opponents as dimensions and value, reason and sentiment. But in the *Tamburlaine,* which discards these opponents in favor of the clash of one ego with another, death assumes the roles of dimension and reason. Life being confined to the first person, death is the second, and, quite literally, when one person addresses himself to another, he kills him. Even though life may signify but little in the alien world of *La Celestina,* Rojas does affirm its continual effort to signify. And the frightening thing about Marlowe's theme is that even this consolation is removed. The *Tamburlaine* seems to be founded on the sinister supposition that life and death are in the last analysis twin modes of senselessness.[54]

Thus, both Marlowe and Rojas turn from a static preoccupation with man to a dynamic vision of human life at war. But there the resemblance ends. Rojas presents war as the process of awareness, a dialogic process involving sentiment and reason as well as the subjective and objective aspects of the human condition. It is defined neither as external clash nor internal indecision; rather, it integrates the two in speech. As we have seen, each word and sentence can express at the same time the innermost sentiments of the self and a wide range of argumentative attitudes, from flattery to violation, towards the other. As a result, in *La Celestina* consciousness, dialogue, and war are substantially identical. War is the process of awareness (the aggressive contact of the individual life with its human or inanimate surroundings) and dialogue (joining by definition these same first and second persons) its unique expression.

Marlowe, on the other hand, only conceives of war externally, as the incessant clash of armies and individuals. It cannot, therefore, be described as a process. It is instead a series of separate instances of violation each of which involves a single moment of recognition in the victim, of conscious realization in death. Hence, Marlowe can make no effort to explore that living continuity of awareness which characterizes war in *La Celestina.* By emphasizing thematically the externality of war, he reduces internal life to a monolith of egoistic passion—that is to say to the barbaric determination of the warrior to win and to express himself at the expense of the enemy. Life has been limited to its own explosive exteriorization, to violation of other life, and if as a result it surpasses the hazards of time and space, it must also forego the discovery of values. Tamburlaine lives in an eternal, yet instantaneous, present and in a space that is as once the universe and a sword's point. Hence he ignores those continuities of duration and dimension which are the great thematic landmarks of *La Celestina.*[55]

Turning to the *Fiammetta,* we may remember that Castro Guisasola suggests that it influenced *La Celestina* (as an antecedent for Melibea's suicide more likely than *Hero y Leandro.*) In Chapter VI Fiammetta describes her attempt to kill herself by jumping from the roof of her house, and, although her reasons for choosing this form of death are her own,[56] there are evident and detailed parallelisms. These include not only the place of her proposed leap, a roof rather than a tower, but also the concealment of intention from the nurse, a concealment comparable to Melibea's deception of Pleberio. More important to us than the possibility of influence, however, is a reminder of the deeper thematic tradition which Boccaccio shared with Rojas. Fiammetta, as usual, is engaged in analyzing herself, in this case the feelings responsible for her suicidal resolution:

Poi gli occhi rivolti per la camera, la quale mai più non sperava vedere, presa da dolore subito il cielo perdei ... e *in me fierissima battaglia* sentive tra' paurosi spiriti e l'adirata anima, i quali lei volenti fuggire a forza tenevano, ma pur l'anima vincendo, e da me la fredda paura cacciando, tutta di focoso dolore m'accese, e riebbi le forze [italics mine]. (p. 159)

We should not, of course, conclude from this that the theme of the *Fiammetta* is war in the same sense as in the *Tamburlaine*. Unquestionably we are dealing once again with love and fortune, transformed in a manner comparable to that of *La Celestina*. But Boccaccio's intuition of love is peculiarly his own. He sees it as helplessly confined within the soul in a continuity of indecision and intimate struggle. The whole narrative course of the *Fiammetta*—indeed its very approach to the problem of communication—involves a constant intellectual coping with the inexplicable and irrational course of love. And at the very time that this is going on, there is the countercurrent of sentimentalization in terms of amorous hopes, sorrows, and fears of whatever conclusions are offered by the reason. Fiammetta lives within a double mystery: what is the inner force which has her in its power and what are the facts of her external situation (her lover's intentions, etc.). And since neither of these mysteries can be solved without prior solution of the other, she can never attain sentimental satisfaction or rational serenity. The struggle is unending, and "infinite lagrime" are its only possible expression. Thus, while Marlowe emphasized thematically the external war of life, the climactic shock of one body or spirit against another, Boccaccio intuits an internal war, the quiet but not less terrible conflict of a spirit divided against itself.

This intimate thematic engagement of sentiment and reason reminds us again of those essays from the *De remediis*—*De discordia anima* and *De ambiguo statu*—which describe internal discord as the most vicious war of all (and which seemed to play a part in Calisto's soliloquy of indecision). It is in accordance with Petrarch's best Stoicism that Fiammetta, by surrendering herself to love, has exposed herself to fortune—an internal fortune with its attendant interlocutors, joy, hope, sorrow, and fear. Thus, Boccaccio, in a manner quite comparable to that of Rojas, creates from the moral doctrine of Petrarch and finds as his theme the alliance of love and fortune in their attack on rational serenity. This theme had been approached by him in *Il filostrato,* but there fortune in verse retained something of its mediaeval externality and personification.[57] Here, on the other hand, the prose narrative is given the single point of view of a fluctuating soul, of a consciousness stripped of its defensive armor in such a way as to permit the complete victory of fortune. All pretense of action or external climax has disappeared (each book contains no more than one or two actual events); dialogue has been drastically reduced (other persons only existing in the mind of Fiammetta);[58] and all is narrated so exclusively in the first person that the very outlines of the world dwindle into nothing (or at best remain in pastoral uncertainty as in Chapter V). As readers we have, like fortune, entered the mind of Fiammetta with its labyrinthine toils of reason and unreason. We have entered it through the wide breach opened by the Petrarchist theme.

In spite of this autobiographical form with its continual use of the first person singular, it is apparent that Fiammetta lives in a manner diametrically opposed to that of Tamburlaine. She does not subject the world to her ego but rather is subjected to it. She lives in the second person of her extreme femininity as completely as does the tyrant in the aggressive first person of his masculinity. Fiammetta's *yo* is opened and helpless, totally subjected, and so absorbs into the intensity of its experience the lives, speeches, and actions of all around her. Thus, Boccaccio's interior warfare—a warfare polar to that of Marlowe—results in a woman who is subject to love, not as a moth seeking out the candle flame, but as a firefly bound to the light within her:

Ecco adunque, o donne, che per gli antichi inganni della fortuna io sono misera; e oltre a questo essa, no altrimenti che come la lucerna vicina al suo spegnersi suole alcuna vampa piena di luce maggiore che l'usato gittare, ha fatto: percio chè dandomi en apparenza alcuno refrigerio, me poi nelle separate lagrime ritornante ha miserissima fatta. (p. 198)

Here is indicated the profound difference between the helpless love of Fiammetta and that of Melibea, as well as the difference in thematic utilization of Petrarch. The Fiammetta who can write these lines is relatively unaffected by the physical delights of love, by the sensual awareness or "gozo" that is central to love-making in *La Celestina*. Even in the brief moments of her satisfaction, Fiammetta is more lovesick than physically ardent, and now we can begin to see why. Thematically she has been denied a body—that is to say, her body only exists for her (and for the reader) insofar as it is reflected in her fluctuating soul. Fiammetta may look at her body and face in the mirror and speculate upon their attractions for her lover (an action which would hardly occur to Melibea as a woman of "carne y hueso"), but in so doing she absorbs it into her mind as one more element of the internal world.[59]

In the same way that the heroine assimilates the realm of the flesh into her mind, the novel is built without the thematic presence of time, space, and value discovered in the outer world. Alien dimensions are, naturally enough, imported by Fiammetta's reason into her internal indecision, but once there, while they may still be alien, they lose their dimensionality. Like Melibea's "deleytosa visión de los nauíos," they are unreal except as they merge with a state of mind. In her well known "esclamazione alla luna" rather than realizing the harsh irrevocability of astral time, Fiammetta merely enters the moon's phases into the panorama of her desperation. She personalizes it by drawing it into herself. As for suicide by hurling herself into space, it is significant that while Fiammetta is capable of dwelling on it as a solution, she is thematically incapable of committing it. To do so would be an effective act, a final making up of the mind.

What is true about dimension is also, paradoxically enough, true about duration. Insofar as the *Fiammetta* is a totally subjective novel and hence a remote ancestor of *Á la recherche du temps perdu,* it does present a variety of internal time and space. Yet this is a strange and unfamiliar duration, a duration purified of all mundane contamination and replacing meaningful experience with sterile emotions and inexplicable passion. Rather than durative, a term which in *La Celestina* makes sense in its intimate conflict with chronology and hollow geometry, it would perhaps be more exact to describe Fiammetta's subjective realm as infinite and eternal—in its suffering. In other words, Fiammetta's love, unlike Melibea's, cannot result in sentimental awareness. She has no world—not even a lover existing as an independent person—in which she can discover value and in terms of which she can project her life and death.

Thus, in the *Fiammetta* there is no thematic encounter of human lives in dialogue, nor of duration and dimension in human life. There is no perspective, no patterning, and no awareness sharpened by desire and impediment. Boccaccio presents, instead, a single human life surrounded by impenetrable mystery and aware of itself only with sentimental distortion and elusive rationalization. Fiammetta, judged from the theme of *La Celestina,* has been trapped in the second person, and so isolated from the world. A creature of memory in which the *yo* is never actual, she can never find either the facts or the values which might give meaning to her tears.[60]

To conclude, a comparison of *La Celestina* to the *Tamburlaine* and the *Fiammetta* reveals the quality of Rojas' art of theme. All three works have one thing in common: in terms of the Petrarchist tradition (a phrase designed to include Machiavelli and Seneca as well as Petrarch himself) they turn their attention from vertical didacticism and its static vision of man to the dynamism of human life in unending struggle. But from this single point of departure the three themes follow divergent paths of preoccupation. Let us return first to the last two. Marlowe sees the struggle of life as external—the strife of body and exalted ego for that elementary victory which is the violation and the eating of the enemy. The *Tamburlaine,* accordingly, is all action and all dramatic monologue in "high astounding terms." There is in it no limitation to life—no time, no space, no reason's caution and precaution, and no fortune—except the ultimate violation of death. Or to say the same thing in another way, since each life has no aspiration, no vocation, beyond the conquest and murder of other lives, that, ironically, becomes its only limitation.

Boccaccio, on the other hand, follows an opposite path. He sees the vital struggle as internal and spiritual, a struggle without victory since his heroine is forced helplessly into the second person by her fluctuation between reason and amorous passion. In the *Fiammetta* there is practically no action and no real climax, for all is limitation, all a labyrinth of impossibilities. Instead of the present time of violation, there is a timeless narration, a narration in which the past is no different from the present and the present no different from the future. No change can ever take place except for deeper and more hopeless enmeshment in the inner toils of reason and passion.[61] This, in turn, leads to the disappearance of all dimensions, not because they are from instant to instant conquered, subdued, and stripped of their power to condition life but rather because they are absorbed by the subject, because they have no purchase on a life occupied only with itself. Fiammetta has lost the ego which might chart a vocational course through time and space and which might retaliate sentimentally against their impossibilities. Unlike Tamburlaine, she has urgent spiritual necessities but she is powerless to convert them into aims.

Both the *Tamburlaine* and the *Fiammetta* are fully thematic in their art. In both the several levels of creation—style, character, structure—are joined in a single organic whole, but, at the same time, both distort the human life they portray. Each is so consequential to its own variety of living conflict, to its own version of the theme, that it becomes to a certain extent tangential to the life of the reader. It is more than a question of verisimilitude or exaggeration. The objection that no tyrant was ever so tyrannical as Tamburlaine and no lover so miserable as Fiammetta is trivial. Rather, precisely because both Marlowe and Boccaccio propose to treat of human life only as alive and in operation, each is confronted with the community of this experience, with the simple fact that he has a reader or auditor actively engaged in the same process. It is not that the stories are incredible but that the theme is incomplete. In each case we realize from within our own lives that something is missing, that essential elements have not been written. Tamburlaine as a legendary tyrant (and so given at least partially in the third person) may act according to his tradition or to the author's desires without any possible objection on anyone's part. But if, thematically, he asserts his existence primarily as a man who is alive, we begin to sense his vital poverty, the foreshortening of his experience as compared to our own.

This is, of course, the danger that Rojas avoids—and with such apparent ease, that without the examples of the *Tamburlaine* and the *Fiammetta,* we might never have realized its existence as such a danger. Rojas' integration of the external with the internal kingdoms of conflict, his constant balancing of first and second persons in living dialogue, his simultaneous preoccupation with duration and dimension (the artistic invention of time, space, and experience), his calculated rhythm of event and reaction to event, his successful juncture of ironical apartness and human understanding, are not to be taken for granted. They render *La Celestina* a European masterpiece of thematic art. Rojas, by centering his attention on spoken awareness not as a mirror of the immediate deed or a remembrance of emotional transition but as a living axis between the world and the self, creates a completed range of experience. Awareness in *La Celestina* (and this is its essential difference from the *Tamburlaine* and the *Fiammetta*) is not a reflection of something else nor is it subsidiary to realms of truth which it cannot penetrate. It is the very center of human life, the terrain where all the forces of vital warfare carry out their reconnaissance, their skirmishes, their battles, and their campaigns.

Thus, it would be inexact to say that Rojas finds a happy middle ground between the thematic extremes of Boccaccio and Marlowe or that his success is a question of ideological thesis, antithesis, and synthesis. Instead, from his artistic distance, from his personal perspective, he integrates their extremes into his own full creation of life. Or to convert the verb into the adjective of Américo Castro, we may say that Celestina in the fullness of her created awareness represents a very Spanish quality: the integral wholeness of her own existence.

CHAPTER SEVEN

THE ART OF GENRE

IN A SENSE, this final chapter will be a conclusion, a gathering together of the several aspects of Rojas' art which have been our concern. It is fitting, therefore, that we begin with a brief meditation on the larger meaning of these essays, the single significance which emerges from them all. In this connection, the notion of *La Celestina*'s originality—a notion stressed by María Rosa Lida de Malkiel in a manner apart from its usual Romantic connotations—has a primary claim to our attention.

Artistically, *La Celestina* is more than original in the usual sense of the word; it is more than a splendid deviant from Aristotle and from Renaissance theories of comedy. As a literary work it is a unique, even a monstrous, creation. Nothing like it has ever been made, and I would almost dare to say, in defiance of Nietzsche, that nothing like it can ever be made again. It is apparent that on every level of artistry the relationship of the writer to the written word is strangely different from those relationships we have been taught (not just by the Renaissance but by our own experience) to recognize as novelistic, lyric, epic, tragic, or comic. In other words, *La Celestina,* by force of its very originality, is without genre. Now in saying this, I do not mean to imply—I could not mean to imply—that Rojas' creation is organically formless or that, lacking a poetic archetype, it is worthless. Such conclusions would involve other definitions of genre than that proposed here. For our purpose, genre is neither a synonym of form nor a traditional and indispensable recipe; it indicates instead a kind of art. It is a way of classifying the creative relationship of author to work.[1] Hence—as Rojas seemed to recognize tacitly when in 1502 he borrowed the hybrid and so monstrous term, *tragicomedia—La Celestina* being artistically unique is necessarily without genre. It is "ageneric," a monster in the sense that Lope de Vega was a monster.

The fundamental condition of this ageneric quality is Rojas' unreserved dedication to dialogue. We have seen in each of the four preceding essays the central importance of dialogue as a distinguishing quality of the work: in style, in characterization from situation to situation, in structure, and finally (when compared to the monologues of *Tamburlaine* and *Fiammetta*) in theme. In effect it is prodigious but true that Rojas' dialogic vision of life is in total organic accord with his means of expression; he has created a war of words which involves not just interchange between the characters but, even more, their exemplary and vital debate with an alien universe. From the most apparently insignificant details of the style to the deepest levels of vision and intent, dialogue is of the essence. It is a final matrix of creation. As a result of this conclusion, I find myself in almost diametric opposition to those who would classify *La Celestina* generically as a dialogue novel. I would maintain that it is without genre precisely because it is so profoundly and so uniquely dialogic.

I express myself in such a personal fashion on this matter not only because of my wonder at *La Celestina*'s ageneric profundity but also because in a previous essay I made a determined effort to isolate dramatic and novelistic strands in the fabric of the dialogue.[2] And for this, the reader may very well want to call me to account. What has happened is not so much that I have changed my mind; rather my perspective towards the problem has shifted radically. Whereas before, I tended to think of genre as a quality or condition of the created work, now I have come to think of it as a quality or condition of the creative process—of the art of Fernando de Rojas. Or to say the same thing in another way, looked at from the point of view of the novel and drama as existing forms, *La Celestina* seems to combine elements of both. But looked at in terms of art, its monstrosity is no longer the result of cross-breeding. It is the necessary product of a creative vision sufficient unto itself and conscientiously in search of its own expression. If my effort to bring out what Herder might have called the "organic unity" of the masterpiece has been at all successful, the traditional generic schism has thereby been denied.

Actually a number of observations made in the course of these essays have prepared for such a conclusion. The statement that *La Celestina* is dimensionally removed from both the novel and the drama should not by this time come as a great surprise. For example, in Chapter II we saw that decorum of language as practiced by Rojas was quite distinct from both that of Cervantes and that of the *comedia* of the Golden Age. In *La Celestina* the elevation of the individual speech seems to be contingent only on the immediate situation of which it forms a part; it does not depend on a more or less fixed definition of character or topic as do the two later forms. This statement may well have seemed arbitrary to the lover of the *Quijote,* given

Cervantes' ability to create independent lives and to play them one against the other. Yet in this very ability, in Cervantes' very practice of irony, we saw a certain definition apparently absent in *La Celestina*. As for the *comedia,* there was little room for argument; according to the most authentic source, the verse level depends on easily recognized topics or varieties of self-expression: *quejas, relaciones, cosas graves,* etc.

Again as far as characterization is concerned, the unprecedented psychology of consciousness which distinguishes the inhabitants of *La Celestina* was shown to be alien to both the novel and the drama. To use Goethe's distinction in the *Wilhelm Meister,* neither the slowly evolving sentiments of the one nor the motivating characteristics of the other are ever totally available to the awareness of the created individual. King Lear cannot know his own senility nor Huck Finn his own tenderness in the same manner that Pármeno and Sempronio know and phrase their own cowardice. The point was this: the former characters—Lear and Huck—exist partially in the third person and so cede something of themselves to author and reader. But in *La Celestina* existence is effectively limited to the first and second persons of dialogue—and to such an extent that we, as readers or critics, continually find ourselves in the incongruous situation of having to hunt out and interpret the characters' definitions of themselves.[3] The question may now arise: What about Fernando de Rojas? Must not he, at least, have had a firm acquaintance with his characters—and in the third person? The question is impossible to answer, but this much can be said: the most sinister aspect of Rojas' irony is the full and intimate knowledge of themselves which he so frequently grants his creations. Unlike Oedipus (known better to Sophocles than to himself) Melibea, Celestina, Calisto, and even Elicia know themselves for what they are; they are aware of their own living commitments to each situation, of their role at any given moment. And when this is not so (for example, Celestina at the moment of her death), the ignorance is usually not so much of the self as of the other. The irony resides, of course, in the fact that this is a dialogic consciousness—an awareness irretrievably linked to speech in its course—and so unavailing for inner salvation or willed redirection of the self.

In the realm of structure, the same idiosyncracy was plain. It was hardly necessary to speak of the novel with its variety of possible structures (usually reflecting the nature and the rhythm of the novelist's intervention), but we did comment on the undramatic or a-dramatic function of act and scene. The act, we observed, belies its name by framing not action but awareness—the key awareness of a central character as revealed in its encounters and situations. Act XII is a striking example with its subordination of a double climax to the acute self-disdain of Pármeno and Sempronio. Here, we must be careful with terminology. It is not that Rojas is a master of motivation and that he accentuates this conscious cowardice in order to prepare psychologically the murder of Celestina. Motivation is a dramatic term and hardly can describe Rojas' intense artistic contemplation of the patterns and trajectories of human consciousness. Greed is evidently the motive for the attack on Celestina, but Act XII, as an act, frames a less definable prerequisite: the field of dialogue—of expressed awareness—of which the deed is merely a minor part.[4] As for the scenes, we observed how little scenic they are, how little spectacle or visual stimulation they afford. Whereas in the drama the usual practice has been to frame action with suitable scenes and divide it into a traditional number of acts, in *La Celestina* the opposite is the case. Precisely because he is not concerned with action, Rojas frames his work in acts and divides it (by a process of more or less unobtrusive segmentation) into dialogic situations. This reversal of the usual structure of the drama is indeed the most evident sign of Rojas' generic originality. His art is that of trellis and vine—an art of life in dialogue skillfully guided to its completion—and never of geometric flower beds or calculated hedgerows.

Finally in the essay on theme we tried to bring out the profound difference between *La Celestina* and its thematic cousins, *Tamburlaine* and *Fiammetta,* one a "protodrama" and the other a "protonovel." I have coined these two terms in order to express the curious approximation of Marlowe and Boccaccio to the forms of drama and novel. Seen from the point of view of the generic literature which followed them, the creations of both are puzzling in their very familiarity to us. They are almost but not quite the way we think they ought to be—as it were, out of focus generically, and so in a sense more elusive in their meaning than the frankly ageneric *Celestina*. Why is this? What is the basic difference between them and the Spanish work? And, above all, how did Rojas maintain the artistic priority of his dialogue against the twin temptations of narrative introspection and poetic self-projection— on the one hand, the temptation of his subject matter and, on the other, that of his words? The answer given was roughly this: that Rojas never allowed either the first person or the second person to escape from its embracement in dialogue and set out on its own. Every word and, indeed, every thought in *La Celestina* is in varying degree dependent on both speaker and listener, determined dynamically by both. But in the *Tamburlaine* and the *Fiammetta* this is hardly the case. In these works, the theme of warfare is accommodated to the single point of view of victimizer or victim. Dialogue can no longer prevail, and in its place are to be found two different sorts of thematic monologue: one a terrifying hymn of violence and the other a terrified narrative of psychological subjection. In other words, the two genres of drama and novel begin to develop precisely at the moment that the author decides upon a point of view which will more or less faithfully define his relationship to the work—which will guide and so classify his artistry. From Marlowe's point of view, we remember, human experience appears to be a flux of incessant warlike action and the fiction he produces tends necessarily towards the dramatic. But from Boccaccio's point of view (in the *Fiammetta*) human experience has a different aspect. Appearing as a timeless passive suffering, the fiction which portrays it tends necessarily towards the novelistic. Neither—and this is in essence the same idea I have tried to express in discussing style, structure, and characterization—maintains or wants to maintain Rojas' prodigious refusal to limit his point of view and so to foreshorten his vision of life.

So much then for a résumé of all that we have already said or implied about the ageneric nature of *La Celestina*. Ultimately our scattered observations come together in an identical conclusion—in marvel at the prodigy of Rojas' dialogic art. But these essays cannot end merely with an exclamation point. In saying all that has been said, I find myself to have made unsuspected commitment, a commitment to state in explicit fashion those tacit assumptions about the nature and origin of literary genre which have guided my thinking. The very use of the term "ageneric" implies an understanding of genre which ought not to be left unexplained—particularly since *La Celestina* had such a decisive role in the birth of the European drama and novel. But before beginning I'want to stress that these are assumptions, not facts, convenient and, I hope, enlightening generalizations, not literary laws or necessities.

Let me begin with that first masterpiece in *La Celestina*'s tradition the *Libro de buen amor* (since the nature of the epic and its relationship to the *Poema del Cid* would take us too far afield). In any case, the *Libro de buen amor,* as Castro brings out so brilliantly in *España en su historia,* must also be thought of as ageneric—like *La Celestina,* a work of literature lacking the attribute of genre. Indeed this lack is so evident in the *Libro de buen amor* that instead of trying to divide it up between novel and drama (or between two and three authors), the more perverse temptation of scholars has been to subdivide it into its sources. It is an effort they would not dare to make with a Shakespeare, a Lope, or even a Cervantes and a Goethe. For these creators, the relationship with the created work is familiar and recognizable, the ultimate mysteries of genius notwithstanding. They are dramatists and novelists, and in spite of the fact that their deepest creativity may never be sounded, responsibility for the surface—the drama or novel as a whole—is plainly theirs. But for the *Libro de buen amor* this is hardly so; it is precisely on its narrative surface, in its immediate artistic relationship to Juan Ruiz, that it is the most puzzling and unfamiliar. Is he didactic or is he not? Does he describe himself or is the famous self-portrait merely literary? And what about the obviously impossible identification of himself with the dramatic character, Don Melón de la Huerta? In view of all these doubts, it is hardly surprising that the effective poetic presence and responsibility of the Arcipreste has been so often denied. What these critics do not realize is that the prodigy of the *Libro de buen amor* is that its poet has absorbed within his poetic *yo* not only all his reading, not only the external world, but also his own face and figure. The work is a prodigious first person in which Juan Ruiz plays all the parts, takes all the roles, and makes all the choices. The poet and his poetry have been totally identified, have become (as far as we are concerned) aspects of each other. Now in such a state of absorption by the first person, genre is obviously impossible, and this includes even those rudimentary mediaeval genres—debates, fables, allegories, *serranillas,* etc.—which are the raw material of Juan Ruiz' new poetic art. The *Libro de buen amor,* in other words, is such an absolutely personal creation, so completely formed in the first person, that it can never be repeated, continued, or even compared.[5] The error of past criticism has been precisely this: to consider the work a kind of anthology of mediaeval topics, to mistake lack of genre for lack of personality.

To go on to the second Arcipreste, the one from Talavera, we find in the *Corbacho* a new kind of creation in the first person. Here, the identification of the writer with what he is writing, the vital flow from the one to the other, seems to occur less as a continuing poetic process than as a sudden accident which happens in the process of teaching. The basic person of the *Corbacho* is, of course, the third—an exemplary third person inherited from mediaeval didacticism; but at times, and given the proper stimulus, the author relinquishes moral arbitration and joins in that kind of living out-burst which we discussed in our essay on style. The difference from the Arcipreste de Hita is clear: in the one case the poet draws the universe into himself; in the other, the moralist relinquishes morality and in a kind of verbal discharge gives life to his human creations. In other words, even though both Arciprestes write solely in the first person, the direction is reversed. One enfolds all about him in the poetic play of his own monologue;

the other is carried out of himself—becoming another *yo*—in a spurting monologue of popular speech. Thus, the Arcipreste de Talavera, in a sense, initiates what might be called the fictional relationship of author and character, a relationship consciously completed by Cervantes and Shakespeare (and hardly speculated upon again before the times of Pirandello and Unamuno). He does something of which neither Juan Ruiz nor the *juglar* of the *Cid* could boast; he makes somebody else out of himself.[6]

Now *La Celestina* carries on where the *Corbacho* leaves off. It adds, as we saw, the second person to the unregulated protoplasmic outbursts of the Arcipreste's ladies, and so discovers the first systematic use of dialogue. Allied to this discovery, of course, is Rojas' thematic preoccupation with the warfare of life, a theme crystallized by the reading of the *De remediis*—with its relentless assignment of man as second person singular to an alien universe. Indeed, it almost appears that the acute awareness of time and space which characterizes *La Celestina* (and which to a certain extent accompanies Petrarch's revival of Stoicism) is the cause of, or at least the condition of, Rojas' ability to create two lives simultaneously. For it is space and time which cement the first and second persons into living situations—dialogic situations. And precisely what Rojas creates in *La Celestina* are not characters or actions but dialogic situations appropriately situated by the speakers' awareness of time and space. The theme of *La Celestina,* then, with its insistence on the dimensional struggle of human life corresponds fully to its dialogic form. Where the two Arciprestes' writing in the first person had either absorbed or ignored dimensions, Rojas, writing in the first and second, makes of them a major constituent of theme. Monologue may be timeless and placeless as the pastoral novel seems to testify, but genuine dialogue is situated. It emerges from one life dimensionally limited and is directed towards another such life. It is in terms of this simple axiom of literature that Rojas achieved his prodigious and ageneric originality.

Spengler may or may not be right when he characterizes western man as "Faustian"—a man forever engaged in understanding and dominating the dimensional universe. But the great modern traditions of novel and drama seem to confirm him by their continuation of *La Celestina*'s temporal and spatial ordering. The novel has been traditionally a journey, a lengthy rise and fall through time and distance, while the drama has been a climactic concentration of deeds in a few hours and a few cubic feet. It is significant, indeed, that the Renaissance should have made a temporal and spatial interpretation of Aristotle and that the unities should at once have plagued Corneille and stimulated Cervantes in his search for narrative freedom. But the word "continuation," should not imply identity. The novel and the drama retain *La Celestina*'s "situation" in alien dimensions but at the same time take this situation more as a point of generic departure than as a central theme. What has happened is not difficult to explain. Whereas in *La Celestina* creation is confined to the first two persons of the vital paradigm, in the *Quijote* and in *King Lear* (to rely only on the greatest) life is made in all three persons. It is simultaneously a *yo*, a *tú*, and an *él*. And when this happens, space and time while still present and still thematic, no longer define the theme exclusively. For Shakespeare and Cervantes use the third person to return from that naked exposure of human *life* which so fascinated Rojas to a new portrayal of *man* in tragic (or novelistic) dignity. In *La Celestina* human life lacks the third person and is subjected to eternal, hopeless, and miserable warfare with its circumstance. It is tragic in its fate and comic in its indignity. But in the greatest novel and drama, full genres with all three grammatical persons integrated to each other, the novelist or dramatist can surpass the never-ending struggle of life and show us the victorious defeat or the desperate victory of man. Dialogue is still essential; space and time are still determinants of structure and fortune; but with the entrance of the third person these things are moulded to an artistic finality beyond themselves. They are organized in a novelistic or dramatic fashion and contribute to a novelistic or dramatic vision of man fully set forth by the artist. The creative absorption of Juan Ruiz has become the creative "ex-pression" of Cervantes and Shakespeare.[7]

To continue these reflections on literary genre—reflections suggested by our reading of *La Celestina*—would, I think lead us into an entirely new book. We would be involved immediately with the distinction of novel and drama, the role of space and time in seventeenth-century tragedy, the failure of the Spanish theatre to continue the intimate vitality of *La Celestina*'s dialogue, and other matters. These things would be interesting, but they are also beyond present capabilities. What matters now is the suggestion that the basic difference between *La Celestina* and dialogue that is fully generic is the absence in the former of the third person—the apparent lack of authorial participation in the presentation of speaker and listener. Previously we have spoken of this human independence, this priority of spoken consciousness, as a central aspect of Rojas' artistry; now we see it as a kind of key to the problem of genre. If *La Celestina* were rewritten by an author interested in controlling (or at least in guiding openly) its characters and circumstance, we might very well expect to find it converted into a novel or drama— or perhaps into a combination of both. As it is, we remain impressed by the almost rigorous lack of genre, the abundance of unique self-shaping life, in the *Comedia* and most of its interpolations.

I mention the sixteen-act *Comedia* specifically for an evident reason. It is that the real difference in artistry between the fifteen original acts of Rojas and the five he added in 1502 is, in my opinion, generic. The principal characters are identical; the style is unmodified; the structure of acts and scenes is apparently the same; and the theme seems to carry on from the original preoccupation. But we may indeed notice some modification in the over-all relationship of creator to created. We may notice the beginnings of genre. We have already spoken of those interpolations designed to reinforce Celestina's characteristic weakness for wine, and we explained them as representing a kind of afterthought on the part of Rojas. The vice of drunkenness had really been developed in conjunction with the picaresque banquet in Act IX, but when Rojas revised his text a few years later he held in his mind an image of the completed character and inserted references to wine whenever they seemed appropriate. The point is precisely this: that I believe the same process to apply to the added acts as a whole. It is, in fact, inconceivable that Rojas could have maintained an identical relationship to his work after an interval of years. It is inevitable that his increased critical consciousness of the nature of his achievement should lead him to some more direct and apparent artistic intervention. And with that, if our thinking about genre is at all meaningful, should come the first tentative fissures in the dialogue, the first hesitant segregation of novel and drama.

Specifically, I would make primary reference to the intrigue spun about Calisto by Areusa, Elicia, and Centurio—an intrigue which has a much greater resemblance to the usual course of events in Roman comedy than either Act I or the remaining fifteen of the *Comedia*. There is, in effect, an encounter of types—dupe, courtesan, braggart—within the ready-made patterns of deceit: the concealing curtain, the boast, the crafty lie. Thus, instead of life known through dialogue, we begin to see dialogue prearranged to fit the exigencies of human definition—of a third person (an *él* or an *ella*) for the first time openly contributory to a sequence of action. Of this change, Rojas' own *argumentos* offer interesting testimony.[8] For example, with reference to Elicia's overhasty relinquishment of mourning and return to her normal existence, he remarks ironically that she lacks "la castimonia de Penelope." Even more evident typification is the comment on Centurio as the reincarnation of a *miles gloriosus:* "E como sea natural a estos no hazer lo que prometen, escúsase como en el proceso paresce." In connection with these hints of comic characterization, the radical change in the behavior of Areusa may also be cited. As has been noted by those critics who would like to relieve Rojas of the responsibility for the added acts, whereas in Act VII Areusa seemed coyly hypocritical and in Act IX, violently rebellious against society, in these added acts she has become a model for the designing courtesan, the perfect *intrigante*. This is true, but less interesting than the change itself (and the mistaken conclusion which may be drawn from it) is Rojas' consciousness of what he has had to do. Unlike an imitator attempting to copy from an original, Rojas is perfectly aware that the process of continuation has resulted in a new Areusa, an Areusa typified for purposes of comedy: "Pues, prima, aprende, que otra arte es esta que la de Celestina; aunque ella me tenía por boua, porque me quería yo serlo." (XVII, 162–63) The dialogue no longer reflects the deep clash of awareness provoked by Celestina but rather the prepared misunderstanding and the minimal motivation of another art—an art which is just beginning to look like the art of comedy.

Along with these incipient changes in characterization and action we may also notice other new tendencies in dialogue and structure. Once the author and reader come to some sort of unspoken agreement as to physiognomy of the speakers in the third person, it becomes possible for these same speakers to disregard the listener, to speak without provision for anyone else's point of view. For example, such an interchange as the following would have been totally impossible in the *Comedia*:

CENT.—... dieron Centurio por nombre a mi abuelo e Centurio se llamó mi padre e Centurio me llamo yo.

ELIC.—¿Pues qué hizo el espada por que ganó tu abuelo esse nombre? Dime, ¿por ventura fué por ella capitán de cient hombres?

CENT.—No; pero fué rufián de cient mugeres.

AREU.—No curemos de linaje ni hazañas viejas. Si has de hazer lo que te digo, sin dilación determina, porque nos queremos yr. (XVIII, 169)

It is evident here that an internally generated trajectory of self-sufficient dialogue is no longer sustained. The trajectory is that of the joke externally generated—the remark directed to the reader and intended for his laughter. In other words, Elicia does not question Centurio because she wants to know the significance of his name; rather it is to set up the reply. We are on the frontiers of theatrical comedy, of a world in which dialogue is designed not for its own sake but for listeners beyond the footlights. Hence, when Areusa returns to the situation at hand there is a certain difficulty and embarrassment; she does not seem to know whether she ought to consider Centurio's explanation as an intentional witticism or not. It is the eternal dilemma of the straight man who must never laugh at the jokes which he inspires. In addition to this new kind of dialogue (centering on the traditional boasts of Centurio), there is at least a hint of theatricality to the structure of the three acts set aside for this intrigue. They are all three short, contingent upon a single setting, and designed to frame action rather than dialogic consciousness. In a sense, the internal structure has become identical with the external. We are confronted with three acts of intrigue appropriately divided and organized, and it is significant that Areusa herself describes what goes on in a word which later became one of the technical terms for theatrical plot: "Ay prima, prima, como sé yo, quando me ensaño, reboluer estas *tramas,* aunque soy moça!"

At the same time that this hesitant trend towards a dramatic (and even theatrical) ordering may be noticed in Acts XV, XVII and XVIII, there is a complementary emergence of novelistic features in the other two. It is precisely in these five added acts that Castro's division (a division with which he now disagrees) of *La Celestina* into planes of literary elevation is best justified.[9] Whereas in the *Comedia* the lives of masters and servants, of *pícaros* and courtly lovers were welded together in dialogic communion, here they begin to separate, to divide themselves between the typed insincerities of intrigue and the total revelation of the self in love. In effect, in Acts XVI and XIX, sentiment is no longer tinctured with argument; the dialogue represents the full blossoming of love, the opening of the *yo,* and its joining with the *tú.* How hard it is for Melibea to dissimulate in Act XVI; how impossible for her to engage in the necessary dialogue of deceit with her mother and father! What has happened is that (as if an anticipation of Goethe's sentimental definition of the novel) Rojas' new vision of Calisto and Melibea as lovers successfully in love renders it almost impossible for him to have them speak on any other terms. As the rest of the cast is typified, given more or less theatrical roles, the two lovers become increasingly novelistic, increasingly immersed in the inner world of their sentiment, increasingly incapable of a purely dialogic relationship with others. Thus, when Calisto remarks to his servants in his first speech of the added acts, "Mis cuydados e los de vosotros no son todos unos," he indicates for us the extent of the generic innovation in 1502. Novel and drama, servant and master, love and deceit, all so firmly united in the *Comedia,* have come undone. Rojas has taken an inevitable step beyond his original creative position and in doing so allows us to witness the birth (or at least the emergence of the possibility) of the two major genres of the coming century.

The act which best displays this new novelistic potentiality is, of course,

Act XIX with its second rendezvous in the garden. Unlike the first such rendezvous (in Act XIV), with its distrust, its overeagerness, its shyness, and its argument, here Rojas presents love as having learned from experience. Both Calisto and Melibea (after the month which Rojas so carefully inserts for them between Acts XV and XVI) are now lovers by definition, knowing lovers who refuse all preoccupations and interests beyond their love.[10] In other words, Rojas' announced intention to lengthen "el processo de su deleyte destos amantes" has resulted in a refinement of experience, an appropriately experienced experience without dialogic urgency. There is, thus, a kind of deceleration, a pastoral languor, a sentimental amplitude, which predicts the novel to come. Along with this, there enters an increased awareness, on the part of the lovers, of the garden around them, the concentric nature—flowers, foliage, moonlight, river, cypresses—which had not been mentioned at all in Act XIV. The characters no longer exist just in a situation but even more in a landscape, a private world given meaning by their love.[11] Since we are reading a record of experience rather than a combat in dialogue, it is only natural that the external world should have a much greater importance than before. As in the pastoral novel, landscape is an indispensable element of this completed—or at least static—adoration. Also significant is the insertion, unthinkable previously, of lyric stanzas which have as their theme this same communion of sentiment and nature (and which at least equal in value those of the *Diana*.)[12] The alternation of verse and prose is in itself an indication of metamorphosis. We are clearly approaching the frontiers of the novel, the genre of sentimentality and immediate experience.

Thus, when Rojas undertook the task of amplifying his work, of bringing its love affair to vital conclusion, he discovered that the generic nature of his creative task was subtly different. On the one hand, in the absence of Celestina the continuing intrigue carried on by Elicia and Areusa tends towards the theatrical and the purely comic—with all the jesting, typification, and scenic maneuver thereby implied. On the other, the love of Calisto and Melibea takes an opposite turn becoming more and more sentimentally self-sufficient, more and more a novelistic experience enfolding landscape and lyricism as well as an almost static dialogue. Since Rojas now knows his characters in the third person, since he has, in effect, known them for years, he can and must return to them with either novelistic or dramatic intentionality. By the very passage of time the generic relationship has been altered. It is true, of course, that this alteration is still implicit, still a shift of emphasis rather than of form. Externally *La Celestina* is ageneric and this holds for the added acts as well as the *Comedia*. Indeed, we could almost say that, within the external identity, the nascent separation in 1502 of novelistic and dramatic threads only tends to confirm our interpretation of this aspect of Rojas' artistry. His uniqueness, his peculiar originality as an artist, has led him to the very threshold of genre—to a sort of personal discovery of the inner significance of the novel and drama.

In conclusion, then, we may note that this intimate surrender to generic literature indicates the reason why Rojas could not initiate a new genre of his own—the "Celestinesque" of dialogue novel. In effect, in spite of numerous attempts, some of them fairly excellent and some of them fairly popular, these imitations remained imitative. Neither Feliciano de Silva nor Ferreira de Vasconcellos (two of the best and most readable), nor any of the others ever managed to accomplish more than a reasonable facsimile of the world of *La Celestina*. Unlike the *Quijote* and the long novelistic tradition which it founded, those works which sought to continue *La Celestina* necessarily imitated it directly. There could be no Celestinesque tradition without a Celestina copied from Rojas, and this involves all the usual processes of sterile caricature, exaggeration, lengthening, etc. But why is this so? Why should Rojas be followed only by a series of more or less brilliant Avellanedas? Precisely because meaningful continuation of *La Celestina,* that is to say continued creation (and not mere reproduction) from its accomplishment, necessarily imposes a consciousness of point of view, an awareness of this or that creative posture. And this in turn, as Rojas himself demonstrates in the additions of 1502, involves a tendency towards either novel or drama. In other words, as long as Feliciano de Silva and the rest imitated the genre of *La Celestina,* as long as they tried to write dialogue novels, they achieved more or less successful imitation and little else. But as soon as they—for example a Delicado and even a Torres Naharro—tried to surpass mere imitation and make original contributions of their own, they show an evident formal trend towards either novel or drama. The thing is inescapable. It is a condition of *La Celestina*'s uniquely ageneric creation. It is a condition of its total dedication to dialogue.

APPENDIX
NOTES
INDEX

THE AUTHORSHIP PROBLEM: FINAL CONSIDERATIONS

In this appendix, I shall make a statement which I carefully refrained from making in the text: the literary evidence brought forward here demonstrates conclusively that the additions of 1502 were written by Rojas. The reason for my previous restraint has already been explained. I realized that the only solution to the authorship question was to transcend it, to surpass it in literary comprehension; and this, in turn, required the acceptance of Rojas' prefatory statements at their face value. But now at the end of the book and within the separate frame of this appendix, these necessities no longer apply. It is now possible to reinterpret our analyses of the interpolations, as evidence indeed as substantial proof— that Rojas was the continuing author. To a reader not yet convinced this change of attitude may seem tautological. First I assume Rojas is the author and on that basis analyze selected passages, and then I turn around and use the results of the analysis to prove my original assumption. I admit the charge fully. The truth is that my certainty resides, first, in Rojas' statement and, second, in my reading experience. It follows that this certainty will not be shared by those who read *La Celestina* in terms of inappropriate aesthetic doctrines. Nevertheless, I am certain, and the supposition of this appendix is that any reader who reaches it in his reading will be equally convinced. Let us agree, then, that Rojas' responsibility for all the changes of 1502 is proved and continue the discussion from there.

This claim to certainty has one obvious effect on the usual chain of reasoning on the authorship question. It renders doubtful the evidence offered by statistical analysis of the language of *La Celestina*. The reader will remember House's reluctant conclusion that there may have been three authors to *La Celestina* because of the substantial variation in stylistic practice in the three major segments of the work. This now being contradicted for the added acts, it seems equally reasonable to go one step further and deny the validity of this approach to Act I.[1] In spite of our willingness to accept separate authorship for Act I, House's failure with the added acts leads us to believe that this is not a matter susceptible to statistical proof. It is still a literary problem.

Let us sum up in this way. There are, House shows, substantial differences in the style of *Comedia* and the style of the added acts; but, since the added acts are unquestionably by Rojas, these differences can only be due to a change of writing habits which occurred between the writing of the first edition and 1502. This was a period of probably four to five years, and if the changes in Rojas' style recorded by House took place in that time, who can deny that Act I, itself, might have been a tentative first version by a youthful Rojas—a first version that was only later completed as the *Comedia?* If time can bring about one stylistic evolution it can bring about another.[2]

At this point, I must make clear that I do not defend this extreme position. I do not claim to have proved or even to have shown that Rojas was the author of the whole of Act I as well as all the rest. Rather I stand on my original acceptance of Rojas' own statements (and will continue to do so as long as ironclad evidence does not invalidate them). But if I choose not to burden myself with the proof which falls to those who would contradict Rojas, I would like to point out that House's results show that linguistic evidence is not in itself decisive. Statistics cannot prove authorship either positively or negatively.

Along with statistics, source studies such as that undertaken by Castro Guisasola seem more or less indecisive for purposes of proof. Even if there were no such exception as that hidden utilization of Petrarch in Act I already discussed,[3] the absence of this or that source or group of sources would only show different needs or a differing variety of creation. It would be absurd to demand that a single author confine himself to fixed linguistic or literary habits along the course of his career. It is probable that Rojas was not the author of Act I, probable because he tells us so, but it is not proved. Act I could have been a first sketch of *La Celestina* written when Rojas was a very young man and completed as the *Comedia* a few years later. Certainly such a hypothesis would explain most of the evidence available—aside from the plain statements of the *Carta.*

It is necessary to insist on this possibility not so much because it is likely but because it allows us to surpass in our thinking a mechanical interpretation of Rojas' role as continuing author. If we are to believe sources and statistics with their arrogant pretense to proof, we must think of Rojas as finding Act I, reading it, getting out a fresh parchment, and sitting down to work. As a result his sources and his language differ measurably—in a fashion which can be measured —from those of the original fragment. To me, given the deep unity of *La Celestina* (a unity which runs beneath the continuing evolution of artistry through the three parts), this is incredible. Menéndez Pelayo could not bring himself to believe that there were two authors, and, while it is dangerous to go that far, his disbelief is understandable. It is indeed difficult to conceive of two authors writing two independent parts. Instead of this, *is it not more likely to assume that Rojas may have rewritten, touched up, or otherwise corrected, the fragment he discovered?* Is it not reasonable to think that he intervened to an appreciable extent in Act I rather than reproducing it as if it were for an edition with notes? We must not let changes in linguistic usage or in frequency of sources disguise this probability.

There are, of course, two arguments which can be marshaled against this supposition. The first is the extravagant praise given in Act I in the *Carta,* praise so sharply in contrast to Rojas' own pretense of modesty, and to his elaborately apologetic revelation of responsibility. The second is the failure to amend the text of the first act in 1502, a failure which has all the appearance of respect for an original text. But these arguments are not at all final. The whole atmosphere of mystification, of extreme humility, of alternate arrogance and timidity, which characterizes the prologue material tends to invalidate them. In other words, while we may not deny Rojas his claim to have continued a previous fragment without positive evidence, it is perfectly permissible to doubt the sincerity of his attitudes and opinions. It is believable that Rojas as a sardonic and harassed *converso* should have disguised the extent of his contribution to Act I with mock apology for one part and mock eulogy for the other. It is an example of duplicity worthy of some of his characters. We may even intuit therefrom the real sense of Rojas' profound treatment of that human reaction to warfare called cowardice.

As for the failure to amend Act I, it had *already been corrected,* and to do so further would only give the show away. Of the few facts we know about Rojas the following are perhaps the most significant: he fled the Puebla de Montalban to avoid the mistreatment of the local nobleman; he was an intellectual, an author, reader, and lawyer; he belonged to a Jewish family in a time of persecution. All of them along with the vision of life embodied in *La Celestina* permit us to suspect that Rojas' pretense of respect for Act I as untouchably perfect was at least partly an effort of self-defense.

Finally we may notice at least three slips in Act I, errors of composition which may well have resulted from momentary carelessness during the process of revision. These three are especially curious from our point of view since they seem to have no parallels in the rest of the text. The first is a reply of Calisto to Sempronio and was noted by H. Warner Allen: "Di pues, esse Adán, esse Salomón, esse David, esse Aristóteles, esse Vergilio, essos que dizes, como se sometieron a ellas?" (I, 50) The point is, of couse, that Sempronio has omitted both David and Virgil from his previous warning even though the usual or commonplace listing of victims of women includes them.[4] A second example is the apparent knowledge of Calisto's love affair displayed by Pármeno even though he is told nothing upon his entrance.[5] And finally there is the apparent misreading of an original text pointed out by Otis Green. It occurs in the following sentence as rendered by Cejador: "... tú ... desesperas de alcançar vna muger, muchas de las quales en grandes estados constituydas se sometieron a los pechos y resollos de viles azemileros e otras a brutos animales. No has leydo de Pásife con el toro, de Minerva con el can." (I, 45) As Green points out, the reference is inexplicable as it stands and should read "Minerva con Vulcán."[6] In all three cases, one is given an impression of failure to assimilate, to digest, an earlier version completely. These are not the sort of errors an original author would be liable to make; rather they suggest a task of rewriting carefully done, but with inevitable slips.[7]

Thus, while there are evident literary differences in the three stages of the work, they do not rule out the likelihood of *effective* single authorship. Certainly, the additions of 1502 are the property of Rojas, while Act I was probably rewritten extensively. Its primitive version was probably not Rojas' (even though there is a possibility that it might be something he began as a very young man and continued later on). These last two statements are, of course, opinions and must be labeled as such. The real truth is that any critic who ventures beyond Rojas' direct statements necessarily is opinionated, and there can be no harm in admitting it here.

THE *ARGUMENTOS*[1]

In the *Prólogo,* Rojas states the basic fact about the *argumentos* in these words: "Que aun los impressores han dado sus punturas, poniendo rúbricas o sumarios al principio de cada aucto, narrando en breue lo que dentro contenía: una cosa bien escusada según los antiguos scriptores usaron." Unlike the first act, the quality of these *argumentos*—their performance of their descriptive function—is so inadequate that Rojas' disclaimer has generally been believed. And rightly so. There is no reason to doubt that both the "argumento de toda la obra" and the *argumentos* to the individual acts were written by another hand. Yet this is, in itself, interesting. It indicates that the *argumentos* may correspond to the vision of *La Celestina* of its first readers—that they are its first recorded criticism. Here is an initial problem. What did the writer of the *argumentos* find important in *La Celestina*? In terms of what literary preconceptions did he interpret it? Or to ask the same questions in a simpler way, how was *La Celestina* read in 1499?

María Rosa Lida de Malkiel has suggested to me orally that the most likely model for the *impressores* were the *argumenta* and scholarly apparatus accompanying those editions of Terence which went into print in the seventies, eighties, and nineties of the fifteenth century in most European countries. It is a notion clearly supported by the precedent mentioned by Rojas, "los antiguos scriptores." Admittedly, in the brief investigation I have made, I have seen no edition of Terence presenting *argumentos* in exactly the same way as *La Celestina*. There are usually initial summaries for each play—"argumentos de toda la obra"—but without special recapitulation at the beginning of the individual act. Instead there is a running commentary in the margin—Donatus, Servius, Calpurnius, etc.— providing moral and critical observations on what is taking place in the dialogue. Nevertheless, since the customary beginning for these comments is "in hac scena" followed by reference to movement and motive, they may very well share the responsibility for the "argumentos" appended to *La Celestina*.[2]

My supposition is, then, that when Rojas sent his manuscript to Burgos in 1499, it was assimilated to the printing tradition which had already come into being for the comedies of Terence. Since I believe it unnecessary to postulate a missing first edition without *argumentos*,[3] I imagine, first, a more or less careful reading of the manuscript—with its "dramatic" division into acts and indication of speakers. This brought the decision to print it in the only way that Fadrique Alemán de Basilea (Friedrich Biel) knew how to print such a work: as he had seen Terence done in the years of his apprenticeship. These suppositions are given greater weight by the English bibliographer, A. W. Pollard, who remarks that even the woodcuts of the 1499 edition were closely imitated from the Grüninger Terence (Strassburg, 1496).[4]

What were the literary preconceptions of this Terentian tradition? As E. W. Robbins brings out clearly,[5] there were none. The Terentian commentators were characterized by their wholly extraliterary moralizing approach—seeing the drama only as a didactic form, a species of "moral action." It is in deep accord with this vision that the writer of the *argumentos* thought of *La Celestina* neither as dramatic (in the sense of being theatrical) nor as novelistic (in the sense of being designed for pleasure reading). Rather it was an active "imitation" of life, a compendium of action in dialogue leading to a morally exemplary conclusion. Thus, in the "argumenta de toda la obra," the most important words are adjectives of moral evaluation, "malo," "casto," "amargo," etc.:

"Por solicitud del pungido Calisto, vencido el casto propósito de Melibea (entreueniendo Celestina, mala y astuta muger, con dos seruientes del vencido Calisto, engañados e por ésta tornados desleales presa su fidelidad con anzuelo de codicia y de deleyte), vinieron los amantes e los que los ministraron en amargo y desastrado fin. Para comienço de lo qual dispuso el aduersa fortuna lugar oportuno, donde a la presencia de Calisto se presentó la desseada Melibea."

Rojas may have here and there in the prologue material claimed moral advantages for his work, and it was only natural that he should do so. But he can hardly be thought responsible for the oversimplification and general inanity of this summary. As he knew only too well, neither did Melibea begin with a "casto propósito" nor were Sempronio and Pármeno "engañados." He must, in fact, have laughed aloud when he read it.

When we turn to the *argumentos* for the individual acts, however, all this goes by the board. There the word, "action," in the notion of "moral action" is the one most heavily underscored. If the "argumento de toda la obra" overstressed the moral patterning of *La Celestina,* these *argumentos* overstress the plot—the bare moral (or immoral) scheme of happening. Their author has failed to realize that this is, as we have seen, the least important aspect of the work he is attempting to summarize. Misled by a doctrinal approach, he is totally blind to Rojas profound and ironical investigation not of action but of reaction, not of doing but of feeling and experience as it is projected into dialogue. We have already remarked on the misleading summary to Act II, and the others are almost as bad. From an historical point of view this is not surprising. But if we as readers want to find out what *La Celestina* is really about these *argumentos* are the last place to which we ought to turn. It is in them that a cast of three-dimensional, living, deeply human characters is first reduced to moral third persons and then thrust into incessant action.

A key indication of the particular inadequacy of these individual *argumentos* is a word repeated in them over and over again, the word "razón." In the *argumento* to Act I, for example, we find it used in three different ways:

"Calisto ... habló con vn criado suyo llamado Sempronio, el qual despues de muchas *razones,* le endereçó a vna vieja llamada Celestina ... Entretanto que Sempronio está negociando con Celestina, Calisto está *razonando* con otro criado suyo, por nombre Pármeno. El qual *razonamiento* dura hasta que llega Sempronio y Celestina a casa de Calisto."

As it is used here, the appropriate synonym for *razonar* is not *pensar* but *hablar,* and it is curious to note that almost every *argumento* has recourse to one or the other of them. Why? Because the writer of the *argumentos* in attempting to outline action exclusively finds whole pages in which nothing happens, pages dedicated to dialogue. As we have seen, it is in these pages that *La Celestina* is at its most Celestinesque, but they are dismissed in the *argumentos* with such phrases as "después de muchas razones" or "estando todos entre si razonando, viene Lucrecia." These are actually the words used to slur over Areusa's outburst on liberty (Act IX) and Celestina's final seduction of Melibea (Act X). The words "razón" and "habla" indicate the failure of the *argumentos* to penetrate into the dialogic substance of *La Celestina.* Their reiterated use reflects the almost palpable reluctance of the work to submit to a definition of "comedy" as "action."

The inadequacy of these *argumentos,* an inadequacy which even our brief examination has made painfully evident,[6] brings up a second problem. It is that of the authorship of the five acts added in 1502. There can be no doubt but that their author (and it is curious that critics have failed to stress the point) is new. The *impressores* charged by Rojas with responsibility for the 1499 *argumentos* leave the scene in 1502. Under these circumstances, we may go on to suppose, Rojas, himself, must have undertaken the task of summary. It might not have occurred to him to include *argumentos* in the first edition (he was, after all, a creator and not a critic) but afterwards, why should he allow another to do this work for him? And if this is so, the change should be clearly visible in the style and technique of the *argumentos* themselves. We can hardly expect to find calculated self-criticism in them—after all they are *argumentos* and nothing more— but if Rojas was in fact their author, they should afford some small insight into the intentions behind the additions.

The specific circumstances of the expansion of *La Celestina* in 1502 make it easy to demonstrate the change of style and approach in the *argumentos.* Since the five new acts are inserted in the middle of Act XIV, its beginning stays as it was, while its end (the fall of Calisto) becomes the end of the *Tragicomedia*'s Act XIX. The result was, of course, that the old *argumento* to Act XIV had to be rewritten to accommodate the new content. The important point is this: when Rojas began to change the *argumento,* he did not just add on a few sentences but rewrote all of it—including the summary of the unchanged beginning of the act. And, in doing so, he affords us the unique privilege of comparing the 1499 and 1502 *argumentos* describing identical happenings. In 1499 the *argumento* in question begins as follows:

"Esperando Melibea la venida de Calisto en la huerta, habla con Lucrecia. Viene Calisto con dos criados suyos, Tristán y Sosia; pónenle el escalera, sube por ella y métese en la huerta onde halla a Melibea. Apártase Lucrecia; quedan los dos solos."[7]

The method is familiar: a detailed outline of action along with an almost resigned reference to the conversation of the characters, "habla con Lucrecia." But when Rojas himself rephrases this in the first sentence of the 1502 *argumento* it has a very different appearance:

"Está Melibea muy afligida hablando con Lucrecia sobre la tardança de Calisto, el qual le auía hecho voto de venir en aquella noche a visitalla, lo qual cumplió, e con él vinieron Sosia e Tristán."

The most notable difference is grammatical, the substitution of one long syntactically complex sentence for the short declarative clauses of 1499. It is a change of style to be found all through the added "argumentos" and seems to imply a refusal to reduce the work to the bare contours of action—to limit it to successive happenings. Rather the effort is to show interrelationship, the webbing of human involvement preceding catastrophe; and for this purpose the grammar of description must have a similar involvement. Even more important from our point of view, however, is the fact that the revised "argumento" does not limit itself to saying, "habla con Melibea," but goes on to tell the reader what Melibea and Lucrecia are talking about and how Melibea feels during the conversation: "Está Melibea muy afligida hablando con Lucrecia sobre la tardança de Calisto ..." For the first time an effort is made to get behind the vacant and evasive verbs, "razonar" and "hablar," and to explain what is really going on in *La Celestina*. And this does not occur here only; it is characteristic of all the 1502 *argumentos*:

"Calisto se retrae en su palacio e quéxase por auer estado tan poca quantidad de tiempo con Melibea ..." (XIV, 114)

"... despídese Elicia de Areusa, no consintiendo en lo que le ruega, por no perder el buen tiempo que se daua, estando en su asueta casa." (XV, 131)

"Pensando Pleberio e Alisa tener su hija Melibea el don de la virginidad conseruado ... están razonando sobre el casamiento de Melibea ..." (XVI, 144)

"Elicia, caresciendo de la castimonía de Penélope, determina de despedir el pesar e luto que por causa de los muertos trae, alabando el consejo de Areusa en este propósito ..." (XVII, 153)

Only Rojas, with his intuitive awareness of the unimportance of plot to his creation, would or could have written the "argumentos" in this way.[8]

There are, furthermore, certain observations in these "argumentos" which illuminate even more sharply the "'intent of the artist"—to use Augusto Centeno's phrase. We may notice, for example, the way in which the *argumento* to Act XVI underlines Melibea's frantic reaction to her parents' misconceptions about her: "... en tan gran quantidad le dan pena las palabras que de sus padres oye, que embía a Lucrecia para que sea causa de su silencio en aquel propósito." It is a summary which approaches the terms of Menéndez Pelayo's praise of the same incident in his defense of Rojas as the continuing author: "¡Qué tormenta de afectos se desata en su alma bravía y apasionada! ... siente oprimido el corazón por el engaño en que viven sus padres."[9] This is a significant coincidence of opinions.

In the *argumento* to Act XIV there is an equally penetrating comment on Calisto's anguished monologue—a comment which explains (perhaps better than any critic has since explained it) the sense of Calisto's sudden crisis of doubt as well as the way he seeks to resolve it:

"Calisto se retrae en su palacio e quéxase por auer estado tan poca quantidad de tiempo con Melibea, e ruega a Febo que cierre sus rayos para auer de restaurar su deseo." (XIV, 114)

Rojas is trying to tell us just this: the sense of Calisto's anguish, his sudden concern for honor and for the death of his servants comes—and can only come—at a time when his desire has been satisfied. The great monologue of Act XIV, perhaps the greatest creative achievement of the additions, was possible only on the morning after the night of love. Both Rojas and Calisto know it; both know that the release from amorous urgency has exposed an underlying ugliness. Hence, the *argumento* alludes to Calisto's solution to his inner conflict, his attempt to "restore" passion artificially. The phrase, "restaurar su desseo," in effect, is a final assessment of Calisto's weakness, his willingness to evade action (revenge or defense of his honor) by retreating into a world of imagination with the phrase we remember: "Pero tú, dulce ymaginación, tú que puedes me acorre. Trae a mi fantasía la presencia angélica de aquella *ymagen* luziente ..." Calisto's solution is the solution of restored desire artificially induced, a Romantic solution, and it is almost savagely exposed for what it is in the *argumento*.

Thus, the *argumentos* of 1502 furnish their own evidence of Rojas' increased critical awareness of the nature of his task.

NOTES

CHAPTER ONE

1. This is reproduced from Foulché Delbosc's critical edition of the *Comedia* in the "Biblioteca Románica" (Macon, 1900). Cejador who is usually referred to here does not include it. The italics are, of course, mine.

2. This is from Cejador's two-volume edition in the "Clásicos Castellanos" (Madrid, 1945). This is the most convenient edition if not the best, and from now on act and page references to it will be found in parentheses following citations. Discrepancies between the text as given here and that of Cejador are the result of a checking of all deletions and interpolations with the text of Foulché Delbosc mentioned in note 1 above. From Act VIII on, page references are to Volume II.

3. Scholars agree that neither Cota nor Mena, for one reason or another, seems to be a likely candidate for responsibility for the first act. Of the two, however, Cota with his tonally and circumstantially parallel poem, *Diálogo entre el Amor y un viejo,* seems to have the preference.

4. *Diálogo de la lengua,* ed. J. F. Montesinos ("Clásicos Castellanos," Madrid, 1928), pp. 177–78.

5. *Diálogo de la lengua,* pp. 176–77.

6. *Variedades o el mensajero de Londres* (London, 1824), I, 226.

7. Foulché Delbosc's criticism may be found in three articles all entitled "Observations sur la *Celestina"* in the *Révue Hispanique* for 1900, 1902, and 1930. The Serrano y Sanz documents were included in his "Noticias biográficas de Fernando de Rojas," *Revista de archivos, bibliotecas y museos,* VI (1902), 245–98.

8. Cejador's opinions are, of course, to be found in the notes and introduction to his edition while House's are specified in note 11. Azorín's essay was first printed in *Los valores literarios* (Madrid, 1913). Delpy, the most recent defender of Foulché Delbosc, has an article in the *Bulletin Hispanique,* XLIX (1947), 261–75, entitled "Les profanations du texte de *La Celestina."*

9. *Orígenes de la novela* (Edición Nacional, Santander, 1942), III, 247.

10. *Orígenes de la novela,* III, 259.

11. R. E. House, M. Mulroney, I. G. Probst, "Notes on the Authorship of the *Celestina,"* *Philological Quarterly,* III (1924), 88. House's previous article announcing his literary support of Foulché Delbosc, "The Present Status of the Problem of Authorship of the *Celestina,"* may be found in the preceding volume of the same periodical.

12. "Notes on the Authorship," p. 91.

13. See S. Gili Gaya's introduction to the *Obras* of Diego de San Pedro ("Clásicos Castellanos") for the change in stylistic habits.

14. Ramón Menéndez Pidal, "La lengua en tiempos de los reyes católicos," *Cuadernos Hispanoamericanos* (1950).

15. At the beginning of his section on *La Celestina,* Menéndez Pidal states categorically, "Rojas mismo añadió cinco autos mas en 1502" and does not bother to refer to the matter again.

16. An additional bit of positive evidence for Rojas' authorship of the added material is the mention of "Mollejar el ortelano" in one of the interpolations in Act XII. This individual—one of Sempronio's past masters—possesses the only non-Latinized name in the work. Hence, it is at least curious to note that according to the witnesses who testified to Rojas' "hidalguia" his family property at Montalbán was known as the "guerta de Mollegas" or "Moblejas." Americo Castro assures me that from a paleographic standpoint the differences in spelling are easily explained. It may very well be that the little incident related by Sempronio—*"E también yo tenía mis questiones con los que tirauan piedras a los páxaros, que assentauan en vn álamo grande que tenia, porque dañauan la ortaliza* (XII, 90)—is a personal reminiscence drawn from Rojas' own childhood.

Since the composition of this chapter, Gina Adinolfi has contributed a splendid monograph, "La *Celestina* e la sua unitá di composizione," to *Filologia romanza* (1954) in which she confirms both my conclusions and approach. I was particularly pleased to see her premise her explanation of the interpolations on Rojas' "più critica coscienza della natura della sua opera" (p. 41).

CHAPTER TWO

1. Naturally, these two kinds of interpolation are not completely separate one from the other. Many of the interpolations designed to reinforce, for example, the arrangement of thematic material also reflect a concern with linguistic circumstance. Nevertheless it is a very useful distinction for our purposes. It gives new importance to a number of textual modifications which have been either disregarded completely or hastily misinterpreted by critics interested in finding support for their authorship theories. Among the corrections which are primarily stylistic, according to the above definition, there are not only additional proverbs and passages of erudition but also what we called Rojas' "minimal self-corrections," deletions and insertions of no more than a word or two. It is with these that we shall begin; it is with these that we may hope to find the most immediate relationship between word and artistry of style.

2. All interpolations are italicized.

3. Stanley M. Sapon, in a Columbia University doctoral dissertation, calculates a percentage of 54.69 for interrogative constructions in *La Celestina,* a percentage corresponding to 736 individual questions.—*A Study of the Development of the Interrogative in Spanish* (Columbus, Ohio, 1951).

4. One is tempted at first glance to distinguish between these two styles in *La Celestina* in terms of the writer. In the one case, he seems to be a calculating intellectual dedicated to a tight and well constructed style; in the other, he seems carried away by

creative inspiration to such an extent that he bursts forth like Rabelais in a new style of vital spontaneity. Such a distinction I believe to be wholly inexact (except perhaps for such passages in Act I as that developing the phrase "puta vieja"). Rojas, in my opinion, manages these two styles consciously and in terms of character and situation. In support of this opinion, I would point out, first, the hidden vitality of the style directed towards the *tú*, its adjustment to the life of the listener beneath the formal coherence of the argument; and, second, the careful gradation of the stylistic breakdown in the above passage of Areusa's. The fact of interpolation is also significant in this connection. In the *Comedia* the speech began with a brief general statement of Areusa's project of independence to be justified by a description of the sad fate of servant girls. Then, as she launches into her subject, she grows more and more worked up and begins to feel as if she herself were a servant, the target of hypothetical insults. At this point, rhyme and reason disappear along with awareness of the circle of listeners, and the living substance of Areusa's indignation invades her language. When this spurt of interior life exhausts itself, as it must, she returns to half-proverbial antitheses and a conclusion beginning with "por esto ..." Rojas, upon rereading this, seems to have felt that he had only expressed Areusa's sentiment negatively. He had shown the momentary outrage, the violent rejection of servitude, but he had not expressed any positive values. If we are to believe Max Scheler, the potentialities of her sentiment in terms of value discovery had not been realized completely. She had not yet discovered the "polar" value. For this reason Rojas inserts a passage that, in the words of Menéndez Pelayo, is both "vivo" and "sabroso." Rapid evocation in imaginary dialogue of the gossip and minimal excitements of a neighborhood give a sense of new and living discovery to the abstractions of liberty, equality, and fraternity. And when Areusa returns from living evaluation out of her own life, she does not attempt reasoned conclusion or summary. Rather she exclaims, paraphrasing Petrarch: "¡O tía, y qué duro nombre e qué graue e soberuio es señora contino en la boca!" She completes not a thought but an implicit evaluation in one of the best sentences of the book. Its poetic force is manifested by a comparison with Petrarch's original: "Durum enim superbumque nomen est dominus." Rojas' use of this style is both calculated and splendid.

5. This adjective was borrowed from the English translation of Martin Buber's *Dialogisches Leben* (Zürich, 1947), a work which attempts to derive a sort of metaphysical communion from the dialogue situation. It is a thematic possibility radically opposed to Rojas' derivation of dialogue from what we shall see to be a theme of war and ultimate human separation.

6. *Corbacho,* ed. José Rogerio Sánchez ("Biblioteca Clásica," Madrid, 1929?), pp. 278–79.

7. We need not accept Sosia's cynical comment on this—"¡Ante quisiera yo oyrte essos miraglos! Todas sabés essa oración después que no puede dexar de ser hecho"—as Rojas' personal interpretation any more than we need to attribute to him Areusa's gross portrayal of Melibea.

8. This includes not only the two Arciprestes but also, as Menéndez Pidal shows, most of the prose and verse of the fifteenth century. Even *La Celestina*'s most illustrious successor, *La Dorotea* is much less clear and logical than its ultimate model.

9. It is significant that in his handling of this problem, Cicero often refers to the practices of the "new comedy."

10. For convenience deletions are bracketed while interpolations are underlined. Deletions will be included wherever possible.

11. Another kind of clarifying interpolation has to do with changes made necessary by the added material, either the five acts or other interpolations. A typical example is the sentence inserted in Melibea's parting speech to Calisto after the first garden scene: *"Sea tu venida por este secreto lugar a la mesma ora, porque siempre te espere apercebida del gozo con que quedo, esperando las venideras noches."* (XIV, 120)

See also the interpolations in Act XX (p. 192) and the *"No tengo ya enojo"* in Celestina's parting thrust to Pármeno and Areusa (VII, 260). This explains her departure in spite of her interpolated desire to remain as a witness to their love. Others are mere clarifications of sense, such as the following: "CEL.—No es cosa mas propia del que ama que la impaciencia. Toda tardança les es tormento. Ninguna dilación les agrada. En vn momento querrían poner en efecto sus cogitaciones. Antes las querrían ver concluydas, que empeçadas. Mayormente estos nouicios *amantes* que contra cualquiera señuelo buelan sin deliberación." (III, 128) In the *Comedia,* the implied antecedent, "del que ama," was so far removed from "nouicios" that the latter might well have been interpreted in its religious sense. Other examples of such specific clarification are "niños de *cuna*" (VI, 123) and "dellos" (IV, 168).

Finally, there is the major group of interpolations designed to clarify meaning in terms of the lives of the speaker or listener. In addition to those studied in detail, we may mention Pleberio's *"a mandar"* (XX, 191), more appropriate to his station, and Pármeno's *"alguna"* (XII, 79) expressing the uncertainty of his fear.

12. Sempronio rejects Calisto's linguistic adornment in dialogue for exactly the same reason that Cicero advises against such language for the successful orator: "in dicendo autem vitium vel maximum sit a vulgari generi orationis, atque a consuetudine communis sensus abhorrere."—Cicero *De Orat.* 1, 3, 12.

13. See note 11.

14. As Castro Guisasola points out, these remarks are taken from Petrarch's "Gratiamque non mediocrem Ciceronis habeo, de cuius tribus exiguis granis tres ingentis aristas messui: ex quibus culto adhibito messis uberior nasci queat. Ita se res habet: doctorum hominum verba praegnantia sunt." The significant thing is not only the extent of adaptation but also the fact that Rojas selected this passage from a part of the *De remediis* far removed from the prologue to the second part. (Dialogue 114).

15. Each of these single words bolsters in its own way the grammatical logic of the thought: "más" introduces a second reason for Pármeno's fear and separates it categorically from the first; *"aparte"* strengthens Celestina's transition from past to future in her thought by further stressing "dexada"; *"que"* subordinates to the idea of old age the conclusion that there is little danger (or hope) of being violated on the way home.

16. Along with these interpolations of grammatical connectives we might list those adverbs giving more precision to time relationships: *agora, al principio,* and *después.* (III, 136; IV, 182; XI, 75)

17. Other examples of summation and conclusion in 1502 are not as unfortunate as the above:

CEL.—Pero pués en mi dicha estaba tu ayrada respuesta, padézcase él su dolor, en pago de buscar tan desdichada mensajera. Que pues en tu mucha virtud me faltó piedad, también me faltará agua si a la mar me enbiara. *Pero ya sabes que el deleyte de la vengança dura un momento y el de la misericordia para siempre.* (IV, 182)

Areu.—... El vientre no se le he visto; pero, juzgando por lo otro, creo que le tiene tan floxo, como vieja de cincuenta años. No sé que se ha visto Calisto, porque dexa de amar otras, que mas ligeramente podría hauer e con quien más él holgasse; *sino que el gusto dañado muchas vezes juzga por dulce lo amargo.* (IX, 33)

These general statements fit into the dialogue not only because of the brevity of the speeches they conclude but also because they derive doctrine from life and present it briefly in a new aspect. Instead of betraying the logic or argument as in the above, they give it more significance. See also "... *pues dizen que ninguna humana passión es perpetua ni durable"* (VIII, 11); *"E si no crees en dolor, cree en color, e verás lo que viene de su sola compañía"* (VII, 252), and others. An example introducing a topic occurs in Act VII:

Cel.—Porque la mocedad en solo lo presente se impide e ocupa a mirar; mas la madura edad no dexa presente ni passado ni por venir. Si tú touieras memoria, hijo Pármeno, del passado amor, que te tuue, la primera, posada, que tomaste venido nueuva-mente en esta cibdad, auía de ser la mía. Pero los moços curays poco de los viejos. Regisvos a sabor de paladar. *Nunca pensays que teneys ni haueys de tener necessidad dellos. Nunca pensays en enfermedades.* Nunca pensays que os puede faltar esta florezilla de juuentud. Pues mira, amigo, que para tales necessidades, como estas, buen acorro es vna vieja conoscida, amiga, madre e más que madre, buen mesón para descansar sano, buen hospital para sanar enfermo, buena bolsa para necessidad, buena arca para guardar dinero en prosperidad ..." (VII, 232-33.)

Celestina argues on the basis of past, present, and future and the interpolation was evi-dently intended to introduce in general terms those arguments applying to the future need of youth for older people. A logical gap is again filled.

18. Only one other interpolation adds more than one proverb: "Cel.—No temo esso, que de día me auiso por donde venga de noche. *Que jamás me subo por poyo ni calçada, sino por medio de la calle. Porque, como dizen: no da passo seguro, quien corre por el muro e que aquél va más sano que anda por llano. Más quiero ensuziar mis zapatos con el lodo que ensangrentar las tocas e los cantos* ..." (XI, 74-75) Here proverbs are used to contribute to the thematic note of space and are not allowed to reproduce themselves as in the one quoted above. The false impression of proverbial quantity in the interpolations is probably due to the fact that proverbs have not usually been distinguished from added conclusions and other erudite material.

19. This tendency has hardly been taken into account by those who go so far as to criticize interpolations of a single proverb, such as the following: "Cel.—No sé quién te abezó tanta filosofía, Sempronio. Semp.—Señor, no es todo blanco aquello que de negro no tiene semejança, *ni es todo oro quanto amarillo reluze."* (VIII, 20) Rojas seems to feel that proverbs, like the swallows and friars above, can hardly stand alone, and that the sentence in the *Comedia* was therefore unbalanced. A glance at several other major works of Spanish literature will support him in this feeling. It is interesting to speculate (since I know of no study of the problem) on the stylistic reasons for the phenomenon.

Each proverb seems to be felt by the speaker or writer to be incomplete in itself; it is a facet of the corpus of folk wisdom rather than a single epigrammatic gem capable of isolated brilliance. This interdependence of proverbs, this reliance one upon another, is perhaps reflected in their poematic style. They are, in a sense, verses of an unwritten poem; and in saying this, I refer not only to the tendency towards internal rhythm and rhyme, but also to the fact that each proverb often endows its particular aspect of wisdom with a poetic charge, that is to say a metaphor. Hence a possible significance for the word "refrán." See E. S. O'Kane, "On the Names of the 'Refrán,'" *Hispanic Review,* XVIII (1950), 1–14. The result is that just as in more formal poetry each metaphor requires and invokes the presence of another, so each proverb depends on the support of the one following it. Truth is communicated not rationally but by semi-poetic intuitions which reinforce each other. Ortega y Gasset implies very much the same thing when he compares proverbs to "almenas" providing a successive defense for the user. Naturally this inherent stylistic tendency can be exaggerated (as in the above example or as in the *Quijote*) and can produce a comic effect; but this confirms rather than denies its existence.

20. Notice the careful deletion of "mayormente en verano" to avoid word repetition with "vna golondrina no haze verano" and that of the introductory clause for Pármeno, "e tal qual es éste," which is no longer useful.

21. Representative deletions of this sort are: "mayormente en verano" in the passage last considered (p. 53) and "por qué me dexaste quando yo te havía de dexar" (XXI, 212) because of the excessive emphasis on the verb "dexar" in its proximity; etc.

22. These figures include as a separate unit of deletion or interpolation not only isolated units but also units following or preceding a change of speaker, even though none of the original text intervenes.

23. It may be argued that this in itself is an over-all principle of style, but such an argument, while true, is beside the point. What matters is that Rojas' dedication to dialogue would seem to deny his artistry as master of the whole. He must have taken a stylistic position towards scene and act as well as speech or he never could have built *La Celestina* as he did build it. It would have remained a conglomeration of living interchange held together by the plot but without a total stylistic significance.

24. See her article, "Four Paradoxes in *La Celestina,*" *Romanic Review,* XXXVIII (1947), 53–68.

25. The inclusion of this phrase in all current texts of *La Celestina,* along with most of the other deletions, is testimony to a mistaken belief on the part of scholars (we have already seen it in the case of Foulché Delbosc) that the oldest version is necessarily the best. Other similar examples of such deletions are "Cristóbal fué borracho" (III, 131) and "O mis grandes servidores" (XIII, 109), a phrase of meaningless pomposity.

26. See the following passage with its often noticed reminiscence of the *Roman de la rose:* "CAL.—¡O desdichado! Que las cibdades están con piedras cercadas e a piedras, piedras las vencen; pero esta mi señora tiene el coraçón de azero. No ay metal, que con él pueda; no ay tiro, que le melle. Pues poned escalas en su muro: vnos ojos tiene con que echa saetas, vna lengua llena de reproches a desuíos, el asiento tiene en parte, que media legua no le pueden poner cerco." (VI, 221) The topic of the cure for love's wounds is also mentioned by Guillaume de Loris (see lines 1724–27).

27. "Comedia de Calisto y Melibea," *Realidad,* V (1949). At a time when the manu-

script for this book was already in the hands of the publisher, I received a copy of Carmelo Samonà's extensive and excellent study of this particular aspect of *La Celestina, Aspetti del retoricismo nella "Celestina"* (Rome, 1953). Taking as a model María Rosa Lida de Malkiel's magistral study of Juan de Mena, Samonà approaches the work from the language, topics, and stylistic traditions available to Rojas. In this sense he completes Castro Guisasola with critical meditation and complements the antithetical approach which I have here chosen. I hope later to be able to comment more extensively on Samonà's interpretation of *La Celestina* in a review.

28. Latin comedy, as has so often been pointed out, offered the most direct model of dialogue usage. But in spite of certain instances in which the dialogue of Plautus or of Terence seems to coincide (Castro Guisasola's listing is probably incomplete) with that of *La Celestina,* the real influence seems to have been more generic than stylistic. Being fundamentally theatrical, there is a tendency in these plays to write with one eye on the desired reaction in the audience. This in turn involves stereotyped characters who are readily predictable and who can be counted on to bring act and play to their appropriate termination. There is, of course, no real problem of decorum, given classic division of styles. Dialogue is, in other words, a mere part of the show, rather than a final stylistic value. Such dialogue could hardly have inspired Rojas' special artistry.

29. Auerbach in the essay on the *Quixote* added to the Spanish translation of *Mimesis* (Mexico, 1951) seems surprised at Sancho's chivalric language on the occasion of presenting the mock Dulcinea to Don Quijote outside of Toboso (Part II, Chapter 10). How much more "unreal" *La Celestina* might seem from this point of view!

30. We might point out as a sign of this difference Cervantes' tendency to betray climactic "literary" moments in the dialogue. His constant counterpoint of literature and life, or—as Castro points out—of "lo particular histórico" and "lo universal poético," never releases decorum completely. He has, in effect, too much fun playing with style to allow each conversation to find its own level.

31. What we have said does not, of course, apply to all of the words attributed to Rojas. We have not discussed the monologues or soliloquies, the prologue material in prose and verse, the song of Lucrecia and Melibea, and the *argumentos* to the added acts (undoubtedly the work of Rojas in comparison to those of the *Comedia*). We shall consider some of these briefly here as a sort of epilogue to this essay.

Aside from those three soliloquies in which topic and action govern style at the expense of individual reaction—in which the speaker is brought up to the level of the transcendent literary moment rather than creating it—the others may be considered to be basically dialogic in their artistry. Among the most important are Celestina's before and after the first interview with Melibea and Calisto's after learning of the death of the servants and after his first night of love. Of secondary importance are such speeches as Pármeno's at the end of Act II. Let us reproduce by way of example Celestina's soliloquy following her success with Melibea:

"¡O rigurosos trances! ¡O cruda osadía! ¡O gran sofrimiento! E que tan cercana estuue de la muerte, si mi mucha astucia no rigera con el tiempo las velas de la petición. ¡O amenazas de donzella brava! ¡O ayrada donzella! ¡O diablo a quien yo conjuré! ¿Cómo compliste tu palabra en todo lo que te pedí? En cargo te soy. Assí amansaste la cruel hembra con tu poder e diste tan oportuno lugar a mi habla quanto quise, con la absencia de su madre. ¡O vieja Celestina! ¿Vas alegre? Sábete que la meytad esta hecha, quando tienen buen principio las cosas. ¡O serpentino azeyte! ¡O blanco filado! ¡Cómo os aparejastes todos en mi favor! ¡O! ¡yo rompiera todos mis atamientos hechos e por fazer ni creyera en yeruas ni piedras ni en palabras! Pues alégrate, vieja, que más sacarás deste pleyto, que de quinze virgos que renouaras. ¡O malditas haldas, prólixas e largas, como me estoruays de llegar adonde han de reposar mis nueuas! O buena fortuna, cómo ayudas a los osados, e a los tímidos eres contraria. Nunca huyendo huye la muerte al couarde. ¡O quántas erraran en lo que yo he acertado! ¿Qué fizieran en tan fuerte estrecho estas nueuas maestras de mi oficio, sino responder algo a Melibea, por donde se perdiera quanto yo con buen callar he ganado? Por esto dizen quien las sabe las tañe e que es mas cierto médico el esperimentado que el letrado e la esperiencia e escarmiento haze los hombres arteros e la vieja, como yo, que alcen sus haldas al passar del vado, como maestra. ¡Ay cordón, cordón! Yo te faré traer por fuerça, si viuo, a la que no quiso darme su buena habla de grado. (V, 193–95)

We may first notice the notes of direction which occur and reoccur all through the monologue. "Diablo," "vieja Celestina," "serpentino azeyte," "vieja," "malditas haldas," "buena fortuna," and "cordón" are all addressed briefly at one point or another in the expression of Celestina's gleeful triumph and relief. Then, too, there is a constant beat of exclamation and a rise and fall of stylistic level as Celestina's language recedes from and approaches her sentiment, as reason and logic translate or break down before the strength of her feeling. Specifically the structure is one of alternation between exclamation and reason, and the expression runs from Celestina's initial fear and recognition of supernatural help through an increasing confidence in her daring and wisdom to a final resolution which is entirely her own. In other words—unlike those more formal soliloquies mentioned above—this speech may be considered, despite the absence of a real auditor, an expression of sentiment at the subjective end of the dialogic range. It and others like it are comparable to Areusa's outburst against mistresses. None of them emerges from the immediate circumstance and all express with fragments of direction and exclamation a sentimental reaction to it—although they may be quite different in decorum and tempo.

As for the *Carta a un su amigo,* and the *Prólogo,* they afford hardly enough textual material for a study of Rojas' expository art of style in the sense that we have studied that of his dialogue. Furthermore, both of them are modeled (and perhaps this is a result of that over-all air of timidity and hesitancy which we have already noticed in them) on Petrarch's prologues to the *De remediis.* The Petrarchist origin of the *Prólogo* has been known since Menéndez Pelayo took the trouble to compare the Rojas text with the prologue to the second book of "remedies" against adverse fortune. But the *Carta* also, although this has never been mentioned specifically, seems to have been inspired by *Petrarch*—this time not by the second, but by the initial prologue to the *De remediis.* The latter is characterized by Petrarch as an *Epistolaris praefatio* directed to his friend, Azzo da Coreggio, who has suffered from fortune but who is proof against it—in much the same way that Rojas' anonymous friend has suffered from love and is now safe. In each case the author proposes his book as intellectual armor which will protect the reader against either love or fortune. Rojas, of course, develops the comparison more fully than Petrarch, who only refers to it in passing several times:

Soli igitur imbecilles ex armati non aequo marte cum implacabili hoste congredimur . . . . Si qua ex me percipi aut sperari potest: ad id maxime respexi: ne armarium evolvere ad hominem hostis suspitionem ac strepitum sit necesse . . . .

Quae vero arci praesidet ratio: his omnibus una respondeat: clypeoque et galea suisque artibus, et propria vi, sed coelesti magis auxilio circumfrementia hostium tela discutiat . . . .—F. Petrarcha *Librorum* (Venice, 1503), Vol. II, fol. 289.

Thus Rojas, when he speaks for himself in didactic or expository prose, seems to lack the daring, the independence, and the willingness to push what is said to its ultimate conclusion—qualities that he possessed when he wrote for his characters. He hides behind the authority and example of Petrarch and in the *Prólogo* mentions Aristotle, Pliny, and Lucan, although they were not present in the *De remediis*. Dialogue, as we have seen, almost writes itself for him, but the task of presenting his own opinion is hazardous and necessarily inconclusive. Nevertheless, a detailed comparison of the two prologues will reveal a number of features reminiscent of the authentic artistry of style we have considered in this essay. That of *La Celestina* while an imitation is far from being a mere copy of Petrarch. Digressions or changes, in the first place, often involve a perceptible break in the *genus nobile* more or less maintained in the original. There is a tendency towards more concrete detail, towards proverbial material, and towards popular language, as in the following two examples:

Pues entre los animales ningún género carece de guerra: pesces, fieras, aves serpientes, de lo cual todo, una especie a otra persigue. El león al lobo, el lobo la cabra, el perro la liebre e, si no paresciesse conseja de tras el fuego, yo llegaría más al cabo esta cuenta. El elefante, animal tan poderoso e fuerte, se espanta e huye de la vista de un suziuelo ratón, e que de sólo oyrle toma gran temor. (I, 19)

Quid quod nullum animal bello vacat? Pisces, ferae: volucres: serpentes homines: una species aliam exagitat: nulli omnium quies data: leo lupum, lupus canem, canis leporem insequitur . . . Quorundam vero tam generosa ferocia et tam nobilis fertur elatio ut ursos aprosque fastidiant, inque solos elephantes aut leones diguentius irruere.

Here the break in language and example is self-evident; it is almost as if Rojas had begun to talk to us through the interstices of his imitation. We may also notice the delicious detail of imagined situation that is original in the following (as well as the extent of change):

Las más aves biven de rapiña, como halcones e águilas e gavilanes. Hasta los grosseros milanos insultan dentro en nuestras moradas los domésticos pollos e debaxo las alas de sus madres los vienen a caçar. (I, 21–22)

Iam qui oro, alii uulpium doli? qui luporum ululatus? quod murmur ad causas? quae coruorum miluorumque circa columbarum domus ac pullorum nidos uigilantia, quod inter se, ut perhibent naturale ac aeternum odium. Alter alterius inuadit nidum effractisque ouis spem prolis interimit . . . (Castro Guisasola, *Obervaciones,* p. 120).

Instead of making an intellectual point Rojas communicates the outrage of this raiding in our own homes and under the mother's very wings.

Finally we may notice the strict logic and brevity imposed by Rojas on Petrarch's lengthy and often chaotically disorganized text. The former's *Prólogo* proceeds from natural or elemental warring to that of the animal kingdom and then to the even greater discord in the world of men. Within the division of animals he separates animals themselves, fish, and birds into separate and successive paragraphs. Petrarch, on the other hand, had presented many of these examples with no attempt at order. Human, animal, and elemental conflicts succeed each other on his pages as they occur to him, but are saved from this dispersion in the imitation. A specific instance out of many is the placing together of the roc and the *milano* although previously they were widely separated. Just as we saw Rojas complete the logic of Celestina's attempt to persuade Melibea to charity, so here a comparison of the two prologues reveals an extraordinary effort towards logical cohesion.

The initial verses in *arte mayor* seem to offer even fewer indications of an original stylistic artistry. They follow the pattern set by Juan de Mena faithfully, even though they may be somewhat less obscure and portentious. Later we shall consider parts of their content, but for now we shall pass them by. The style of the verses of Act XIX will also be taken up at the proper time. See note 12, Chapter VII.

CHAPTER THREE

1. *La Nación* (Buenos Aires, 16 January, 1949).

2. In *Don Quijote, Don Juan, La Celestina* most conveniently available in the "Colección Austral." See also F. Rauhut, "Das Dämonische in der *Celestina*," *Homenaje a Vossler* (Munich, 1932).

3. Américo Castro in his major essay on Cervantes' artistry, "Incarnation in Don Quixote" (*Cervantes across the Centuries*, New York, 1947), proposes a similar fluidity of being for the inhabitants of the novel: "In accord with the same vital ontology, Don Quixote is alternately insane, rational, simpleton, clown, 'beast,' magnificent orator, firm or vacillating in the consciousness of himself, etc., according to the vital situation in which he finds himself immersed." (pp. 160–61) Yet even in the *Quixote*, this fundamental requirement of fictional life is not as radical as in *La Celestina*. The third person exists precisely because Cervantes plays with it so effectively and so charmingly, whereas for Rojas, I woud maintain, it is just not there.

4. The description of Melibea often coincides, as has been observed, with that offered by Don Amor of doctrinally desirable women. See María Rosa Lida de Malkiel's comments on the extension and significance of this pattern in "Notas para la interpretación, influencia, fuentes, y texto del *Libro de buen amor*," *Revista de filología hispánica*, II (1940).

5. This utilization of an apparently trite commonplace to express a personal and authentic reaction or evaluation is, as we shall see in our chapter on theme, typical of *La Celestina*. It is continued in the interpolation which immediately follows the above: "*No quiero en este mundo, sino día e victo e parte en parayso. Avnque los ricos tiene mejor aparejo para ganar la gloria, que quien poco tiene. No ay ninguno contento, no*

ay quién diga: harto tengo; no ay ninguno, que no trocasse mi plazer por sus dineros. Dexemos cuydados agenos e acostémonos, que es hora. *Que más me engordará vn buen sueño sin temor, que quanto thesoro ay en Venecia.*" (VII, 262–63) Here "mi plazer" and "mi sueño" become what Castro would call a vital "surtidor" for the "fontezicas de filosofía" of which Rojas speaks in his *Carta.*

6. It is unnecessary to reproduce this famous passage with its lengthy list of classical precedents—again springing from sentimental authenticity and involving an appropriate elevation of style. It may be found, of course, in Act XVI.

7. The artistic consequence of this climactic moment will be considered in Chapter V.

8. In the interpolation Rojas stresses for Pármeno a form of rationalization that in the *Comedia* was only implied in the word *locos.* I refer to his feeling of superiority, his disdain for the folly of his master. Pármeno must despise Calisto personally as well as justify his treason in terms of society. This note of a personal break with Calisto is confirmed by the direct address in the last sentence of the interpolation: "Pues anda ... que ... te espulguen!" Pármeno's anguished desperation as a *yo* is more directly expressed with this than with the reasonings of the original.

9. In Act XII, after the evident success of Celestina's negotiations, there is a moment in which Calisto and Pármeno meet again in terms of the first situation: "CAL.—... ¿Qué te parece, Pármeno, de la vieja, que tú me desalauas? ¿Qué obra ha salido de sus manos? ¿Qué fuera hecha sin ella? PARM.—Ni yo sentía tu gran pena ni conoscía la gentileza e merescimiento de Melibea, e assí no tengo culpa. Conoscía a Celestina e sus mañas. Auisáuate como a señor; pero ya me parece que es otra. Todas las ha mudado." (XII, 93) Here, Calisto obviously expects Pármeno to have changed his opinion. It is a moment of triumph which winds up the earlier argument and disposes of it for good. Pármeno can, as a result, admit his change and attribute it to mistaken judgment without sacrificing the *tú* to which he has been committed.

10. This was foreseen in Act I. At the end of the act, when Pármeno had agreed to friendship "aunque ... espantado," Sempronio answered: "SEMP.—Pues calla, que yo te haré espantar dos tanto. PARM.—¡O Diós! No ay pestilencia mas eficaz, qu'l enemigo de casa para empecer." (I, 112) Pármeno's tentative effort to make peace is never followed out but instead allowed to lapse at this first arrogant reception. He is in no state to affirm a friendship with anyone, let alone Sempronio.

11. Rojas is so aware of the need of confirming this intermediate phase of Pármeno's consciousness that (in addition to the above exchanges and others in the same act), he allows even Calisto to notice that something is wrong with him. We are given an almost graphic picture of Pármeno through Calisto's eyes: "CAL.—¡Corre! Pármeno, llama a mi sastre ... PARM.—¡Assí, assí! A la vieja todo ... e a mí que me arrastren ... CAL.—¡De qué gana va el diablo! No ay cierto tan malseruido hombre como yo, manteniendo moços adeuinos, reçongadores, enemigos de mi bien. ¿Qué vas, vellaco, rezando? Embidioso, ¿qué dizes, que no te entiendo? Ve donde te mando presto e no me enojes ..." (VI, 218)

12. At this point Pármeno's reaction is limited to an aside: "No la medre Diós más a esta vieja, que ella me da plazer con estos loores de sus palabras." But the dart has been firmly fixed and, as we shall see, finally contributes to the death of Celestina.

Rojas' premeditation of this expanded treatment of Claudina—the potential importance which he saw in the brief mention of her in Act I—is made clear by Celestina's explanation of it to Sempronio in Act III: "... acordéle quien era su madre, porque no menospreciase mi oficio; porque queriendo de mí dezir mal, tropeçasse primero en ella."

13. The several reservations (mentioned above) to this full identification of Pármeno and Sempronio are hardly sufficient to give a true picture of his independent life after Act VIII. Rojas is too careful and too consequential an artist to allow the role of Pármeno (or that of anyone else) to descend to the level of caricature. But whatever personal contributions Pármeno does make to the dialogue after this point necessarily refer to past situations. The situation of Act XI, for example, repeats Act VI on different terms just as situation three for Pármeno was a remake of situation one. The same dialogic situations cannot help, as we saw, but repeat to a certain extent the same dialogue. Another significant case of renovation of Pármeno's past sentiments occurs at Celestina's death in Act XII. "CEL.—E tú, Pármeno, no pienses que soy tu catiua por saber mis secretos e mi passada vida e los casos que nos acaescieron a mí e a la desdichada de tu madre. E avn assí me trataua ella, quando Diós quería. PARM.—No me hinches las narizes con essas memorias; si no, embiart'é con nueuas a ella, donde mejor te puedas quexar." (XII, 102) Pármeno's desperation seems to return in full force at this mention of the earlier means of his spiritual destruction, and he is the first to raise his hand against Celestina. But at the same time, and this is the point I tried to make above, Pármeno is engaged in no new living growth, no new process which merits Rojas' full artistic attention. Hence he is given relatively few lines or is used to underline in comic repetition the cowardice and cynicism of Sempronio. The end of his significant trajectory effectively occurs in Act VIII. After that it is only a question of an occasional reminiscence.

14. In relation to the above utilization of Bergson for the understanding of Rojas' artistry, it is interesting to remember the initial citation from Heraclitus. Even though Petrarch is clearly the intermediate source, Heraclitus was still as close a philosophical approximation as Rojas could have found for his own intuition of life. Recently Eduardo Nicoll in his *Historicismo y existencialismo* (Mexico, 1950) has attempted to answer Bergson's own protests against relating his thought to that of Heraclitus: "Cuando Bergson protesta de que su filosofía se confunda con la de Heráclito revela que dejó pasar inadvertida la significación profunda del pensamiento heracliteana, la que precisamente justifica su actualidad ante el problema del ser y el tiempo. Pues todo el esfuerzo de Heráclito tendió a buscar en lo cambiante mismo el principio de su cambio ..." (pp. 35–36)

15. In an article written for the *Revista de filología hispánica,* VII (1945), 147–59, entitled "Tiempo y género literario en *La Celestina.*" The peculiar phenomenon of two times in the work, which led to the assumption of a subconscious life for Calisto and Melibea, will be discussed in the essay on theme.

16. Further confirmation of this psychology of consciousness is furnished by the surprisingly small part played by dreams in a work paying so much attention to love. Calisto does mention in Act VI, "En sueños la veo tantas noches ... ," but the very simplicity of this direct dream vision only confirms our point.

17. *Revista de Guatemala* (1945).

18. An edited reproduction of García Bacca's concluding paragraphs will explain the above reservations. He is much less interested in *La Celestina* as a work of art than in finding illustrations for his "Hispanic consciousness" in it:

"La conciencia real de verdad es la conciencia sentimental, y sería más correcto decir que *conciencia es sentimiento,* porque sentimiento es esencialmente un *sentirse.* [He refers back to his discussion of Heidegger.]

"El instinto filosófico español, el del pueblo ... inventó esas maravillosas frases de la *Celestina,* que son todo un programa de *conciencia real,* de criterio metafísico para saber *cuando somos* y *cuanto somos.* Porque ... el sentimiento, y cada sentimiento a su manera y grado, no solamente nos hace *notar* que somos reales, sino nos hace *estar siendo* reales, y siéndolo y notándolo en nosotros, para nosotros mismos. [This suggests that secret of creating literary lives more real, according to Unamuno, than that of the author consists of adequate expression of sentiments.]

. . . .

"Unamuno, tan español, sostendrá que no es precisamente el sentimiento del *goce* el que no haga *sentirnos* y *ser mas reales,* sino el sentimiento de *agonía,* el *sentimiento trágico* de la vida ...

"Es claro que, radicalmente tan español es Unamuno como Celestina, pues para ambos, sin gazmoñerías ni falsos recatos, conciencia es *conciencia sentimental,* hombre es ser que se siente y existe sintiéndose, porque se siente ye en la medida que se siente. No existe en rigor *conciencia* intelectual; y los intentos historicos que se han hecho ciertamente para darle la supremacia en el hombre han sido en detrimento de su realidad misma, que nunca el hombre se nota menos hombre que cuando discurre, intuye ideas, hace ciencia abstracta.

. . . .

"Celestina suelta a continuación otra frase de malicia metafísica infinitamente mayor que la primera [the first was "así goze de mí"]: *así goce yo de esta alma pecadora. ¿Cuál es el valor metafísico, en que grado nos hacen* ser reales *y* sentirnos reales *los goces pecaminosos del alma?*"

This interesting question is never answered; García Bacca closes instead with a suggested parallel from Baudelaire:

> "Un phare ironique, infernale,
> Flambeau des graces sataniques,
> Soulagement et gloires uniques
> La conscience dans le mal."
> —*Fleurs du Mal,* "L'Irrémediable"

It was necessary to reproduce so much of this article because, in spite of the fact it does not deal primarily with *La Celestina* as a work of art, much of what is there present is immensely suggestive to us. García Bacca's peculiar approach only hints at what he might think about our problems.

19. There is, as we shall see, a possible parallel with Pleberio who replaces her as the aged character after her death but, even in this, her artistic domination is manifest.

20. The first mention of wine in the *Comedia* is relatively brief and occurs in Act IV when Celestina explains its consolation for her poverty: "Que con mi pobreza jamás me faltó, a Dios gracias vna blanca para pan e vn quarto para vino ..." Again it is not strange to the dialogic context.

21. Those quoted above and in note 20.

22. Admittedly in other cases the added sentences seem much more artificial than the above. Too often exaggeration of a single trait of character overpowers the sentiment and argument appropriate to the situation (for example, the interpolation following the sentence mentioned in note 20, IV, 171). Overemphasis is an almost irresistible temptation for an author who corrects—with full consciousness—a work which had been created intuitively.

23. For example, the disgusted interpolation at the end of Act II or the absurdly elevated, "No me indignes, Sempronio, con tan lastimeras razones ..." which corresponds to his sentimental repletion in Act VIII. In general for the rest of the cast it is difficult to isolate interpolations primarily related to art of character—precisely because character does not exist alone, because it is related to other aspects of Rojas' art. When Calisto says, for example, "... Mañana haré que vengo de fuera, si pudiera vengar estas muertes; si no pagaré mi inocencia con mi fingida absencia *o me fingiré loco, por mejor gozar deste sabroso deleyte de mis amores, como hizo aquel gran capitán Ulizes por euitar la batalla troyana e holgar con Penélope su muger*" (XIII, 113), the addition not only brings out and emphasizes the "sentimentalization" of honor at the moment just prior to love's completion (a "trait" appropriate to Calisto) but also establishes a clear "structural" contrast between the ending of this act and that of the next. The ease of Calisto's escape from his obligations, his readiness for any excuse, is underlined in order that the later anguish at loss of honor may take on full meaning. The interpolation, thus, helps the reader focus the second monologue in terms of the first. Character, style, and structure are hardly separated in Rojas' mind. The exception to this is, of course, Celestina who came to fascinate her author as an individual.

24. Along with the evident relationship to the character of Celestina, this interpolation also reflects that general preoccupation with space which acts as a premonition for the four deaths by falling. It has, as we shall see, thematic significance.

25. When Celestina is explaining to Pármeno in Act VII the trials and humiliations inflicted on Claudina as a result of her witchcraft, one of her sentences in the *Comedia* reads as follows: "Algo han de sofrir los hombres en este triste mundo para sustentar sus vidas." Rojas on rereading this in 1502 added two words which signify his ironical intention in giving Celestina a special "vocational" consciousness: "y honrras." The description which follows this interpolation further establishes that identity of vocation, self-awareness, and honor which distinguishes Celestina (and her vision of Claudina) from Calisto, Melibea, Sempronio, and all the others: "... En todo tenía gracia. Que en Dios e en mi conciencia, avn en aquella escalera estaua e parecía que a todos los debaxo no tenía en vna blanca, según su meneo e presencia. Assí que los que algo son como ella e saben e valen, son los que más presto yerran. Verás quien fué Virgilio e qué tanto supo: mas ya haurás oydo cómo estouo en vn cesto colgado de vna torre, mirándole toda Roma. Pero por eso no dejó de ser honrrado ni perdió el nombre de Virgilio." (VII, 243–44) It is a passage which lies deep in the Spanish tradition which produced the splendid if caricaturesque description of "el Buscón's" uncle on the scaffold.

26. Madariaga perceives the special nature of Celestina's characterization but in such a way as to forbid its investigation. "Celestina está concebida y descrita con una riqueza de detalles quizá mayor que la de los demás personajes por ser el mas pintoresco."— "Discurso sobre Melibea," *Sur,* No. 76 (1941), pp. 38–69. This notion is in accord with

his general subordination of Celestina to Melibea and his effort to find examples of inefficiency which will reduce Celestina in importance. In a cast which is without character such playful comparison of roles can go on indefinitely. It would be as easy to make a case for the artistic supremacy of any one of the other principals of *La Celestina*.

CHAPTER FOUR

1. This list evidently can make no provision for those situations which are choral in nature—that is to say those which involve a rapid shift of dialogue from one group to another and often, as well, a mutual overhearing between groups. There may be other possible grounds for minor disagreement, due to the flexibility of Rojas' movement from situation to situation. These matters will be discussed in the second part of this essay dealing with the internal structure of scenes.

2. This distinction is noted acutely by F. M. Torner in an article printed in *El Nacional* (Mexico, D.F., 21 March, 1948): "Si don Juan es satánico, también es satánica Celestina, aunque no con el satanismo pueril que pudieran conferirle sus conjuros, brevajes y filtros. Todo eso es la tramoya ostensible y superficial de otro satanismo mas auténtico cuyos recursos mas poderosos no son las retortas y los matraces de la magia sino como fuerza espritual que es la palabra insinuante y viscosa que empieza por inquietar y acaba por persuadir."

3. For a discussion of the style of this passage see note 31 of Chapter II.

4. See Friedrich Leo, *Der Monolog im Drama* (Abhandlungen d. K. Ges. d. Wiss. zu Gottingen, Phil.-hist. Kl. N. F. Band 10, Berlin, 1908), for the correlation of act divisions in the New Comedy with monologues. There it seems primarily to be a matter of the halting of dialogic action when a single speaker remains on the stage. Monologues do not as in *La Celestina* possess major structural importance; rather, they indicate a lessening of theatrical tension and occur in moments of rest and transition.

5. Those who object to this interpolation and include it (along with others in the same act) among their major reasons for believing in a second author for the additions of 1502 consistently fail to realize its contribution to the structure of the act—an act dedicated to choral emphasis on states of consciousness already achieved. It is not a portrait of Melibea as such but rather a further inking in of Celestina's pride in having been able to dominate the situation. The implied image, Melibea as the wounded bull and Celestina as the *diestra* ("bulliendo los miembros," "herida de aquella ... frecha," "acoceando con los pies," "yo, arrinconada, encogida"), was prepared for in the original text: "Cal.—¿Qué cara te mostró al principio? Cel.—Aquella cara, señor, que suelen los bravos toros mostrar contra los que lançan las agudas frechas en el coso ..." (VI, 206)

6. Rojas is careful to continue this into the last scene when Lucrecia and Celestina have left the revelry and are preparing to proceed towards Melibea's house. In dialogue which seems at first glance designed only to advance the plot (to prepare the reader for Melibea's changed state of mind) Lucrecia reveals herself completely: "Por cierto, ya se me hauía oluidado mi principal demanda e mensaje con la memoria de esse tan alegre tiempo como has contado e assí me estuuiera vn año sin comer, escuchándote e pensando en aquella vida buena, que aquellas moças gozarían, que me parece e semeja

que estó yo agora en ella." (IX, 49) A few lines later she expresses a resentment towards Celestina's *falsedad* which further marks her as existing in a state of mind (in relation to herself and to her listener) comparable in feminine terms to that of Pármeno prior to Act VIII. This comparison becomes explicit in Act X after Celestina notices it: "Nunca me ha de faltar vn diablo acá e acullá: escapóme Diós de Pármeno, topóme con Lucrecia." The point is that within the terms of Rojas' art even the most utilitarian interchange must be written in such a way as to relate to the structure of consciousness which is the act. Here our understanding of Lucrecia is completed as earlier our understanding of Elicia and Areusa had become complete.

7. The act closes with the usual punch line not of action but of consciousness when Alisa expresses her worry at the reappearance of Celestina: "ALI.—... Guarte, hija, della, que es gran traydora ... MELIB.—¿Dessas es? ¡Nunca más! Bien huelgo, señora, de ser auisada, por saber de quién me tengo de guardar." (X, 65) After this Melibea is irrevocably lost. We should not, however, interpret this passage as a sort of conscious admission of a desire previously held in the subconscious—as does Madariaga:

La escena a solas entre Celestina y Melibea está tan sembrada de maravillas y de atisbos geniales que para hacerle justicia habría que comentarla línea a línea y palabra a palabra. La correspondencia entre los delicados pensamientos y soterrañas emociones manejados por ambas mujeres y el lenguaje simbólico revelador y encubridor a la vez de lo que pasa en el ser amoroso que la entrometida va gradualmente y no sin sufrimiento abriendo al amor es tan perfecta, tan increíblemente "moderna" en su penetración del subconsciente, que puede considerarse este diálogo como una desfloración psíquica de la doncella preparatoria de la desfloración carnal."—*Discurso sobre Melibea*, pp. 59–60.

Against this interpretation we submit not only the theory of character previously proposed but also the full self-awareness of Melibea's initial soliloquy.

8. It may be argued that both Sempronio and Pármeno doubt the truth of her story, but they do so after the fact. Her actual news, the details of what passed between her and Melibea, are not, in themselves, important to them. After the preliminary success of the first interview, the report is less interesting than the interpretation.

9. The original had read: "... pues tan buen recabdo traygo, que te traygo muchas buenas palabras de Melibea e la dexo a tu servicio." Even though the original stimulus for the change in text may well have been the unseemly approximation of the two "traygo's," there is no question but that Rojas took advantage of the necessary change to stress the intentional rapidity and brevity of the act.

10. This is true with the exception of a brief situation inside Melibea's house after Pleberio and Alisa are awakened.

11. This apparent reminiscence from Rojas' own boyhood (see Chapter I, note 16) was inserted to balance a similar anecdote of Pármeno's in the *Comedia* and so to stress again the identity of the two: "Tragada tenía ya la muerte, que me parescía que me yuan dando en estas espaldas golpes. En mi vida me acuerdo hauer tan gran temor ni verme en tal afrenta, avnque he andado por casas agenas harto tiempo e en lugares de harto trabajo. Que nueue años serví a los frayles de Guadalupe, que mill vezes nos apuñeáuamos yo e otros. Pero nunca como esta vez houe miedo de morir." (XII, 90)

12. Although not structurally important, it would be well to mention one other fatal mistake of Celestina in this situation. It is her mention to Pármeno of his mother, a

touch of the whip which had brought him to heel in the past but which now further infuriates him. (See Chapter I, note 3.) It is one more symptom of Celestina's failure to realize the profound crisis of consciousness of the servants, the real crisis of this act. Whenever she says such things as "Que bien sé donde nasce esto, bien sé e barrunto de que pie cozqueays" what follows demonstrates how far from the truth she has strayed. Not only are women mysterious to men in *La Celestina,* but, here, the wisest woman of them all completely fails to understand men.

13. "Fernando de Rojas, su obra de humanidad española y de arte renacentista," *Boletín de la Academia Argentina de letras,* XII (1943), 132.

14. It must be remembered, of course, that Rojas was not responsible for the *argumentos* and their stress on location as the place of action. He saw location rather as an element of situation and in this follows rigorously the practice of Act I and of the New Comedy (although, there, indications of place often seem to be announced artificially). In addition to the example given above, we may remember that in the first deception of Sempronio by Celestina and Elicia, we do not learn that Crito has been hidden upstairs until Sempronio hears steps "allá arriba."

15. "El tiempo y el género literario en la *Celestina,*" pp. 149–50.

16. *Ibid.,* p. 149.

17. This, as we have already seen, is also true in the early editions for the frequent asides.

18. Exceptions are "vermejas letras" (III, 150), "posturas blancas y coloradas" (VI, 227), "verdes prados" (VIII, 22), "coloradas colores de tu gesto" (X, 52), "calças de grana" (XII, 99), "rubicundos labios" (XIV, 129), "ruuia color" (XVII, 155). We may compare this scarcity with such outbursts of polychromy in *La Dorotea* as the following: "En tiempo de Claudio (si no miente Plinio) trajeron a Roma un fénix, y dicen que era de la grandeza y proporción de un águila; el cuello dorado y resplandeciente, el cuerpo purpúreo, la cola cerúlea, distinta de rosadas plumas, o que en ella estaban formadas rosas, como en la cola del pavón los ojos, y coronado de diversos rayos de otras más sútiles de varios cambiantes y tornasoles." (IV, Escena primera) We, therefore, cannot agree with Ramón Sender when he compares *La Celestina* to Valle Inclán's "esperpentos" and identifies their treatment of color:

La Celestina era irrepresentable por las mismas razones que los esperpentos de Valle—no porque fuera demasiado larga o porque acabara demasiado mal o porque su realismo pudiera ser procaz e indecente—era irrepresentable porque estaba concebida no como una estructura homogénea con sus realidades aparentes y determinantes, sus ruedecillas interdependientes y compleja exactitud, sino como una acumulación de masas de color estáticas y fijas. (En el caso de *La Celestina* el color es un fin también en si mismo)..."
—"La gestación literaria en Valle Inclán," *Cuadernos Americanos,* LXII (1952), 270–81.

19. This is, of course, typical of popular speech and frequently occurs in Spanish and other European ballads. Examples are so familiar that they need not be given here.

20. Other examples are: "dorada frecha" (VI, 214), "pan blanco" (VIII, 17), "negro traygo el coraçón" (XV, 134), "manos como la nieve" (XIX, 174), and, used as a symbol of old age, "tus blancos cabellos" (XXI, 201). And there are quite a few more.

21. There is a note of intimacy in the second garden scene and perhaps in the hushed interchange between Pármeno and Sempronio in Act XII. Also one might point out

the jerky cadence of Sempronio's efforts to question Celestina as she hurries along jubilantly in Act V.

Let us illustrate this last point in greater detail. Sempronio's speeches are consistently short as if uttered while hurrying along after Celestina. Hers, on the other hand, are somewhat longer, giving the impression that she has stopped to answer him:

> CEL.—... mientras más tardasse, más caro me costasse.
>
> SEMP.—Por amor mío, madre, no passes de aquí sin me lo contar.
>
> CEL.—Sempronio amigo, ni yo me podría parar ni el lugar es aparejado. Vente comigo. Delante Calisto oyrás marauillas. Que será desflorar mi embaxada comunicándola con muchos. De mi boca quiero que sepa lo que se ha hecho. Que, avnque ayas de hauer alguna partizilla de prouecho, quiero yo todas las gracias del trabajo.
>
> SEMP.—¿Partezilla, Celestina? Mal me parece eso que dizes.
>
> CEL.—Calla, loquillo, que parte o partezilla, quanto tú quisieres te daré ... (V, 196–97)

In the above we can sense Celestina's movements, her attempts to get on about her business. She essays a rapid argument and starts away, but in her haste provides Sempronio with another doubt and a resulting question. This is again disposed of hastily and so on, as he continues "royéndole las haldas" in vain hope of satisfaction. We can even perceive how the last sentence of each of Celestina's speeches must trail off in sound as she turns to leave. Thus, the "paradillas de rato en rato" which Pármeno observes from the window are present in the peculiar rhythm of the dialogue. Nevertheless, it is again the state of consciousness—the alternate expression of curiosity and impatience—which interests Rojas and not primarily the accompanying motion (as it might have been in a novel).

22. For example, Sempronio's "no passes de aquí" in note 21, above.

23. This is not the first example in Act I of spatial structure. The first dialogue of Sempronio and Calisto is outside of space and time (after brief mention of the latter's lounging in the "sala") and is written, as we have seen, less as an encounter of consciousnesses than as a burlesque of certain topics. But the situation at Celestina's house which follows does use a spatial barrier, the first and second floors, as a means of displaying the feminine guile which so frustrates Sempronio. Then, the quadruple encounter at Calisto's door goes on to develop the technique in a more definitive manner.

24. We are now in a position to understand better the paradox of gesture and expression without facial or corporal setting for them. Just as the speakers of *La Celestina* fail to notice people or objects except insofar as they are related to the immediacies of the situation, so in this case the face and body are taken for granted while the attitude assumed momentarily by the same face or body, an attitude charged with situational meaning, is reflected without delay in words. The physiognomy exists in the third person; gestures and expressions in the first and second.

25. See also pages 147 and 148 for the contribution of these passages to the structure of the act.

26. Similar examples may be found in Act V (situation 2, p. 196), Act VII (situation 2, p. 247), Act VIII (situation 1, p. 7; situation 3, p. 19), Act IX (situation 1, p. 24; situation 2, p. 27), Act XII (situation 1, p. 76), Act XIII (situation 1, p. 107), Act XIV (situation 2, p. 119).

CHAPTER FIVE

1. Pedro Salinas, *La poesía de Rubén Darío* (Buenos Aires, 1948); José Ortega y Gasset, "Ideas sobre Pío Baroja," *Obras Completas* (Madrid, 1946), Vol. II; Augusto Centeno, *The Intent of the Artist* (Princeton, 1941).

2. Salinas points out, for example: "Sería error grave querer deducir el tema del poeta de los hechos de su biografía y no de los actos de su creación. Tampoco se le debe tomar por las ideas o creencias del escritor; se hallan sin duda, condicionadas temporalmente, por él, pero sin ser él" (p. 49).

And Centeno with different terminology makes a similar point: "For while there is a *total* and *single intent* which pervades the work of art and overflows into other works of the same creator or into other works created in the same style, there also is a multiplicity of *particular intentions* present in each given work. Such intentions are concretely realizable and, once realized, the intention itself has been completed and exhausted. . . . The intentions are always conscious; the intent, largely, although not completely unconscious" (p. 22).

3. See, for example, the following interchange from Act XI: CAL.—Sí, que Melibea ángel dissimulado es, que viue entre nosotros. SEMP.—¿Todauía te buelues a tus eregías? (p. 73)

4. The well-known phrases are as follows: "elegante estilo," "sotil artificio," "auisos y consejos," "lisonjeros e malos siruientes e falsas mugeres hechiceras." We may note the inadequacy of this last reference to characterization. As a result of the stress on thesis, Celestina, Pármeno, and Sempronio are reduced to third-person silhouettes of their own lives, mere shadows of their full dialogic existence. It does not necessarily follow that Rojas had no deeper appreciation than this of the nature and achievement of his own artistry of character. Rather, emphasizing for the public the moral justification of the thesis, he was led inevitably to this simplification. The phrase stands as a warning to future critics.

5. *Observaciones sobre las fuentes literarias de "La Celestina"* (Madrid, 1924).

6. Aristotle is the source for this tripartite classification, according to Castro Guisasola.

7. See Theodore Spencer, *Death and Elizabethan Tragedy* (Cambridge, 1936). Spencer is particularly concerned with Shakespearian revitalization of the language of these topics, a reworking comparable to that of a Calderón. But it was precisely such rewording that Rojas' art neither required nor made possible.

8. *Meditaciones del Quijote, Obras* (Madrid, 1950), I, 321.

9. As is indicated above, even Juan Ruiz was not free, to the extent that Rojas was free, to give inner artistic pattern and significance to his borrowed commonplaces. Juan Ruiz might transfuse the mediaeval patterns which were the raw materials of his art with his creative and created personality, but, since he himself was the one true life, or character, of the *Libro de Buen Amor,* he had no other points of human reference in terms of which to arrange them. As a result, his artistry not only invents an autobiography but possesses, in itself, such qualities of human life as duration and experience. This experience is not of the real world but of the artistic circumstance, precisely *lugares comunes* of all sorts. Thus, for example, the successive "serranilla" experiments

are experiences of the *Libro* itself. And the *Pamphilus* is in the same way converted from an objective drama to a pseudo-experience in the first person. There is no question but that each commonplace is integrated to Juan Ruiz' art, yet that integration is accomplished more by stylistic metamorphosis than by ironical juxtaposition. Juan Ruiz never achieves, (and this is no denial of his greatness) that creative distance which allowed Rojas to arrange his complex of living situations, patterns and trajectories.

10. For example, Celestina's observations on death in Act IV: "Tan presto, señora, se va el cordero como el carnero"; and Sempronio's on the temporal and temporary nature of human concern in Act III "Todo es assí, todo passa desta manera . . ."

11. Calisto cries out, for example, in Act XIII: "¡O fortuna, quánto e por quántas partes me has combatido . . .!" Even Celestina recognizes its power over her: "La ley es de fortuna que ninguna cosa en un ser mucho tiempo permanesce . . ." (Act XII)

12. The role of the *mundo* in the work is much more difficult to justify and constitutes precisely one of the major difficulties for those who would so interpret Rojas' intentions. As we shall see later on, "mundo" (borrowed like the other two from Petrarch) was stressed in Act XXI because of an apparent dissatisfaction with "amor" and "fortuna" as effective explanations of what had been created. It seems to be an all-inclusive commonplace and thus provides for a multiude of omissions.

13. H. O. Patch in *The Goddess Fortuna* (Cambridge, Mass., 1927) comments at length on the traditional partnership of these two. The reference to the Alexandrine novel is confirmed by H. O. Taylor in *The Classical Heritage of the Middle Ages* (New York, 1911) by now a classic itself. Taylor stresses the early appearance of fortune in this novel in contrast to the destiny, integrated to character, of the Greek tragedy. As an absolute force and definable only as a blind chance, it results in a series of enamored puppets who carom without resistance about the Mediterranean world. In the seventeenth century love and fortune seem to exhaust their impetus of significance. As commonplaces they have become commonplace. In Elizabethan England, for example, the very title *The Rare Triumphs of Love and Fortune* is an indication of triviality and as early as 1583. Nevertheless, the equation of *La Celestina* with this tradition does not seem to offer any doubt to E. J. Webber in his article, "Tragedy and Comedy in the Celestina" *Hispania*, XXXV (1952), 318–20. He notices the coincidence of the falling of Calisto and the others and the doctrinaire falling from happy estate, but he does not see the radical difference between the two. His conclusion is that in *La Celestina* there is a mixture of two distinct styles: a series of "tragic falls" within the "romantic obliviousness of comedy."

14. W. Farnham, *The Medieval Heritage of Elizabethan Tragedy* (Berkeley, Calif., 1936), p. 157.

15. Farnham, p. 157.

16. A typical example is the following passage from the beginning of the poem. Troilus, still immune himself castigates the folly of lovers:

> " 'O veray fooles! nyce and blynde be ye.
> Ther nys nat oon kan war by other be.'
>
> And with that word he gan caste up the browe
> Ascaunces, 'loo! is this nat wisely spoken?'
> At which the god of love gan loken rowe

Right for despit, and shop for to be wroken.
He kidde anon his bowe nas nat broken,
For sodeynly he hitte hym atte fulle,
And yet as proud a pekok kan he pulle.

O blynde world, O blynde entencioun . . . ."
—*The Book of Troilus and Criseyde,* ed.
R. K. Root (Princeton, 1926); lines 202–11

The external force of love, the god rather than the sentiment, is like fortune, a temptation to thesis. Chaucer certainly does not mean us to take this literally, as his later subtle presentation of Troilus' interior passion brings out. And yet by the very use of the image, the thesis has been launched.

17. This interpretation was also made by the *impressor* who was responsible for the "Argumento de toda la obra": "... vinieron los amantes en amargo y desastrado fin. Para comienço de lo cual dispuso la aduersa fortuna lugar oportuno, donde a la presencia de Calisto se presentó la desseada Melibea."

18. H. Warner Allen discusses this same problem in his introduction and appendix to the Mabbe translation (*Celestina,* Broadway Translations, London, 1924). Considering that the intention of Rojas was to castigate "the passion that leaves the ground to lose itself in the sky," he regards the *Comedia* as defective "in that the catastrophe is not really motivated by what precedes." This fault, he thinks, was corrected in the *Tragicomedia,* "although Centurio did not intend . . . fatal results." In my opinion, however, the very fact that Rojas provides for but docs not employ death by retribution is evidence of his intention to stress its accidental nature. By constructing an ineffective plot for revenge, he underlines with ironical contrast his very lack of thesis.

19. The above remarks on fortune and its fall are treated with an irony comparable to that of any other isolated commonplace. For example, Sempronio's remark about Celestina not quoted above, "Que quien con modo torpe sube en lo alto, mas presto cae que sube," chains this truth to the rascality of its source. And the same thing is true of most of the other cases (including that of Sosia whose warning, "de cayda vamos" does not take into account the fact that the worst has already happened). From the point of view of a moralist of fortune such as Petrarch, Sempronio and Sosia fear their respective *caydas* without realizing that they have already fallen. The only reference completely free of irony is, perhaps, Pármeno's observation about Calisto after the latter kneels down to Celestina: "Deshecho es, vencido es, caydo es; no es capaz de ninguna redención, ni consejo, ni esfuerzo." (I, 92)

20. The reference, like most of the *Prólogo,* is taken from the *De remediis.* Nevertheless, since Rojas (as we have seen) rejected more of Petrarch's prologue than he translated, it is significant that he should keep and emphasize this item. By "emphasize" I mean the insertion of such details as "cargado de todas sus xarcias" and "con el meneo de su vuelo caen" which are not in the original.

21. One of the unrealized possibilities of *La Celestina* is, perhaps, emphasis on the falcon's flight through space with its ultimate and purely unpredictable dive into Melibea's garden. When the great motion picture which the work calls for is made, an effective opening scene would be this circling flight with glimpses of the several heights later to be fatal. T. Spoerri in his "Elements d'une critique constructive" (*Trivium,*

1953) speaks of this same verticality in space as a possible theme ("projet du monde") without particular reference to *La Celestina*.

22. Among the more recent efforts is the monograph by José Ramos Díaz entitled *Algo más que tenerías* (Salamanca, 1950) which defends Salamanca. Ramos Díaz explains away the "nauíos" by pointing out that it is incorrect to isolate geographical references from the "espíritu que mueve la obra toda"—that is to say, from the theme. As a result, Melibea's "idealism reinforced with passion" (as opposed to Celestina's "realism") is supposed to cause her to see the shallops of the Tormes as ships. It is a process which is explained as comparable to that of the *Quixote*. While Ramos Díaz' point of departure—the primordial importance of the theme for all critical problems—is beyond question, such a division of characters is a simplification. As I tried to show in a previous chapter, Rojas' intent is to intermingle and equate his characters and never to divide them categorically. Each life in *La Celestina* has in its own way and on its own terms its own idealization of reality and its own (defeated) realization of ideality.

23. In *The Goddess Fortuna* Patch describes the "fortune of the seas" as a typical species of the larger commonplace. He mentions, for example (p. 37), a mediaeval illustration taken from Barbier de Montault's *Traité d'Iconographie Chrétiènne* (Paris, 1890): "In one of the Vatican pictures she is represented on the sea with a boat, a sail, and an oar, 'car la fortune vient du commerce maritime.' "

24. It is interesting to note that Lope continues the theme of falling in *La Dorotea* with Gerarda's death. Even more, he specifically relates the physical fall to that of Fortune:

"FELIPA—¡Cómo han quedado aquellas honradas tocas!

CELIA—Las tocas sanas: ¡así lo estuviera la cabeza! Pero puédese consolar, que murió cayendo como aquellos a quienes levanta la fortuna." (Act V, Escena duodecima)

Lope treats this coincidence of meaning as a mere play on words in accordance with the semi-burlesque *ingenio* of the whole scene. The deep thematic preoccupation of Rojas has been reduced to a witty aside (hardly distinguishable from the substitution of "salada" for "dulce" in the preceding passage). We may also notice that Lope has joined to this final fall one of the commonplaces attributed by Rojas to Celestina, that of fondness for wine. Gerarda dies (ironically enough, as is noted at length in the dialogue) by fainting and falling into the "cueva" as she goes to look for water to revive Dorotea. Thus, in *La Dorotea* an aspect of the theme of *La Celestina* has been dredged to the surface by the literary intuition of Lope and is there redisplayed in terms of an entirely new artistry.

25. *Jorge Manrique* (Buenos Aires, 1947), pp. 97-98.

26. That Rojas was aware of this thesis (a thesis still artistically valid for Gil Vicente and others) is hardly open to question. When he does, in effect, introduce some reference to it, his manner is careless and utterly without serious conviction:

"ELIC.—Por Dios, dexemos enojo e al tiempo el consejo. Ayamos much plazer. Mientra oy touieremos de comer, no pensemos en mañana. También se muere el que mucho allega como el que pobremente viue e el doctor como el pastor e el papa como el sacristán e el señor como el sieruo e el de alto linaje como el baxo e tú con oficio como yo sin ninguno. No hauemos de viuir para siempre. Gozemos e holguemos que la vejez pocos la veen e de los que la veen ninguno murió de hambre." (VII, 262)

The context of these remarks indicates as usual the ironical twist given them by Rojas— his Cervantine refusal to allow his characters to mouth theses. Just as Sancho uses ascetic commonplaces on death to his own advantage and from his own point of view (*Quixote,* II, 20), so Elicia clearly adjusts Death's final equation of men to her own slothfulness. It would be even more difficult to build a case for Death as the thesis than for Fortune.

27. Marcial José Bayo in a recent article ("Nota sobre *La Celestina*," *Clavileño,* 1950) notices the difference between Rojas' presentation of death and that of the *Danza de la muerte*. He attributes it, however, to the "resonancia" of Jorge Manrique's *Coplas*— a "resonancia" particularly evident in Act XXI. In the *Coplas,* he points out, "La muerte es paso y no acabamiento," and so lacks its previous vengefulness, "el resentimiento del individuo anónimo." Moreover, in spite of *La Celestina*'s "posición agnóstica" there is at least a suggestion that fame may provide an antidote to death:

"Ninguno perdió lo que yo el día de oy, avnque algo conforme parescía la fuerte animosidad de Lambas de Auria, duque de los ginoveses, que a su hijo herido con sus braços desde la nao echó en la mar. Porque todas estas son muertes que, si roban la vida, es forçado de complir con la fama." (XXI, 208–9)

This is a fine point, but it does not take into account the fact that the disappearance of death as a vengeful commonplace is much more complete in *La Celestina* even than in the *Coplas*. Whereas the latter proposes antidotes to death, the former, as we shall see, relieves it of all positive import or moral meaning. In the world of Rojas, death has become a senseless casualty and nothing more.

28. As in the case of Elicia's brief dance of death, references to death by the characters usually occur in connection with some prescription for the good life. When, for example, Celestina insinuates argumentatively to Melibea, "Tan presto, señora, se va el carnero como el cordero ..." (IV, 270), it is only in order to suggest the desirability of surrender to love.

29. The rapport of these two was first developed by Laín Entralgo in an essay I have been unable to obtain. To refute Quevedo and Heidegger (from this particular point of view) we might reread Andreyev's *The Seven that were Hanged* with its hair-raising analysis of the unrealizability of death. Kenneth Burke in a recent article, "Thanatopsis for Critics," *Essays in Criticism,* II (1952), 369–75, studies the repercussions of this unknowability on poetic use of death as topic or image.

30. As for death as transition (rather than gleeful destruction as in the *Danza*), it is ignored in *La Celestina*. Unlike Chaucer, Rojas makes no provision for the moment after death. The ultimate fate of the soul (like the ultimate value of each life) remains unassessed, and if both Calisto and Celestina cry "confession," no moral is drawn from their failure to receive it. We may assume that damnation is inevitable but (aside from Pármeno's warning in Act I that Calisto will lose his soul) the text nowhere confirms the assumption. Pleberio's significant unconcern with Melibea's future may also be noted. Thus, lack of confession in *La Celestina* does not necessarily imply eternal punishment. It is instead a reflection of a thematic lack of "official" death. Death is a mere termination of life, an end of meaning, and has no positive or negative significance in

itself. Menéndez Pelayo and others have related Rojas' failure to concern himself with the consequences of death (and particularly of suicide) to his Judaism. For our special purposes the thematic implications are more interesting.

31. In general, references to temporality in *La Celestina* are not given the same ironical display as references to other commonplaces. When Pleberio reminds us of Jorge Manrique by remarking, "Alisa, amiga, el tiempo, según me parece, se nos va, como dizen, entre las manos. Corren los días como agua de río," (XVI, 144) the irony is purely dramatic. It does not as in other cases reside in the juxtaposition of the particular intention and the general truth. Rather it stems from the fact that we know (while Pleberio does not) that his plans for Melibea's marriage are a month too late.

32. There are certain passages in *La Celestina* which could almost be interpreted as fables in reverse, that is to say, passages in which animal traits are converted in image to those of human beings. The implied comparison of Melibea's wrath to that of a bull is the most familiar example. Although this technique is frequent in satire (and even in Balzac), Rojas seems to have had no such intention. Rather the enormity of her passion in the eyes of Celestina invites stylistic expansion beyond the limited sphere of man.

33. We may detect the same point of view when both Calisto and Melibea, preoccupied with the consequences of their love (for the one, a loss of honor, for the other, of virginity), speak of "breue deleyte." (XIV, 119, 123) But in spite of this momentary change in point of view, both as a rule situate themselves within "deleyte" raised to spaceless and timeless "gloria." From here they may, in effect, either castigate or ignore dimensionality. The living opposition to this attitude is that of Elicia who, as we have seen, reduces all things, especially love, to the moment: "Son passadas quatro horas después ¿e hauíaseme de acordar desso?." (XI, 75) Elicia accepts the brevity of delight as a matter of course and, for that very reason, cannot fully realize time's alien nature until Celestina's death. In this sense, she serves as a thematic foil for Calisto and Melibea.

34. Time is present not only on the level of structure and situation, where it often appears as a preoccupation with lateness (for example, Calisto's nervous clockwatching while waiting for his midnight rendezvous), but also (as is thematically appropriate) in intimate involvement in the style. One of the most effective images of *La Celestina* is contained in a remark of Pármeno criticizing his master's fulsome praise of Melibea: "Ya escurre eslauones el perdido. Ya se desconciertan sus badajadas. Nunca da menos de doze; siempre está hecho relox de mediodía." (VI, 210)

35. In the following definition of love copied from Petrarch, "Es vn fuego escondido, vna agradable llaga, vn sabroso veneno, vna dulce amargura, vna delectable dolencia, vn alegre tormento, vna dulce e fiera herida, vna blanda muerte" (X, 59), the phrase "dulce e fiera herida" is Rojas' own insertion.

36. *Orígenes de la novela*, p. 381.

37. *Etica*, Madrid (1942), II, 33. The italics are in the original. Scheler's use of "acto de amor" as the subject seems to represent a purposeful avoidance of the noun, "love," with its passionate implications.

38. This distinction has, of course, little to do with the popular distinction between sentimental (that is to say, superficially emotional) as against passionate (that is to say deep, sincere, and lasting) love. We are here less interested in measuring love quantitatively than we are in establishing points of view. For those who still may

question our terminology, Jean Maisonneuve (*Les Sentiments,* Paris, 1948, p. 26) offers a convenient distinction between sentiments and emotions:

"On distinguerait ainsi des joies et des tristesses, des craintes et des désirs de caractère émotif, et des attitudes désignées par les mêmes termes, mais dépourvus de cette espèce d'affolement, de déroutement qui caractérise les émotions. Et il semble qu'ici precisement, le terme de sentiment serait précieux ... L'amour peut comporter des états de crise: attente, jalousie, volupté, de'ordre émotif; on ne saurait dire que l'amour, en soi, est une émotion. La peur elle-même n'est pas nécessairement émotive, dans la mesure où elle inspire seulement des reactions controlées de précautions ou de defense. Tous ces éxemples nous conduisent à voir dans les émotions des phénomènes affectifs au cours desquels l'individu se trouve en quelque sort "désadapté" en présence d'une situation; tandis que les phénomènes auxquels nous réservons le nom de sentiments, seraient des attitudes adaptées aux circonstances variées de notre éxistence. Le sentiment serait donc comme le résultat d'une osmose *entre le moi el le monde,* état subjectif certes, mais en contact avec le non-moi, et partiellement determiné de l'extérieur."

If passionate love may be defined as coming from this "non-moi extérieur" (from the point of view of rational consciousness), emotional love, on the other hand, is recognizably transient and subjective. Emotions accompany sentiment but lack its longer duration and peculiar variety of awareness. Thus, Calisto's rapture on the garden wall can hardly be ascribed to an excess of emotion. Rather it is a moment into which the full experience of his love is expressed and by means of which he is opened to the "non-moi," of music, landscape, physical beauty, and above all to the incomparable value of Melibea as a person. On the other hand, as we shall see, it is quite frequent for the characters of *La Celestina* to interpret their emotional states as grand passions for which they are not responsible.

39. *L'amour et l'Occident* (Paris, 1939).

40. The rapprochement of contemporary terminology to a past creation is a hazardous and delicate operation. It carries with it the danger of distortion of both elements insofar as it suggests equation of disparate perspectives. In this case, I have chosen to use concepts inherited from Scheler, Guyau, and Bergson apart from their systematic rigor in an effort to describe one aspect of Rojas' theme. As a description it is both anachronistic and inexact; yet both failures may be excused if our comprehension of Calisto's sentimental evasion of time and space is thereby increased.

41. This essay originally in *La nouvelle révue française* (Vol. XIV) was reprinted by Thibaudet in his *Refléxions sur la critique* (Paris, 1939).

42. This comparison should, of course, not be taken to mean that Rojas influenced either Flaubert or Proust. The stylistic resemblance noticed above is, after all, both partial and remote. Rather, Rojas in this first thematic exploration of human life as such could not help but verge upon the preoccupations of those who in later centuries were to continue his work.

43. See the essay on Flaubert in the work previously mentioned (note 41 of this chapter). For a fuller treatment of the temporal paradox of *La Celestina,* consult my *"El tiempo y el género literario en "La Celestina," Revista de filología hispánica,* VII (1945), 147-59. In that article the attempt was made to relate directly the existence of two times to problems of genre—an attempt that was premised on a faulty understand-

ing of the theme. To speak of the fusion of novel and drama may be tolerated as ex post facto criticism, but from the point of view of art, it tends to obscure *La Celestina*'s fundamental creative unity and to confuse what we shall term here its ageneric character. An adequate intuition of the theme is an indispensable prerequisite for any discussion of genre. An attempt to resolve the same paradox may be found in Manuel Asensio's "El tiempo en *La Celestina*," *Hispanic Review*, XX (1952), 28–43. His assumption that an undetermined length of time is supposed to have passed between the first and second situations of Act I seems to me to be completely unjustified, insofar as he tends to identify the requirements of literature with those of life. My detailed reply to his conclusions appears in a later issue of the same review.

44. In the *comedia* of the Golden Age the phrase "el otro día" is frequently sinonymous with "ayer," and we may assume that this is what Rojas intended here.

45. In the added acts when the theme was verging upon the frontiers of conscious artistry, Rojas inserts a month of time between Acts XV and XVI in order to provide adequate time for the experience of completed love. But the existence of "muchos e muchos días" in sentimental duration alongside the *Comedia*'s two days of dialogue reveals even more effectively that same irreconcilable conflict of sentiment against dimension which is to end (on the level of action) in the lovers' fatal emergence into a world of perspective and solid geometry after the timeless and spaceless idyll of their "gloria." Whether Rojas was aware of it or not, his theme results in two times, times which differ not only in length but in essence, almost as the enclosed garden and the exposed "açotea" offer two opposed spaces. It is necessary that we distinguish these two currents of thematic time from other apparently comparable instances. In *Troilus and Cressida*, for example, the time of action is some three years; yet overlaid upon it is what might be called a time of metaphor based on images derived from seasonal change. On this level the varying sentimental moods result in a sort of poetic year beginning in the early spring and ending in the winter of Cressida's betrayal and Troilus' death. Thus, one flow of time is vertical and belongs to the realm of mediaeval commonplace (with its emphasis on cyclical destiny) while the other is horizontal and follows the dramatic movements of the characters. Unlike *La Celestina* with its internal and external discrepancy, the division in the *Troilus* is one of immanence against transcendence. Still both occur in an artistic world for deeply artistic reasons and serve to show the futility of explanations basing themselves on the equation of art with life. See H. W. Sams, "The Dual Time Scheme in Chaucer's *Troilus*," *Modern Language Notes*, LVI (1941), 94–100.

46. In the text, for all its argument and all its dimensional hazards, the struggle is never mentioned directly. Rojas is creatively much more preoccupied by the trees than with the ultimate shape of the forest, and it is precisely for this reason that a discussion of the theme must be so carefully undertaken. The very few indirect references include Celestina's answer to Areusa's complaint that the only pleasures of mistresses is quarreling: "Que los sabios dizen: que mas vale una migaja de pan con paz, que toda la casa llena de viandas con renzilla." (IX, 43) Another typical brush of the text with the theme is Pármeno's interpolated excuse for cowardice:

Que no querer morir ni matar no es couardía, sino buen natural. Estos escuderos de Pleberio son locos: no desean tanto comer ni dormir como questiones e ruydos. Pues más locura sería esperar pelea con enemigo que no ama tanto la victoria e vencimiento, como la continua guerra e contienda. (XII, 88)

47. See pp. 48-49.

48. See Chapter II, note 31.

49. The fact of adaptation from Petrarch does not in itself deprive the *Prólogo* of thematic significance. The charge of plagiarism is, of course, anachronistic and seems even more empty when we remember that Rojas both identified and substantially reworked his source. The second prologue of the *De remediis* was chosen, as we shall see, precisely because it was profoundly interesting to Rojas, because it gave words to his own intuition. It is less easy, however, to answer Cejador's accusation of disproportion, the disproportion of universal conflict presented only to explain divergent opinions about the *Comedia*. This disproportion does exist (although it does not necessarily prove that Rojas was not the author of the *Tragicomedia*) and has to be taken into account when relating the *Prólogo* to the theme.

50. This proposed *Weltanschauung* might very well be related to Rojas' Judaism, a possibility which I am not equipped to investigate. My only purpose in mentioning the social and historical environment is to illustrate an intuition of the theme, and in doing so I become increasingly conscious of the immense debt I owe to Américo Castro. It is for him to speak with authority on these matters.

51. Even more out of the question than the third person singular (that is to say, a defined role) as a manner of living socially is the first person plural, the "nosotros" of the mediaeval community. This social possibility proposed by Martin Buber (see Chapter II, note 5) is, of course, the first to disappear in a state of disintegration. What is significant is the way Rojas goes beyond this preliminary stage to the collapse of individual definition itself.

52. *The Civilization of the Renaissance in Italy*, II, 1.

53. This, of course, does not mean the rebellion of Espronceda or the Romantic interpretation of *La Celestina* recently refurbished by J. M. Gutiérrez Mora ("Lo romántico en *La Celestina*," *Et Caetera*, 1950). We might better propose a post-mediaeval variety of consciousness within which Burckhardt's Renaissance, Romanticism, Neo-Classicism, the Baroque, and others all might fit and which, in *La Celestina*, has its own Celestinesque characteristics. Among these characteristics is the above counterpoint of perdition to salvation, a matter to which we shall refer again and which, we shall see, did find echoes in the Italian Renaissance in spite of Burckhardt's historical optimism.

CHAPTER SIX

1. It is possible, of course, to define the tradition of *La Celestina* not just in terms of the evolution of its art of theme but rather as including the whole literary background of its author. This task has been admirably accomplished by Menéndez Pelayo with his usual anticipation of contemporary concerns. Unfortunately, however, his broader view of the nature of tradition led him to underestimate if not ignore the thematic contribution of Petrarch. He did not realize that the efficient tradition is that to which an author has recourse in order to understand his theme. This, as we shall see, is an entirely different matter from the mere assimilation of literary atmosphere and material. For a discussion of the above aspect of Diderot's aesthetics, see J. Doolittle,

"Criticism as Creation in the Work of Diderot," *Yale French Studies,* II (1949), 14-23.

2. The mention of Heraclitus was taken literally from the *De remediis* in spite of Rojas' claim to have found "esta sentencia *corroborada* por aquel gran orador e poeta laureado, Francisco Petrarcha ..." This pretense to personal erudition may not be to Rojas' credit, but taken by itself it has little significance either for the art of theme or problem of authorship.

3. Only the most evident seem to have been listed by Castro Guisasola. See note 31 for a subtle reminiscence of the *De remediis* that was overlooked by him. And there are very probably others.

4. *Orígenes,* pp. 340, 344.

5. *Giornale storico della letteratura italiana,* XLIV (1904), 313–14.

6. For example, Castro Guisasola, who denies the possibility that the *Prólogo* might be a statement of thesis and who insists that Rojas' object was "únicamente justificar algunas modificaciones introducidas en la primitive *Comedia.*"—*Observaciones,* p. 136.

7. See F. Simone "Note sulla fortuna del Petrarca en Francia nella prima metá del Cinquecento," *Giornale storico della letteratura italiana,* CXVII (1950), 1–59; also W. Fiske, *Bibliographical Notices* (Florence, 1888), Vol. III.

8. It is evident that a full treatment of the *De remediis'* significance for its time should include evidence not only of its wide reading and frequent translation but also of the assimilation of its vision and doctrine by reflective literature. This does not mean full thematic utilization as in *La Celestina.* I know of no comparable case except Boccaccio's *Fiammetta* considered (along with Marlowe's *Tamburlaine*) later in this chapter. Rather what seems to be called for is a study of the *De remediis'* direct influence. F. Simone (see note 7) offers valuable indications of this sort, but his work is admittedly incomplete both in range and in intention. There must be quite a. few other examples comparable to the verses of Jean Meschinot cited by Huizinga in *The Waning of the Middle Ages* (London, 1924), Chapter II:

> O miserable et très dolente vie!
>
> .   .   .   .
>
> La guerre avons, mortalite, famine;
> Le froid, le chaud, le jour, la nuit nous mine;
> Puces, cirons et tant d'autre vermine
> Nous guerroyent. Bref, miserere domine
> Noz mechans corps, dont la vie est très court.

Curiously enough, Huizinga equates this apparently Petrarchist sensibility with the pessimism of Deschamps as expressed in his "Temps de douleur et de temptacion / Ages de plour, d'envie et de tourment ..." written some "three quarters of a century before." What seems to have happened is that the diffuse and general pessimism of the late Middle Ages, as exemplified in Deschamps, has been crystallized lyrically in terms of the Stoic war of inner and outer worlds, the warfare of the *De remediis.* According to Dilthey, this was precisely the ambition of Petrarch: "Er wollte der originale Lebens-philosoph seiner Zeit sein." Dilthey discusses Petrarch's philosophical pretensions at some length in his *Auffassung und Analyse des Menschen im 15. und 16. Jahrhundert.*

9. *Orígenes,* p. 341.

10. *Jorge Manrique,* p. 86.

11. *The Mediaeval Heritage*, pp. 47–50. Farnham pays particular attention to Boccaccio's *De casibus* and passes over the *De remediis* rapidly. He is primarily interested in tracing the tragic story—catastrophe and its enigmatic causation—back from Shakespeare and Marlowe. From this point of view, the tragic dilemma of the sixteenth and seventeenth centuries as intuitively foreseen by Petrarch seems elusive and hardly pertinent.

12. For example, E. Hoepfner in his introduction to Volume II of the *Oeuvres de Guillaume Machaut* (Paris, 1911) remarks:

"L'auteur anonyme des *Regles de seconde rhetorique* fait remarquer à propos de Fortune que 'plusieurs poètes ont closé sur ceste matière pour ce que tousjours ara son cours.' Et, en effet, les poèmes et les traités à ce sujet pullelent littéralement surtout depuis la fin du XIIIme siècle dans la littérature française parmi les contemporains plus ou moins rapprochés de Machaut."

13. The style with its revival of Senecan antithesis seems to have been equally attractive in its novelty. Unfortunately I am hardly qualified to speak of this.

14. Petrarch considered that Seneca was the author. The attribution has since then been disallowed.

15. This comparison is not entirely fair to the *Consolations* in which the author from time to time manages to take his own part. Boethius' ripostes are not as violent (nor as amusingly childish) as those of Juan Ruiz when angered at Don Amor, but he does reveal himself in an interesting fashion. Only at the end does he collapse completely before the dialectic of Philosophy.

16. This is true to such an extent that while Farnham refers to the chapter headings of Twyne's translation—"The Flourishing Years," "The Goodlie Beauties of the Body," etc.—as "Elizabethan," they are, nevertheless, more or less accurate renderings of the original Latin.

17. Whether or not we choose to term these innovations Renaissance characteristics within a mediaeval lesson is of little moment. The important thing is to grasp their function. This same counterpoint of attitude towards the world is stressed by Farnham and Salinas in connection with the *Secretum*. The following (from José Luis Romero's monograph on the Middle Ages) will serve as a general resumé:

"En el ambiente de crisis que caracteriza a la baja Edad Media, la concepción del mundo acentuó su bipolaridad al romperse el equilibrio establecido sobre la preeminencia de lo espiritual, de lo referido al trasmundo, de lo que pertenecía a la ciudad celeste. Ese equilibrio no se constituyó sobre nuevas bases, sino que, simplemente, los elementos encontrados permanecieron en presencia, oponiéndose o complementándose en síntesis transitorias e inestables. La contemporaneidad de Boccaccio y Santa Catalina de Siena tiene el valor de un símbolo.—*La Edad Media* (Mexico, 1949), p. 197.

18. See p. 22.

19. As Patch points out, Petrarch specifically (and somewhat unnecessarily) denies belief in fortune in his letter to Tomas de Garbo.

20. García Bacca in the article previously cited recalls the Stoic image of man as a "ciudad sitiada" and goes on to compare the contents of the world to archers attacking him. From this, the root meanings of *ob-jectum* and *sub-jectum* may be developed.

García Bacca does not, however, relate this Stoic version of consciousness to that of the inhabitants of *La Celestina*.

21. It must be admitted that Petrarch does not assert the alien nature of the universe in as uncompromising a fashion as Rojas. On several occasions he states his belief in providence, but since providence is unknowable the circumstance of his individual seems quite as alien as that of *La Celestina*.

22. See P. Barth, *Los estoicos* (Madrid, 1930), p. 64.

23. As far as the *De remediis* is concerned, such misfortunes as blindness and imprisonment are defended only in order to console man's natural fear of them.

24. See Barth, *Los estoicos*, p. 57.

25. I am hardly in a position to take sides with those who affirm or those who deny Boethius' influence on the *Troilus*. What is interesting for us is the continued presence in it of the verticality—the vertical pattern of preoccupation—of the *Consolations*, in spite of the variant conclusions. The problem of fortune has been approached in the same way after some eight centuries. In any case, as students of the matter point out, Boethius was a central influence on most mediaeval treatments of fortune. The fifth book of the *Roman de la rose* is one of numberless examples.

26. See L. Zanta, *La renaissance du stoicisme au XVme siecle* (Paris, 1914). Naturally Seneca was well known during the Middle Ages and long before his Petrarchist revival. Yet precisely because his work was presented as a collection of excerpts (*florilegia*), there was no total understanding of his doctrine.

27. See Centeno's *Intent of the Artist*.

28. The reference to the "regocijados conbites de las bodas y sus danzas" calls to mind once again the paintings of Breughel with their subtle grossness of attack on the sensibility. Rather than exultation in a direct and newly achieved vision of the world, in Breughel we find the same recognition of the intolerable presence of sensation—a kind of incarnated pessimism. This, in turn, helps us to understand the effect Rojas wished to achieve with Pleberio's lament—"los verdaderos lloros de los padres." It is not just a statement of Stoic ideology but rather a direct and purified rending of the spirit. We are also reminded of Huizinga's masterful evocation of "The Violent Tenor of Life" with all its harsh contrast and aggressive polychromy. Significant for *La Celestina* (and Act XII in particular) is the following paragraph:

"The contrast between silence and sound, darkness and light, like that between summer and winter, was more strongly marked than it is in our lives. The modern town hardly knows silence or darkness in their purity, nor the effect of a solitary light or a single distant cry."—*The Waning of the Middle Ages*, p. 2.

We must not forget that in reading the dialogue of *La Celestina* we are participating in the fifteenth century sense of life.

29. This may be clarified by remembering our previous distinction between passion and sentiment—one blind and shut within itself and the other in intimate communication with the world and its values. It is true that the Stoics of antiquity were particularly concerned with passions (thought of as excesses of instinct or natural appetite) and their domination by reason. Such a conflict could be settled from within and did not require the intervention of alien time and space. The universe was not per se estranged from man, although it might seem so to a mind overwrought with passion.

The *De remediis,* on the other hand, by opposing reason to sentiment not only portrays consciousness as locked in intimate and unending struggle but also requires the invention of a "mundo ageno y estraño" to counteract the attraction of values discovered sentimentally in the immediate circumstance. Hence, the garden (sentimental circumstance) against the fatal roof top (alien space) at the end of *La Celestina.* The new sentimental enemy seemed to require a new and more frightful weapon of defense.

30. See the classic account in Burckhard'ts *Civilization* (IV, 3). This awareness of dimensions is particularly acute in the prologue to the second part of the *De remediis,* the prologue which so fascinated Rojas. It is there, as we shall see, that Petrarch seems most conscious of his subterranean innovations into Stoicism. Also from time to time in the text there are to be found passages such as the following, presenting the special dimensionality of landscape:

"Dolor—Soy condenado a ceguedad perpetua. *Razón:* No verás ahora los valles llenos de arboledas, los airosos montes, los floridos céspedes, las sombrías cuevas, las claras fuentes, los corrientes ríos, los verdes prados, ni lo que dizen que es mas hermoso que todo lo otro, la compostura del rostro humano, pero tampoco verás los montones de cieno ... (*De caecitate,* F. Madrid, fol. CXLIII)

31. Comparison of the following two passages shows a variety of influence somewhat more subtle than that considered by Castro Guisasola. The author of Act I succeeds in reapplying effectively the series of sounds offered him by Petrarch:

"¿... quién no padece las guerras de las *aves* nocturnas, de los buhos y lechuzas, y el demasiado velar de los *perros* que ladran a la luna ...? Llévase también a esto el ruido que las *ranas* de noche hazen ... Pues el reposo del día no es mayor, antes las cigarras gritadoras y el graznido de los cuervos y roznidos de los *asnos* impiden, así mismo el *balido* de las ovejas y el bramido de los *bueyes* ... Y también los tristes *cantares* conque los cardadores y *peinadores* halagan sus trabajos, y la desabrida musica de los *arcadores* y *tejedores,* y los roncos soplidos de las fuelles de los *herreros* y el agudo son de sus *martillos.* (*Epistolaris praefatio,* F. Madrid, fol. LXXXI)

Si passa por los *perros,* aquello suena su *ladrido;* si está cerca las *aves,* otra cosa no cantan; si cerca los *ganados, balando* lo pregonan; si cerca las *bestias,* rebuznando dizen: ¡puta vieja! Las *ranas* de los charcos otra cosa no suelen mentar. Si va entre los *herreros* aquello dizen sus *martillos.* Carpinteros e armeros, herradores, caldereros, *arcadores,* todo oficio de instrumento forma en el ayre su nombre. *Cántanla* los carpinteros, péinanla los *peinadores, texedores.* (I, 68)

32. According to Castro Guisasola, this is not true of the beginning of Act II, but this is a matter more significant for his personal authorship speculations than for us.

33. Glancing over the other borrowings from Aristotle, as well as those from Seneca and Boethius, it is evident that they have been chosen to fit the topic—the subject or commonplace under discussion. Aside from a few phrases and short sentences, a third reminiscence of Aristotle is the analysis of the motives for friendship ("bien," "proucho," and "deleyte"; see p. 6). As for Seneca, there is the passage beginning, "Como Séneca nos dize, los peregrinos tienen muchas posadas y pocas amistades ... (I, 100) while others refer to such matters as poverty and virtue. Finally, Boethius contributes Sempronio's "Miserable cosa es pensar ser maestro el que nunca fué discipulo" (I, 52) and one or two other learned vauntings.

34. We may estimate the intensity of Calisto's vital engagement by the shortness of his replies when arguing (although not on other occasions) in comparison to the wordy disquisitions of the servants.

35. Even Celestina, as we have seen, begins her intrigue with the intention merely to deceive and cheat Calisto. Only in Act IV with its epic "Yr quiero" does she engage herself fully in the action.

36. Castro Guisasola gives Boethius as a partial source, but in any case these remarks are parallel to the essay in the *De remediis* entitled *De origine generosa*. Compare the following to the text as reproduced above:

"*Gozo*—Nací noble. *Razón*—Ya te dije que el verdadero noble no nace; mas hacese.

Gozo—A lo menos esta nobleza que mis padres me dejaron es grande. *Razón*—También te dije que la nobleza no se halla naciendo, mas viviendo. Un bien veo aquí, que no te faltarán familiares ejemplos de virtudes y domésticas guías cuyas pisadas hayas miedo de errar." (F. Madrid, fol. XIII)

37. The complementary Stoic argument is made by Calisto when he points out in the above passage that, while objectively valid truth may be distorted and used for private purposes, ultimately it must prevail. Accordingly, the realm of *opinión*, which cannot change truth, must adjust itself to it.

38. Pármeno, in his muttered reply to these remarks, seems to interpret them as expressing a feeling of insecurity in Calisto. He realizes that his master is attempting to rationalize his dependence on Celestina—and that is the reason for the effort to explain away her devastating description in Act I: "¿Ya lloras? Dualos tenemos ...? The effect of irony is of course strengthened by this indication of the half sob which must have accompanied Calisto's miserable invocation of the commonplace.

39. *Orígenes*, pp. 340–41. I have indented the quotations for easy reference.

40. The preceding sentence, "Rara es la bonança en el piélago," was taken directly from the *De remediis*.

41. At this point Rojas introduces an interpolation which further illustrates Calisto's total lack of fortitude. It is the reference to "Ulixes"—an attempt to excuse his inaction by asserting an apocryphal epic precedent.

42. I would, of course, agree with Menéndez Pelayo in his rejection of Petrarch's influence but for very different reasons.

43. The third pattern of character, that of condition or class, was established in Act I and, as far as the servants are concerned, has many possible sources of inspiration. Nevertheless, the following excerpts will have a familiar ring for any reader of *La Celestina*:

"*Dolor*—Tengo siervos muy malos, tragones, ladrones, mentirosos, y desvergonzados.

Razón—¿Qué menester es contar tanta abundancia de títulos? Di siervos y habrás dicho cuanto hay en ellos ... *Dolor*—De muchos siervos soy cercado. *Razón*—... los siervos aunque sean buenos (lo que yo tendría por milagro) si son muchos nunca bien sirven, porque siempre entre si discordan, murmuran y alteran. Mira el uno a las manos del otro y huelga entre tanto ... tiene por gran honra hacer del señor y piensa que ninguna cosa hay mas honesta que no hacer nada."

Reason then goes on to advise that those who become servants because of their extreme poverty and humble background (e.g., Sosia) are more likely to be diligent and faithful. The conclusion follows:

"Echa de tu casa los que fueren hermosos, los muy peinados, y a los que del gesto o de ingenio se precian y entre pocos rudos y desharrapados vivirás mas seguro." (*De seruis malis*, F. Madrid, fol. CIII–CIIII)

In exactly the same way, Cejador's suggestion that the affair of Calisto and Melibea may be an outgrowth of *De gratis amoribus* may not be without some justification. There is specific mention of the blasphemies of lovers, and Celestina's famous definition of love ("... es un fuego escondido ...") is derived from it.

44. Rojas continues to refer to Petrarch and the *De remediis* in interpolations to particular passages—see among other examples, "*Las riquezas no hazen rico, mas ocupado* ..." from Act III—which he is interested in completing. This makes the failure to look to Petrarch in the added acts all the more striking.

45. In this connection we may notice that several of the specific references to Petrarch have to do with the calculated repetition of earlier stages of the thematic evolution. For example, when Calisto at the beginning of the second soliloquy argues, "No ay hora cierta ni limitada ni avn vn solo momento ..." he reminds us of the doctrinaire time of Stoicism and not the dimensional time—more terrible because more alien—which he is soon to recognize. Again when Pleberio says, with another quotation from Petrarch, "Alisa amiga, el tiempo según parece se nos va como dizen entre las manos ..." he thinks of himself as motionless, a Stoic rock of consciousness around which time flows. He has not yet appreciated the thing that Calisto discovered at the end of his soliloquy: that he himself is conditioned dimensionally and that the "ygual curso" of time involves him beyond any possibility of remedy.

46. My primary source for these statements is already somewhat dangerous to cite because of its date of publication. It is R. W. Battenhouse's book on the *Tamburlaine* and its criticism, *Marlowe's "Tamburlaine"* (Nashville, Tenn., 1941)

47. I take the liberty of suggesting that both possibilities might have been applicable, although Machiavelli and Seneca are undoubtedly the major purveyors of Marlowe's thematic tradition. If Marlowe did read the *De remediis* in translation its second prologue must have fascinated him in much the same way as it did Rojas.

48. Marlowe, *Plays* (Everyman's Library, London, 1950), p. 54.

49. One large class has to do with the eating of human flesh, and another gives new significance to such inherited images as "the horned moon." More elusive than those quoted above are the two following:

> Thou hast procured a greater enemy
> Than he that *darted* mountains at thy head.
>
> (p. 98)

Here, mountains are visualized poetically in only one form—as sharp peaks fit for metaphorical conversion into arrows or darts. Again, and even more daringly, angels take on the same role as pointed missiles:

> To see the devils mount in angels' thrones
> And angels dive into the pools of hell!
>
> (p. 114)

M. B. Smith's catalogue of Marlowe's imagery classifies by content rather than by poetic action or function and so is hardly useful for our purposes. See *Marlowe's Imagery and the Marlowe Canon* (Philadelphia, 1940).

50. In this connection it is interesting to note that the only time the word "violence" occurs in the play it has the most usual meaning of "violation":

> Injurious tyrant, wilt thou so defame
> The hateful fortunes of thy victory
> To exercise upon such guiltless dames
> The violence of thy common soldier's lust?
>
> (p. 104)

51. Many of these features, violence, passion, monologues of sheer self-expression seem to have been inherited directly from the non-theatrical tragedies of Seneca. There is, however, one essential difference between Marlowe and Seneca: for Seneca everything is subordinated to stylistic effect, to style considered as a value on its own terms, while for Marlowe the thematic intuition is primary. Many students of Marlowe will claim that this presentation of the *Tamburlaine* is an exaggeration to the point of caricature. Certainly, the relationship between Tamburlaine and Zenocrate is quite opposed—I should say, placed in purposeful counterpoint—to the lives and relationships described above. Yet if Tamburlaine and Zenocrate are supposed to accentuate the thematic violence of the whole by their personal tides of tenderness, they are also as a pair somewhat inexplicable and incongruent. This is also true in the case of the love of Theridamas for Olympia, even though the former is not too far removed from the urge to violate. Finally, these critics might point to such evident characterizations as that of the Governor of Babylon, the weak Mycetes, the cowardly and sensual son Calyphas, and others. Yet all these, ranged in structural counterpoint around the figure of Tamburlaine, seem foolish and ridiculous in their opposition to him. Their failure to predict the results of conflict between their characters and his ego shows them to be lacking in the most elementary powers of deduction. One might apply in reverse Alfonso Reyes' keen generalization that in the Middle Ages the autobiographical *ego* is in itself foolish and ridiculous. In this thematic world of violation, it is not the *ego* which is at a disadvantage but the *ille*.

52. After writing this my attention has been called to E. Seaton's "Marlowe's Map," *Essays and Studies*, X (1924), 13–35, which demonstrates the use of a specific map in the composition of the *Tamburlaine*. Like Tamburlaine himself, Marlowe seems to have been stimulated by maps. Each saw in them much more than guides to geographical location. They were rather metaphors of mundane power, both poetical and military. In reading the *Tamburlaine* one has the impression that the map is a part of the creative process and that Tamburlaine lives and campaigns on a map, a map that has become poetry.

53. Marlowe, as is evident in the episode of Sigismund, is careful not to involve himself with Christianity. It is for this reason that the only structure of belief that is pitted against Tamburlaine—and defied by him successfully on so many occasions— is Mohammedanism. This was a convenient fulfillment of the thematic need to pit the irresistible force of the exploding ego against an inadequate providence. We should take

care to remember that this is a function of theme and bears no necessary relation to Marlowe's personal atheism—or his lack of it.

54. Hence, death is referred to at the end as the rebellious slave of Tamburlaine. It accomplishes what no man could accomplish; it reduces him from an "I" to a "thou" and then violates him with its murderous dart. In Tamburlaine's delirium, death is personified but in a way far removed from the mediaeval emblem.

55. Simone Weil in her article, "The Iliad or the Poem of Force," (*Politics*, 1945) might well have chosen the *Tamburlaine* for her literary point of departure. Whereas violence and force with their inevitable dehumanization of both aggressor and victim is only one aspect of the *Iliad*'s epic theme—of its consideration of heroism—in the *Tamburlaine,* as we have seen, war is limited to this single aspect. Homer delves deeply into the living reaction of his heroes to the senselessness of their belicose milieu, while Marlowe, taking an opposite tack, eliminates the heroic quest for meaning. He emphasizes only the external violence of warfare. It is in the final sense more true of Tamburlaine than of Achilles to say: "The conquering soldier is like a scourge of nature. Possessed by war, he, like the slave, becomes a thing—over him words are as powerless as over matter itself."

56. These involve a purposeful approximation of fortune's fall to a spatial fall (similar to those of *La Celestina*):

"Ma oltre a tutti questi modi m'occorse di Perdici la morte, caduto dell'altissima arce cretense, e questo solo modo mi piacque di seguitare per infallibile morte e vota d'ogni infamia, fra me dicendo: io dell'alte parti della casa gittandomi, il corpo rotto in cento parti, per tutti e cento renderò l'infelice anima maculata e rotta a tristi Iddii, nè fia chi quinci pensi crudeltà o furore in me stato di morte, anzi a fortunoso caso imputandolo, spandendo pietose lagrime per me, la fortuna maladiranno."—G. Boccaccio, *Opere volgari* (Firenze, 1829), VI, 155.

57. *Il filostrato* is generally recognized as an early work, a condition which may account for the difference in theme. Nevertheless, the classic comparison of *Il filostrato* and Chaucer's *Troilus* reveals Boccaccio's relative lack of stress on external fortune. His thematic evolution towards the *Fiammetta* apparently has already begun, and we may surmise that Petrarch contributed to the final expression of this theme in much the same way as in *La Celestina.*

58. It is interesting to note that the nurse, who speaks as the voice of Fiammetta's reason, contributes much more to what little dialogue there is than does either the husband or the lover.

59. The lack of "gozo" or "deleyte" as we know them in *La Celestina* is manifest in the following:

"Certo se io dicessi che questa fosse la cagione per la quale io l'amassi, io confesserei che ogni volta che ciò nella memoria mi tornasse mi fosse dolore a niuno altro simile; ma in ciò mi sia Iddio testimonio, che cotale accidente fu ed é cagione menomissima dell'amore che io li porto ...' (p. 32)

Fiammetta begins with physical love, and her novel continues long after it is over. There is nothing in her comparable to that slow growth to ardor in Melibea.

60. In this connection, it is worth noting that Rojas' one important borrowing from the *Fiammetta* (aside from the circumstances of Melibea's suicide) occurs at that uncer-

tain moment when Melibea, after having consented to meet Calisto, is waiting for him in the garden. At this point Calisto (like Fiammetta's Panfilo) is still a figment of her imagination, a creation of longing, rather than a person whom she loves:

"Mas, cuytada, pienso muchas cosas que desde su casa acá le podrían acaecer. ¿*Quién sabe si él, con voluntad de venir al prometido plazo en la forma que los tales mancebos a las tales horas suelen andar, fué topado de los alguaziles noturnos e sin le conocer le han acometido ... O se ha caydo en alguna calçada o hoyo donde algun daño le viniesse? Mas, ¡o mezquina de mí! ¿Qué son estos inconuenientes que el concebido amor me pone delante e los atribulados ymaginamientos me acarrean?*" (XIV, 115)

The falling "en alguna calçada o hoyo" is Rojas' particular thematic danger and was inserted by him. But the last two sentences in which the mind feels its own isolation in terms of a love that has not yet been experienced (in the *Fiammetta* the experience was long past) is taken almost word for word from the Salamanca, 1496, translation. Later on Melibea, certain from within her love, forgets the futility of imaginative fears, and the *Fiammetta* no longer serves as a source.

61. Fiammetta tells us at the very beginning of her narrative that "Io avanti non vinta da alcuno piacere giammai, tentata da molti, ultimamente vinta da uno, ed arsi ed ardo, e servai e servo più che altra facesse giammai nel preso fuoco. (p. 13) This change-lessness corresponds fully to Boccaccio's thematic version of war. Insofar as time is eliminated by the force of love, this sentence introduces the whole.

Since these pages were written, Harry Levin's critical study of Marlowe, *The Over-reacher* (Cambridge, Mass., 1954), has been published. In it I was pleased to find the following remarks on *Tamburlaine,* remarks which authoritatively and brilliantly contribute to my interpretation of the theme:

Driven by an impetus toward infinity and faced with the limitations of the stage, the basic convention of the Marlovian drama is to take the word for the deed. Words are weapons; conflict perforce is invective, verbal rather than physical aggression; through musters and parleys, wars of nerves are fought out by exchanging boasts and parrying insults. . . . Dialogue does not flow in *Tamburlaine;* characters converse in formal monologue, accumulating to rhetorical lengths; the text consists mainly of set pieces or purple passages, rather loosely strung together by short bits of awkward verse and functional prose. . . . Marlowe contrives his own sound effects, manipulating a language which is not simply a means of communication but a substitute for representation. Magniloquence does duty for magnificence.

Hence the hero is a consummate rhetorician and, conversely, weakness is represented as speechlessness. (p. 44)

To support these remarks, Levin quotes images similar to those I have here analyzed, for example, "Go stout Theridamas, thy words are swords", "his piercing instruments of sight", "perswade at a sodaine pinch", etc.

CHAPTER SEVEN

1. Ultimately, as recent criticism seems to recognize, this definition of genre must involve the relationship of author and work with reader or apprehender. Genre involves artistry but, at the same time, necessarily surpasses it by involving as well the historical

life of the work. I do not stress this for *La Celestina* precisely because, in spite of its splendid artistry, its history as a masterpiece (its relationship with generations of readers) has been so frequently unsatisfactory.

2. See "El tiempo y el género literario en *La Celestina*," *Revista de filología hispánica,* VII, 147-59.

3. One curious result of this is the constant debate carried on by critics as to the character of almost everyone of the principal characters: Celestina, Calisto, Melibea, the servants. One might almost define *La Celestina* as a work in which characterization is an open problem by the very terms of its art. Hence these debates are interesting but ultimately futile; they correspond to an attempt to read the work as if it were dramatic and novelistic and so overlook its deepest ageneric marvel.

4. That paradox stressed by don Juan Valera, Calisto's failure to seek a licit path to Melibea, is a striking example of Rojas' lack of concern with motivation in the accepted sense of the word. What matters are the sentimental awarenesses of the lovers in love, not *why* they act in this way or that. Rojas, like L. Vives in his *Tratado del alma,* is interested in how the soul works, not in defining it with adequate motivation. It should also be noted that this lack of concern involves not just the first act and the first author but the whole. At no point, not even when Melibea in Act XVI rejects matrimony in favor of love, does Rojas even think it worth while referring to this purely dramatic inconsistency. The requirements of the drama just do not occur to him.

5. A full discussion of this interpretation would require much more than a paragraph. May I refer the reader to reflections of mine on *España en su historia* entitled "The Juvenile Intuition of Juan Ruiz" (*Symposium,* 1950), In that article I tried to show how the problem of determining and classifying Juan Ruiz' intention (i.e., his generic relationship to his work) can never be solved because it is based on faulty assumptions. The *Libro de buen amor* is a work of poetic play, play in the sense that children play, not of classifiable intention or intentions. It is a work of pretending and of fun in which the mood brings into itself (as the child into his game) both the objective world and objective intentions. We can also explain in the same way one of the most evident characteristics of the work, the almost childish delight of the poetic ego at its own technical skill. There is all through the work the repeated appeal of the child: "See how I do"; in this case, "See how well I can versify; look at me write variations on the *serranilla* pattern." The lack of genre in the *Libro de buen amor* thus corresponds to a joining together of poet, poetry, and process of poetic creation under the single aegis of the first person. Juan Ruiz' play has turned our usual concepts of literary creation inside out.

6. I need not mention here various sorts of fiction in the third person—tales, fables, parables, etc.—if only because they do not commit the author to surpass the role of narrator. He may do this, of course, and in many cases generic literature arises from the innoculation of these ageless patterns with life in first- and second-person immediacy. But I am not here attempting to analyze the birth and growth of genre in terms of literature as a whole, as an independent phenomenon to be studied historically. Rather I am concerned with describing outside of history the ageneric tradition of *La Celestina* and of illustrating therefrom a concept or definition of genre. It is my hope that this concept will be enlightening; even though the way the novel and drama seem to have come about in Spain may be quite unlike what happened in other nations and periods.

7. This explains that curious simulation of genre which caused us to describe the

Tamburlaine and the *Fiammetta* as "protogeneric." In both these works creative emphasis on a single person produced an effect of consistency which gave the illusion of character or personality in the third person. Tamburlaine's single ego expression, for example, not only allows him to dominate time, space, and fortune but also establishes his fixed image for a possible audience. Actually, however, we saw how, in this universe of war, character is either nonexistent or ridiculous. What really differentiates men is the force of their ego. But before closing this note, I want to insist again that this emphasis is creative, not grammatical. There is dialogue in the *Tamburlaine* and people are addressed in the second person and so on. But the grammar of significance, what Kenneth Burke might call the "grammar of motives," has a paradigm of a single person—a paradigm so consistent as to give an impression of dramatic character.

8. See Appendix B.

9. *Santa Teresa y otros ensayos* (Madrid, 1925).

10. This careful insertion of time is accomplished by a break in the sequence of the action (the only one of its kind) and the insertion of at least three references to "un mes" by Melibea in Act XVI. This process is, of course, quite different from the illogical junction of durative and mechanical time in the *Comedia* and is in itself an indication of the increased generic consciousness of Rojas. We may note, however, a malicious divergence as to the use of this month of time on the part of the two sets of characters. Whereas Melibea asserts that Calisto visits her every night ("jamás noche ha faltado"), Sosia paints a different picture: "Ni menos, auía de yr cada noche, que aquel officio no çufre cotidiana visitación ... en vn mes no auemos ydo ocho veces ..." It is a sign not so much of illogic and self-contradiction as of Rojas' continuing refusal to posit truth upon facts. Comically Calisto is weak as a man; novelistically he is totally dedicated to love; and both things (like the two times in the *Comedia*) are true at the same time. At any rate, in neither statement need we infer a deliberate lie. What has happened is that each genre demands its own history.

11. It is these qualities of Act XIX that inspired the sensibility of Jorge Guillén to recreate the rendezvous in his *Huerto de Melibea*. The wealth of suggested but not completely realized possibilities of experience lead directly to this uniquely authentic continuation of *La Celestina*. That Guillén's is a lyric rather than a novelistic continuation is of secondary importance; the garden rendezvous is novelistic from our point of view precisely because it adds lyric awareness of experience to its dialogic sequence. See *Inventario, 1953.*

12. The most elementary sort of formal analysis will reveal the skill of Rojas as a lyric poet; only continuing doubt as to authorship has kept these verses from their place among the "hundred best." We may mention, for example, this extraordinarily vital metaphor with its graphic portrayal of love's physical urgency and its suggestion of the theme of warfare:

> Saltos de gozo infinitos
> da el lobo viendo ganado;
> con las tetas los cabritos,
> Melibea con su amado.

We ought also to point out the tight growth of the poetic concept from stanza to stanza, a procedure which in Rojas is not surprising. "Cara" in the first stanza suggests "vista" in the second; "saltar" (with its mournful note of prediction) suggests the "saltos" of the third; and "amado" at the end of the third becomes the key word in the fourth. It would be impertinent on the basis of these few lines of poetry to try to analyze Rojas' lyric artistry, but I think that they do show certain qualities which are recognizable from our study of the dialogue.

APPENDIX A

1. I refer not only to House's observations (mentioned in Chapter I) but also to Ruth Davis' *New Data on the Author of Act I* (University of Iowa Studies, 1928) and to J. V. Montesino Samperio, "Sobre la cuantificación literaria," *Revista nacional de cultura* (1947), both of which separate statistically the first act from the rest. As regards the added acts, Miss Davis does not investigate them and Montesino Samperio accords them tentatively to Rojas. Since the latter's results for the added acts do not seem to contradict our own literary proof, the temptation is to give him more credit for his work on Act I. Nevertheless since no one has yet taken the trouble to compare and correlate his work with House's, and since House is so obviously wrong in relation to the added acts, it is reasonable at present to consider the whole statistical approach as doubtful. As long as a period of time can be thought of as intervening between the writing of one act and another (as in the case of the added acts and the *Comedia*) there will very probably exist stylistic variations which will register statistically. Changes in writing habits do not require a second author necessarily.

2. Here two comments need be made, one favorable and the other unfavorable to this hypothesis.

The first is that an analysis of House's statistics shows a perceptible progression of linguistic tendencies from the first act, through the *Comedia* and into the added acts. For almost every factor studied the fifteen acts of the *Comedia* stand statistically in between Act I and the added acts. For example, in Act I, according to House, there is a "strong tendency towards the use of 'le' for both persons and things." Then, in Acts II to XVI of the *Comedia* "lo" begins to be used for things, while in the additions " 'lo' has gained decidedly in popularity." In other words, even though House would reject such a conclusion from his statistics, it would appear at least possible that what he tabulates is the record of a continuing stylistic evolution of a single person.

The unfavorable comment has to do with Rojas' age. From the sparse documents that have been unearthed, we know the following facts: in 1525 Rojas' wife was thirty-five years old; he was mayor of Talavera in 1538; and he died in 1541. These facts would lead us to believe that in 1498—the probable date of the *Comedia*—Rojas was a very young man. If we estimate that he was sixty-one when he died and that he was ten years older than his wife he would have been only twenty at that time. This matter of youthful creation has been discussed at length by Menéndez Pelayo and others and we need not repeat their arguments. But it is awkward to have to propose an even earlier date for Rojas' writing of Act I. The only possible solution is to suppose that Rojas may have been twenty or even twenty-five years older than his wife. This would result in some such imaginary chronology as the following:

Born 1470?
First Act 1492?
Comedia 1497–98?
Added Acts 1502

3. See Chapter VI, note 31.

4. As Cejador points out, the full listing is given in the *Corbacho*.

5. This is noted by M. J. Asensio in the article previously cited as evidence of an intentional time lapse between the first and second scenes. This is difficult to accept in view of Sempronio's surprise at being given the same information.

6. O. H. Green, *"Celestina,* Auto I, 'Minerva con el Can,'" *Nueva Revista de Filología Hispánica* (1953).

7. So also might be explained the linguistic archaisms which appear from time to time in this act and which have been so frequently noticed.

APPENDIX B

1. The first version of this appendix was rewritten in the form of a paper delivered at the Modern Language Association meeting in Chicago in 1953. I then made the mistake of submitting it as an article to *Romance Philology* with the idea of reprinting it at the proper time. This, as I say, was a mistake because the appropriate authorities at the California University Press refused to permit any such transferral. They have, however, allowed me to rewrite some parts of the original as well as to quote it extensively. In doing so, I have reconverted the paper and article to the point of view of an appendix; that is to say, it has been rewritten with the reader of this book in mind.

2. H. I. Marrou, "La division en chapitres des livres de la *Cité de Dieu,"* *Mélanges J. de Ghellinck,* I (1951), 247–48 remarks: "L'idée que nous est familière de faciliter l'accès d'une oeuvre par un plan synoptique convenablement divisé et pourvu de sommaires généraux était tout à fait étrangère à l'esprit antique: elle est chez nous un héritage de la scolastique médiévale et de sa technique de la *divisio."* As Marrou goes on to point out for the evolution of printed editions of St. Augustine, this represents a gradual development. The same thing is true of Terence, the amount of whose commentary becomes unwieldy by the middle of the sixteenth century.

3. The primary reason for proposing an edition prior to 1499 is the phrase, "con sus argumentos nuevamente añadidos," which appears in the title to the sixteen-act edition of 1501. Since the *argumentos* to the individual acts are included in the 1499 edition, this seems to indicate a prior edition without them. While this may be the case, I suggest that it is based on too rigid an interpretation of the word "nuevamente." We know from the 1502 *Prólogo* that the *argumentos* were in fact *añadidos* by the printers; hence that part of the above phrase is self-explanatory. As for "nuevamente," it could easily be an awkward reference to the same intervention. In other words, whoever wrote the 1501 title (probably also on the missing 1499 folio) might merely have been trying to distinguish between the original text and the "new" *argumentos* just added to it. It may not have occurred to him at all that "nuevamente" would be misleading to a reader who had not seen the manuscript in its original form—without *argumentos.* But even if

there were a pre-1499 edition the above assumptions are not invalidated. Fadrique Alemán must have in any case been the printer referred to in the prologue. Otherwise we should have to postulate two lost editions!

4. See *Fine Books* (New York, 1912). As far as a layman's eye can judge these matters, the *Celestina* woodcuts resemble those of a number of other editions of Terence as well.

5. E. W. Robbins, *Dramatic Characterization in Printed Commentaries on Terence* (Urbana Ill., 1951).

6. At this point it is natural to ask: are the *argumentos* (and critical apparatus) to Terence aesthetically more adequate than those to *La Celestina?* My answer would be that they fail in another way. They fail—and here I am relying on Robbins' study—by insisting on the exemplary and didactic virtues of plays written for Roman entertainment. Yet this is an historical failure, in the deepest sense the failure of the mind of the Middle Ages to evaluate correctly its Classical past, and so cannot be charged to any one individual or set of circumstances. Furthermore, since the plays of Terence were designed for theatrical action, presentation of them as moral or even rhetorical action is often quite accurate. In other words, if the *argumenta* to Terence betray the original intent, the *argumentos* to *La Celestina* betray the text itself. In one case, the failure amounts to an historically significant interpretation; in the other, it is not so much a matter of interpretation as of misunderstanding.

7. This *argumento* is appended by Cejador in a note (Vol. II, p. 114).

8. María Rosa Lida de Malkiel, after reading my manuscript, has suggested another significant difference: "Aunque la materia sea resbaladiza (y aunque *negocio* no era tan prosaico en el siglo XV como lo es hoy), no puedo menos de contrastar 'Acabado su negocio ...' (1499) con 'E después que cumplió su voluntad ...' (1502): una vez más el autor de los argumentos de 1499 atiende al sucederse de la acción, mientras el autor de los argumentos de 1502 señala la conexión anímica de la obra. Pues ese Calisto que ha satisfecho su voluntad es quien, lógicamente, aparece hastiado y arrepentido, y sólo tras un proceso nada espontaneo logra 'restaurar su desseo' en el soliloquio del mismo acto XIV."

9. *Orígenes,* p. 270.

INDEX

ACT I: absence of Petrarch, 169–70; retouched by Rojas, 210–11; errors in, 211

Act XII: structure, 100–104; scene construction in, 115–16

Additions of 1502: reveal new creative point of view, 14–15; Petrarch's role in their composition, 179–81; their trend towards genre, 202–6; Rojas proved author, 209; their "argumentos" by Rojas, 214–16

Adinolfi, Gina, 219

Aeschylus, 104

Animal kingdom: used for didactic illustration, 135–36; exempt from Fortune, 162; provides for fables in reverse, 240

Areusa: purposefully changed in 1502, 202–4

Argumentos: irrelevant to Rojas' intentions, 89; unwieldy example for Act XII, 99–100; authorship of, 212–16

Aristotle: concept of structure inapplicable, 88; concept of scene inapplicable, 105; as a source for Act I, 169–70

Artifacts: contribute to structure of scenes, 107

Auerbach, Erich: concept of realism inapplicable, 223

BAUDELAIRE, Charles: comparable consciousness of evil, 229

Bergson, Henri: clarifies characterization, 74; duration and sentiment, 144; Nicoll asserts relation to Heraclitus, 228

Blanco White, José María: authorship opinions, 9

Boethius: on Fortune, 159, 246

Breughel, Peter: theme of space, 130; his sense of life illustrated by Petrarch, 246

Burckhardt, Jacob, 152–53

Burke, Kenneth, 239, 254

CALISTO: as a lover, 142; anguish revealed in Act XIV *argumento,* 216

Carcel de amor. See San Pedro, Diego de

Carta of 1501: as literary criticism, 4

Cast: subdivisions of, 58–61; presents Stoic patterns of femininity and old age, 166–67

Castro, Américo: clarifies characterization, 76; concept of integralism, 193; discusses "vital situations" in Cervantes, 226; theme of Rojas' Judaism, 243

Castro Guisasola, F.: discusses commonplaces, 121; asserts Petrarch's importance as a source, 156; contradiction of his authorship evidence, 210

Celestina: special role of, 81; presentation in Act I, 82; domination of the title, 83; interpolations in her speeches, 83–87; compared to Trotaconventos and Gerarda, 87; her role in the structure of Acts III, IV, and V, 93–95; most deeply explored in Act VII, 96–97; explanation of her murder, 103; friendship for Claudina, 145–46; as Satanic, 231

Centeno, Augusto: concept of theme, 119; "intent" and "intention," 235

Centurio: as a comic figure, 202–4

Cervantes, Miguel de: the "decorum" of the *Quijote,* 44–45, 54, 195–96; thesis and theme in the *Quijote,* 120; his irony compared to Rojas', 123; his use of the *Amadis* as compared to Rojas' of Petrarch, 175; "man" as his subject, 201; unlike Rojas founds a genre, 206

Cicero: clarifies Rojas' oratorical use of logic, 42; concept of decorum, 44, 47

Color: absence of, 108; references to, 233

Comedia: Use of "decorum," 54, 196; direction of its dialogue, 53

Commonplaces: not to be taken out of context, 121; in Pármeno's trajectory, 122; in Elizabethan theater, 122, 235; Salinas' explanation of their role, 132; final metamorphosis of, 150; suitability of Petrarch's presentation of them, 172–78; in *Libro de buen amor,* 235–36

Consciousness: as basis for non-Freudian psychology of characters, 75–76; contrasted to that of Racine and Descartes, 76–77, 79; in trajectories and patterns of character, 78–80; exemplary quality of, 80–81; chorus of in Act VI, 96; feminine varieties in Act IX, 97–98; of cowardice in Act XII, 101–3; of light and dark, 108–9; of space, 107, 110; conditioned by space and time, 136–37; of love, 141, 144; as conflict and struggle, 146–49, 151, 168; Stoic definition of, 162, 245–46

Corbacho: style of, 26–31; structure of, 118; as "ageneric," 199–200

Cosmetics: stylistic importance of, 23

Cota, Rodrigo de, 6

DANZA de la muerte: absence of its thesis, 132; not taken seriously, 238–39

Death: violence of, 133–34; loss of importance, 132–34; in *Tamburlaine,* 187–88; *Danza* motif, 238–239; influence of Jorge Manrique in its presentation, 239; its unknowability, 239; does not lead to afterlife, 239–40

Decorum, 48–50

Deletions: of "decorum," 46

Delicado, Francisco, 206

De remediis fortuitorum: a source for Petrarch, 159

Diálogo de la lengua. See Valdés, Juan de

Diderot, Denis, 155–56

Dilthey, Wilhelm, 168, 244

Don Quijote. See Cervantes, Miguel de

Dorotea, La: use of color in, 233; Fortune's fall in, 238

Dreams: minor role of, 228

EDITIONS of *La Celestina,* 3–7

Eliot, Thomas Stearns, 155

Exclamations: stylistic importance of, 22–23

FALLS: in the dialogue, 128–29; in the prologue material, 129–30. *See also* Space *and* Fortune

Farinelli, Arturo, 156–57

Farnham, Willard: analyzes *Troilus,* 126; defends the *Secretum,* 158

Ferreira de Vasconcelos, Jorge, 206

Fiammetta: as a source, 188–89; theme of, 189–93; as a "protonovel," 197–98

Flaubert, Gustave, 145

Fortune: as a thesis, 123–25; treated ironically in Act IX, 127; converted into space, 128–30; importance of in Petrarch's time, 158–59; Petrarch's presentation of, 159–68; in the *Tamburlaine,* 187; bibliography, 236;

additional examples of the fall, 237–38, 251

Foulché Delbosc, Raymond, 9–10

Freud, Sigmund: his psychology inapplicable, 75

Friendship: sentimental style of expression, 145–46

GARCÍA BACCA, Juan David: discusses Heidegger, 78–79; sees Rojas as purveying "Hispanic consciousness," 228–29

Gestures: as an aspect of dialogue, 23; seen through space, 113–14; relation to facelessness of characters, 234

Goethe, Johann Wolfgang von: distinguishes novel from drama, 196

Guillén, Jorge: lyric recreation of *Huerto de Melibea,* 254

HEIDEGGER, Martin: clarifies characterization, 77–78

Heraclitus: suggestive comment on, in *Prólogo,* 36, 118; defines theme as struggle, 149; Nicoll asserts relation to Bergson, 228

Herder, Johann Gottfried, 195

House, Ralph Emerson: authorship opinions, 11–12; authorship conclusion disputed, 209–10

Huck Finn: incompletely aware of self, 196

Huizinga, Johann: clarifies fifteenth century sense of life in Act XII, 246

INTERPOLATIONS: as indicative of artistry, 15–16; their classification, 18, 51–52; of dialogic direction, 18–20; of clarity, 31–33, 220; of logic, 37–41, 220–21; of decorum, 46–51; of characterization for Celestina, 83–87; of cowardice in Act XII, 100–103; of structure, 92, 96, 231–32; of spatial freedom, 106; of spatial fear, 129; of freedom in Areusa's outburst, 218–19; of character, 230

Interrogatives: stylistic importance of, 22–23, 218

Irony: compared to Cervantes', 123; derived from commonplaces, 123, 175; not dramatic, 196; in Act XVI, 240

KING LEAR: fully characterized, 57; theme of space in, 130; incompletely aware of self, 196, 201

LEO, Friedrich, 231

Levin, Harry: discusses *Tamburlaine,* 252

Libro de buen amor: treatment of theses in, 123; as "ageneric," 198–99, 253; personal assimilation of commonplaces, 235–36

Lida de Malkiel, María Rosa: characterizes Calisto, 57; stresses Rojas' originality, 194; suggests Terence editions as model for *argumentos,* 212; analyzes *argumento* to Act XIV, 257

Light and dark: manifested through consciousness, 108–9

Love: as a thesis, 123–25, 139; in conflict with time, 136–39; provides sentimental awareness, 141; as durative, 144; in *Fiammetta,* 189–91; in *Troilus,* 236–237; sentimental variety defined, 240–41

Lyric stanzas: analyzed in garden scene, 254–55

MACHAUT, Guillaume: theme of Fortune, 126; vertical structure, 159

Machiavelli, Niccolo: in Marlowe's tradition, 182, 192

Madariaga, Salvador de: on Cervantine decorum, 54; interprets Melibea, 230–31, 232

Maeztu, Ramiro de: characterizes Celestina, 57

Maisonneuve, Jean: distinguishes emotions and sentiments, 240–41

Malherbe, François de: his concept of "clarté" inapplicable, 34, 53

Marlowe, Christopher. *See Tamburlaine*

Martínez de Toledo, Alonso. *See Corbacho*

Melibea: dominates Act X, 98–99; as a lover, 142–43; in additions, 204–5; conscious revealed in *argumento* to Act XVI, 215; Madariaga's interpretation of, 230–31, 232

Mena, Juan de: as authorship candidate, 6, 217

Menéndez Pelayo, Marcelino: authorship opinions, 10; interprets role of love, 140; clarifies social background, 152; denies importance of Petrarch, 156–58; his Petrarch opinion disputed, 174–75

Menéndez Pidal, Ramón: authorship opinions, 12–13

Meschinot, Jean, 244

Mollejar el ortelano: biographical significance for Rojas, 218, 232

Motivation: Rojas' lack of interest in, 196–97

NICOLL, Eduardo. *See* Bergson, Henri

OEDIPUS REX: fully characterized, 57; incompletely aware of self, 196

Ortega y Gasset, José: concept of theme, 119; concept of creative distance, 122–23; clarification of proverbial style, 222

PÁRMENO: trajectory of his existence, 65–73; structure of Act II centered on him, 92–93; with Sempronio the central consciousness of Act XII, 100–104; references after Act VIII, 227, 228

Petrarch, Francesco: importance in Rojas' tradition, 156–57; *Secretum meum* defended by Salinas and Farnham, 158; presentation of Fortune, 159–63; his sensibility, 164–65; his vision of time, space, and consciousness, 167–68; furnishes theme for his time, 168–69; in Act I, 169, 247; in the remaining fifteen acts of the *Comedia,* 171–78; in 1502 additions, 179–81; in *Fiammetta* and *Tamburlaine,* 182; in prologue material, 224–26, 243; range of influence, 244; vision of servants, 247–48

Poema del Cid: theories of divided authorship, 6; its dialogue, 26

Proaza, Alonso de: gives key to authorship cipher, 5; preoccupied with oral clarity, 33–34

Prólogo: Petrarch's influence on, 6, 180, 243; its note of fear, 7; as tacit expression of the theme, 149–50

Pronouns: stylistic importance of, 20–21

Proust, Marcel: sentimental search for Albertine, 144; discusses Flaubert, 145; *Fiammetta* in his novelistic tradition, 191

Proverbs: poetic quality of, 221–22

RABELAIS, François: style, 52; narrative structure, 118

Racine, Jean: concept of love: 143

Ramos Díaz, José, 238

Robbins, Edward: interprets commentators of Terence, 213, 257

Roman de la rose: treatment of thesis in, 123; Rojas' adaptation of its allegory, 245

Romero, José Luis, 245

Rougemont, Denis de, 143

Ruiz, Juan. *See Libro de buen amor*

SALAS BARBADILLO, Jerónimo, 181

Salinas, Pedro: concept of theme, 119; interprets mediaeval commonplaces, 132; concept of tradition, 155; defends *Secretum meum,* 158

Samoná, Carmelo, 222–23

San Pedro, Diego de: change in stylistic habits, 12; style of compared to Rojas', 43–44; vision of love, 142

Sapón, Stanley Martin, 218

Sartre, Jean Paul: clarifies characterization, 64, 75; his sensibility compared to Petrarch's, 164–65

Scenes: Rojas concept of defined, 104–5

Scheler, Max: concept of sentimental awareness, 77; theory of sentimental love, 140–41

Seaton, Edith, 250
Sender, Ramón, 233
Seneca: revived by Petrarch, 161; surpassed by Petrarch, 165–66
Serrano y Sanz, Manuel, 9
"Siglo de Oro": Rojas as forerunner of, 54
Silva, Feliciano de, 206
Silvio Piccolomini, Eneas, 155
Simone, France, 244
Situations: as building blocks of acts, 89–91; in Act VI, 95–96; in Act XI, 99; defined by Nicoll, 105
Social background, 152
Soliloquies: structural use of, 90, 104; Pleberio's, 123–25, 133; Calisto's 138–39; Celestina's, 223–24; as used in New Comedy, 231
Sophocles. *See Oedipus Rex*
Space: as three dimensional, 105–6; urban vacancy of, 107; as atmosphere or environment, 110, 234; as distance or barrier, 110–13; as surrogate for Fortune, 138–30; as expressed thematically, 131; Petrarch's vision of, 167–68; in *Tamburlaine*, 186–87; in Fiammetta, 191; its situation of dialogue, 200; as central condition of modern genres, 200–201
Spencer, Theodore, 235
Spengler, Oswald, 200–201
Spitzer, Leo: defines style, 17–18; concept of perspectivism, 56
Spoerri, Theophil, 237–38
Stoicism: Petrarch's revival of, 161–63; Petrarch's innovations in, 164–68; in character patterns, 176–77; frees characters from typification, 178
Stylistic adornment, 34–35

TALAVERA, Arcipreste de. *See Corbacho*
Tamburlaine: theme of, 182–88, 192–93; as a protodrama, 197–98; characterization in,
250; clarified by Simone Weill, 251; interpreted by Harry Levin, 252
Taylor, Henry Osborne, 236
Terence: fifteenth century editions stimulate "argumentos", 212–13; misinterpreted in Middle Ages, 257
Theatrical concept of structure, 116–18
Time: preoccupation with time of day, 114, 137; from thesis theme, 134–35; in conflict with love, 136–39; as paradoxical, 146–47, 241–42; in *Tamburlaine*, 186; in *Fiammetta*, 191; situates dialogue, 200; as central condition of modern genres, 200–201; opposing attitudes towards, 240; in imagery, 240
Torres Naharro, Bartolomé, 206
Tristan et Iseult, 143–44
Troilus and Cressida: Love and Fortune theses, 126, 242; thematic need of Petrarch, 164; use of time in, 242
Twain, Mark. *See* Huck Finn

UNAMUNO, Miguel de: clarifies characterization, 67; tragic sense of life compared to Celestina's sinful sense, 229

VALDÉS, Juan de: authorship opinions, 8; defines style, 16–17
Valera, Juan, 253
Valle Inclán, Ramón María del, 233
Vega, Lope de. *See Comedia and Dorotea*
Vicente, Gil, 238
Vives, Luis, 253
Vossler, Karl, 75

WEIL, Simone, 251
World: as a thesis, 123–25

ZANTA, Luigi, 246
Zeno, 166
Zola, Emile, 110